UQ HOLDER!

KEN AKAMATSU

vol.14

CHARACTERS

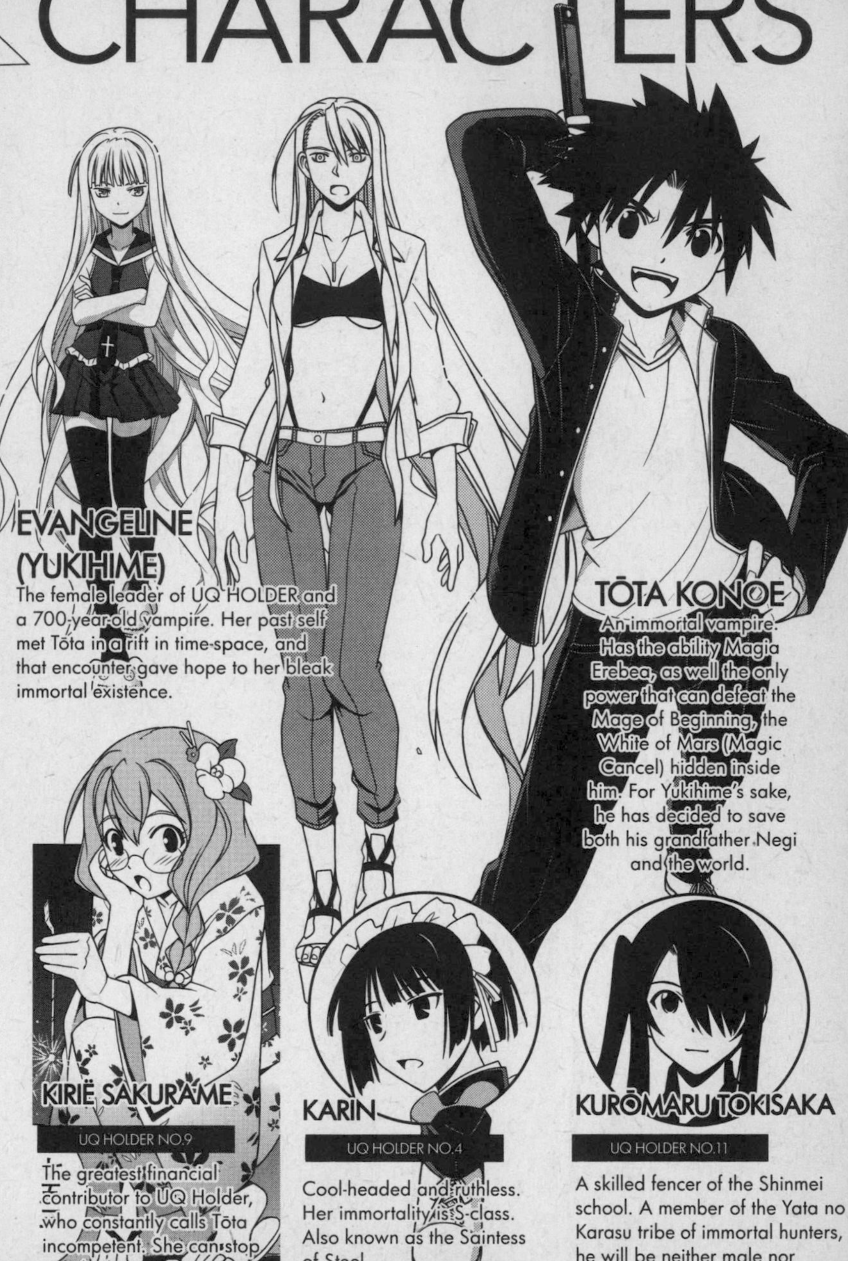

EVANGELINE (YUKIHIME)

The female leader of UQ HOLDER and a 700-year-old vampire. Her past self met Tōta in a rift in time-space, and that encounter gave hope to her bleak immortal existence.

TŌTA KONOE

An immortal vampire. Has the ability Magia Erebea, as well the only power that can defeat the Mage of Beginning, the White of Mars (Magic Cancel) hidden inside him. For Yukihime's sake, he has decided to save both his grandfather Negi and the world.

KIRIË SAKURAME

UQ HOLDER NO.9

The greatest financial contributor to UQ Holder, who constantly calls Tōta incompetent. She can stop time by kissing Tōta.

KARIN

UQ HOLDER NO.4

Cool-headed and ruthless. Her immortality is S-class. Also known as the Saintess of Steel.

KURŌMARU TOKISAKA

UQ HOLDER NO.11

A skilled fencer of the Shinmei school. A member of the Yata no Karasu tribe of immortal hunters, he will be neither male nor female until his coming of age ceremony at age 16.

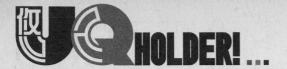

UQ HOLDER! ...

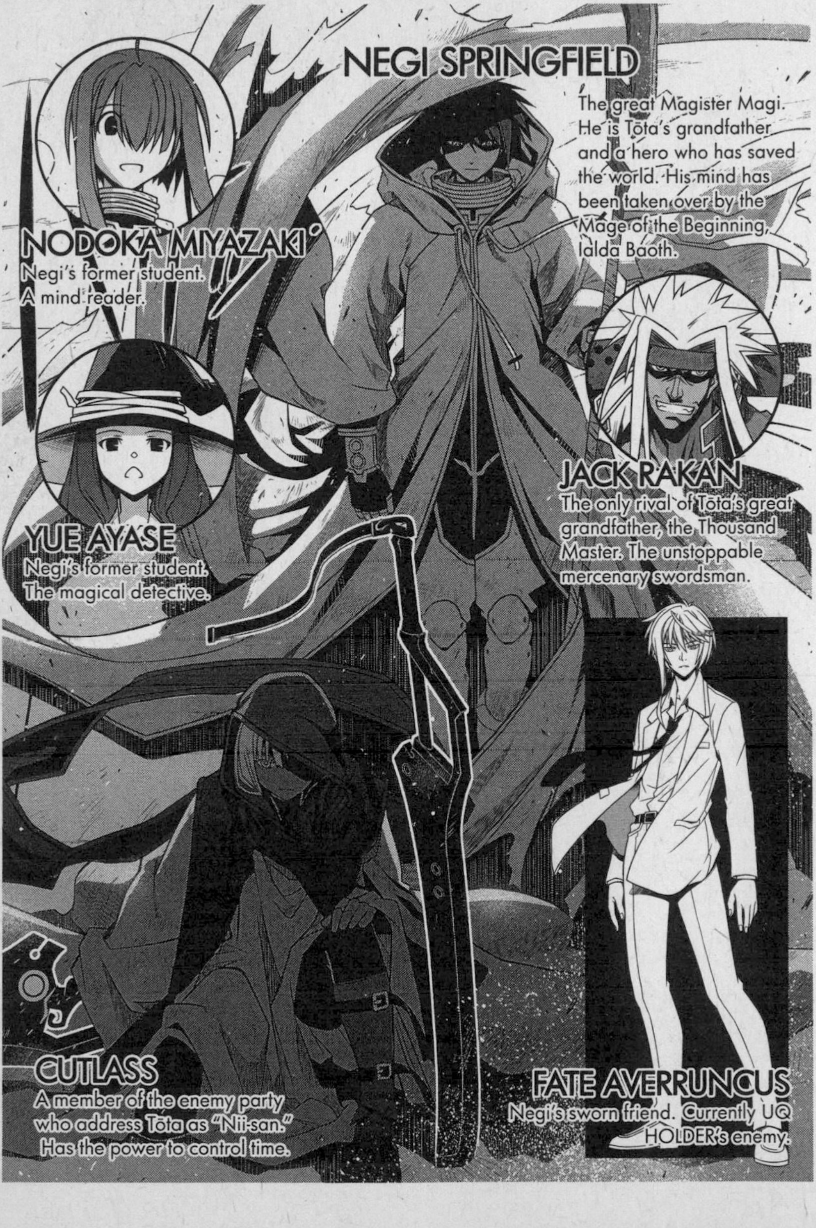
NEGI SPRINGFIELD
The great Magister Magi. He is Tōta's grandfather and a hero who has saved the world. His mind has been taken over by the Mage of the Beginning, Ialda Baoth.
NODOKA MIYAZAKI
Negi's former student. A mind reader.
JACK RAKAN
The only rival of Tōta's great grandfather, the Thousand Master. The unstoppable mercenary swordsman.
YUE AYASE
Negi's former student. The magical detective.
FATE AVERRUNCUS
Negi's sworn friend. Currently UQ HOLDER's enemy.
CUTLASS
A member of the enemy party who address Tōta as "Nii-san." Has the power to control time.

THE STORY SO FAR

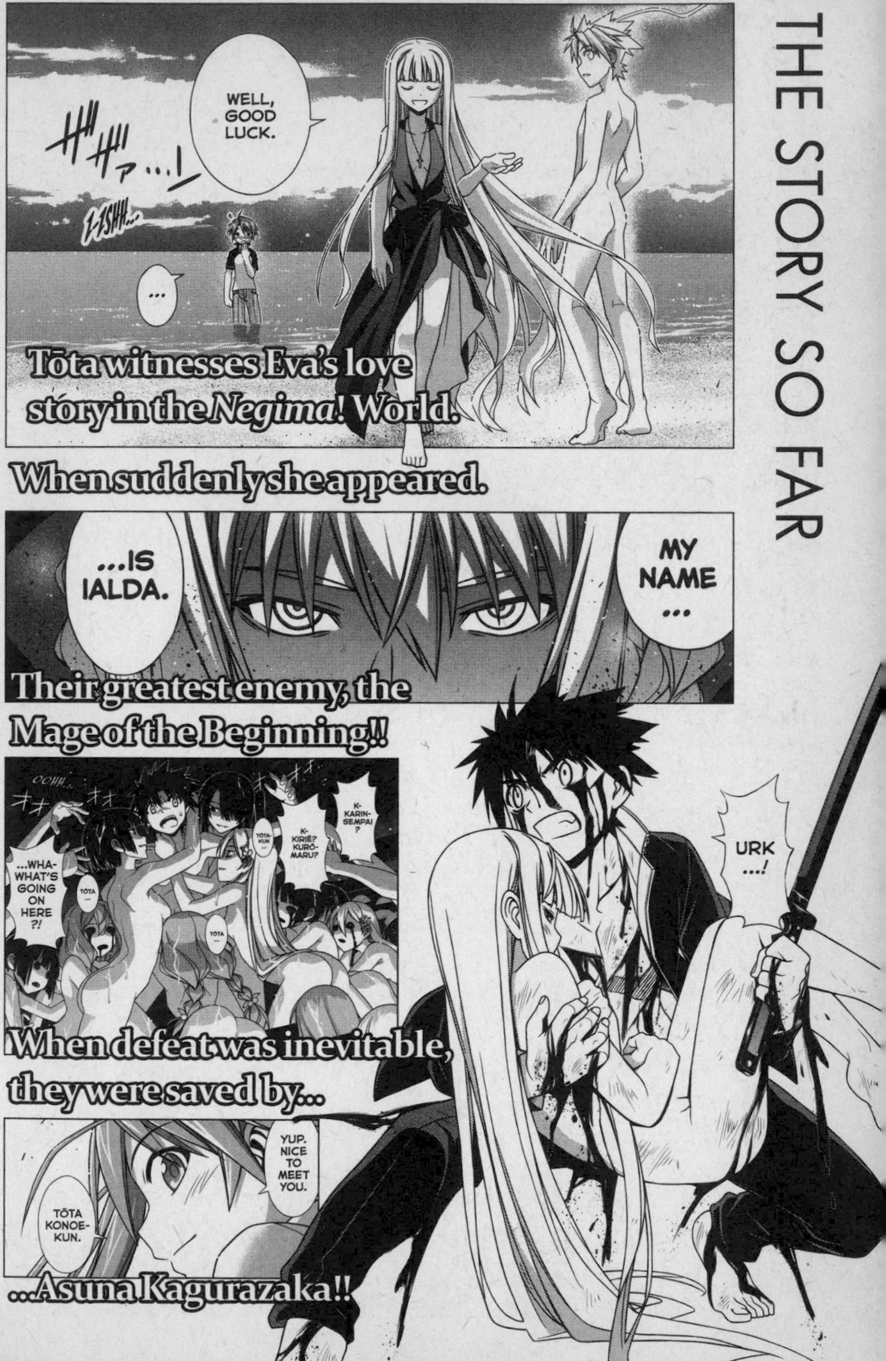

WELL, GOOD LUCK.
Z-ZSHH...
...
Tōta witnesses Eva's love story in the *Negima*! World.
When suddenly she appeared.
MY NAME...
...IS IALDA.
Their greatest enemy, the Mage of the Beginning!!
URK ...!
OOHH...
K-KARIN-SEMPAI?
K-KIRIÉ? KURŌMARU?
TŌTA-KUN...
...WHA-WHAT'S GOING ON HERE?!
TŌTA...
TŌTA...
When defeat was inevitable, they were saved by...
YUP. NICE TO MEET YOU.
TŌTA KONOE-KUN.
...Asuna Kagurazaka!!

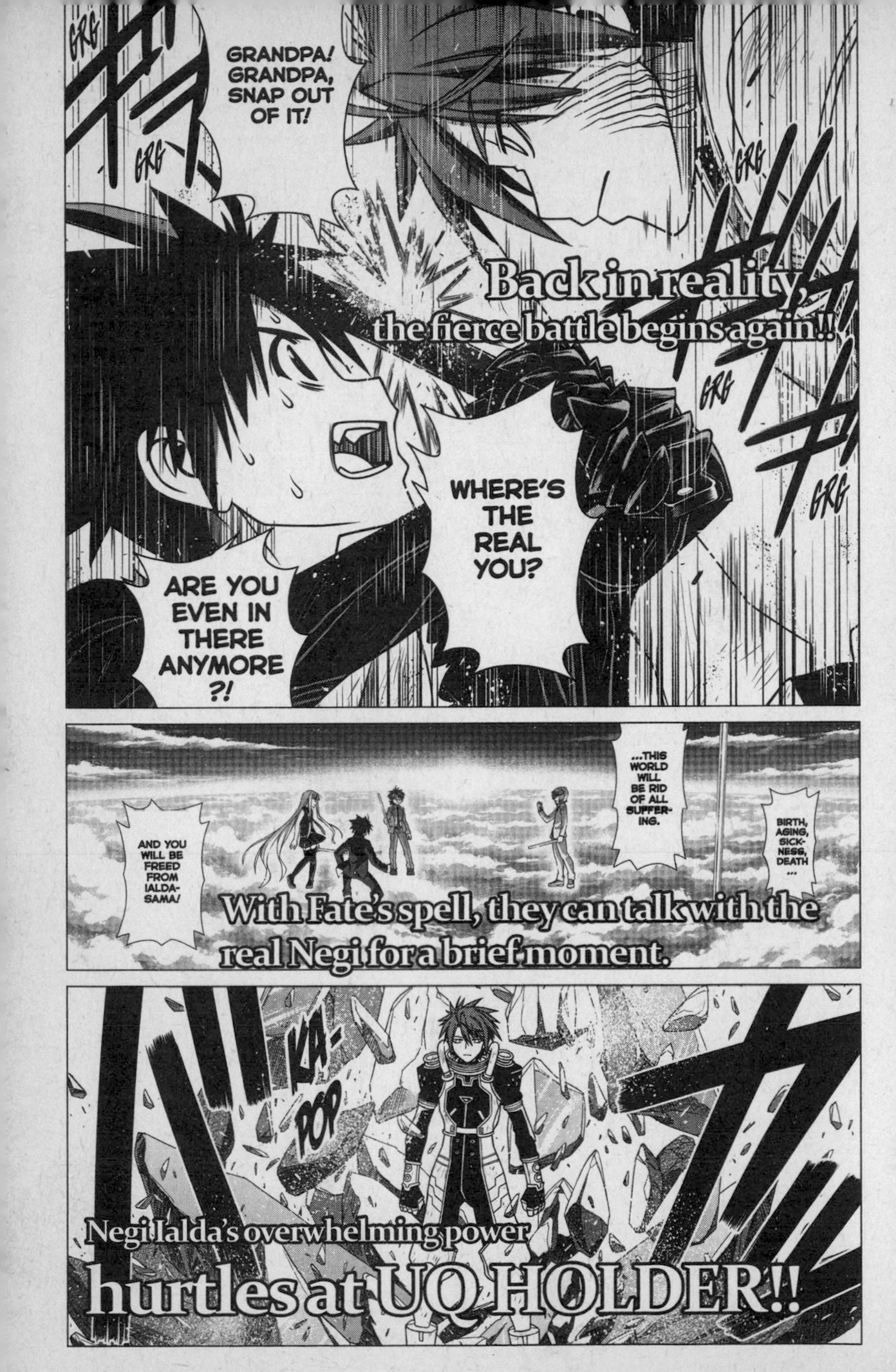
GRG
GRANDPA! GRANDPA, SNAP OUT OF IT!
Back in reality, the fierce battle begins again!!
WHERE'S THE REAL YOU?
ARE YOU EVEN IN THERE ANYMORE ?!
BIRTH, AGING, SICK-NESS, DEATH ...
...THIS WORLD WILL BE RID OF ALL SUFFER-ING.
AND YOU WILL BE FREED FROM IALDA-SAMA!
With Fate's spell, they can talk with the real Negi for a brief moment.
KA-POP
Negi Ialda's overwhelming power hurtles at UQ HOLDER!!

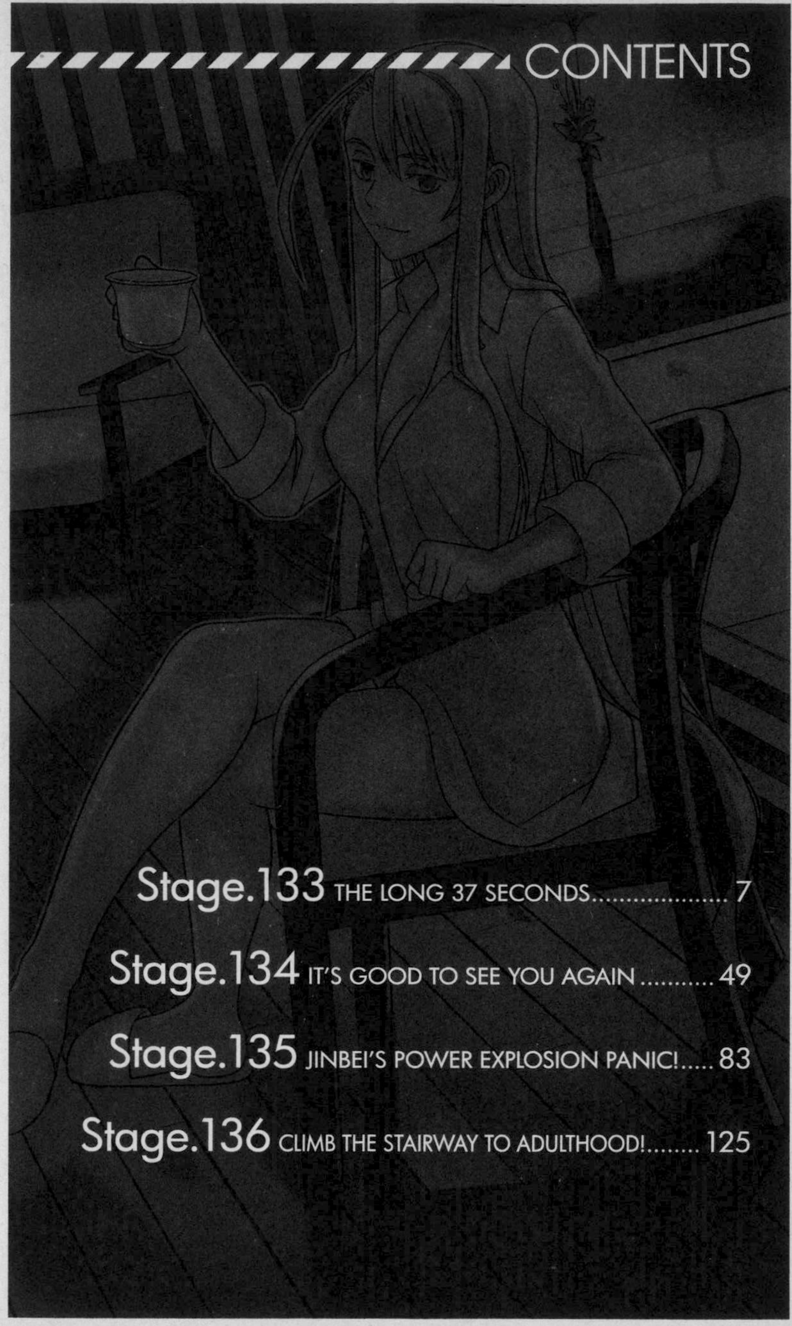

CONTENTS

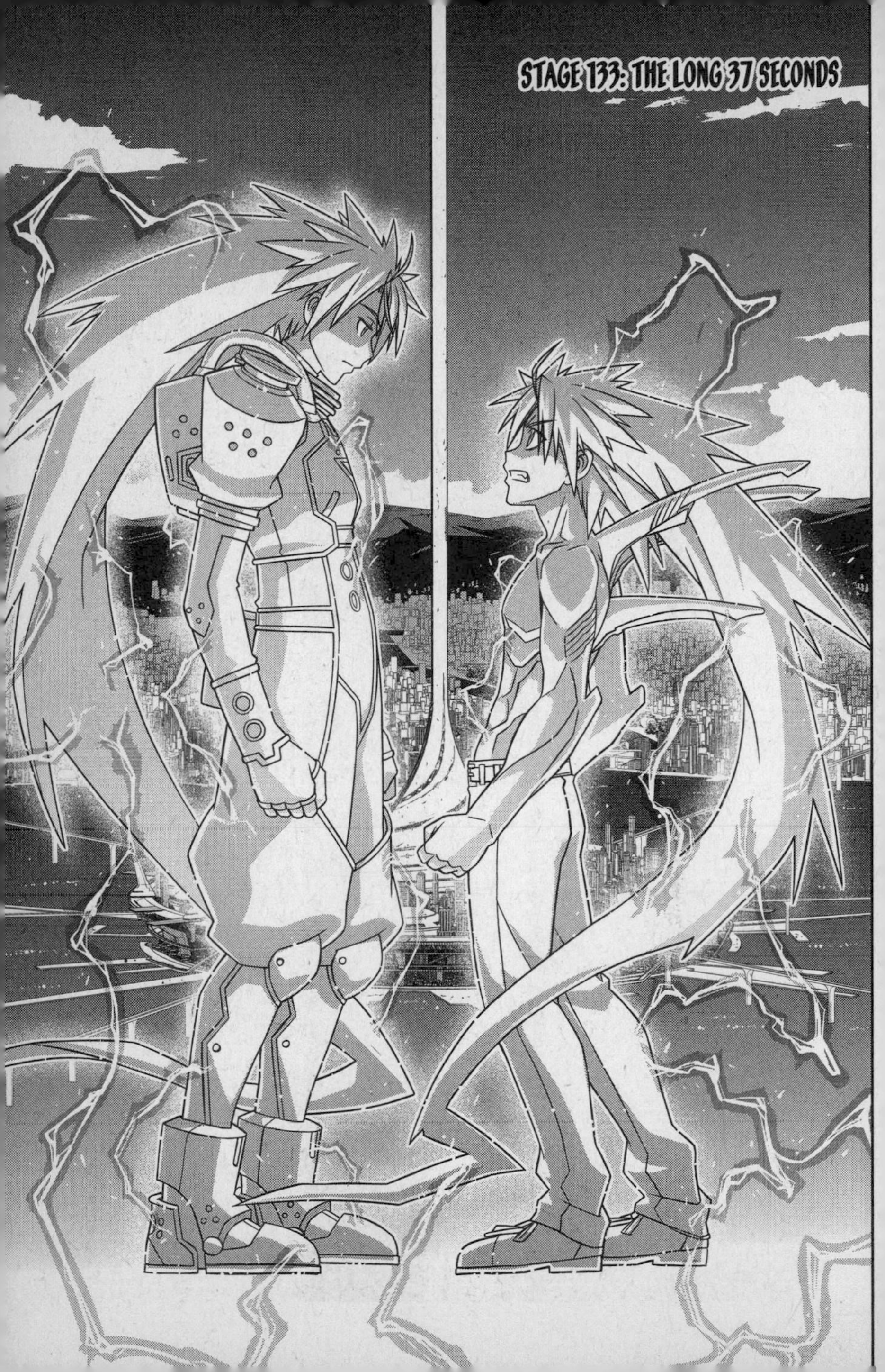
STAGE 133: THE LONG 37 SECONDS

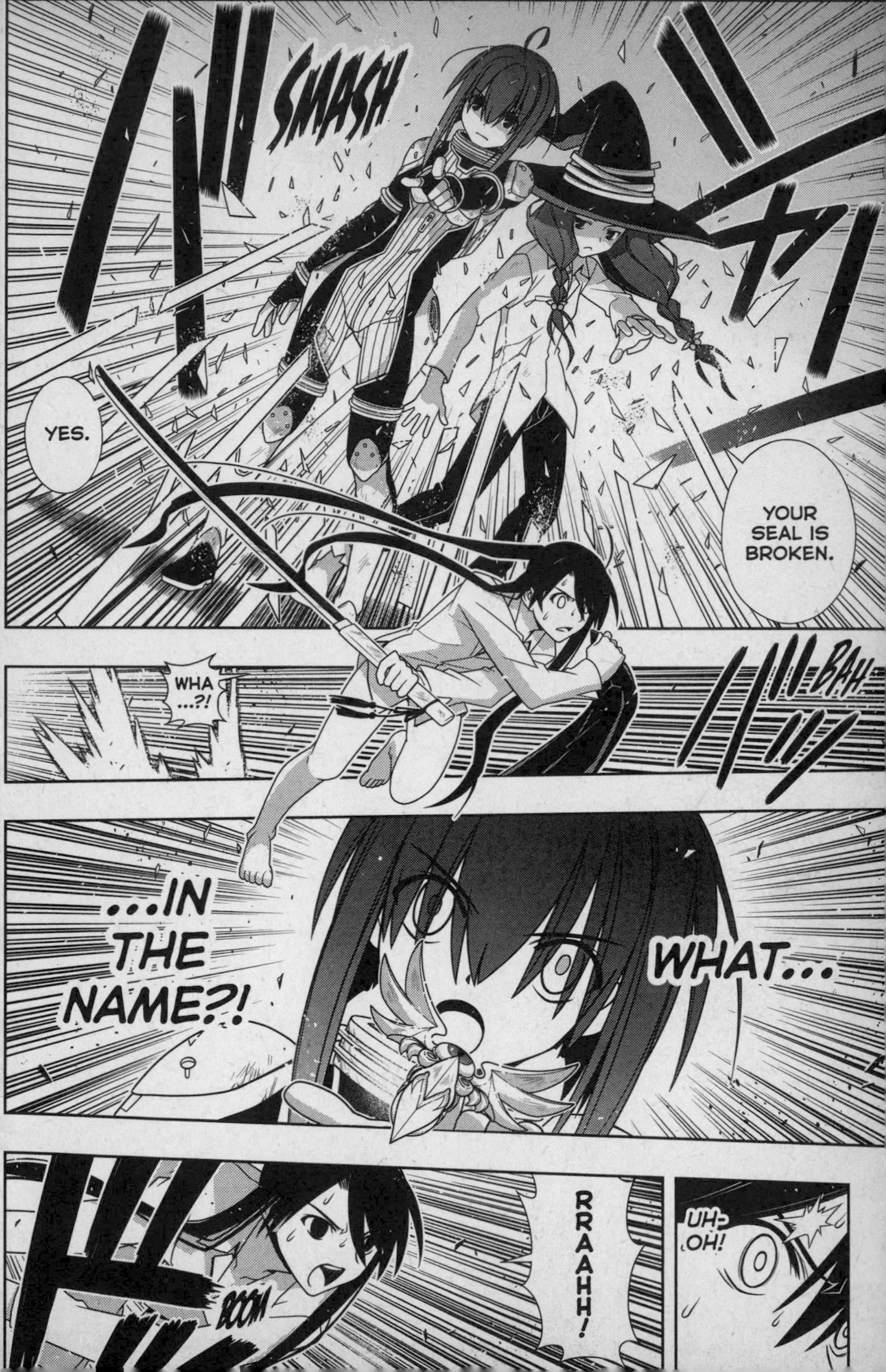
SMASH
YOUR SEAL IS BROKEN.
YES.
BAH
WHA ...?!
WHAT...
...IN THE NAME?!
UH-OH!
RRAAHH!
BOOM

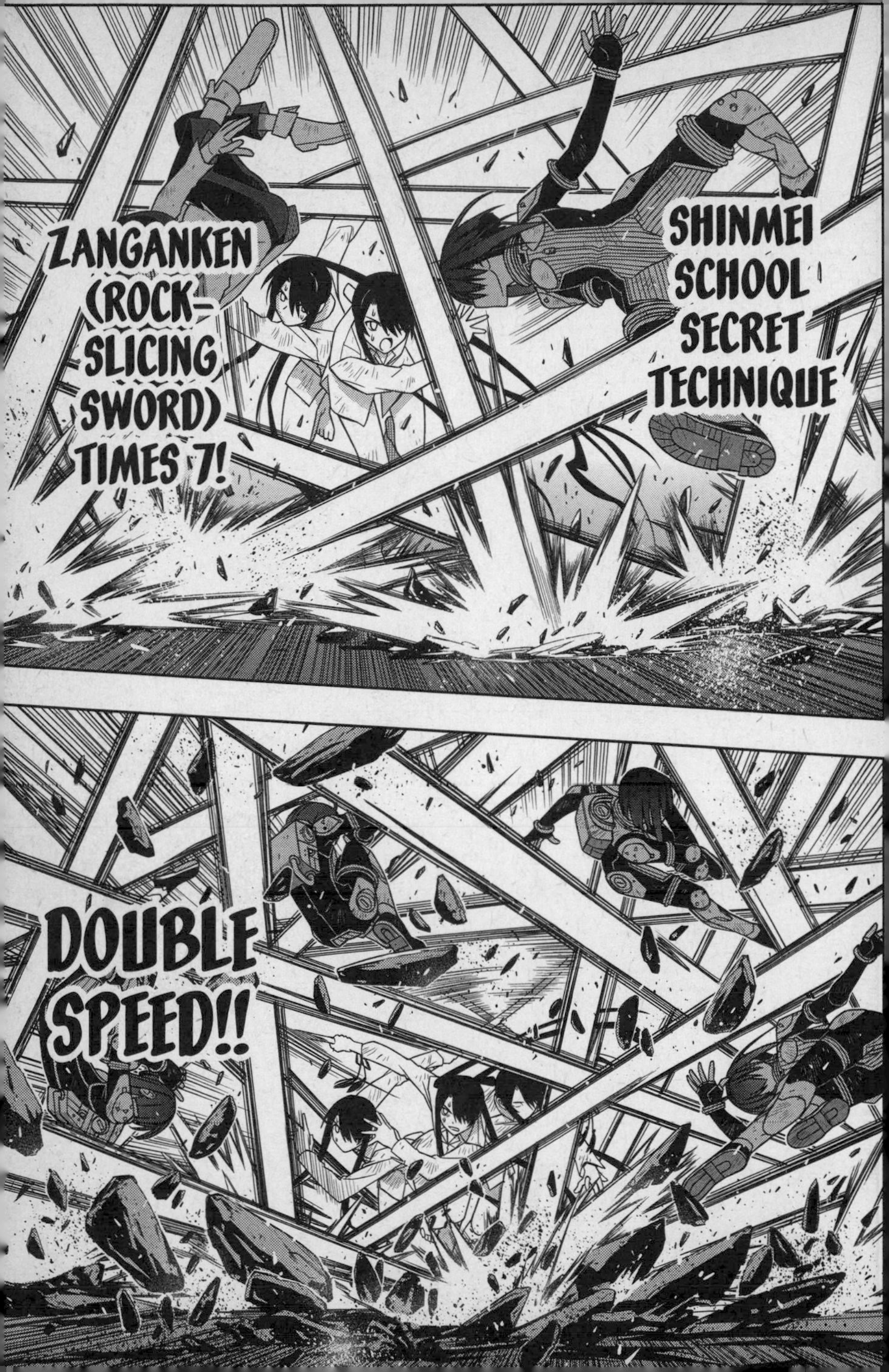
SHINMEI SCHOOL SECRET TECHNIQUE
ZANGANKEN (ROCK-SLICING SWORD) TIMES 7!
DOUBLE SPEED!!

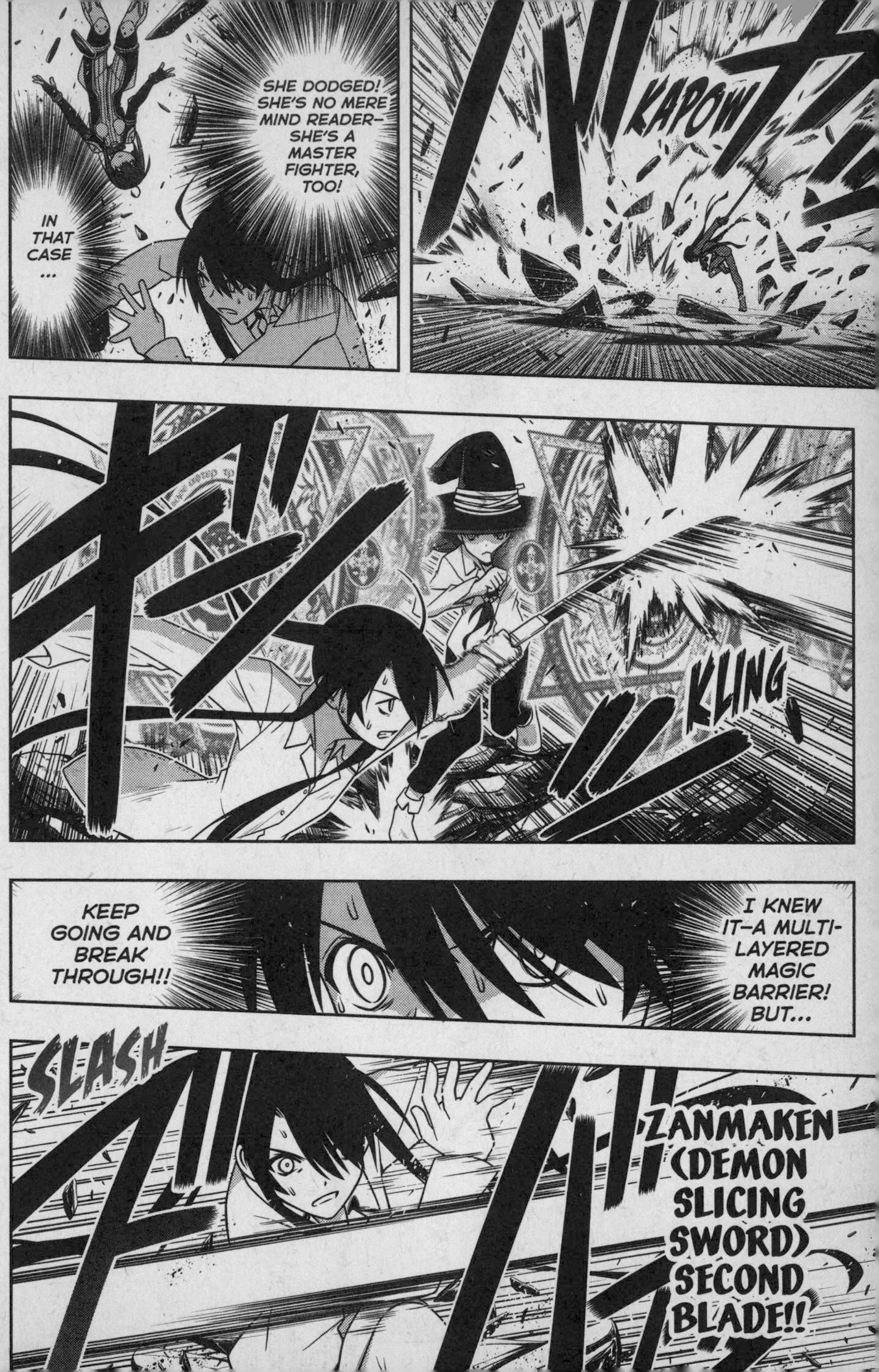
KAPOW
SHE DODGED! SHE'S NO MERE MIND READER– SHE'S A MASTER FIGHTER, TOO!
IN THAT CASE ...
KLING
I KNEW IT–A MULTI-LAYERED MAGIC BARRIER! BUT...
KEEP GOING AND BREAK THROUGH!!
ZANMAKEN (DEMON SLICING SWORD) SECOND BLADE!!
SLASH

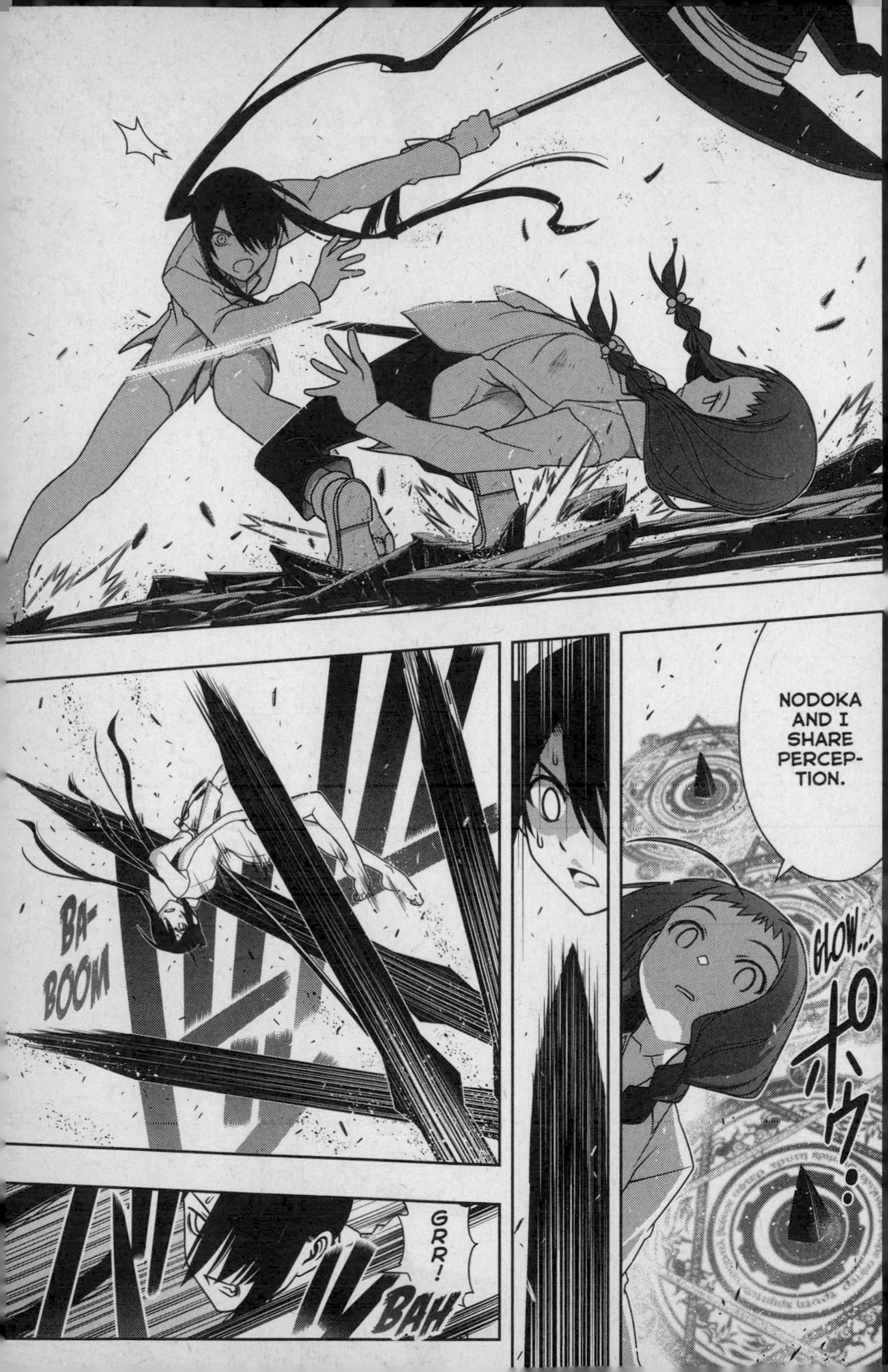
NODOKA AND I SHARE PERCEP-TION.
GLOW...
ポゥ…
BA-BOOM
GRR!
BAH

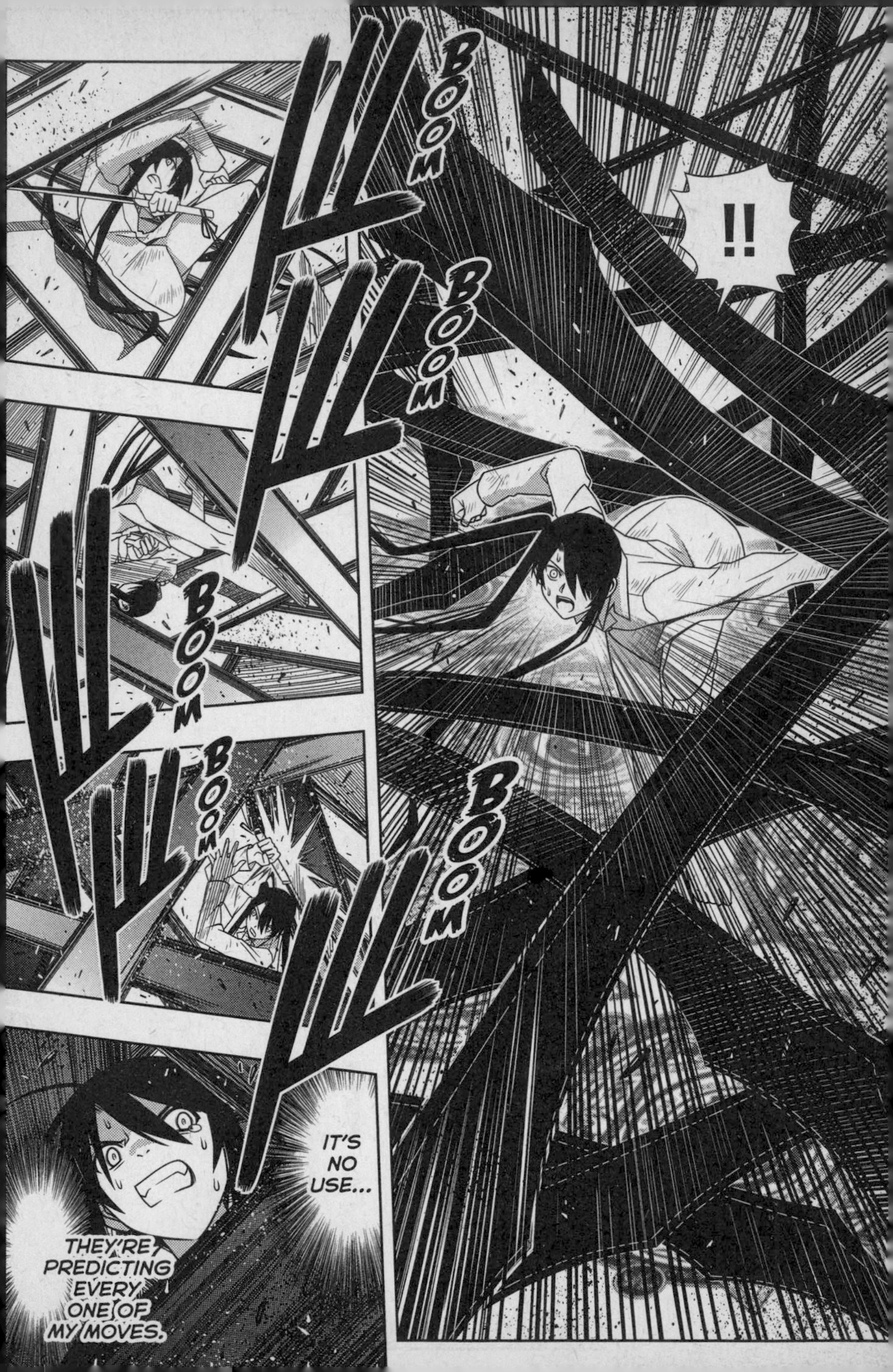
!!
BOOM
BOOM
BOOM
BOOM
BOOM
IT'S NO USE...
THEY'RE PREDICTING EVERY ONE OF MY MOVES.

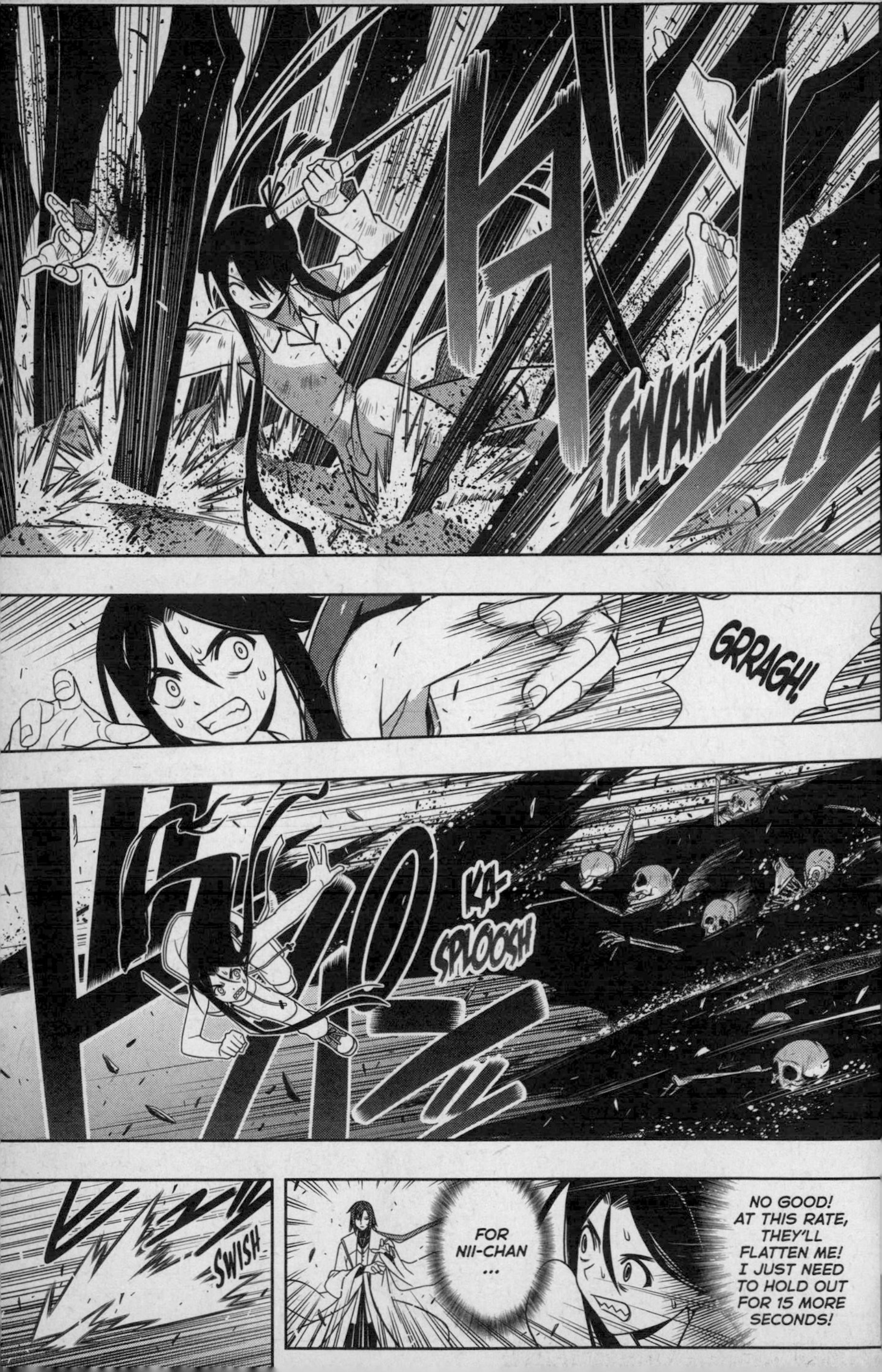
FWAM
GRRAGH!
KA-SPLOOSH
NO GOOD! AT THIS RATE, THEY'LL FLATTEN ME! I JUST NEED TO HOLD OUT FOR 15 MORE SECONDS!
FOR NII-CHAN ...
SWISH

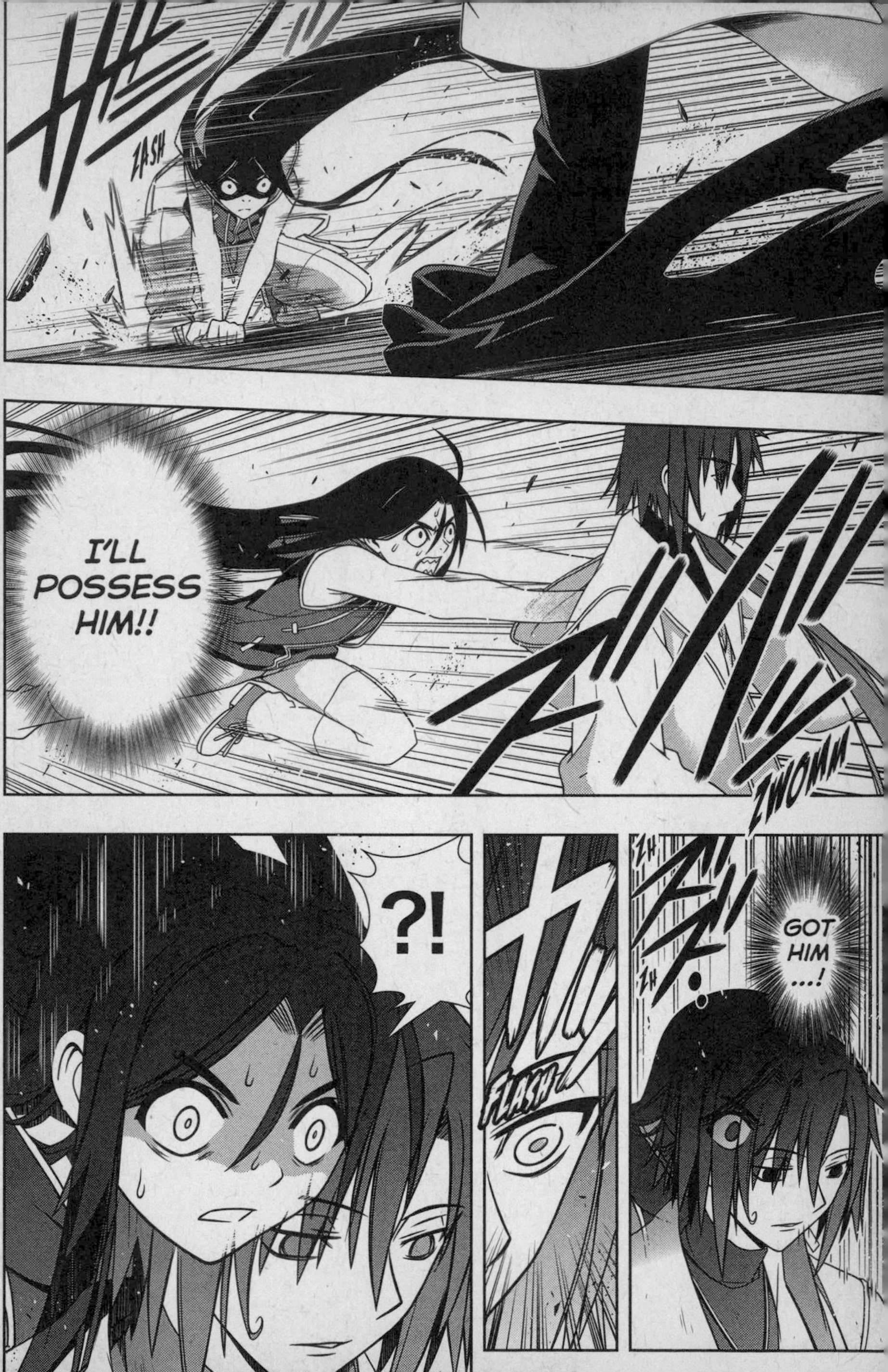
ZASH
I'LL POSSESS HIM!!
ZWOMM
ZH
ZH
GOT HIM ...!
FLASH
?!

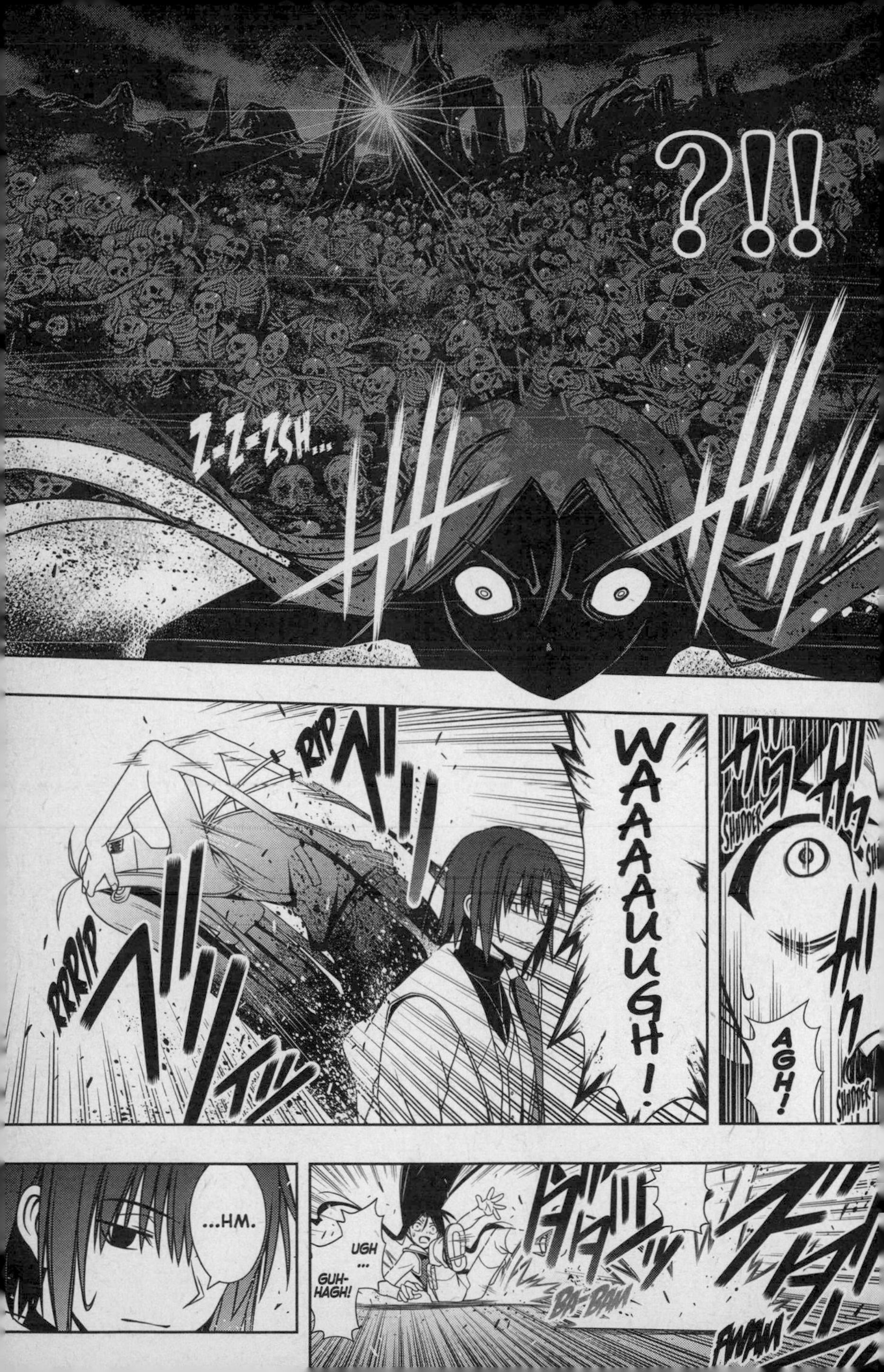
?!!
Z-Z-ZSH...
SHUDDER
AGH!
SHUDDER
WAAAAAUUGH!
RIP
RRRIP
BA-BAM
UGH...
GUH-HAGH!
...HM.

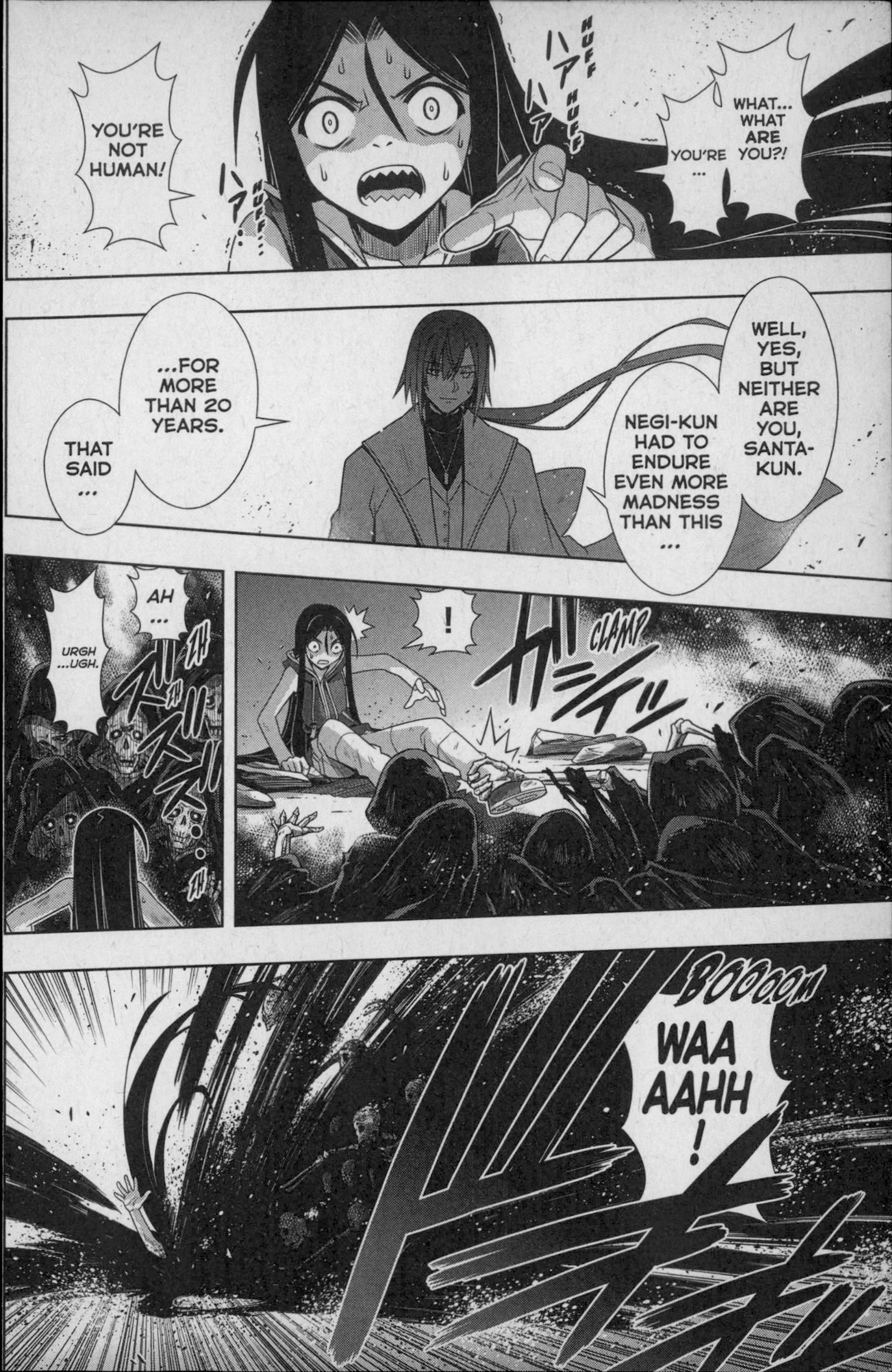
WHAT... WHAT ARE YOU?!
YOU'RE ...
HUFF HUFF HUFF...
YOU'RE NOT HUMAN!
WELL, YES, BUT NEITHER ARE YOU, SANTA-KUN.
NEGI-KUN HAD TO ENDURE EVEN MORE MADNESS THAN THIS ...
...FOR MORE THAN 20 YEARS.
THAT SAID ...
CLAMP
!
AH ...
URGH ...UGH.
BOOOOM
WAA AAHH !

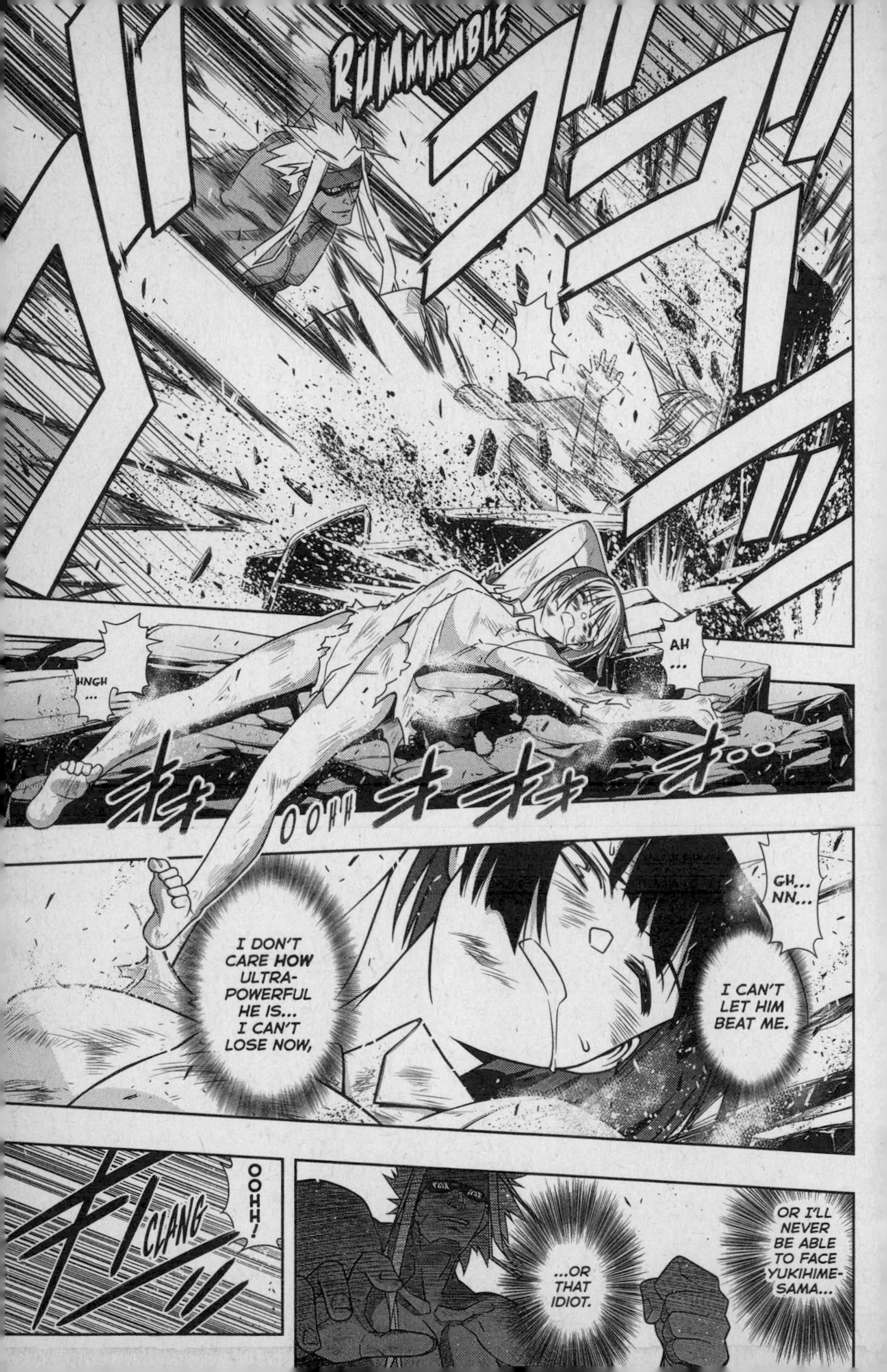
RUMMMMBLE
AH ...
HNGH ...
OOHH
GH... NN...
I DON'T CARE HOW ULTRA-POWERFUL HE IS... I CAN'T LOSE NOW,
I CAN'T LET HIM BEAT ME.
OR I'LL NEVER BE ABLE TO FACE YUKIHIME-SAMA...
...OR THAT IDIOT.
OOHH!
CLANG

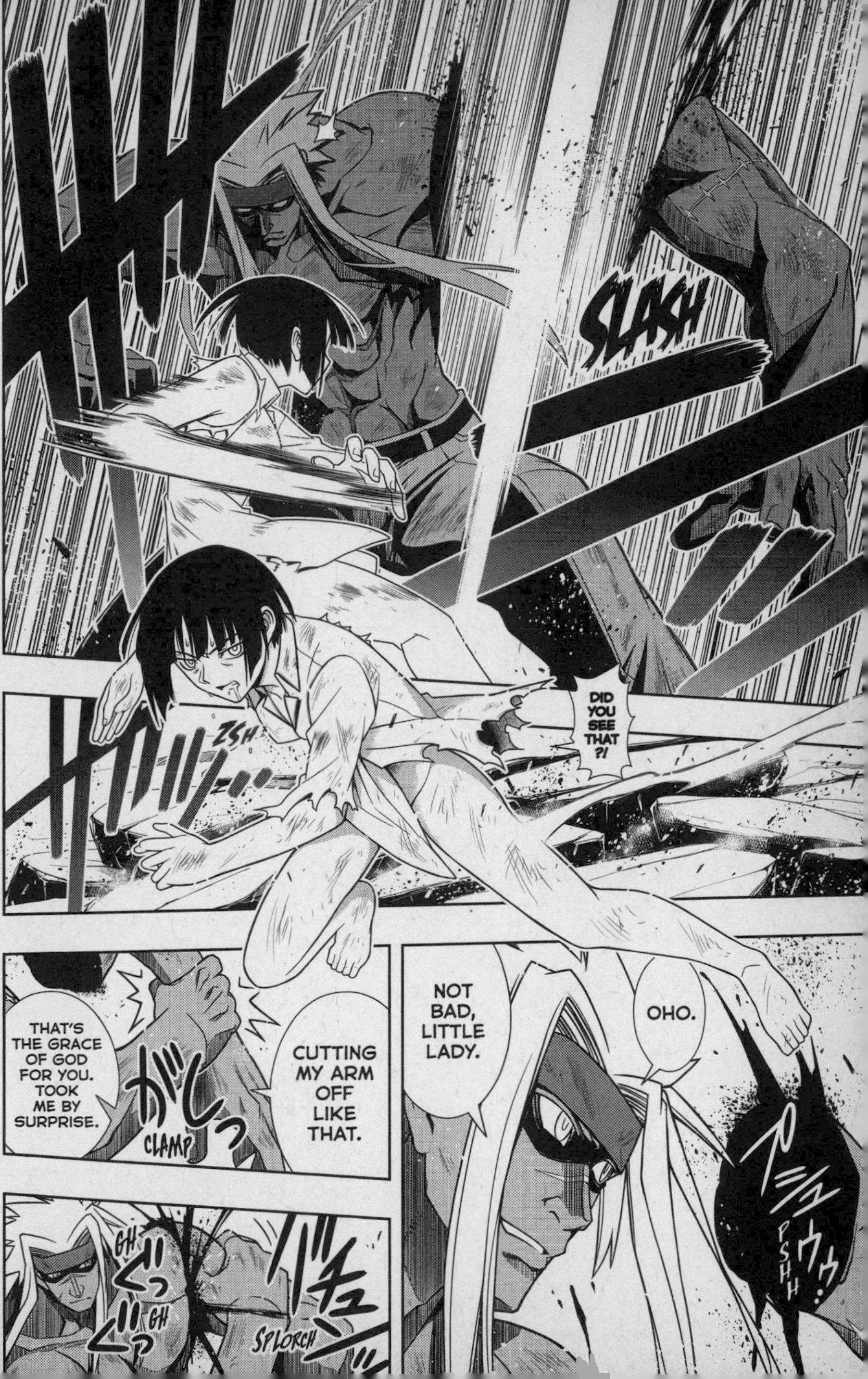
SLASH
DID YOU SEE THAT?!
ZSH
OHO.
NOT BAD, LITTLE LADY.
PSHH
CUTTING MY ARM OFF LIKE THAT.
THAT'S THE GRACE OF GOD FOR YOU. TOOK ME BY SURPRISE.
CLAMP
SPLORCH
GH
GH

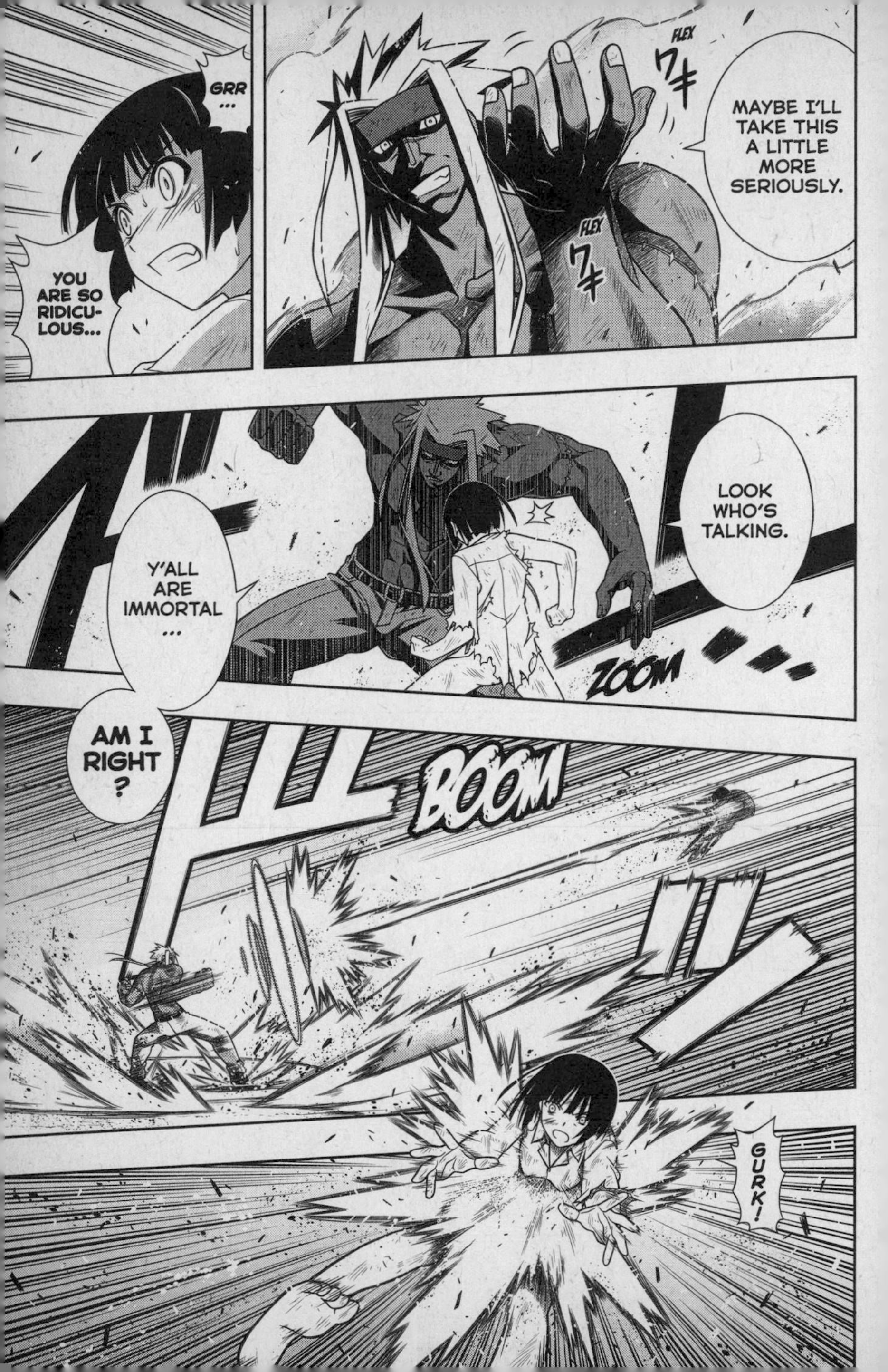
FLEX
ワキ
MAYBE I'LL TAKE THIS A LITTLE MORE SERIOUSLY.
FLEX
ワキ
GRR ...
YOU ARE SO RIDICULOUS...
LOOK WHO'S TALKING.
Y'ALL ARE IMMORTAL ...
ZOOM
AM I RIGHT ?
BOOM
GURK!

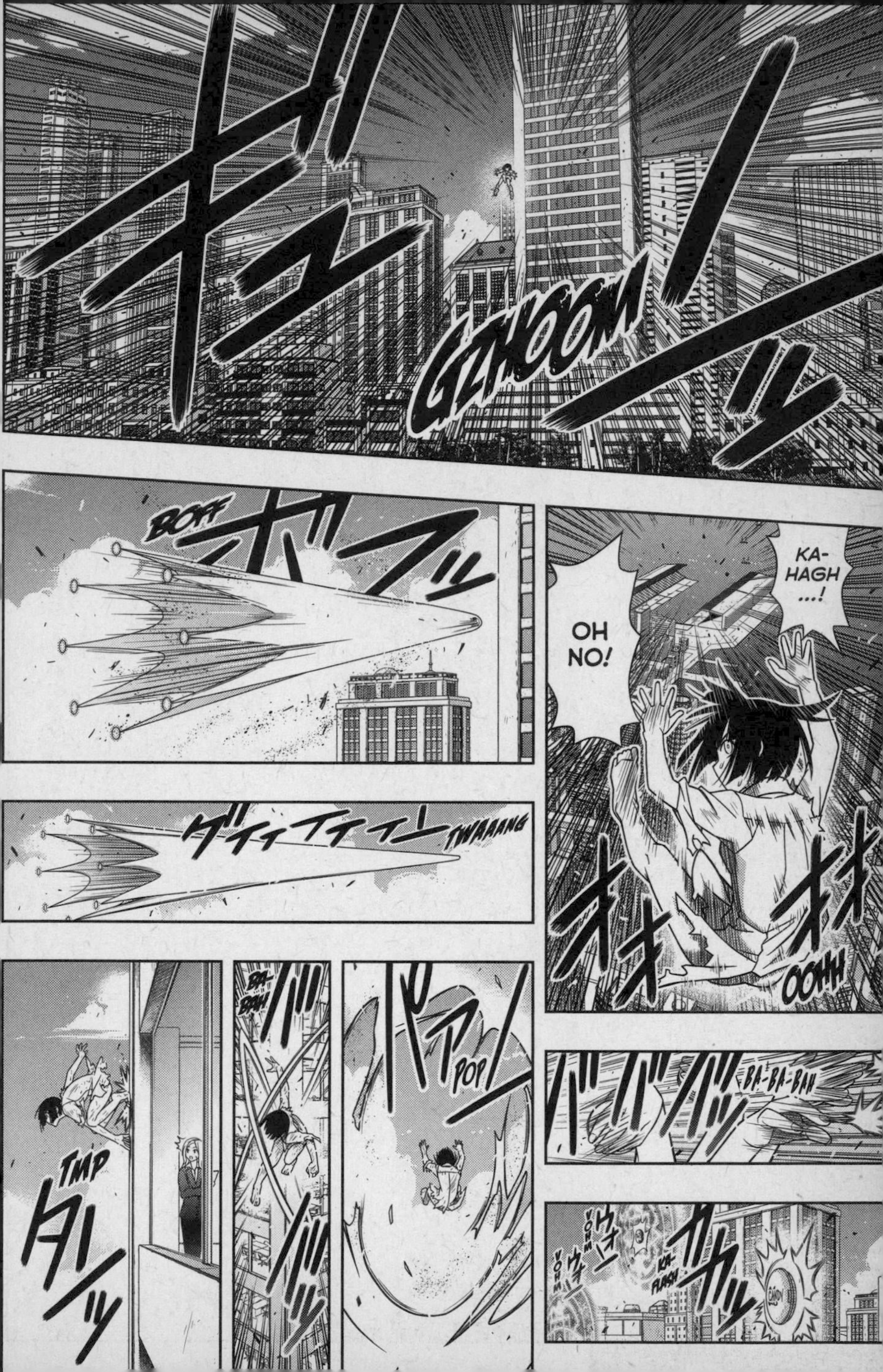
GZHOOM
KA-HAGH...!
OH NO!
OOHH
BOFF
TWAAANG
BA-BA-BAN
VOHM
VOHM
VOHM
KA-FLASH
POP
BA-BAN
TMP

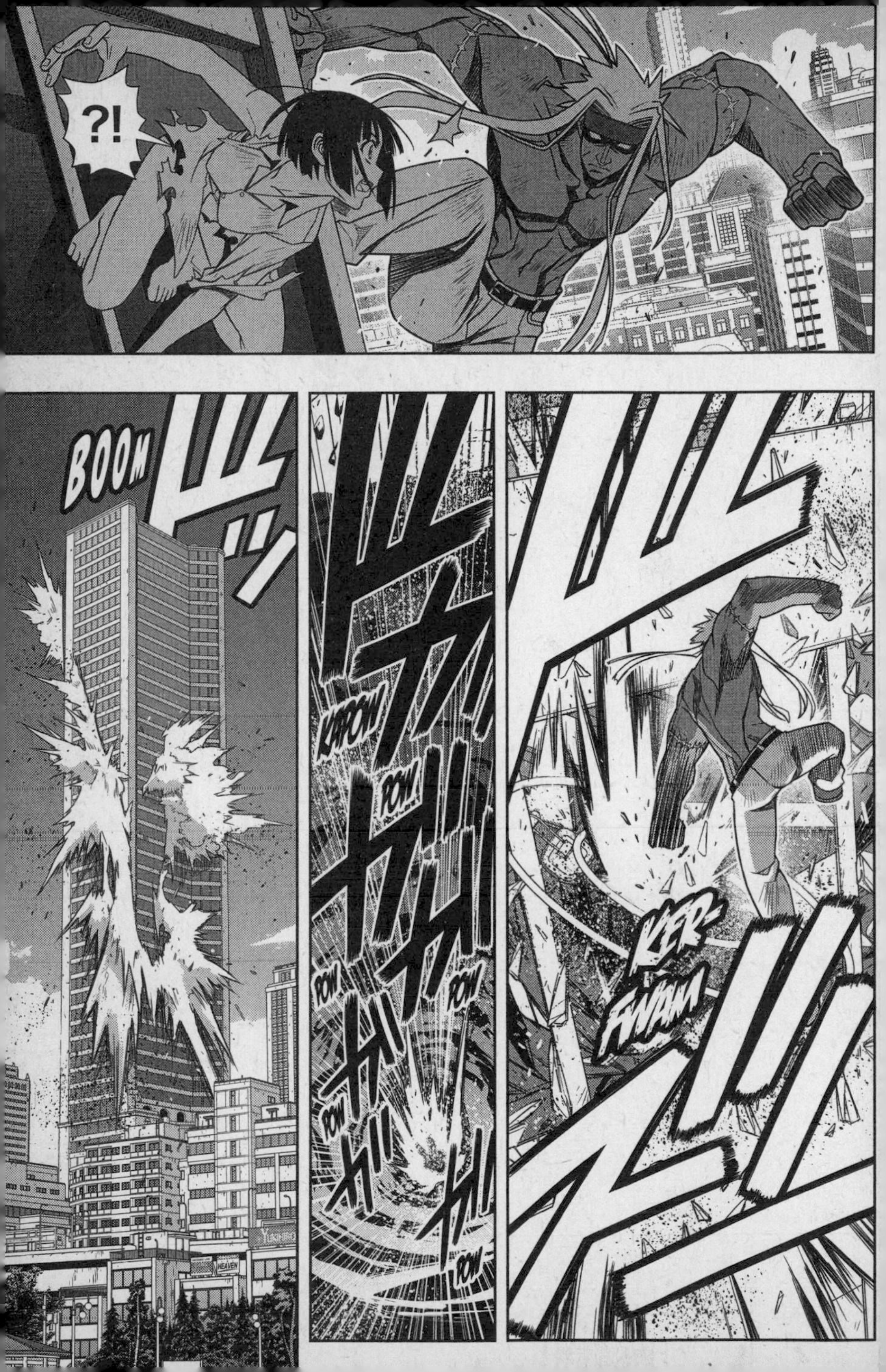
?!
KER-
FWAM
KAPOW
POW
POW
POW
POW
POW
BOOM

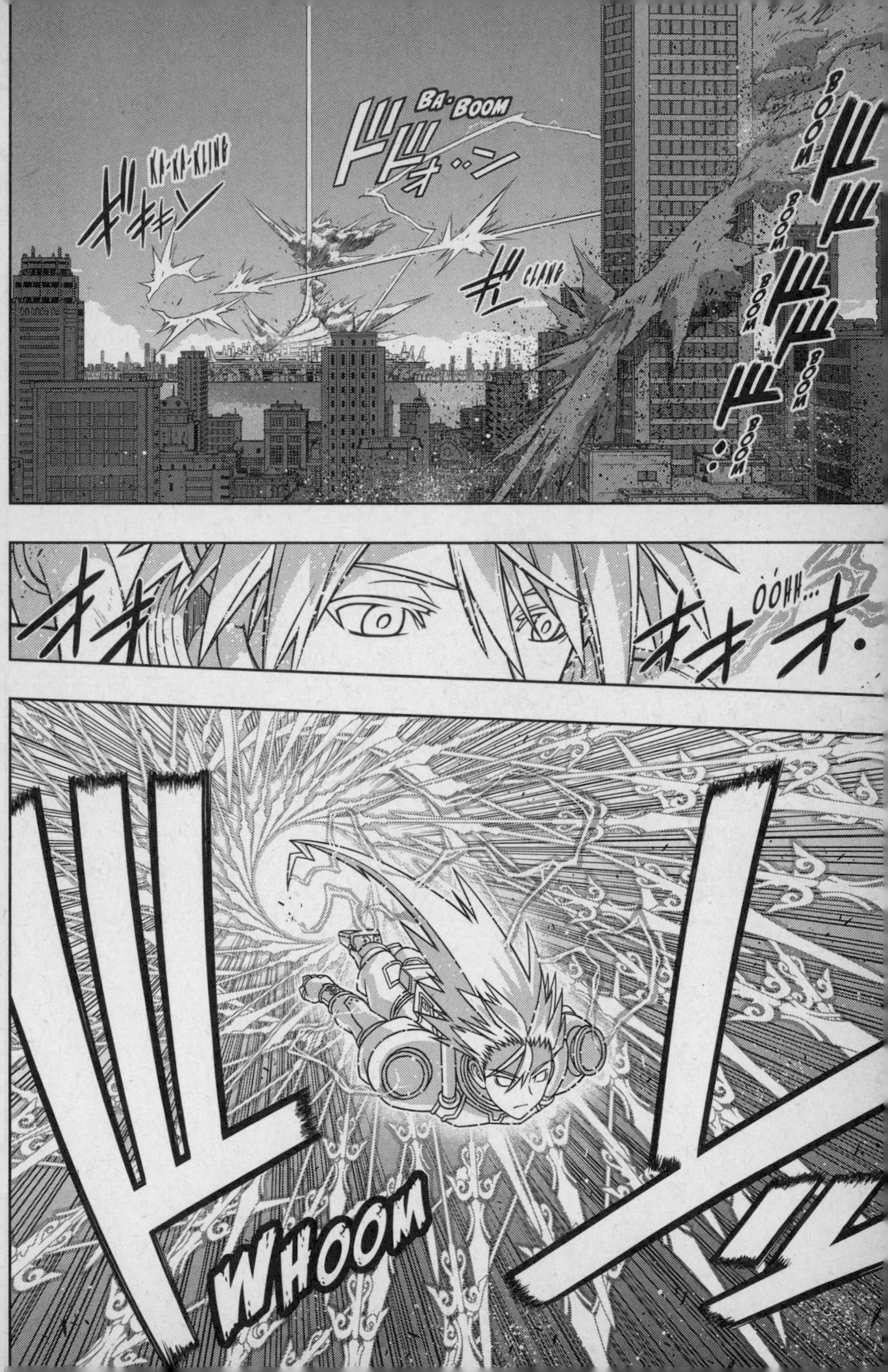
ドドドドド‥
BOOM BOOM BOOM BOOM BOOM
ドドォ‥ン
BA-BOOM
ギ
CLANG
ギキキン
KA-KA-KLING
オオオ‥
OOHH...
オオ
ドン
WHOOM

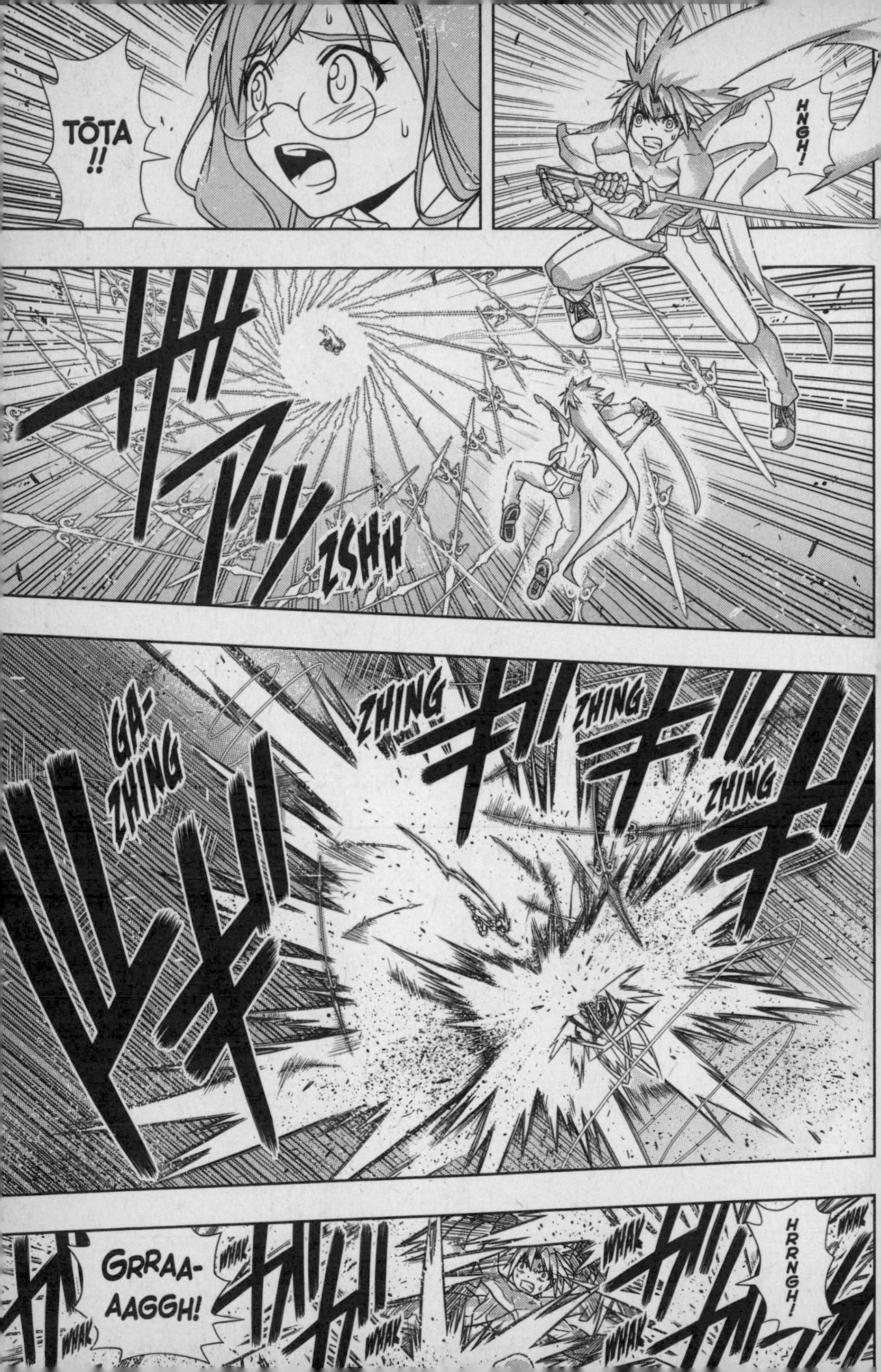
HNGH!
TŌTA !!
ZSHH
ZHING
ZHING
ZHING
GA-ZHING
HRRNGH!
WHAK
WHAK
WHAK
WHAK
WHAK
GRRAA-AAGGH!
WHAK

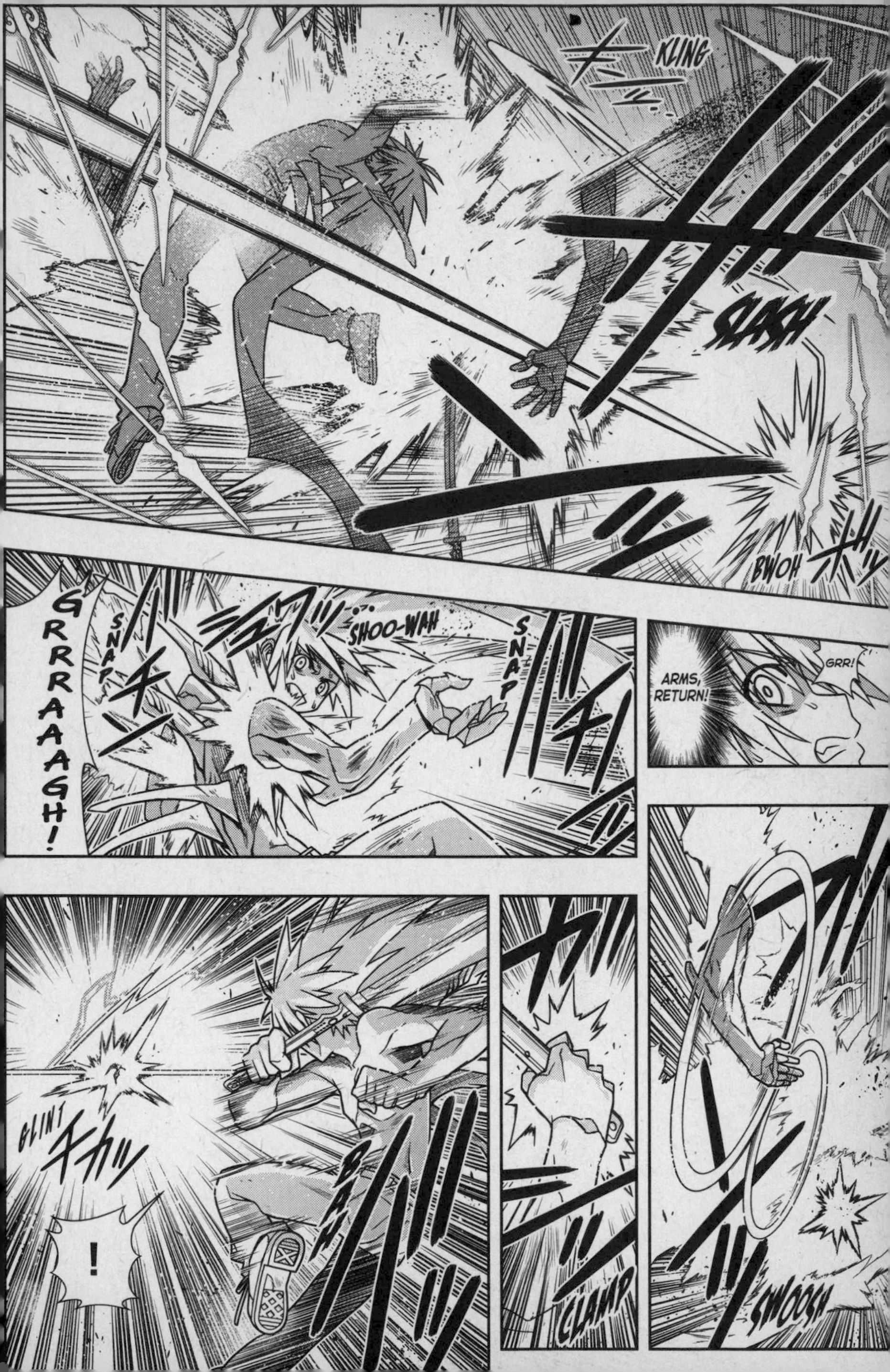

KLING
SLASH
BWOH
GRR!
ARMS, RETURN!
SNAP
SHOO-WAH
SNAP
GRRRAAAGH!
SWOOSH
CLAMP
GLINT
!

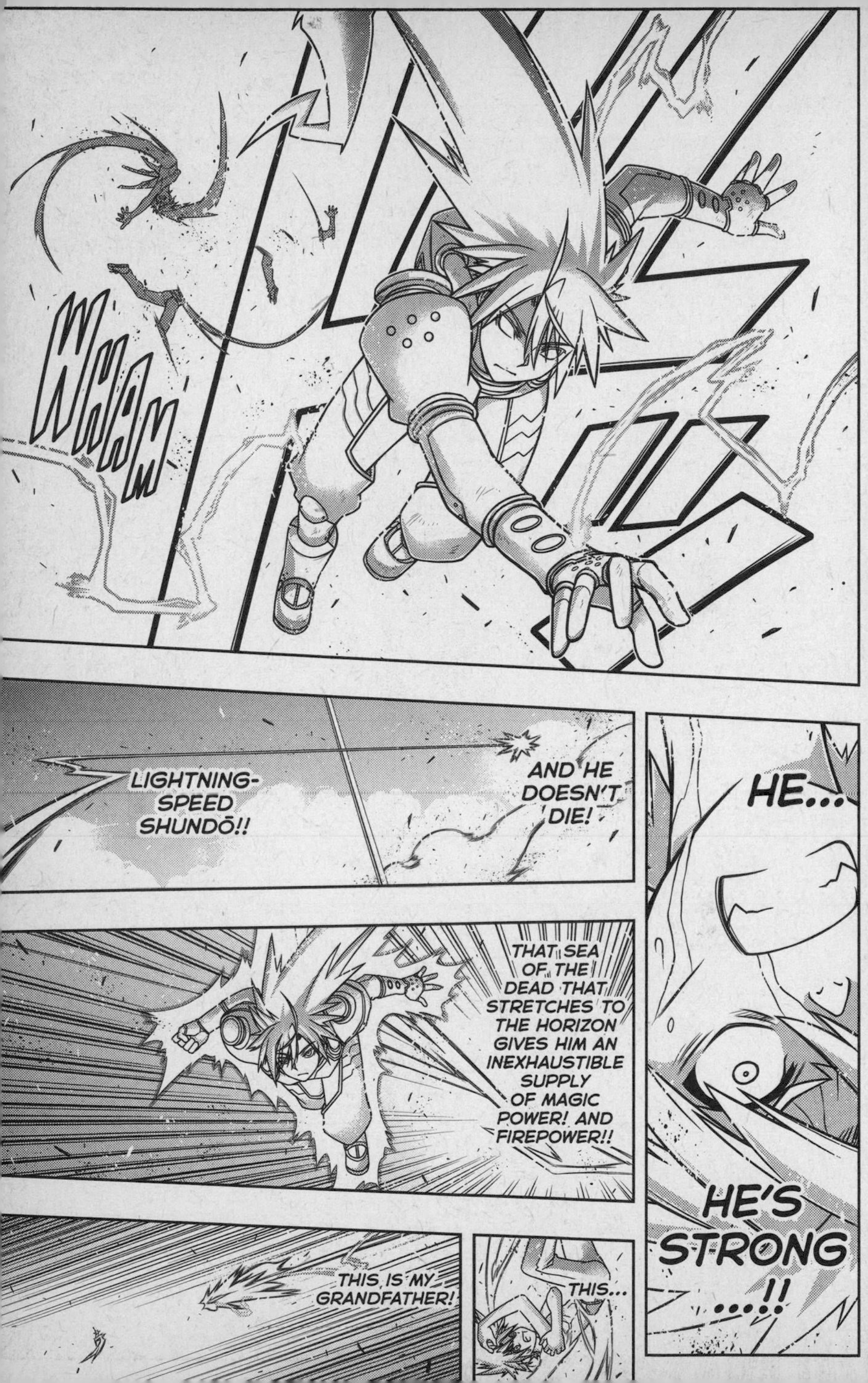
HE...
HE'S STRONG ....!!
AND HE DOESN'T DIE!
LIGHTNING-SPEED SHUNDŌ!!
THAT SEA OF THE DEAD THAT STRETCHES TO THE HORIZON GIVES HIM AN INEXHAUSTIBLE SUPPLY OF MAGIC POWER! AND FIREPOWER!!
THIS...
THIS IS MY GRANDFATHER!

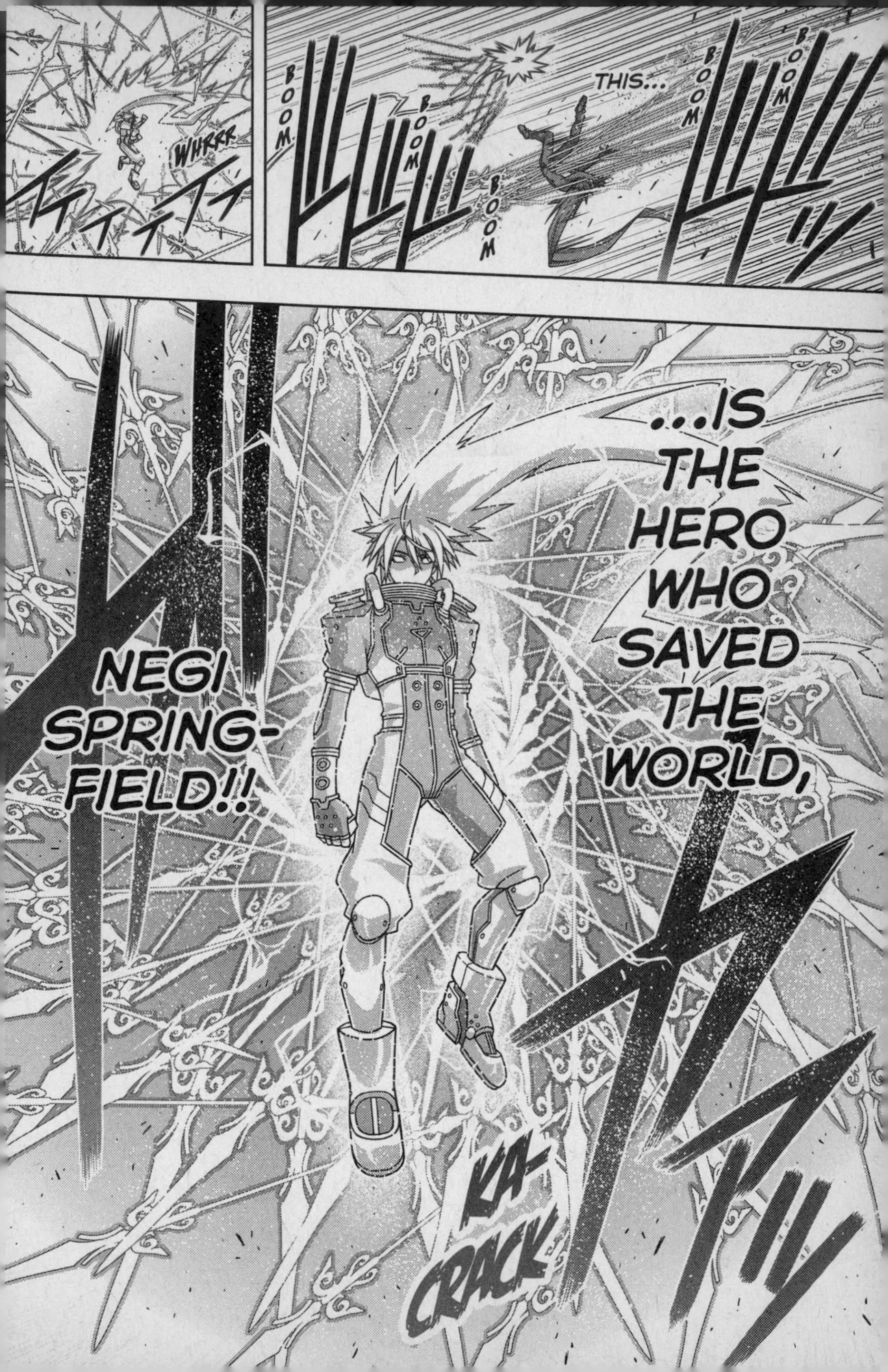
BOOM
BOOM
THIS...
BOOM
BOOM
BOOM
WHRRR
...IS THE HERO WHO SAVED THE WORLD,
NEGI SPRING-FIELD!!
KA-CRACK

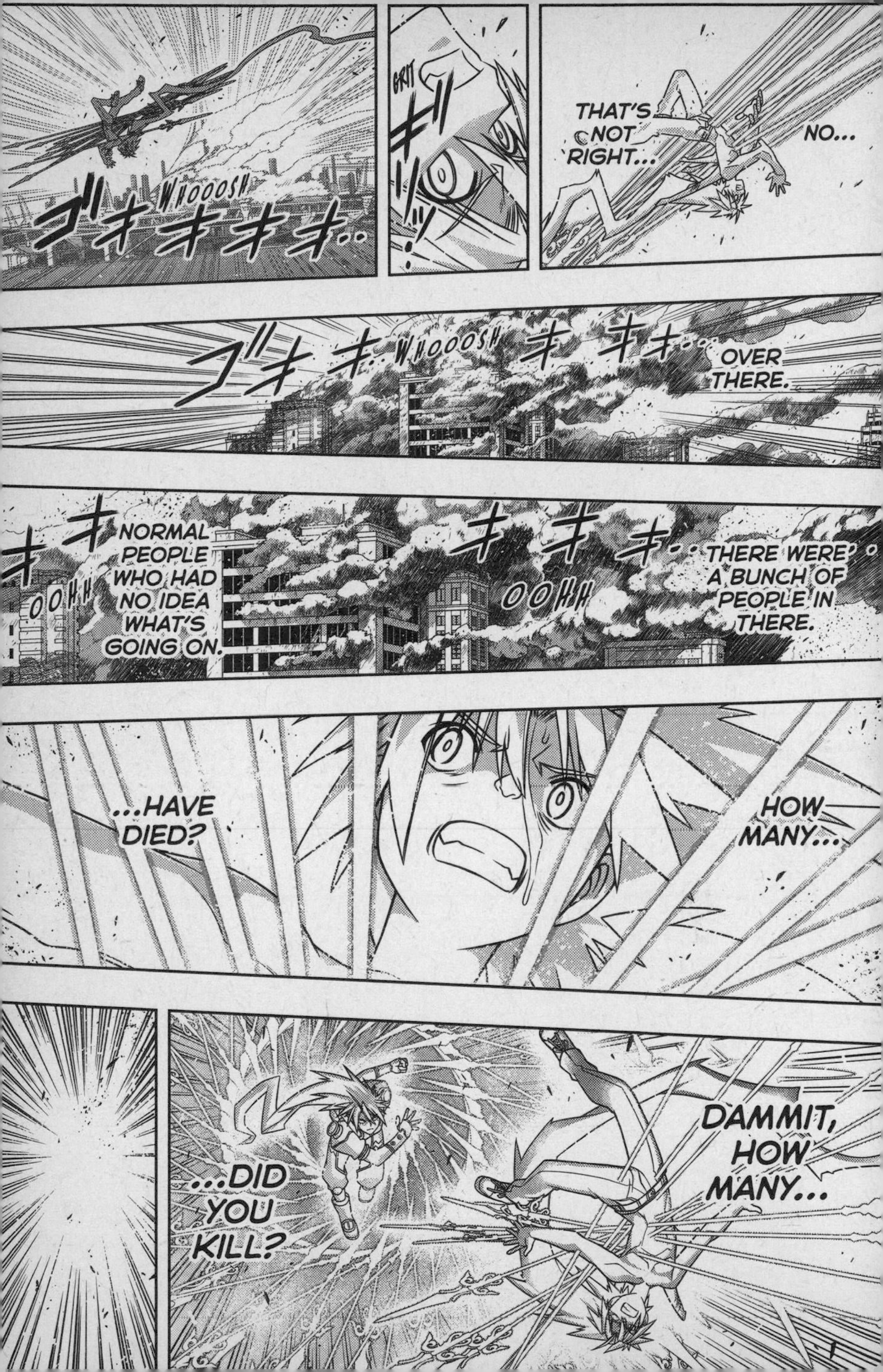
NO...
THAT'S NOT RIGHT...
GRIT
WHOOOSH
OVER THERE.
WHOOOSH
THERE WERE A BUNCH OF PEOPLE IN THERE.
OOHH
NORMAL PEOPLE WHO HAD NO IDEA WHAT'S GOING ON.
OOHH
HOW MANY...
...HAVE DIED?
DAMMIT, HOW MANY...
...DID YOU KILL?

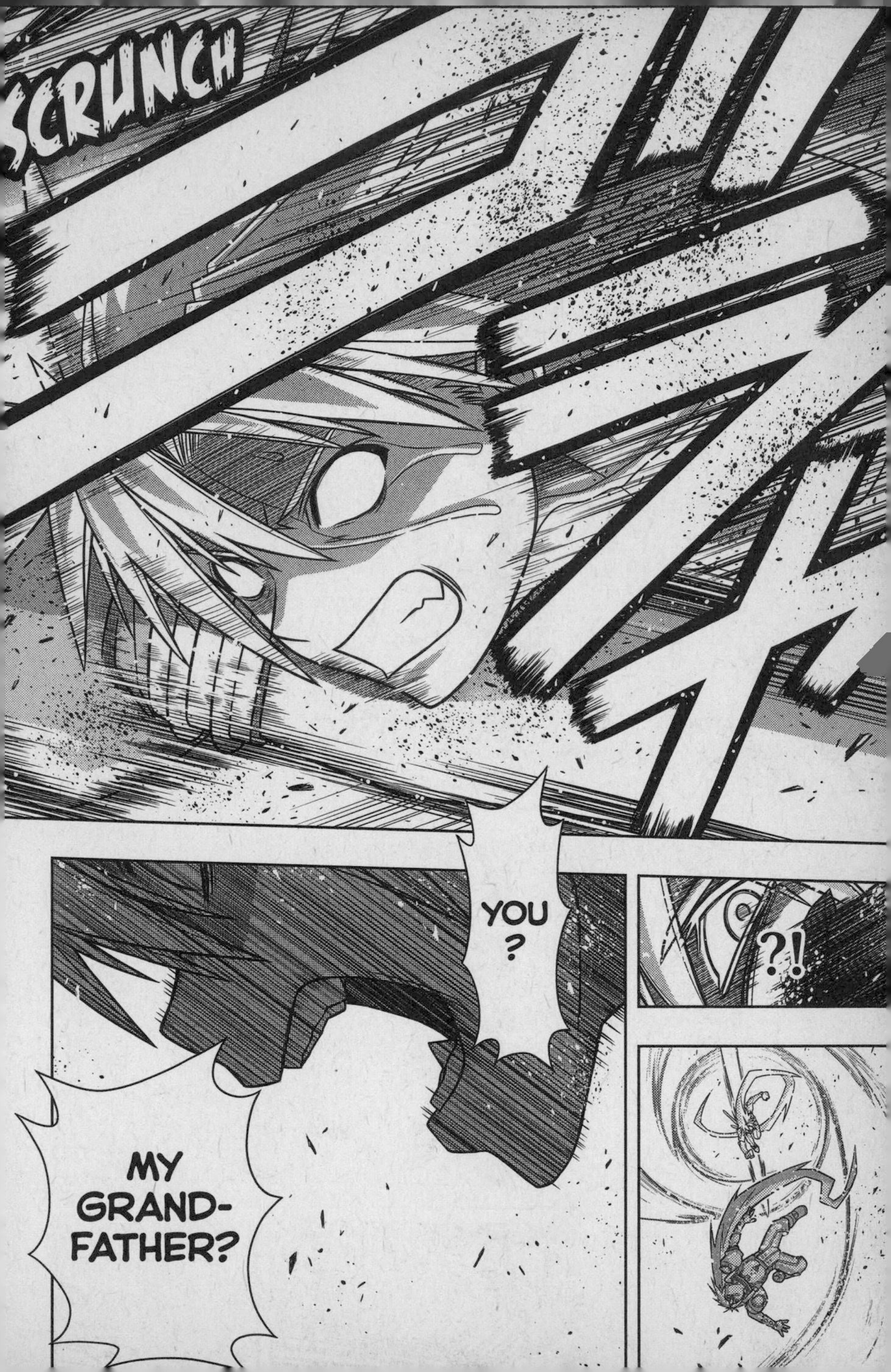
SCRUNCH
?!
YOU ?
MY GRAND-FATHER?

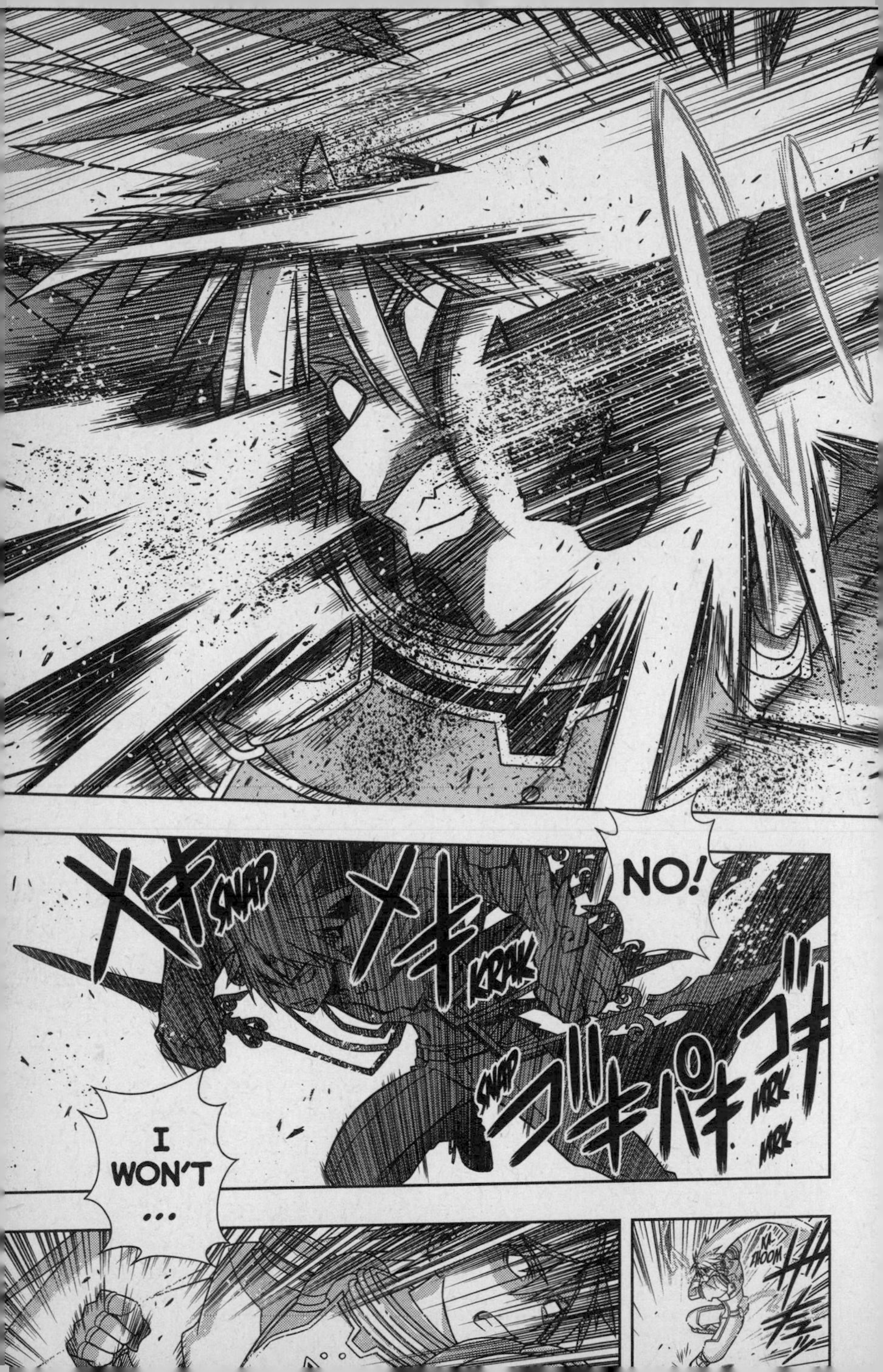
NO!
MRK
MRK
MRK
SNAP
KRAK
SNAP
I WON'T ...
KA-THOOM

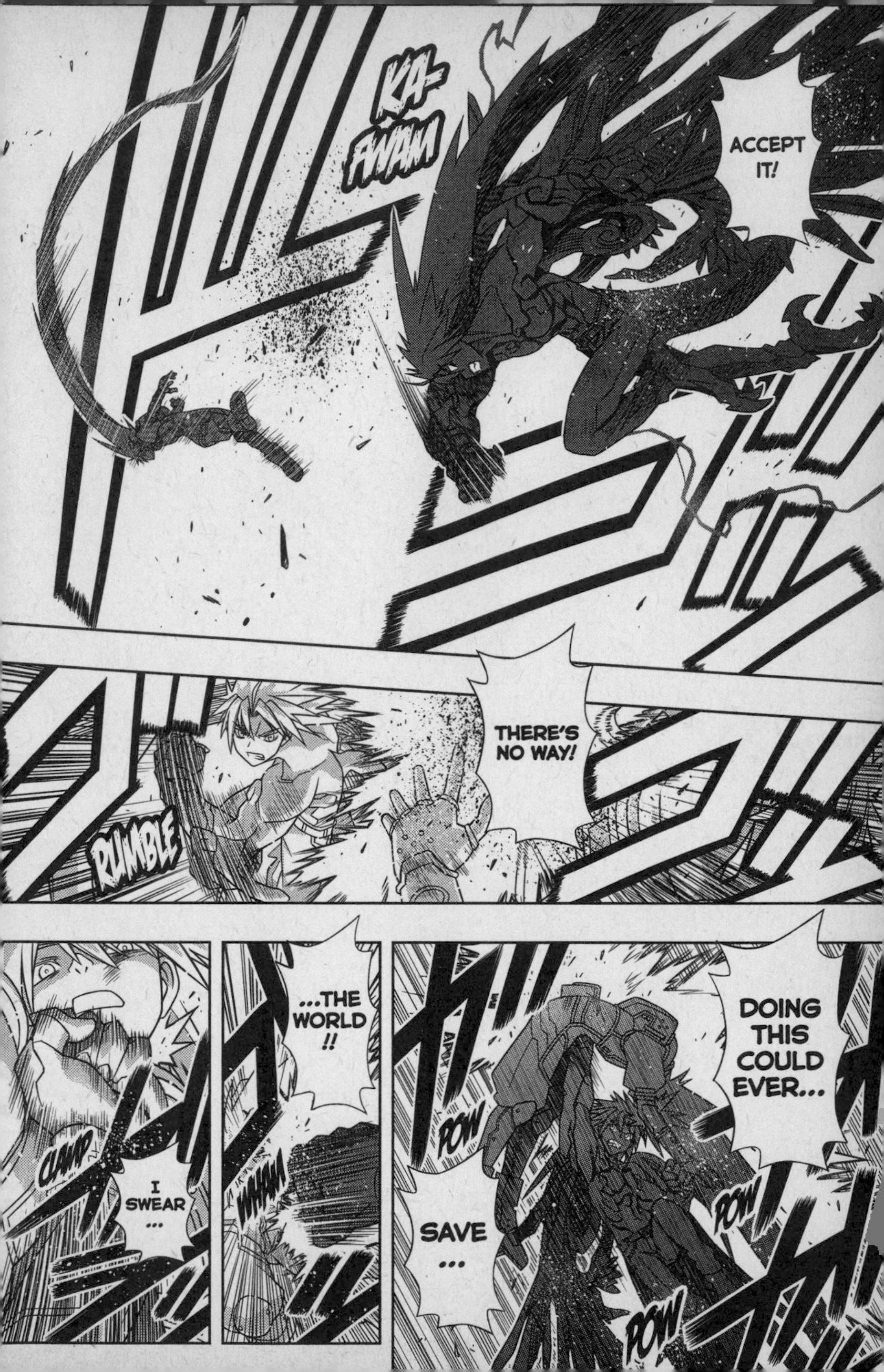
ACCEPT IT!
KA-FWAM
THERE'S NO WAY!
RUMBLE
DOING THIS COULD EVER...
POW
SAVE ...
POW
POW
...THE WORLD !!
WHAM
CLAMP
I SWEAR ...

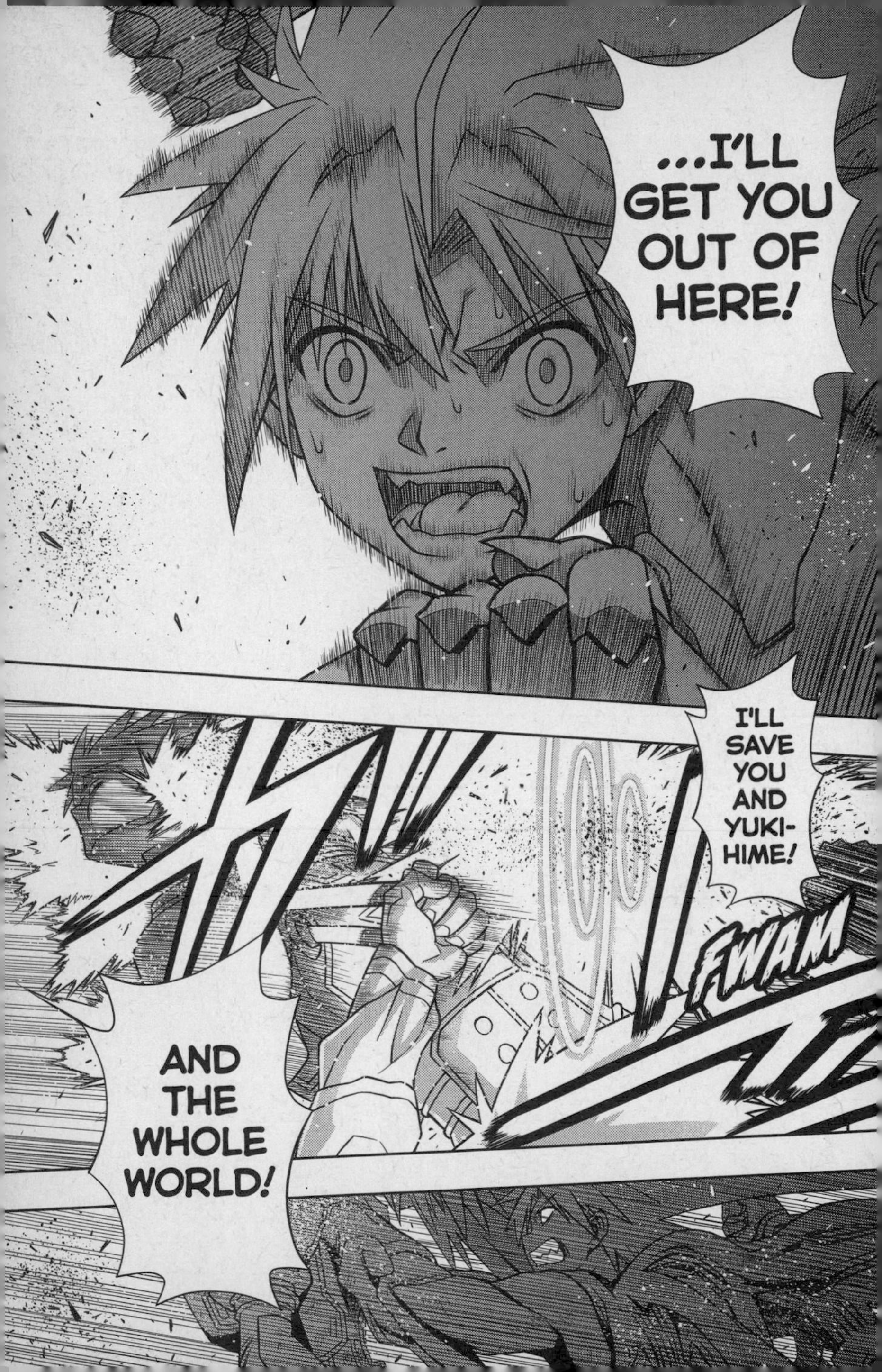
...I'LL GET YOU OUT OF HERE!
I'LL SAVE YOU AND YUKI-HIME!
FWAM
AND THE WHOLE WORLD!

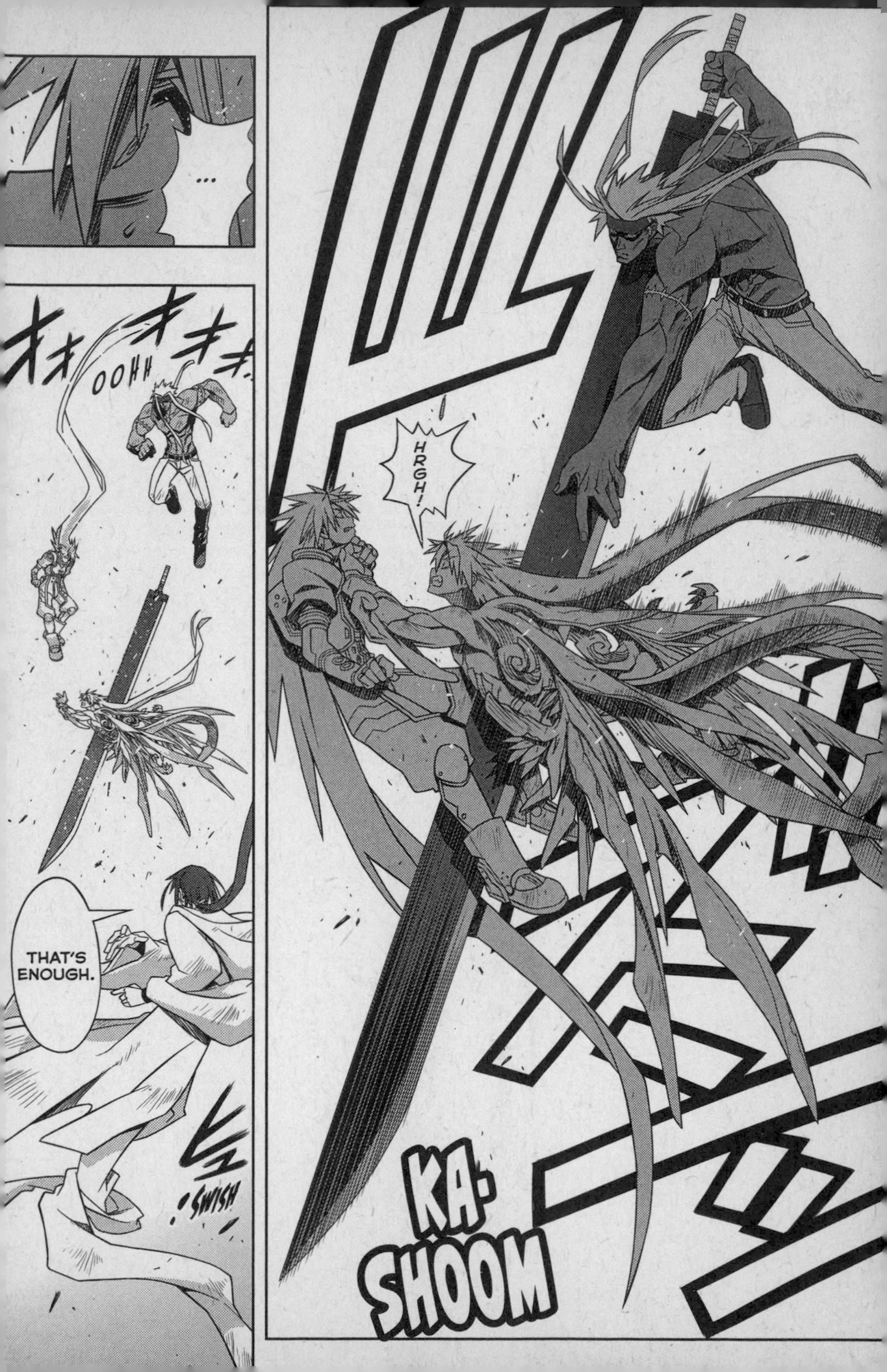
HRGH!
KA-SHOOM
...
OOHH
THAT'S ENOUGH.
SWISH

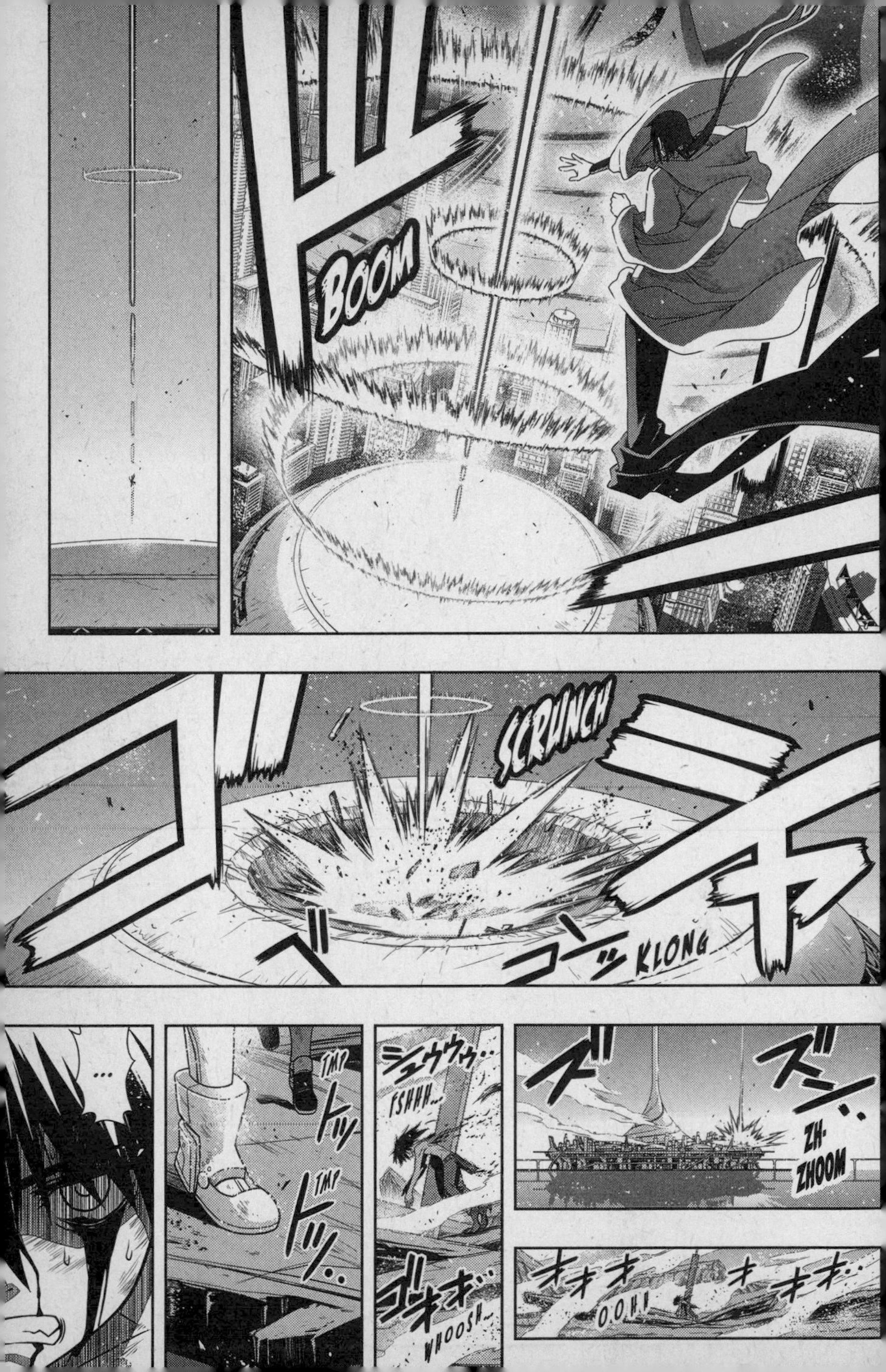

BOOM
SCRUNCH
KLONG
ZH-ZHOOM
OOHH
シュウウ…
FSHHH…
WHOOSH…
TMP
TMP
…

OOHH

KA-KRAK

TŌTA ...!

NII-CHAN ...

TŌTA-KUN !!

BLAST IT...

WHAK

I'M SORRY ...

COUGH! OH NO...

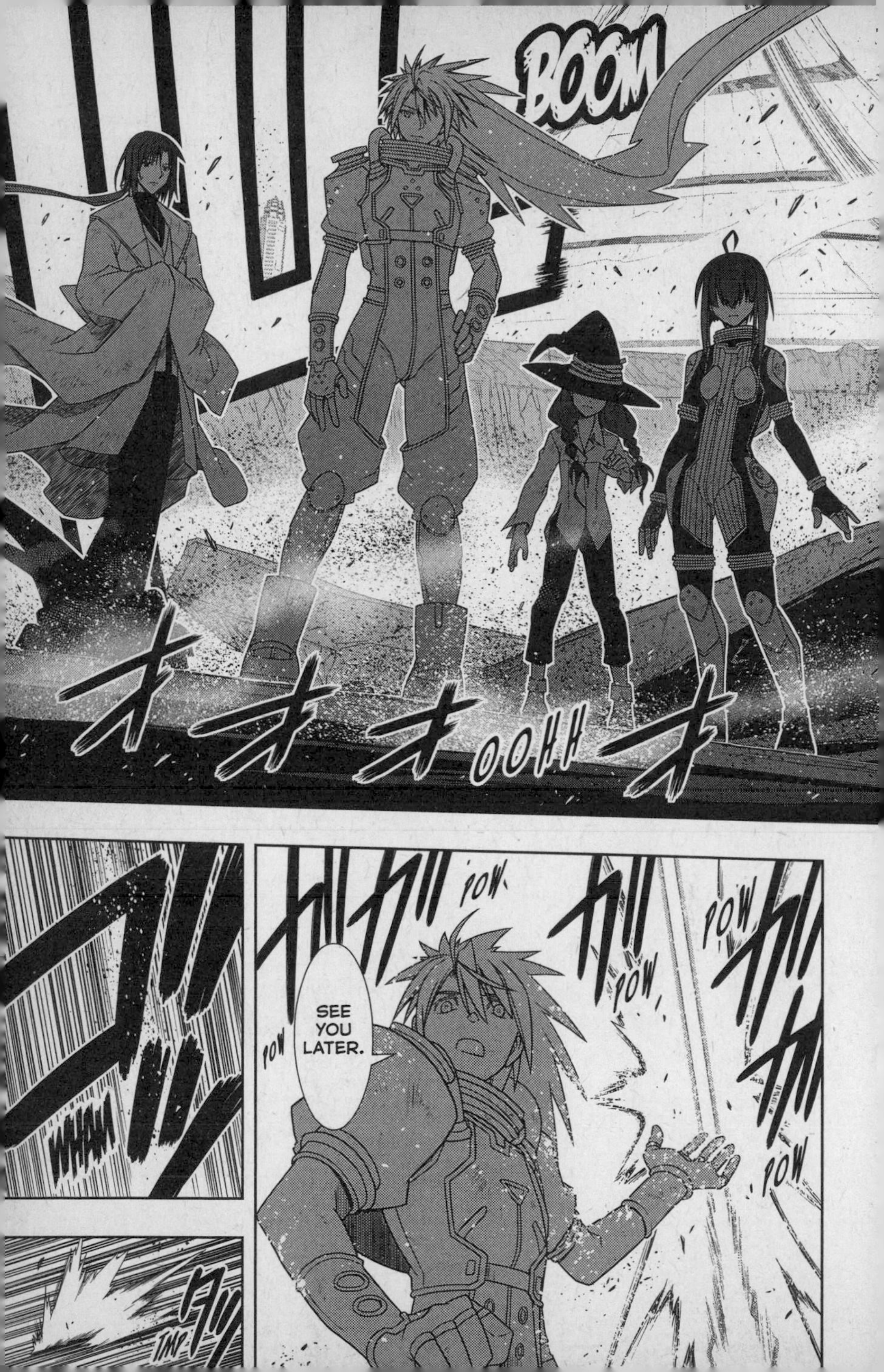

BOOM
OOHH
POW
POW
POW
SEE YOU LATER.
POW
POW
WHAM
TMP

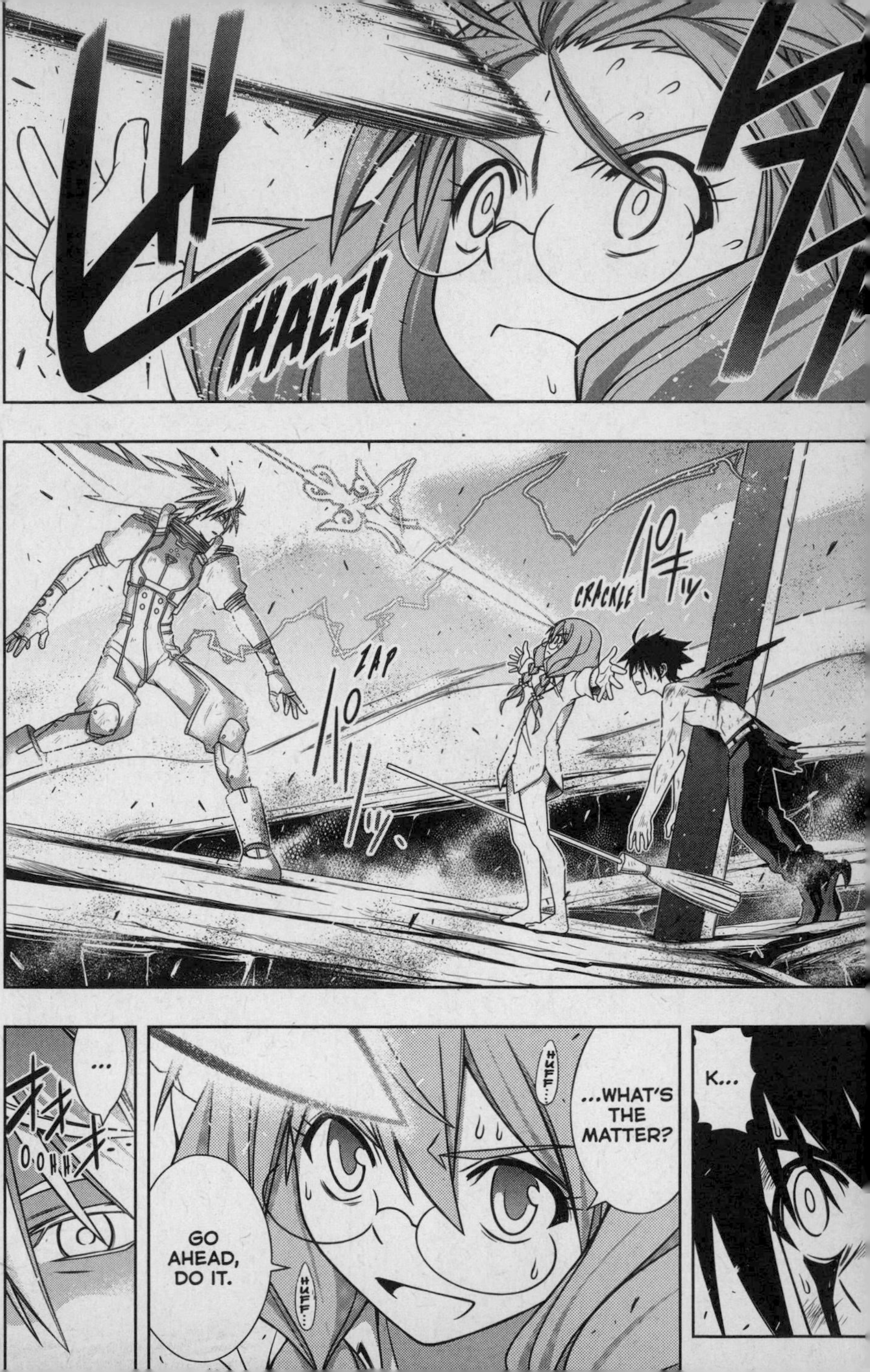

HALT!
CRACKLE
パキッ
ZAP
パリッ
K...
...WHAT'S THE MATTER?
HUFF...
GO AHEAD, DO IT.
HUFF...
...
OOHH

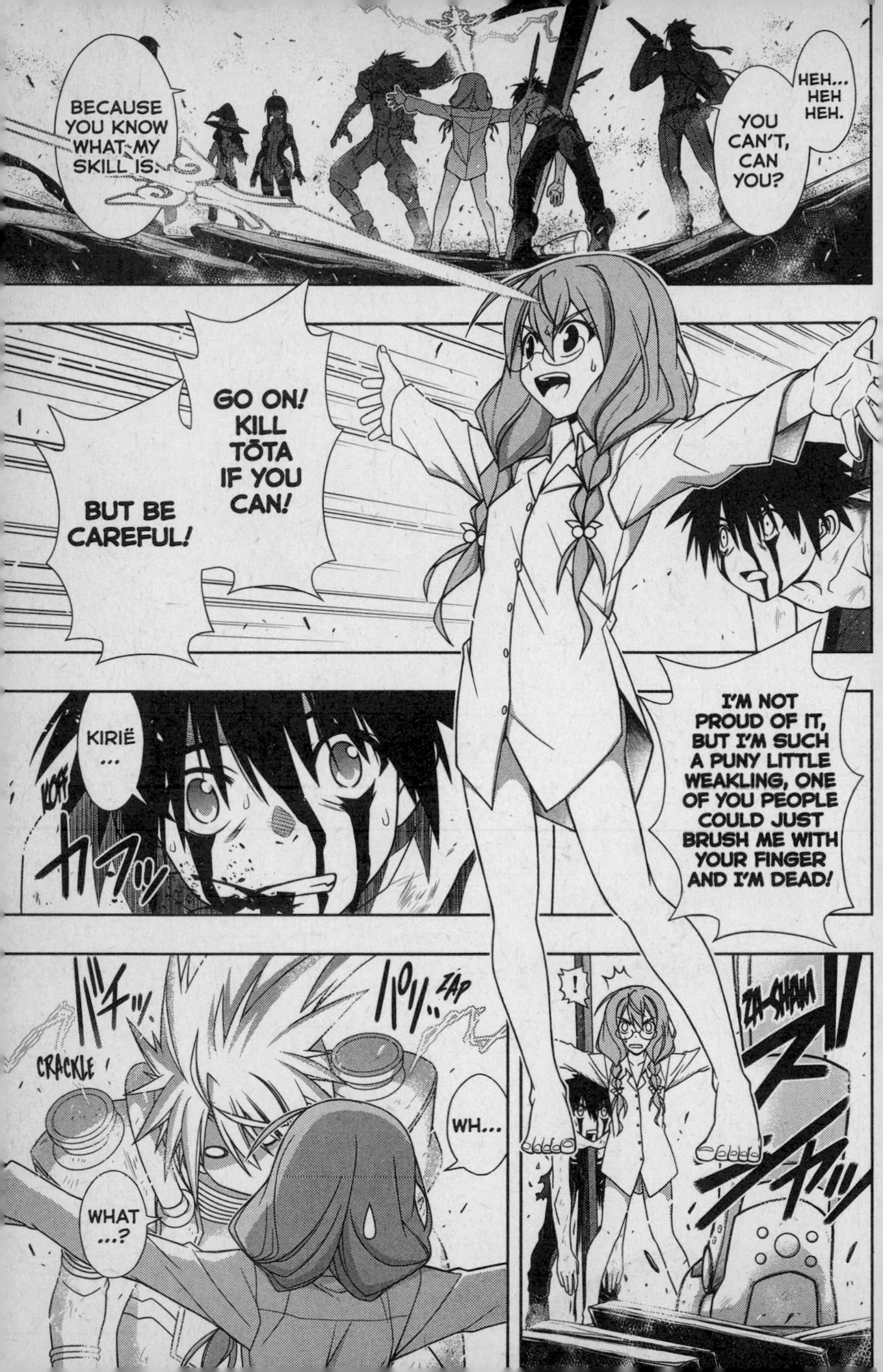
HEH... HEH HEH.
YOU CAN'T, CAN YOU?
BECAUSE YOU KNOW WHAT MY SKILL IS.
GO ON! KILL TŌTA IF YOU CAN!
BUT BE CAREFUL!
I'M NOT PROUD OF IT, BUT I'M SUCH A PUNY LITTLE WEAKLING, ONE OF YOU PEOPLE COULD JUST BRUSH ME WITH YOUR FINGER AND I'M DEAD!
KIRIË...
KOFF
カフッ
!
ZA-SHAAA
パリッ
ZAP
WH...
バチッ
CRACKLE
WHAT...?

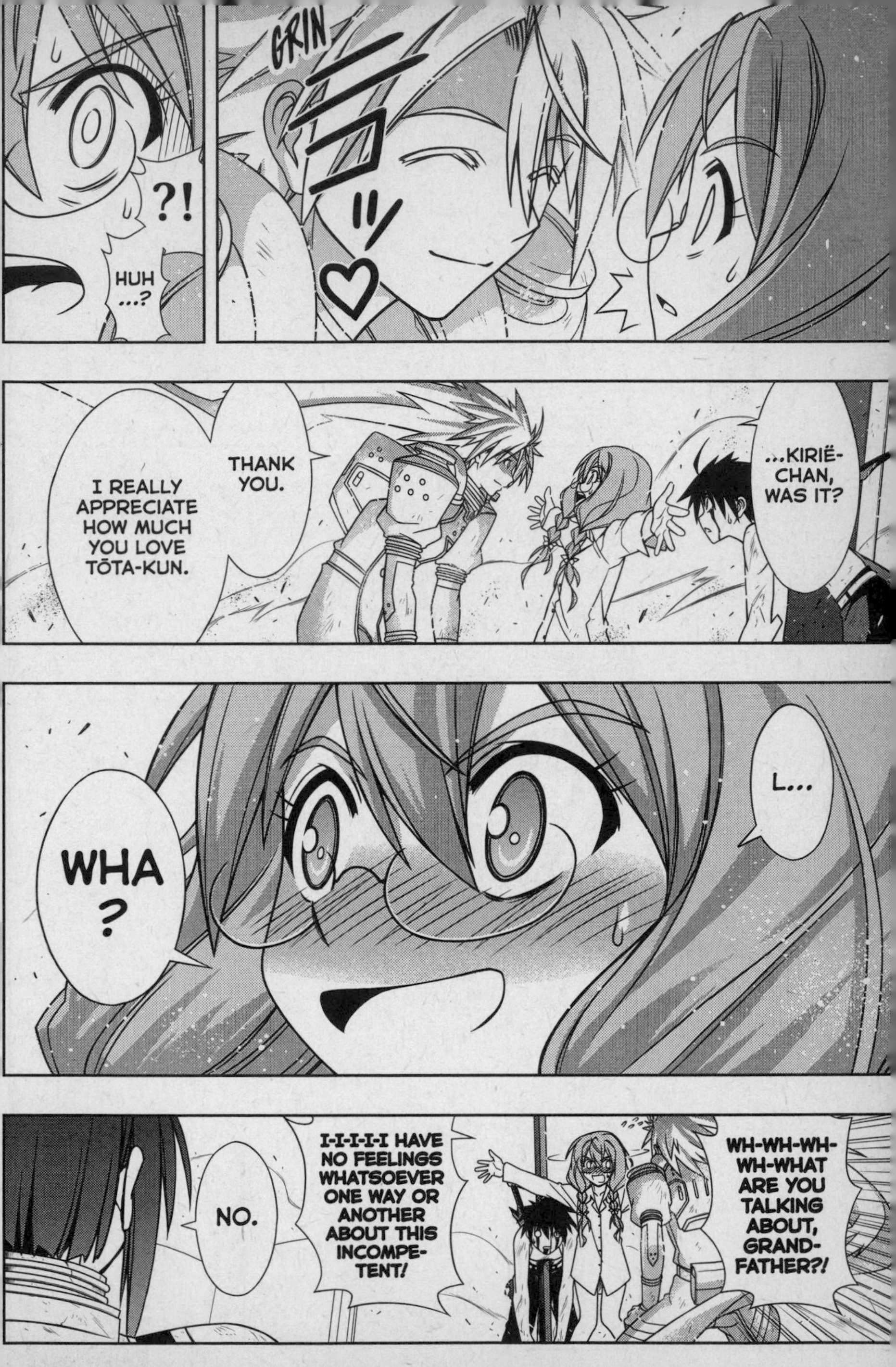
GRIN
?!
HUH ...?
...KIRIË-CHAN, WAS IT?
THANK YOU.
I REALLY APPRECIATE HOW MUCH YOU LOVE TŌTA-KUN.
L...
WHA ?
WH-WH-WH-WH-WHAT ARE YOU TALKING ABOUT, GRAND-FATHER?!
I-I-I-I-I HAVE NO FEELINGS WHATSOEVER ONE WAY OR ANOTHER ABOUT THIS INCOMPE-TENT!
NO.

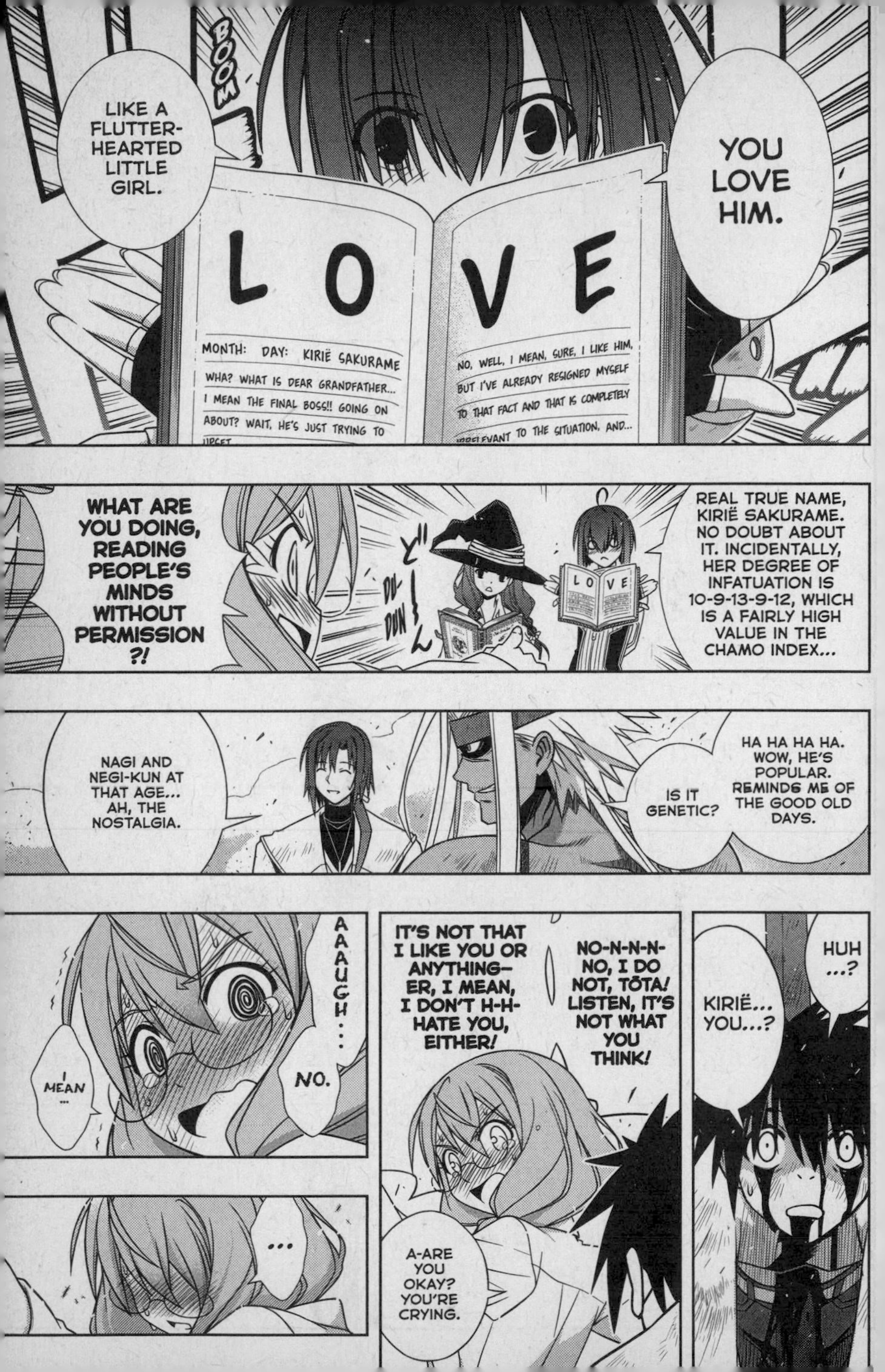
YOU LOVE HIM.
BOOM
LIKE A FLUTTER-HEARTED LITTLE GIRL.
LOVE
MONTH: DAY: KIRIË SAKURAME
WHA? WHAT IS DEAR GRANDFATHER... I MEAN THE FINAL BOSS!! GOING ON ABOUT? WAIT, HE'S JUST TRYING TO
NO, WELL, I MEAN, SURE, I LIKE HIM, BUT I'VE ALREADY RESIGNED MYSELF TO THAT FACT AND THAT IS COMPLETELY IRRELEVANT TO THE SITUATION, AND...
REAL TRUE NAME, KIRIË SAKURAME. NO DOUBT ABOUT IT. INCIDENTALLY, HER DEGREE OF INFATUATION IS 10-9-13-9-12, WHICH IS A FAIRLY HIGH VALUE IN THE CHAMO INDEX...
LOVE
DU-DUN
WHAT ARE YOU DOING, READING PEOPLE'S MINDS WITHOUT PERMISSION?!
HA HA HA HA. WOW, HE'S POPULAR. REMINDS ME OF THE GOOD OLD DAYS.
IS IT GENETIC?
NAGI AND NEGI-KUN AT THAT AGE... AH, THE NOSTALGIA.
HUH...?
KIRIË... YOU...?
NO-N-N-N-NO, I DO NOT, TŌTA! LISTEN, IT'S NOT WHAT YOU THINK!
IT'S NOT THAT I LIKE YOU OR ANYTHING—ER, I MEAN, I DON'T H-H-HATE YOU, EITHER!
A-ARE YOU OKAY? YOU'RE CRYING.
AAAAUGH...
NO.
I MEAN...
...

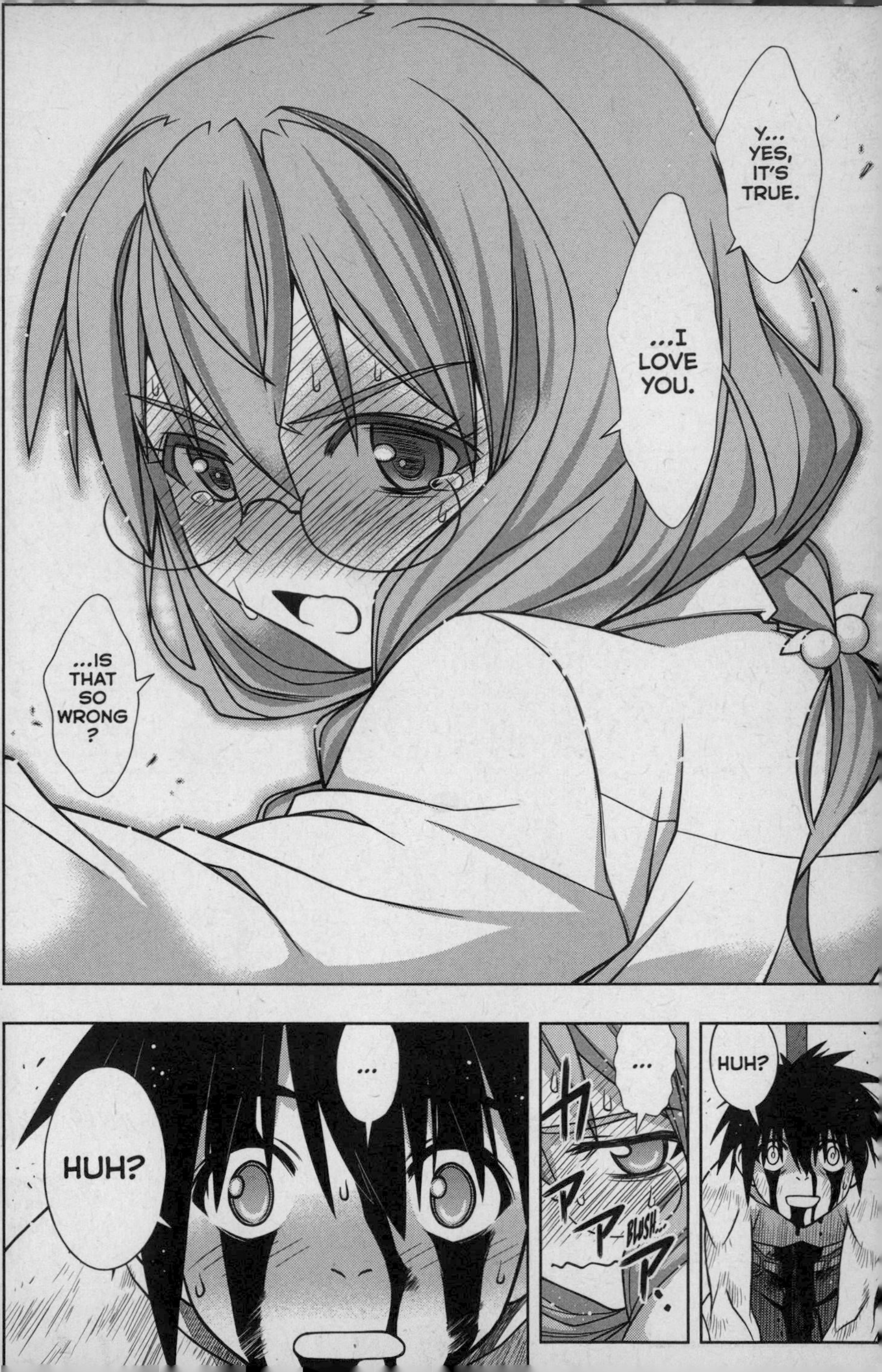
Y... YES, IT'S TRUE.
...I LOVE YOU.
...IS THAT SO WRONG?
HUH?
...
BLUSH...
...
HUH?

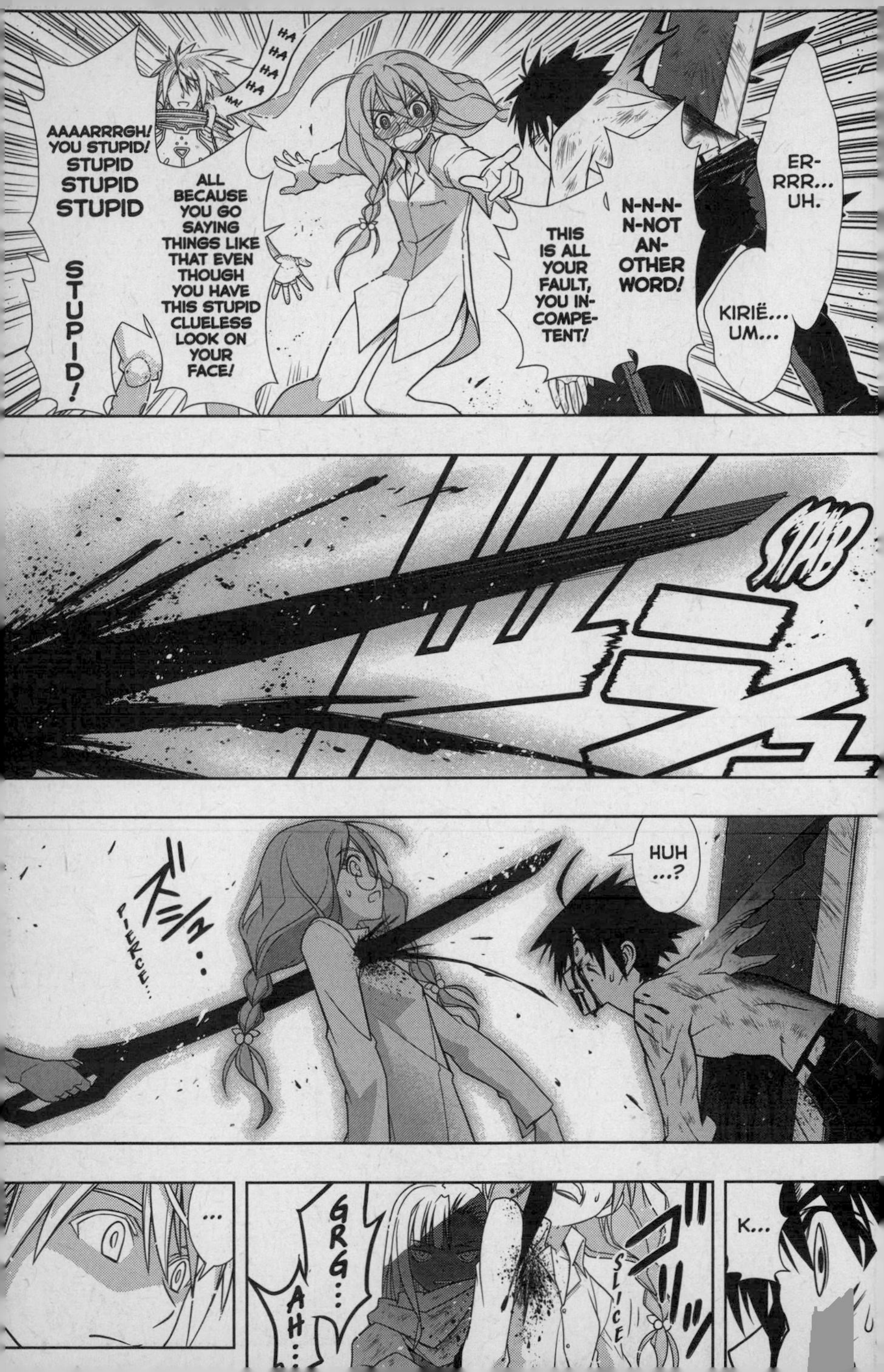
ER-RRR... UH.
KIRIË... UM...
N-N-N-N-NOT AN-OTHER WORD!
THIS IS ALL YOUR FAULT, YOU IN-COMPE-TENT!
HA HA HA HA HA!
ALL BECAUSE YOU GO SAYING THINGS LIKE THAT EVEN THOUGH YOU HAVE THIS STUPID CLUELESS LOOK ON YOUR FACE!
AAAARRRGH! YOU STUPID! STUPID STUPID STUPID
STUPID!
STAB
HUH ...?
PIERCE...
K...
SLICE
GRG...
AH...
...

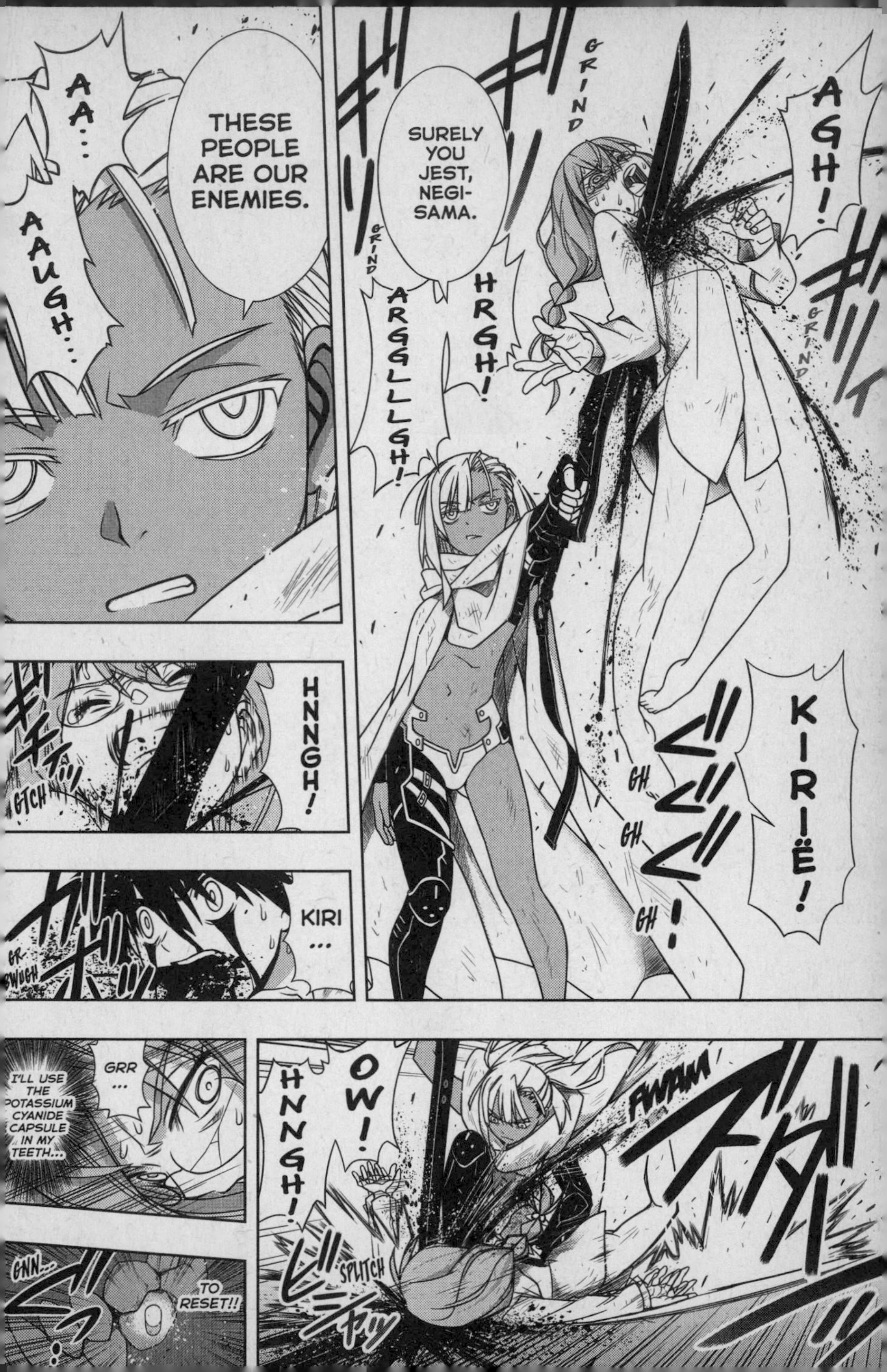
AGH!
GRIND
SURELY YOU JEST, NEGI-SAMA.
GRIND
HRGH!
ARGGLLLGH!
GRIND
KIRI-Ë!
GH
GH
GH
THESE PEOPLE ARE OUR ENEMIES.
AA...
AAUGH...
HNNGH!
GTCH
KIRI...
OW!
HNNGH!
SPLITCH
GRR...
I'LL USE THE POTASSIUM CYANIDE CAPSULE IN MY TEETH...
GNN...
TO RESET!!

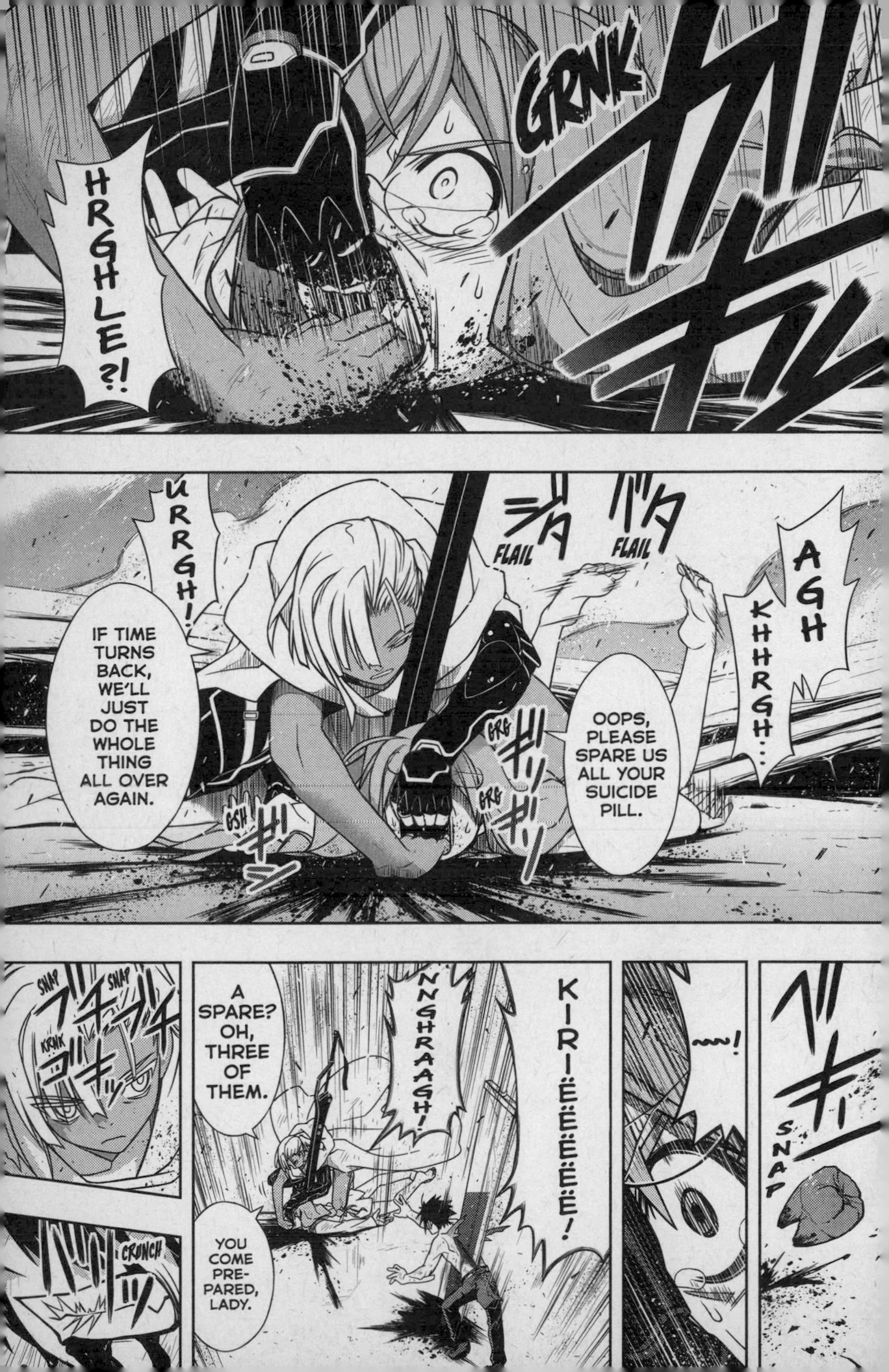
GRNK
HRGHLE?!
AGH
KHHRGH...
OOPS, PLEASE SPARE US ALL YOUR SUICIDE PILL.
FLAIL
FLAIL
GRG
GRG
GSH
URRGH!
IF TIME TURNS BACK, WE'LL JUST DO THE WHOLE THING ALL OVER AGAIN.
SNAP
~~~!
KIRIEEEEE!
NNGHRAAGH!
A SPARE? OH, THREE OF THEM.
YOU COME PRE-PARED, LADY.
SNAP
SNAP
KRNK
CRUNCH
~~~

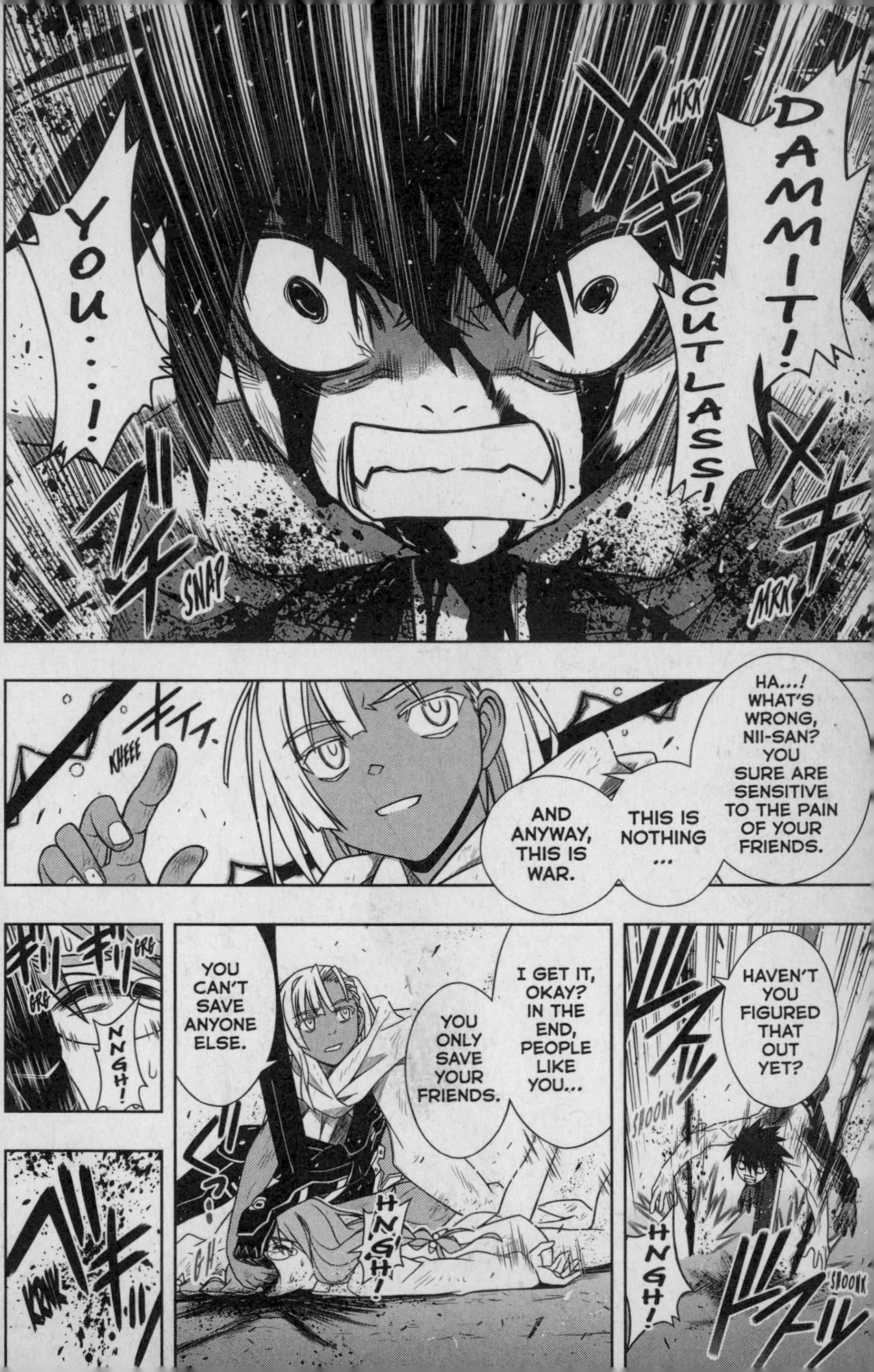
DAMMIT!
MRK
CUTLASS!
YOU...!
SNAP
MRK
HA...! WHAT'S WRONG, NII-SAN? YOU SURE ARE SENSITIVE TO THE PAIN OF YOUR FRIENDS.
THIS IS NOTHING ...
AND ANYWAY, THIS IS WAR.
KHEEE
HAVEN'T YOU FIGURED THAT OUT YET?
SHOONK
HNGH!
SHOONK
I GET IT, OKAY? IN THE END, PEOPLE LIKE YOU...
YOU ONLY SAVE YOUR FRIENDS.
YOU CAN'T SAVE ANYONE ELSE.
HNGH!
GH
GRG
GRG
NNGH!
KRNK

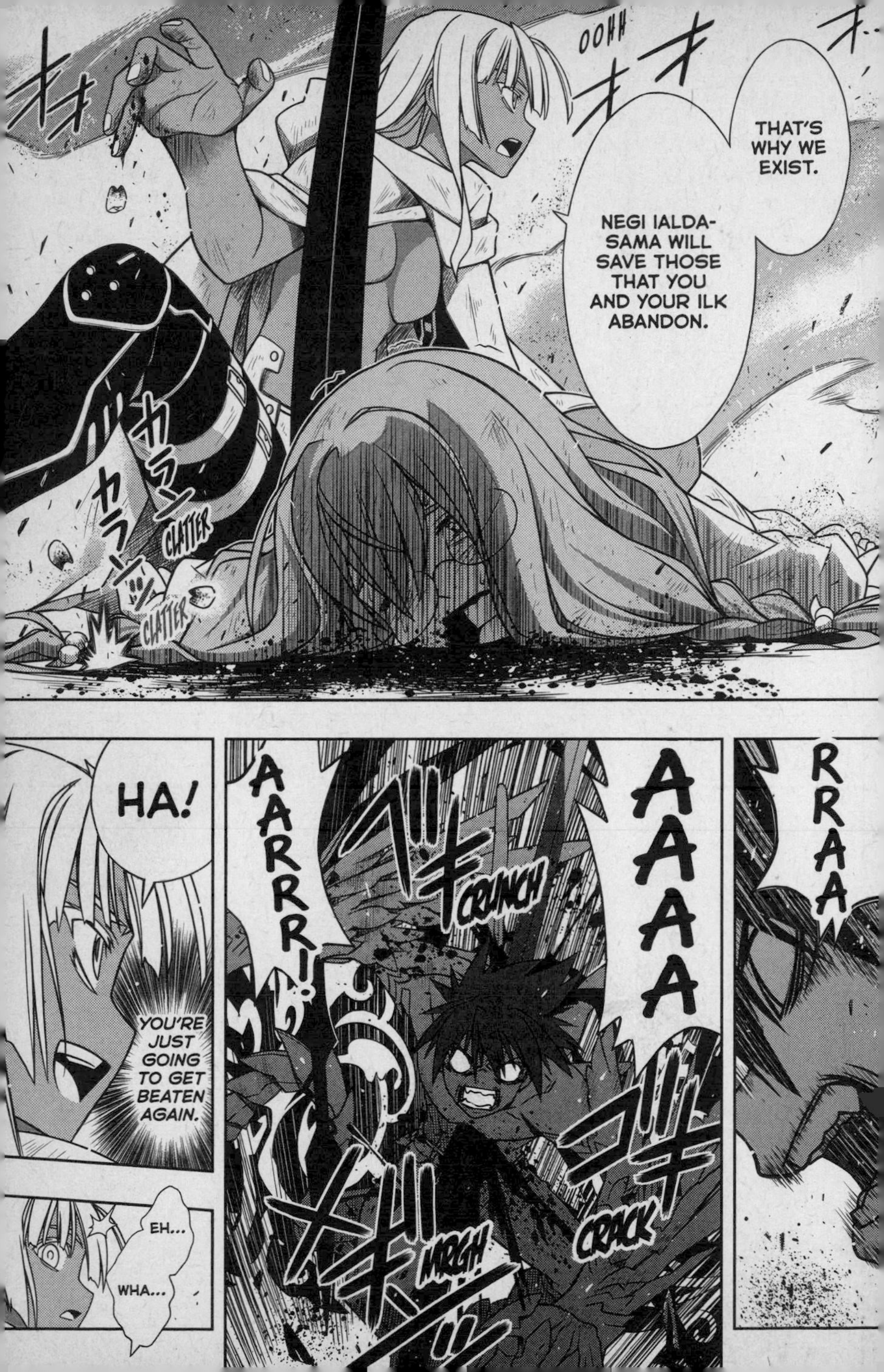
OOHH
THAT'S WHY WE EXIST.
NEGI IALDA-SAMA WILL SAVE THOSE THAT YOU AND YOUR ILK ABANDON.
カラン
CLATTER
カラン
CLATTER
RRAA
AAAA
CRUNCH
CRACK
AARRRR!
MRGH!
HA!
YOU'RE JUST GOING TO GET BEATEN AGAIN.
EH...
WHA...

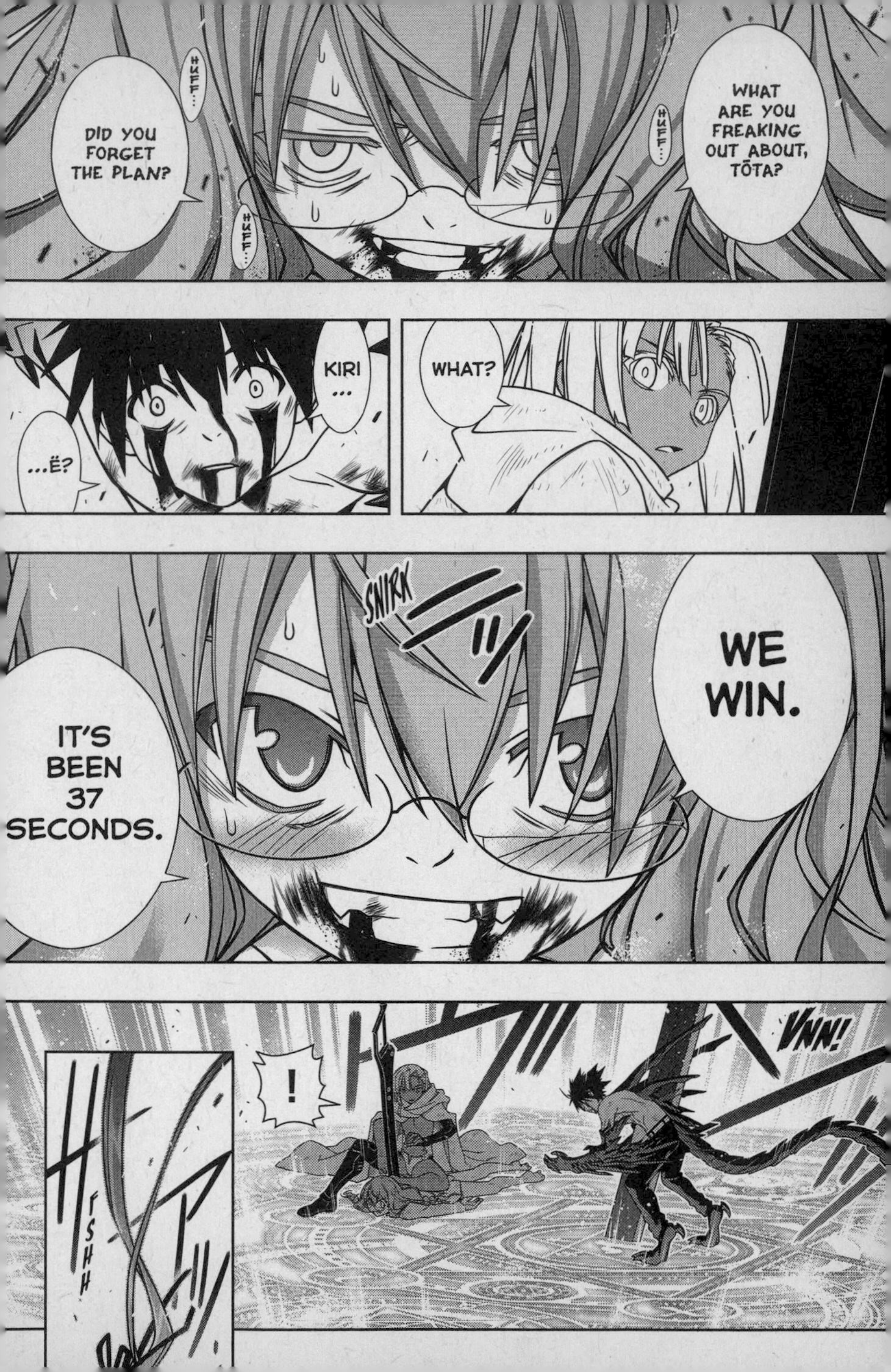
WHAT ARE YOU FREAKING OUT ABOUT, TŌTA?
HUFF...
HUFF...
DID YOU FORGET THE PLAN?
HUFF...
WHAT?
KIRI ...
...Ë?
SNIRK
WE WIN.
IT'S BEEN 37 SECONDS.
VNN!
!
FSHH

悠久 UQ HOLDER!

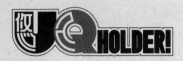

UQ HOLDER!

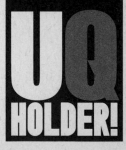

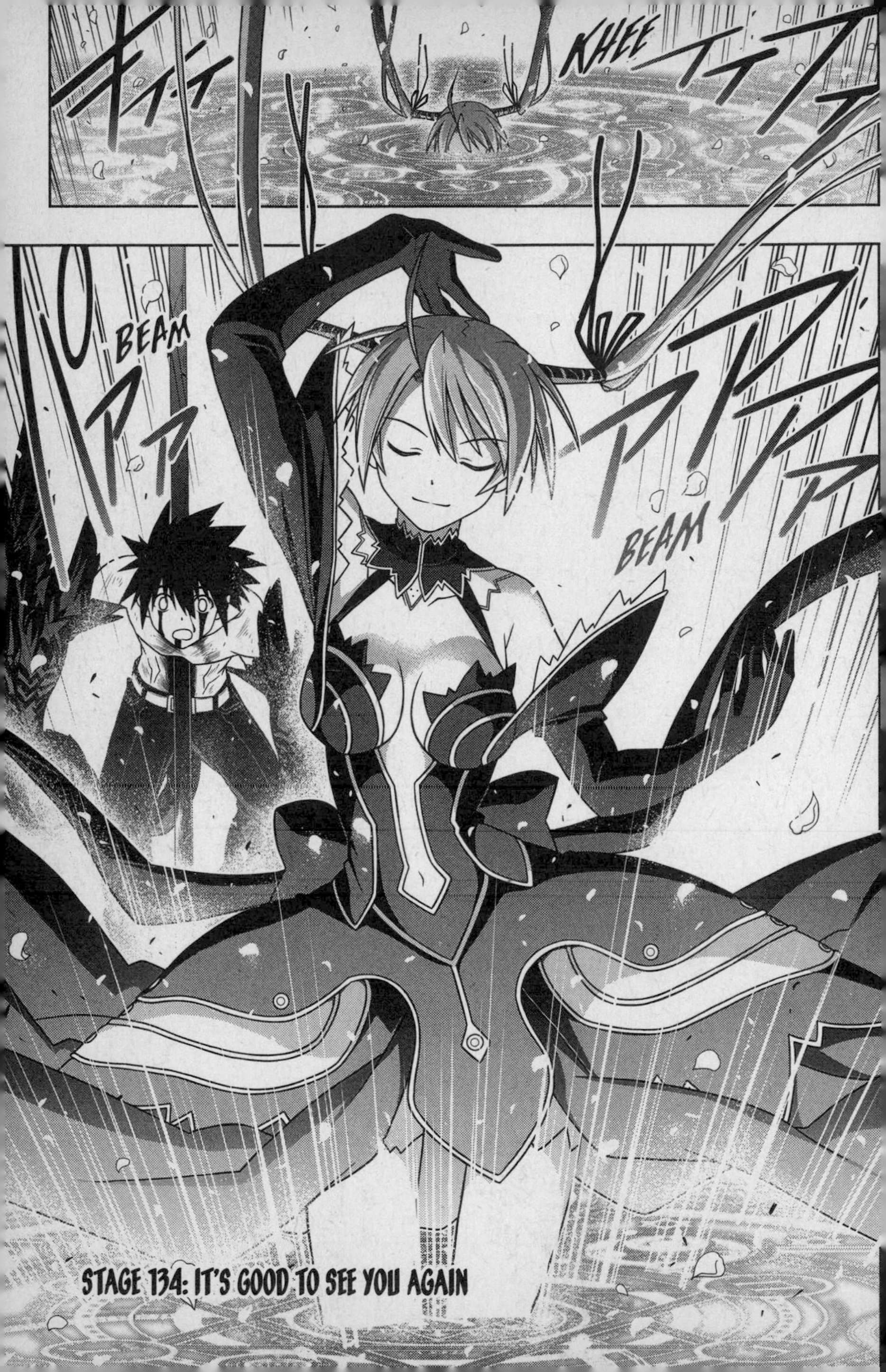
KHEE
BEAM
BEAM
STAGE 134: IT'S GOOD TO SEE YOU AGAIN

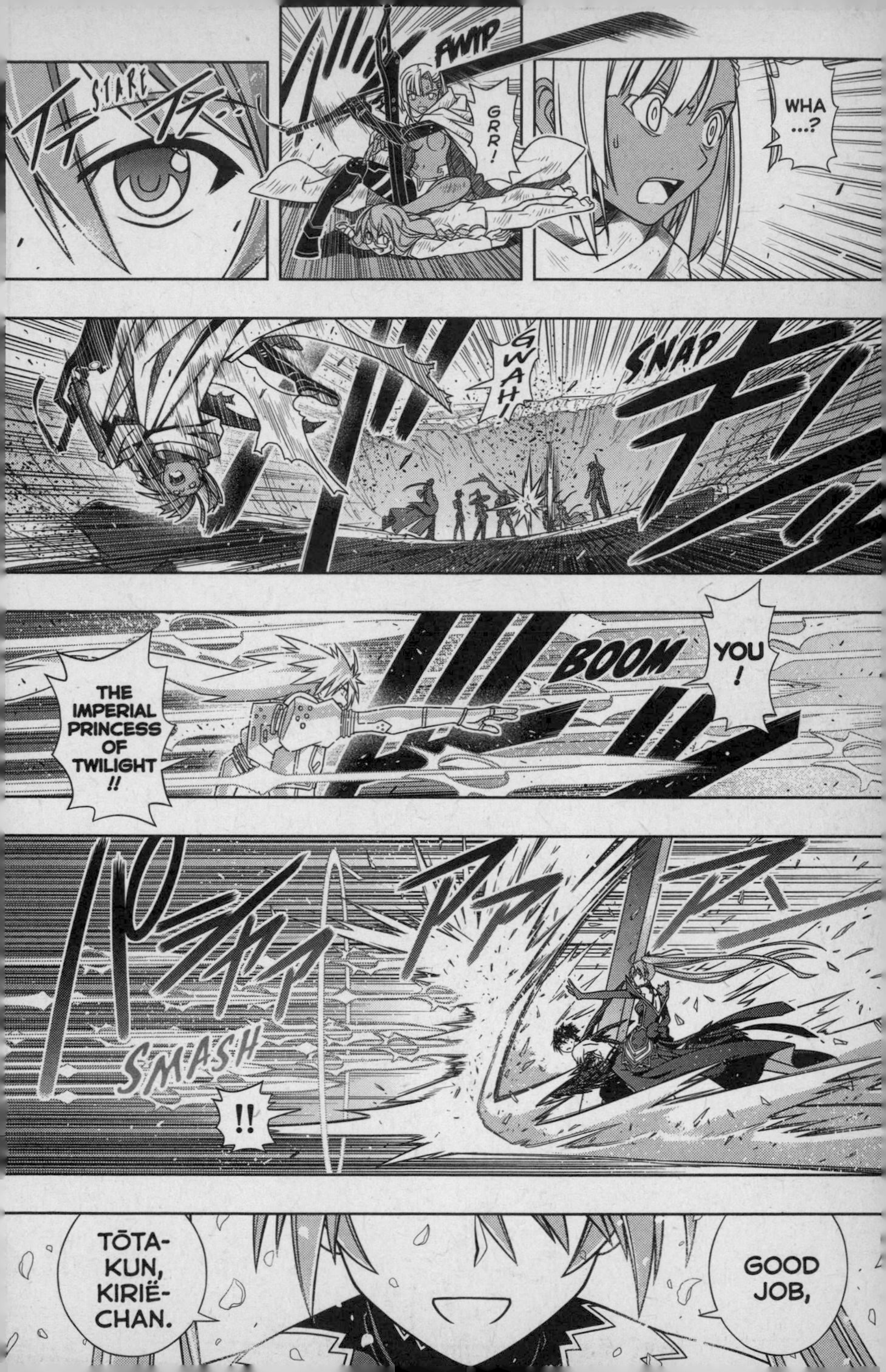

WHA ...?
FWIP
GRR!
STARE
SNAP
GWAH!
YOU!
BOOM
THE IMPERIAL PRINCESS OF TWILIGHT!!
SMASH
!!
GOOD JOB,
TŌTA-KUN, KIRIË-CHAN.

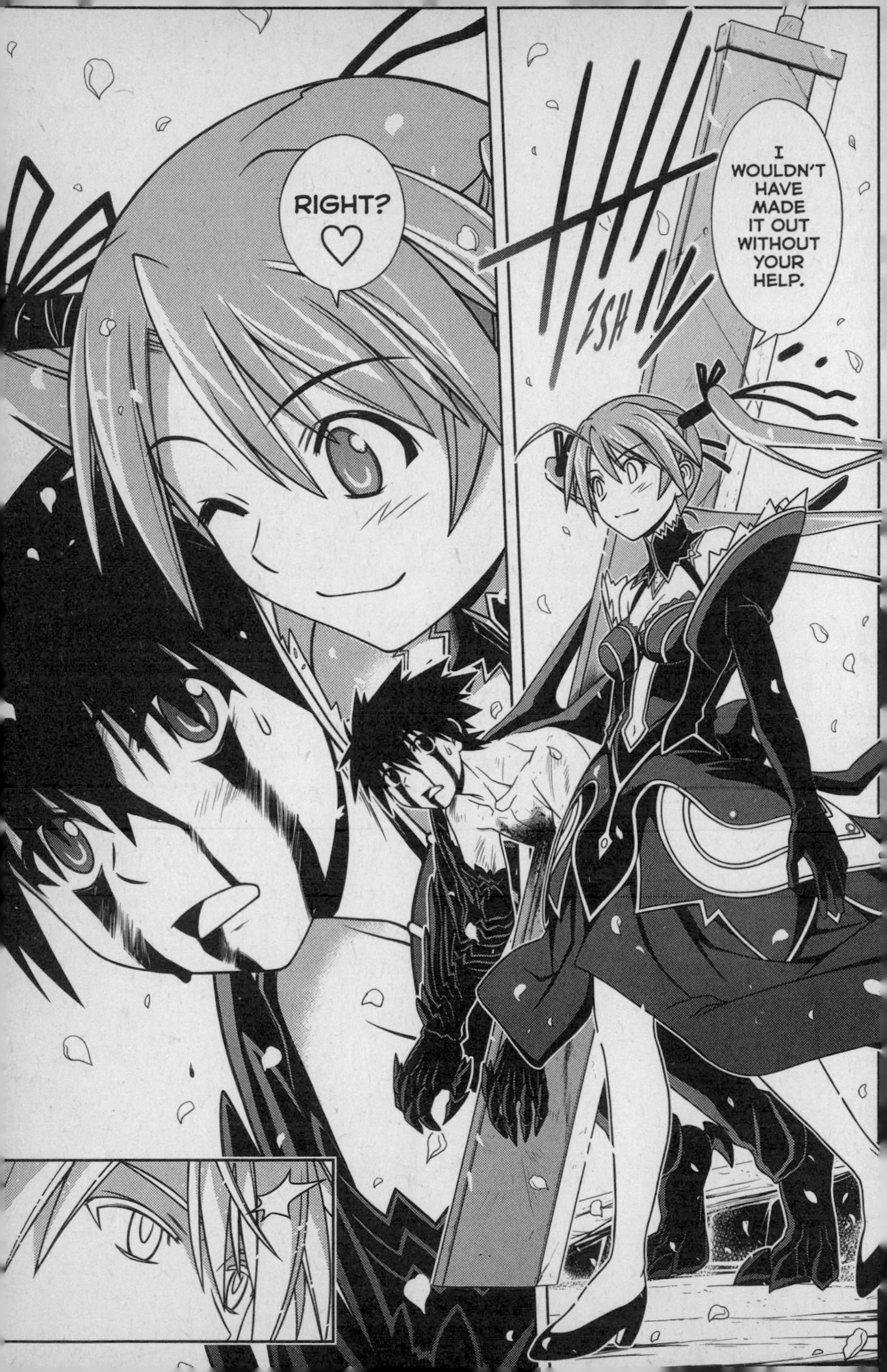
I WOULDN'T HAVE MADE IT OUT WITHOUT YOUR HELP.
ZSH
RIGHT? ♡

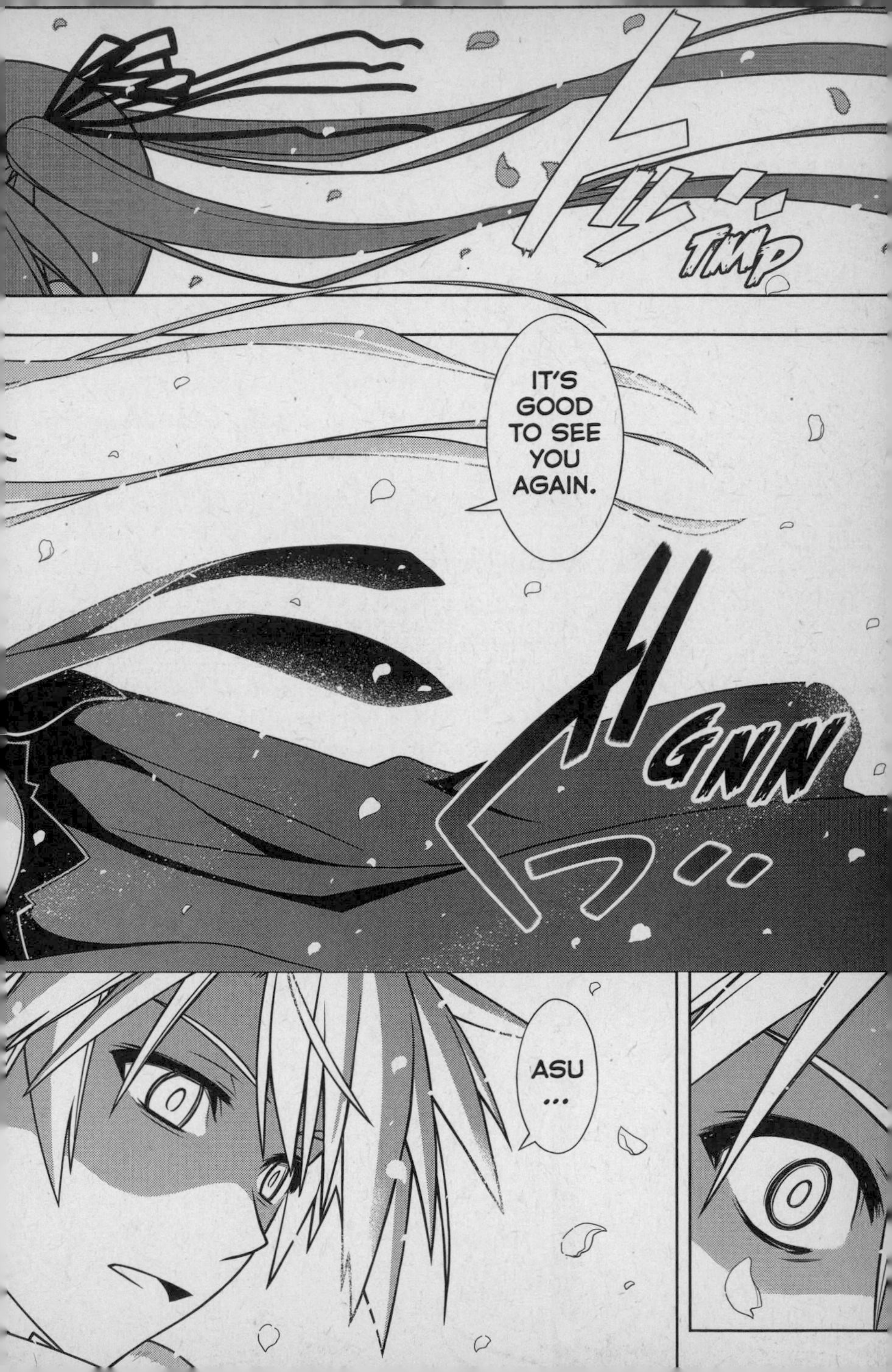
TMP
IT'S GOOD TO SEE YOU AGAIN.
GNN
ASU ...

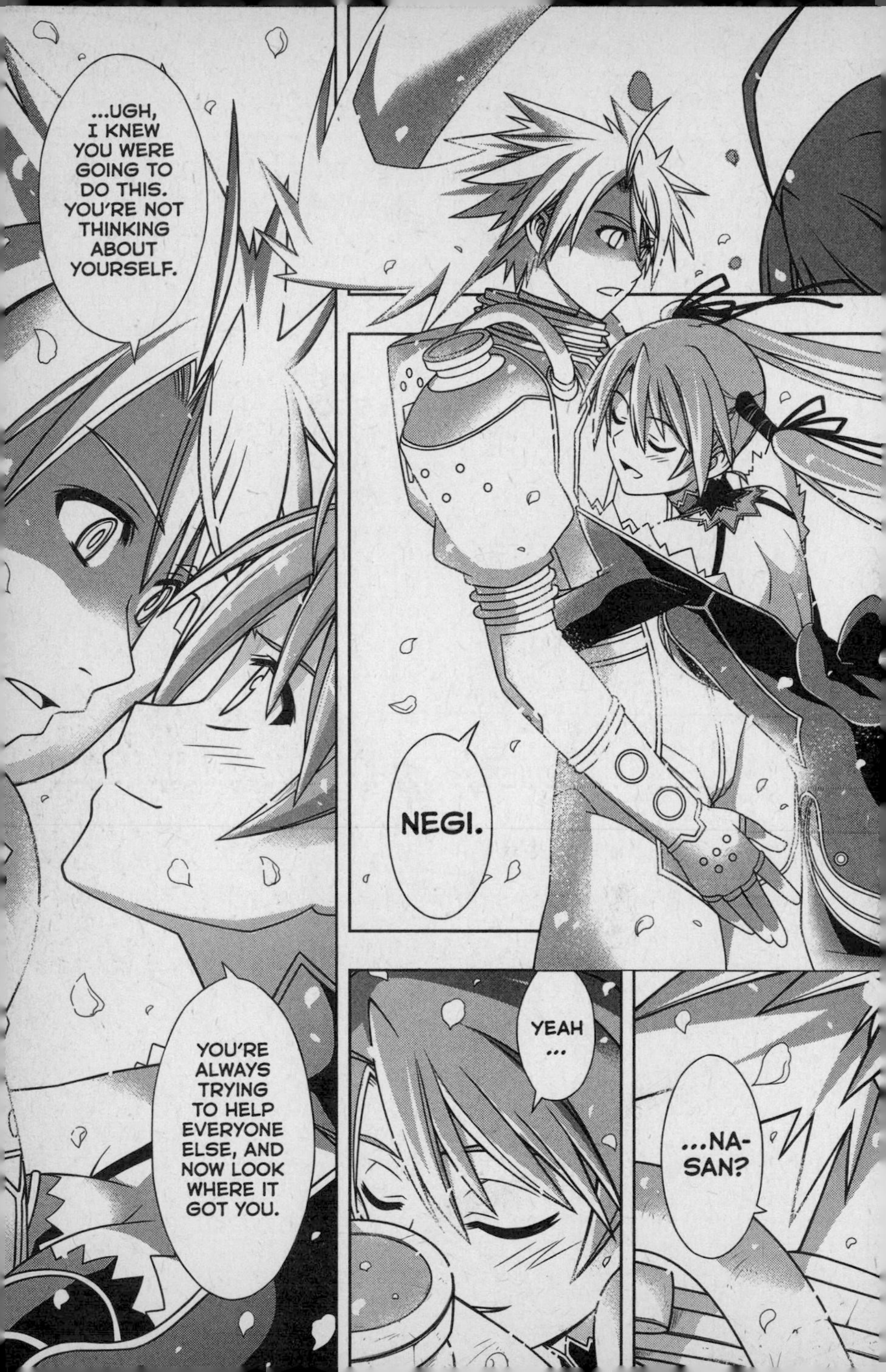
NEGI.
...NA-SAN?
YEAH ...
...UGH, I KNEW YOU WERE GOING TO DO THIS. YOU'RE NOT THINKING ABOUT YOURSELF.
YOU'RE ALWAYS TRYING TO HELP EVERYONE ELSE, AND NOW LOOK WHERE IT GOT YOU.

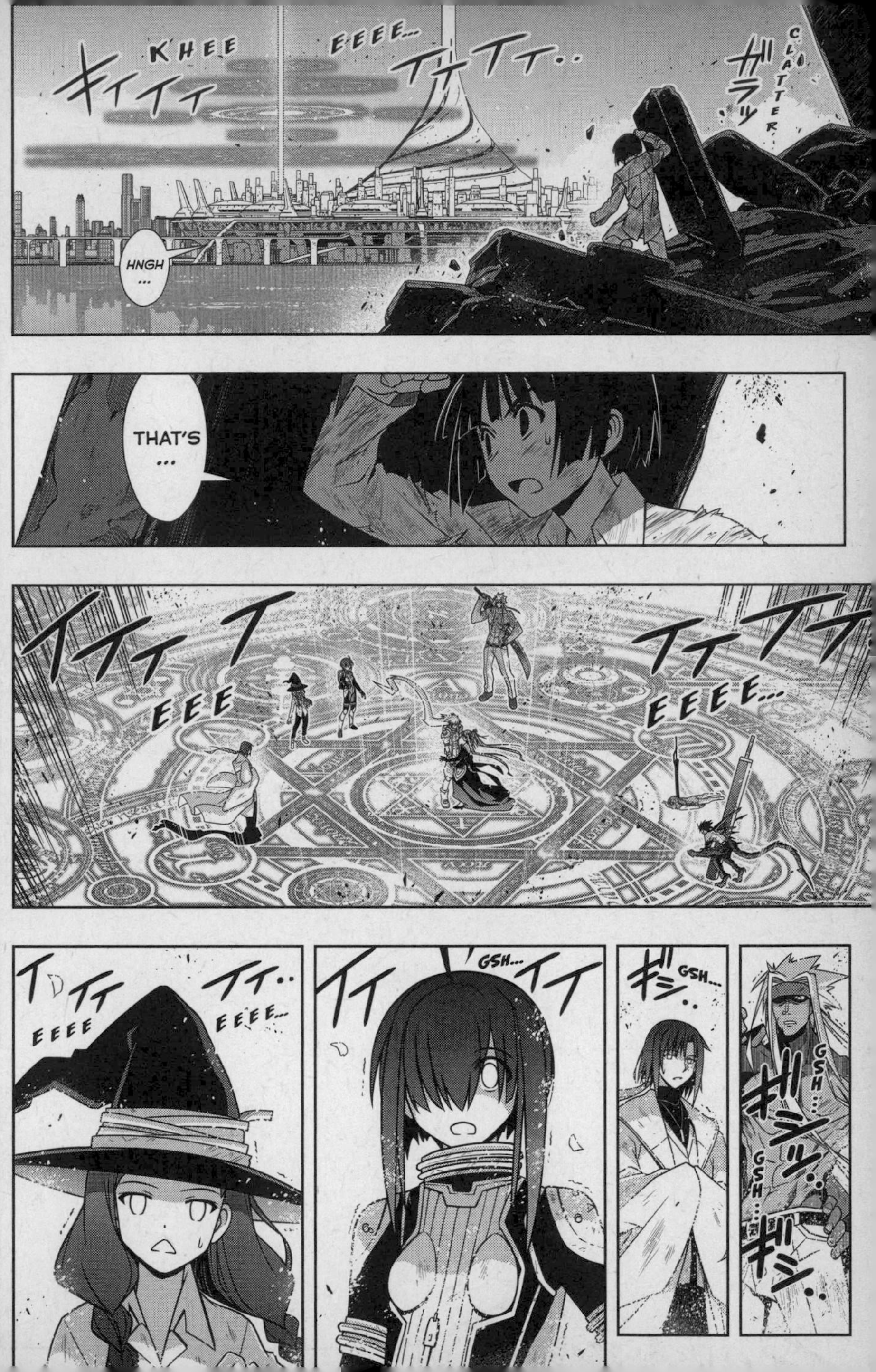

CLATTER
EEEE...
KHEE
HNGH...
THAT'S...
EEEE...
EEE
GSH...
GSH...
GSH...
GSH...
EEEE...
EEEE

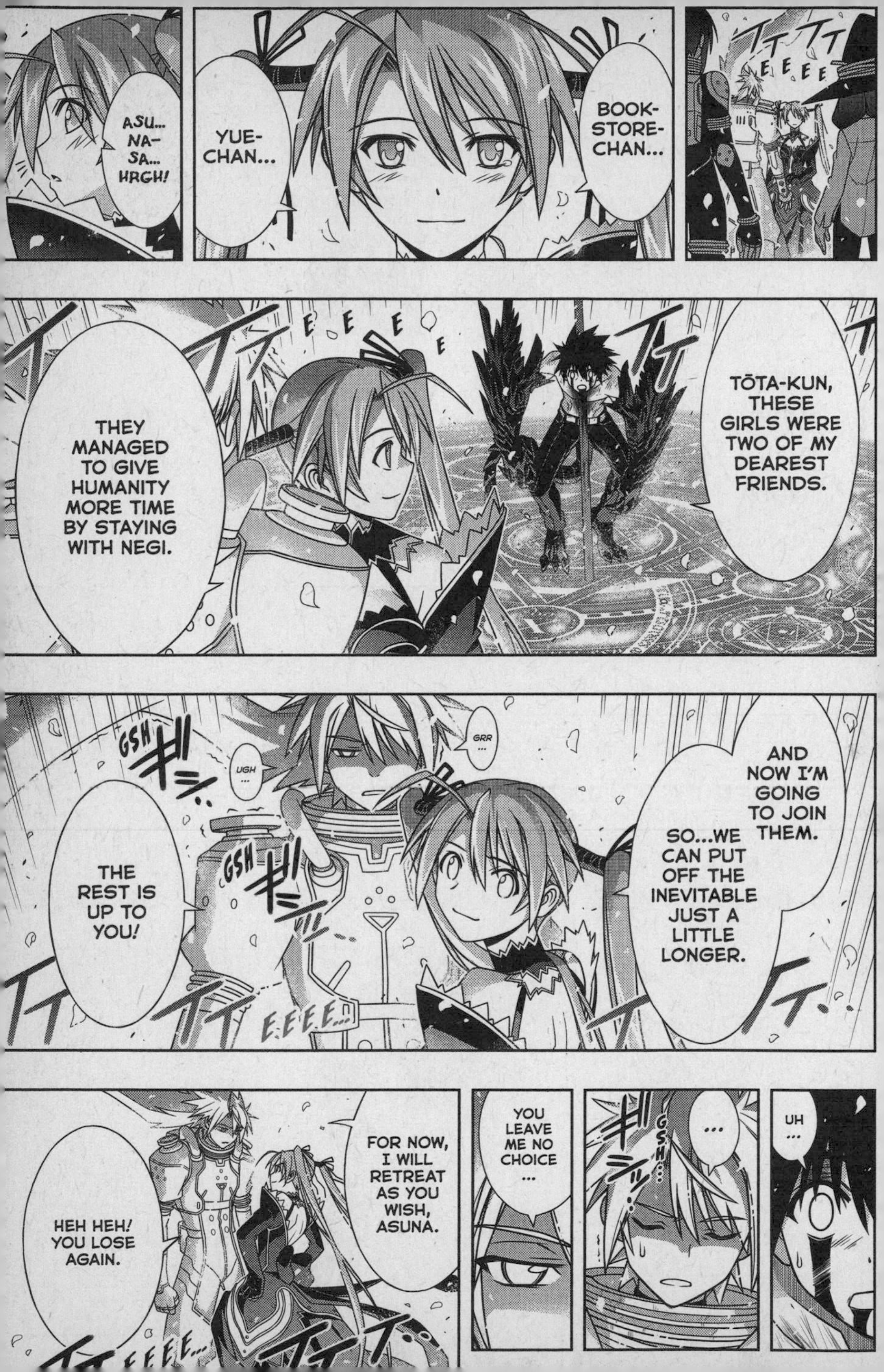
EEEE
BOOK-STORE-CHAN...
YUE-CHAN...
ASU... NA-SA... HRGH!
TŌTA-KUN, THESE GIRLS WERE TWO OF MY DEAREST FRIENDS.
THEY MANAGED TO GIVE HUMANITY MORE TIME BY STAYING WITH NEGI.
EEEE
AND NOW I'M GOING TO JOIN THEM.
SO...WE CAN PUT OFF THE INEVITABLE JUST A LITTLE LONGER.
GRR ...
UGH ...
GSH
THE REST IS UP TO YOU!
GSH
EEEE...
UH ...
...
GSH...
YOU LEAVE ME NO CHOICE ...
FOR NOW, I WILL RETREAT AS YOU WISH, ASUNA.
HEH HEH! YOU LOSE AGAIN.
EEEE...

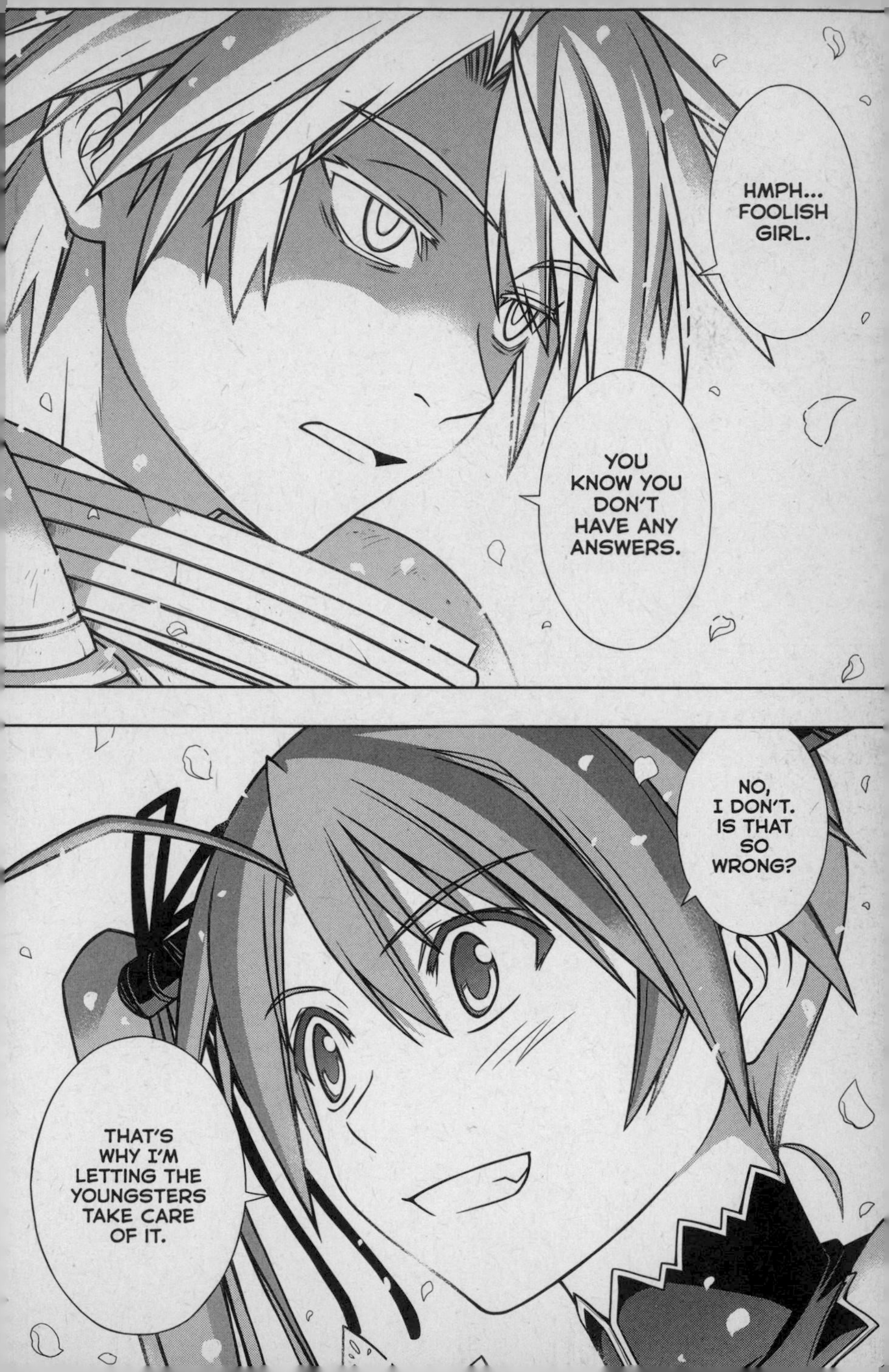
HMPH... FOOLISH GIRL.
YOU KNOW YOU DON'T HAVE ANY ANSWERS.
NO, I DON'T. IS THAT SO WRONG?
THAT'S WHY I'M LETTING THE YOUNGSTERS TAKE CARE OF IT.

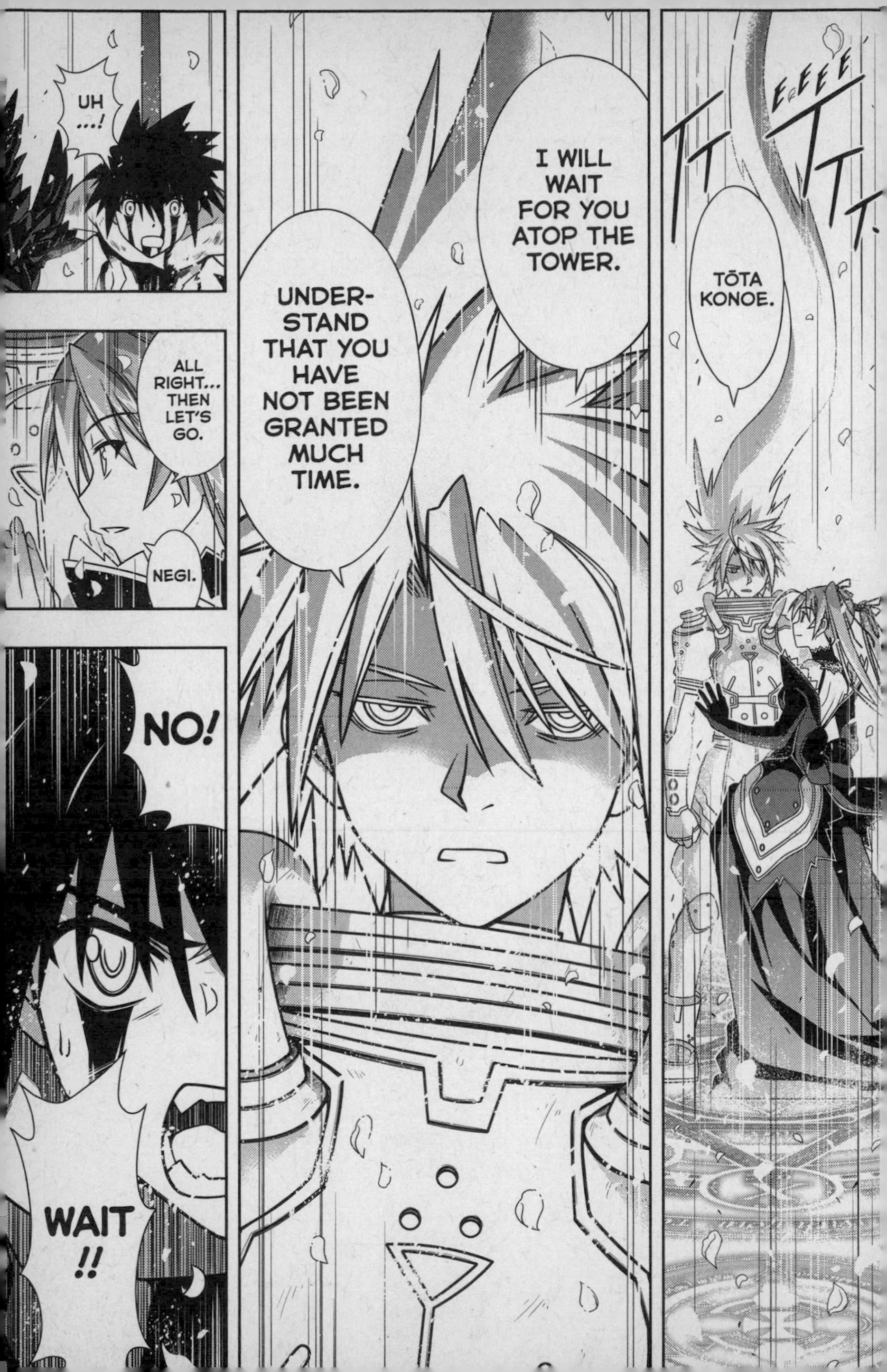
TŌTA KONOE.
I WILL WAIT FOR YOU ATOP THE TOWER.
UNDER-STAND THAT YOU HAVE NOT BEEN GRANTED MUCH TIME.
UH ...!
ALL RIGHT... THEN LET'S GO.
NEGI.
NO!
WAIT !!

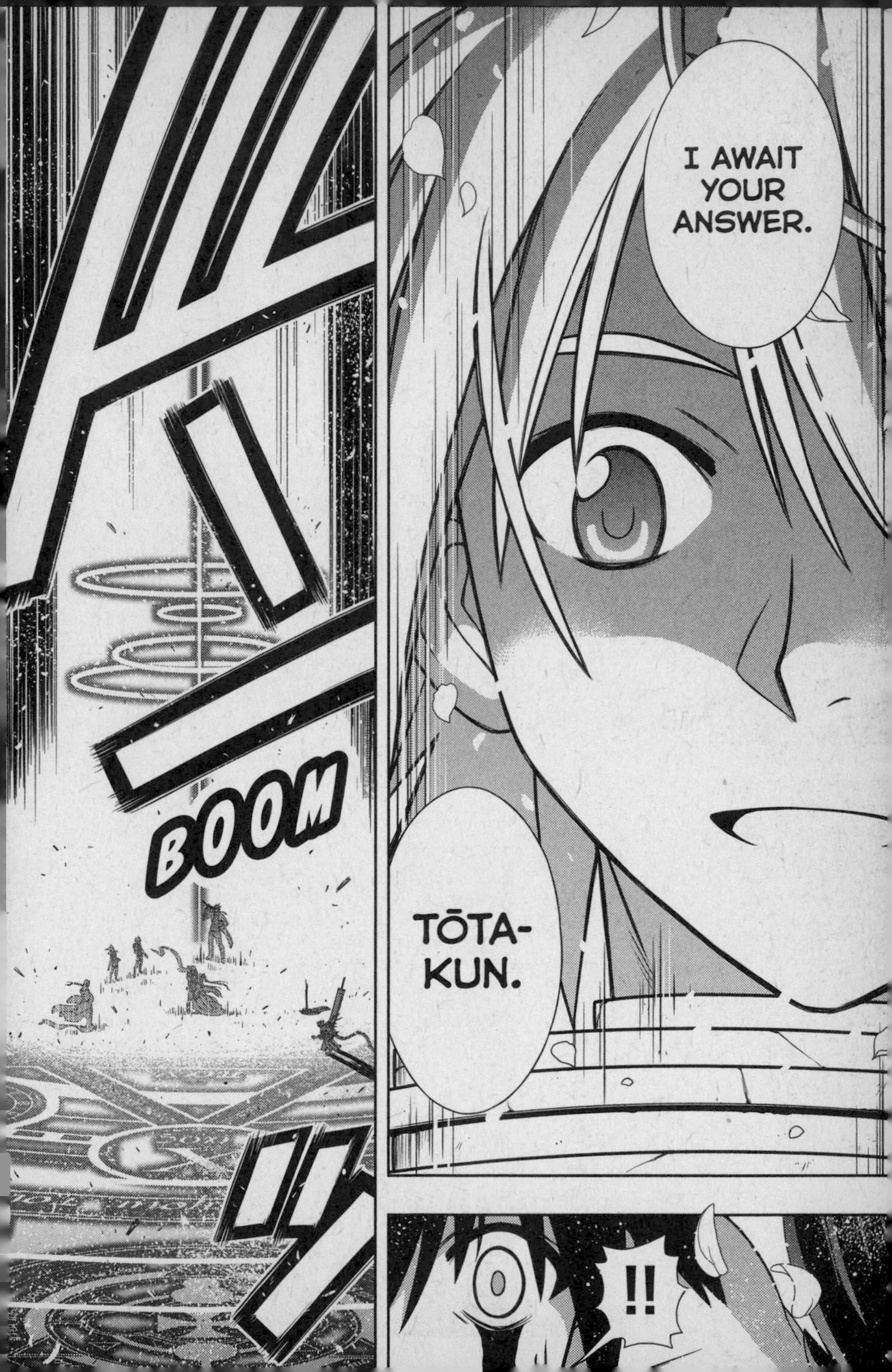
I AWAIT YOUR ANSWER.
TŌTA-KUN.
!!
BOOM

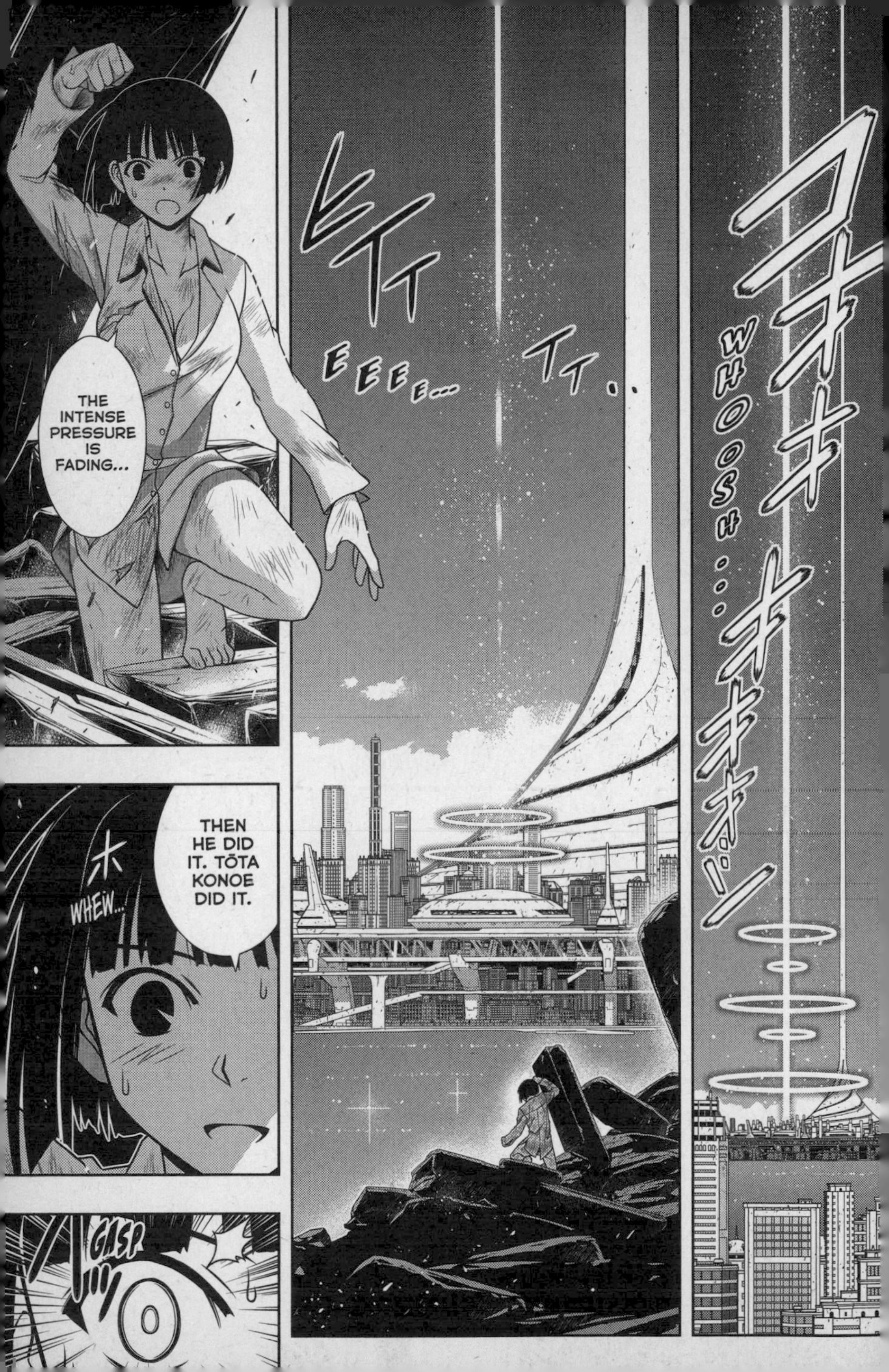

WHOOSH...
EEEE... TT..
THE INTENSE PRESSURE IS FADING...
WHEW...
THEN HE DID IT. TŌTA KONOE DID IT.
GASP

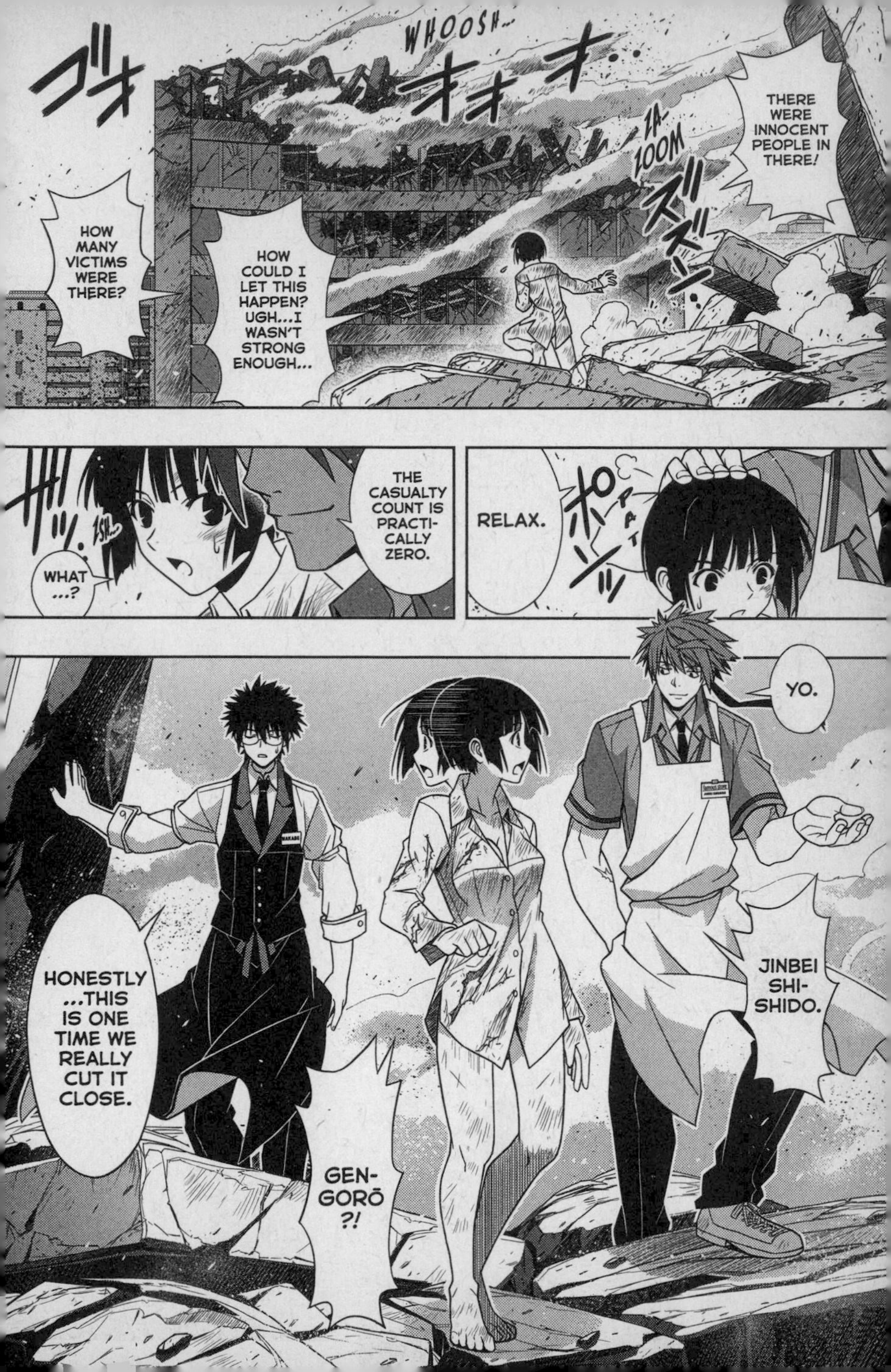
WHOOSH...
THERE WERE INNOCENT PEOPLE IN THERE!
ZA-ZOOM
HOW COULD I LET THIS HAPPEN? UGH...I WASN'T STRONG ENOUGH...
HOW MANY VICTIMS WERE THERE?
PAT
RELAX.
THE CASUALTY COUNT IS PRACTICALLY ZERO.
WHAT ...?
YO.
JINBEI SHI-SHIDO.
HONESTLY ...THIS IS ONE TIME WE REALLY CUT IT CLOSE.
GEN-GORŌ ?!

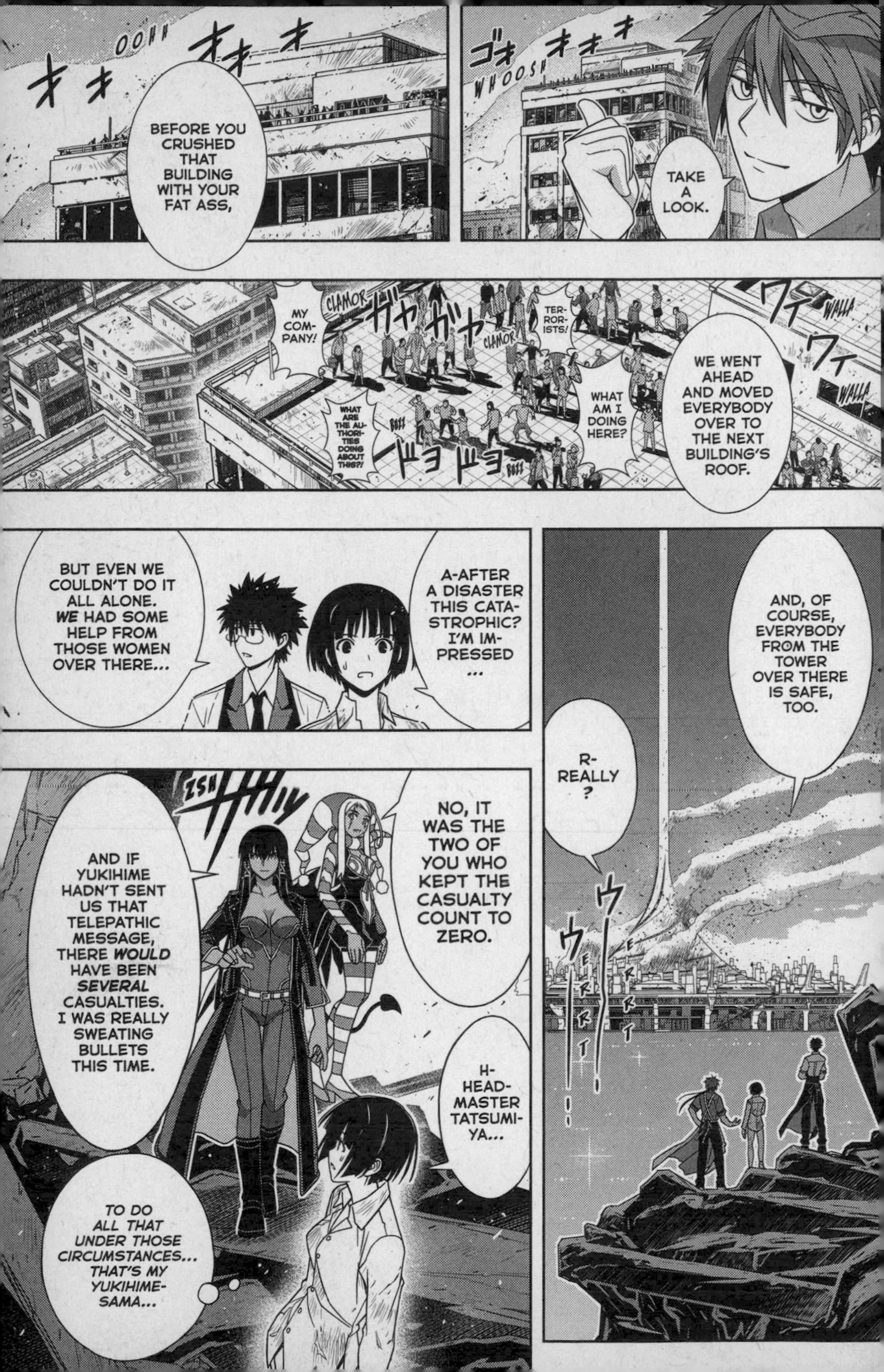

ゴオ オォォ
WHOOSH
TAKE A LOOK.
OOHH
オォ オォォ
BEFORE YOU CRUSHED THAT BUILDING WITH YOUR FAT ASS,
WE WENT AHEAD AND MOVED EVERYBODY OVER TO THE NEXT BUILDING'S ROOF.
WALLA
ワイ ワイ
TERRORISTS!
WHAT AM I DOING HERE?
CLAMOR
ガヤ ガヤ
MY COMPANY!
WHAT ARE THE AUTHORITIES DOING ABOUT THIS?!
BOZZ
ドヨ ドヨ
AND, OF COURSE, EVERYBODY FROM THE TOWER OVER THERE IS SAFE, TOO.
R-REALLY?
ウー ウー
A-AFTER A DISASTER THIS CATASTROPHIC? I'M IMPRESSED...
BUT EVEN WE COULDN'T DO IT ALL ALONE. *WE* HAD SOME HELP FROM THOSE WOMEN OVER THERE...
ZSH
ザッ
NO, IT WAS THE TWO OF YOU WHO KEPT THE CASUALTY COUNT TO ZERO.
AND IF YUKIHIME HADN'T SENT US THAT TELEPATHIC MESSAGE, THERE *WOULD* HAVE BEEN *SEVERAL* CASUALTIES. I WAS REALLY SWEATING BULLETS THIS TIME.
H-HEADMASTER TATSUMIYA...
TO DO ALL THAT UNDER THOSE CIRCUMSTANCES... THAT'S MY YUKIHIME-SAMA...

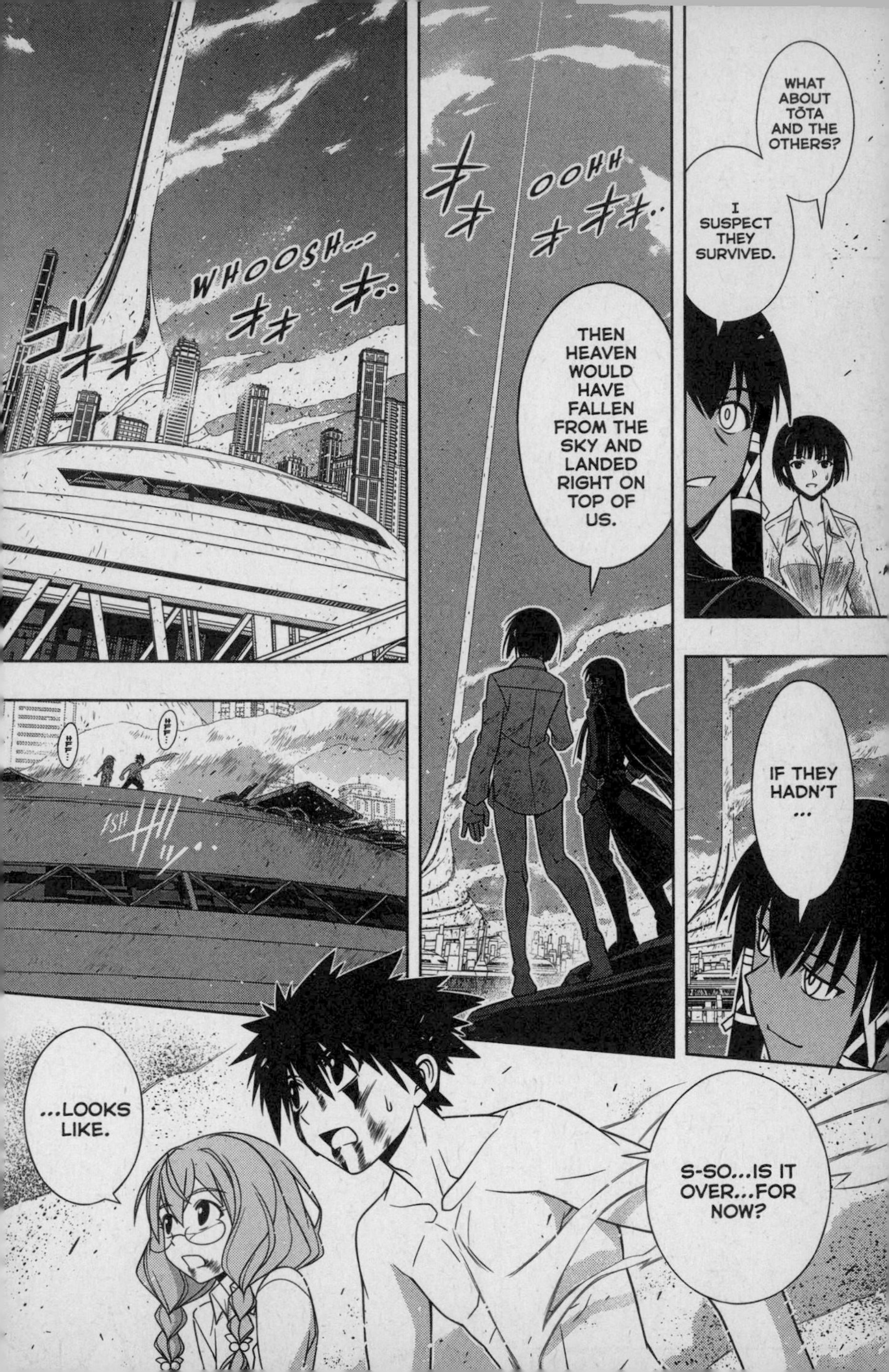
WHAT ABOUT TŌTA AND THE OTHERS?
I SUSPECT THEY SURVIVED.
IF THEY HADN'T...
OOHH
THEN HEAVEN WOULD HAVE FALLEN FROM THE SKY AND LANDED RIGHT ON TOP OF US.
WHOOSH...
S-SO...IS IT OVER...FOR NOW?
...LOOKS LIKE.

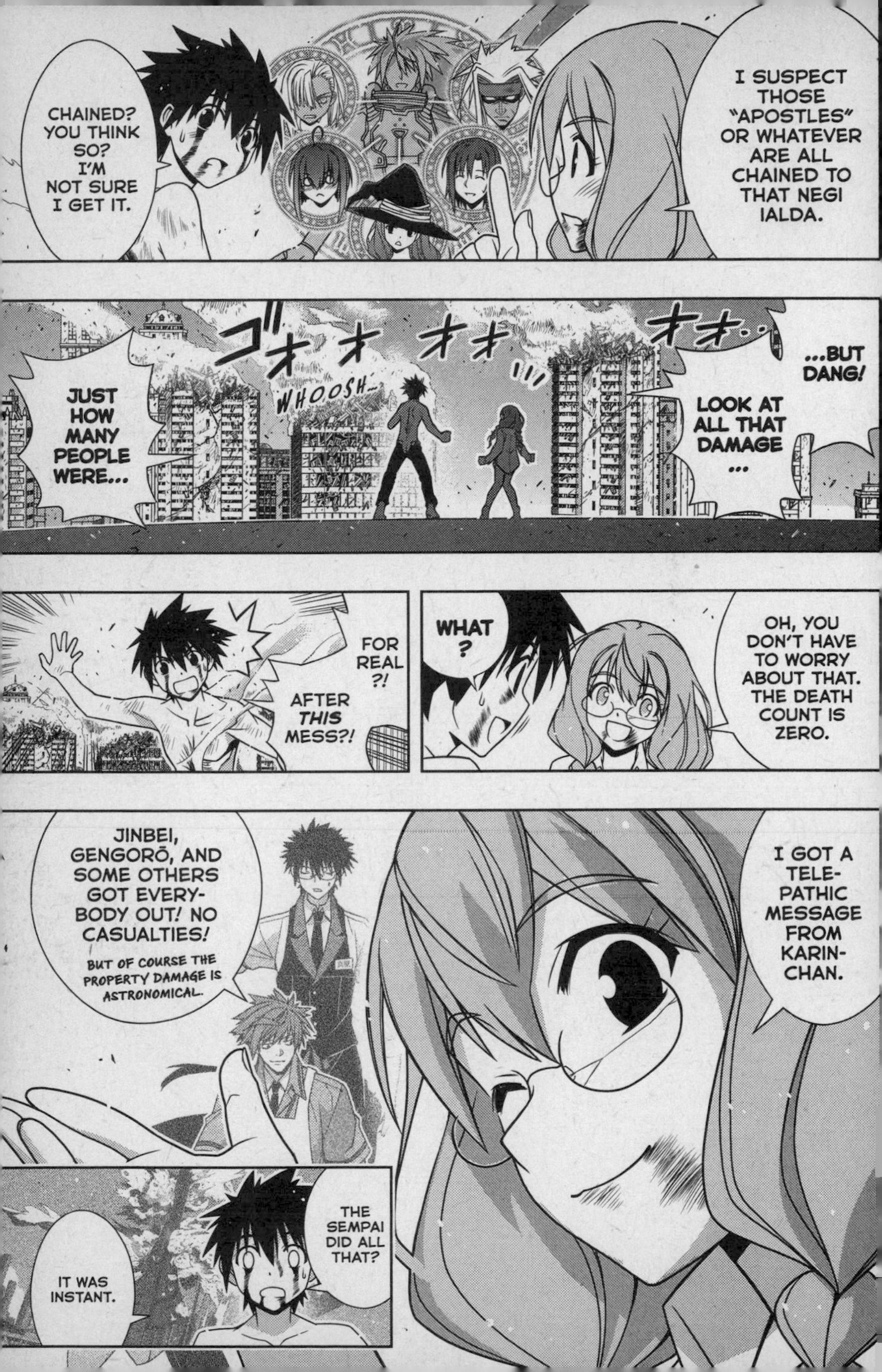
I SUSPECT THOSE "APOSTLES" OR WHATEVER ARE ALL CHAINED TO THAT NEGI IALDA.
CHAINED? YOU THINK SO? I'M NOT SURE I GET IT.
...BUT DANG!
ゴオオ オオ オオ‥
LOOK AT ALL THAT DAMAGE ...
WHOOSH...
JUST HOW MANY PEOPLE WERE...
OH, YOU DON'T HAVE TO WORRY ABOUT THAT. THE DEATH COUNT IS ZERO.
WHAT?
FOR REAL?!
AFTER THIS MESS?!
I GOT A TELE-PATHIC MESSAGE FROM KARIN-CHAN.
JINBEI, GENGORŌ, AND SOME OTHERS GOT EVERY-BODY OUT! NO CASUALTIES!
BUT OF COURSE THE PROPERTY DAMAGE IS ASTRONOMICAL.
THE SEMPAI DID ALL THAT?
IT WAS INSTANT.

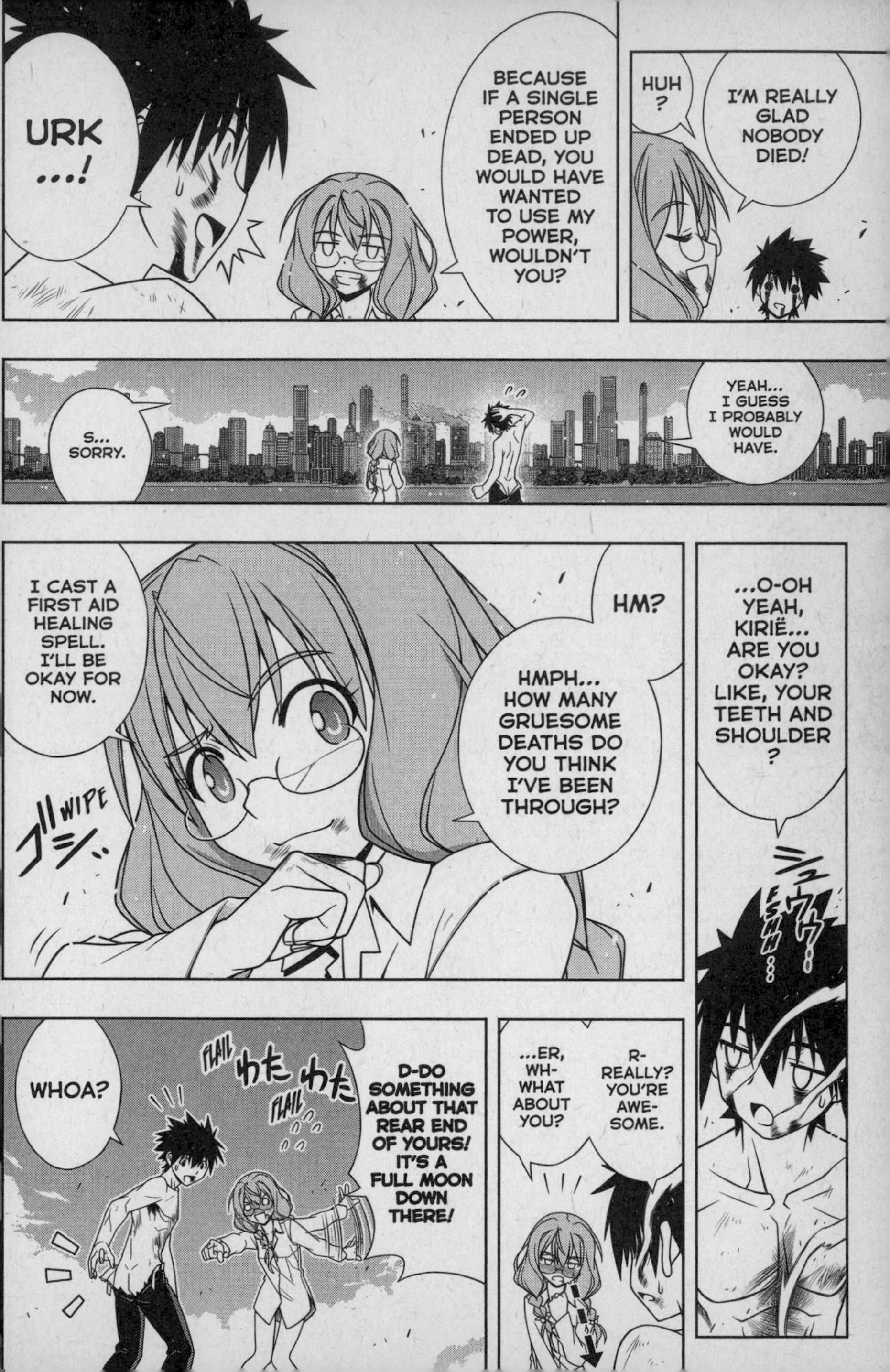
I'M REALLY GLAD NOBODY DIED!
HUH?
BECAUSE IF A SINGLE PERSON ENDED UP DEAD, YOU WOULD HAVE WANTED TO USE MY POWER, WOULDN'T YOU?
URK...!
YEAH... I GUESS I PROBABLY WOULD HAVE.
S... SORRY.
...O-OH YEAH, KIRIË... ARE YOU OKAY? LIKE, YOUR TEETH AND SHOULDER?
FSHH...
HM?
HMPH... HOW MANY GRUESOME DEATHS DO YOU THINK I'VE BEEN THROUGH?
I CAST A FIRST AID HEALING SPELL. I'LL BE OKAY FOR NOW.
WIPE
R-REALLY? YOU'RE AWE-SOME.
...ER, WH-WHAT ABOUT YOU?
D-DO SOMETHING ABOUT THAT REAR END OF YOURS! IT'S A FULL MOON DOWN THERE!
FLAIL わた
FLAIL わた
WHOA?

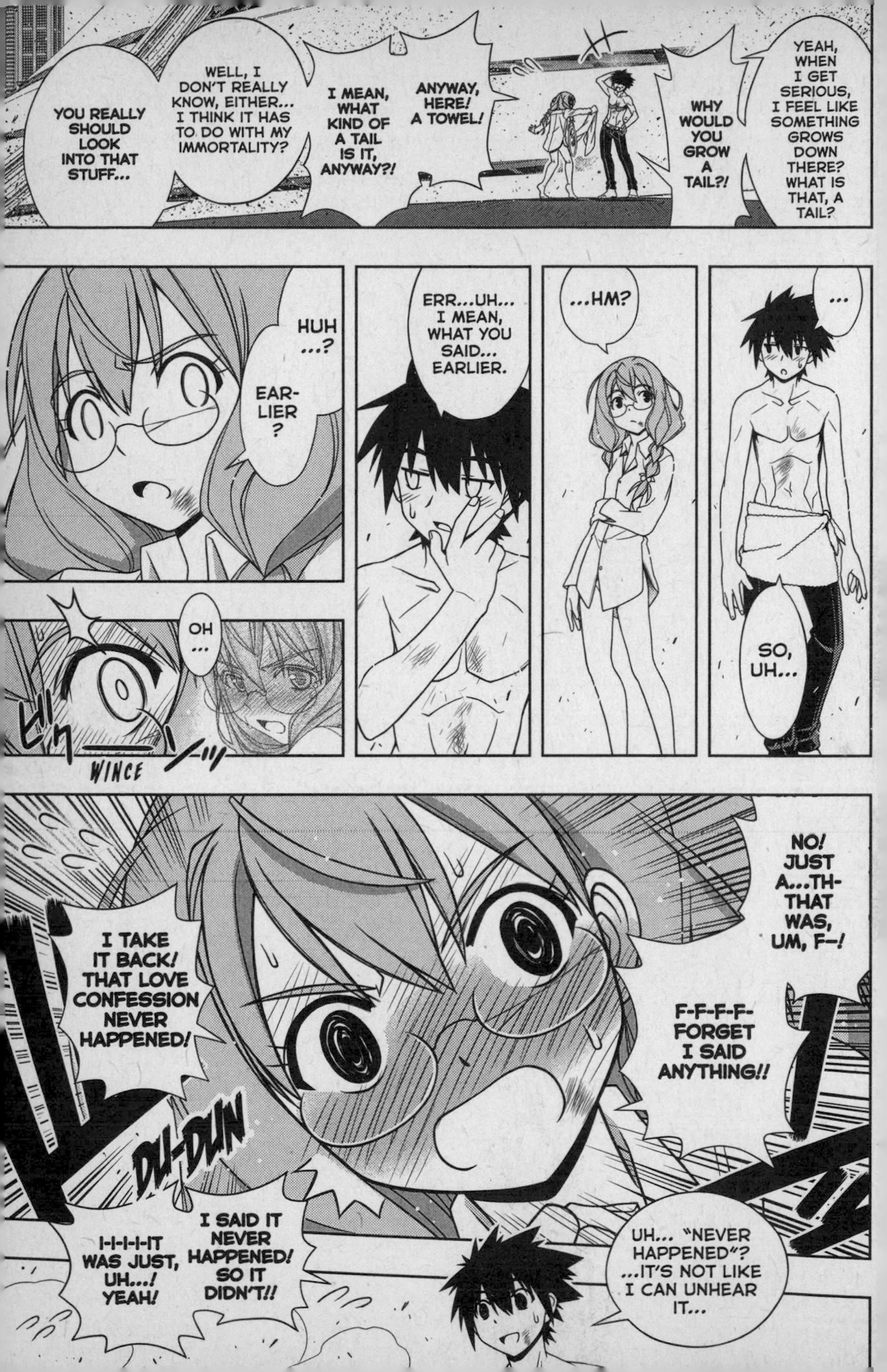
YEAH, WHEN I GET SERIOUS, I FEEL LIKE SOMETHING GROWS DOWN THERE? WHAT IS THAT, A TAIL?
WHY WOULD YOU GROW A TAIL?!
ANYWAY, HERE! A TOWEL!
I MEAN, WHAT KIND OF A TAIL IS IT, ANYWAY?!
WELL, I DON'T REALLY KNOW, EITHER... I THINK IT HAS TO DO WITH MY IMMORTALITY?
YOU REALLY SHOULD LOOK INTO THAT STUFF...
...
SO, UH...
...HM?
ERR...UH... I MEAN, WHAT YOU SAID... EARLIER.
HUH...?
EAR-LIER?
OH...
WINCE
NO! JUST A...TH-THAT WAS, UM, F--!
F-F-F-F-FORGET I SAID ANYTHING!!
I TAKE IT BACK! THAT LOVE CONFESSION NEVER HAPPENED!
DU-DUN
UH... "NEVER HAPPENED"? ...IT'S NOT LIKE I CAN UNHEAR IT...
I SAID IT NEVER HAPPENED! SO IT DIDN'T!!
I-I-I-I-IT WAS JUST, UH...! YEAH!

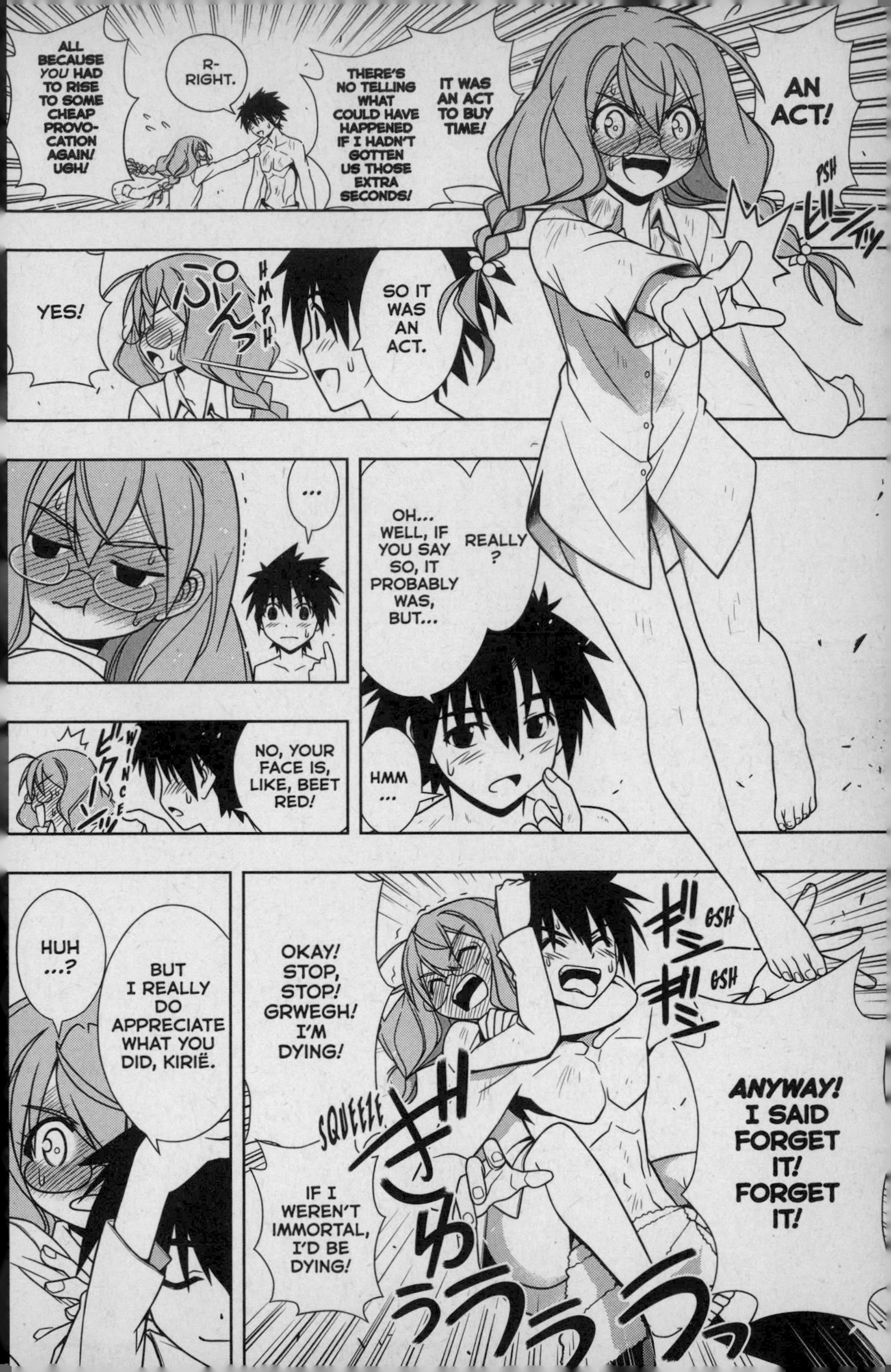
AN ACT!
PSH
IT WAS AN ACT TO BUY TIME!
THERE'S NO TELLING WHAT COULD HAVE HAPPENED IF I HADN'T GOTTEN US THOSE EXTRA SECONDS!
R-RIGHT.
ALL BECAUSE *YOU* HAD TO RISE TO SOME CHEAP PROVOCATION AGAIN! UGH!
SO IT WAS AN ACT.
HMPH
YES!
REALLY?
OH... WELL, IF YOU SAY SO, IT PROBABLY WAS, BUT...
...
HMM...
NO, YOUR FACE IS, LIKE, BEET RED!
WINCE
ANYWAY! I SAID FORGET IT! FORGET IT!
GSH
GSH
OKAY! STOP, STOP! GRWEGH! I'M DYING!
SQUEEZE
IF I WEREN'T IMMORTAL, I'D BE DYING!
BUT I REALLY DO APPRECIATE WHAT YOU DID, KIRIË.
HUH...?

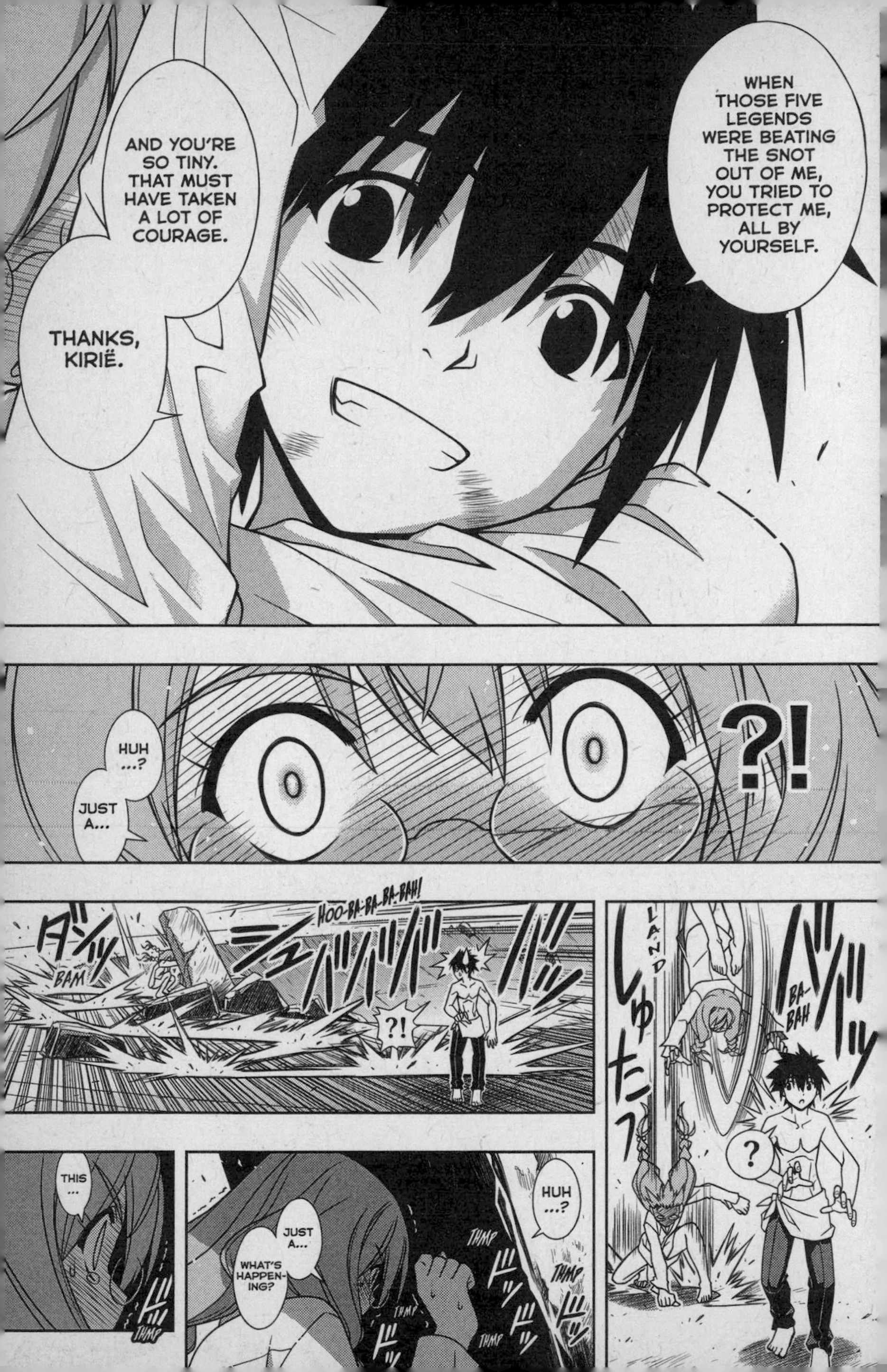
WHEN THOSE FIVE LEGENDS WERE BEATING THE SNOT OUT OF ME, YOU TRIED TO PROTECT ME, ALL BY YOURSELF.
AND YOU'RE SO TINY. THAT MUST HAVE TAKEN A LOT OF COURAGE.
THANKS, KIRIË.
?!
HUH ...?
JUST A...
LAND
BA-BAH
?
HOO-BA-BA-BA-BAH!
BAM
?!
HUH ...?
JUST A...
WHAT'S HAPPENING?
THMP
THMP
THMP
THMP
THIS ...
THMP

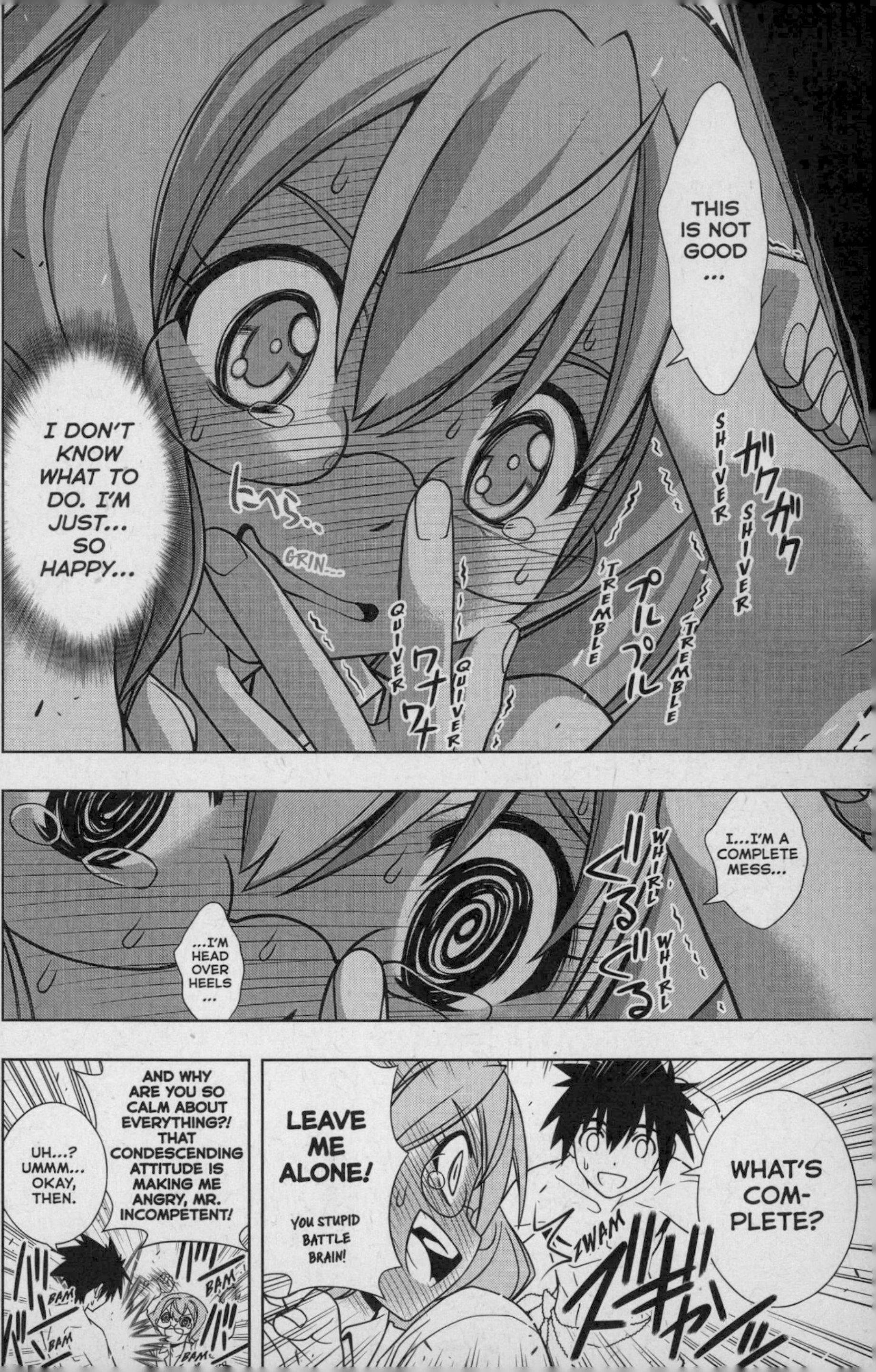
THIS IS NOT GOOD ...
I DON'T KNOW WHAT TO DO. I'M JUST... SO HAPPY...
SHIVER SHIVER
TREMBLE TREMBLE
QUIVER QUIVER
GRIN...
I...I'M A COMPLETE MESS...
...I'M HEAD OVER HEELS ...
WHIRL WHIRL
WHAT'S COM-PLETE?
ZWAM
LEAVE ME ALONE!
YOU STUPID BATTLE BRAIN!
AND WHY ARE YOU SO CALM ABOUT EVERYTHING?! THAT CONDESCENDING ATTITUDE IS MAKING ME ANGRY, MR. INCOMPETENT!
UH...? UMMM... OKAY, THEN.
BAM BAM BAM BAM

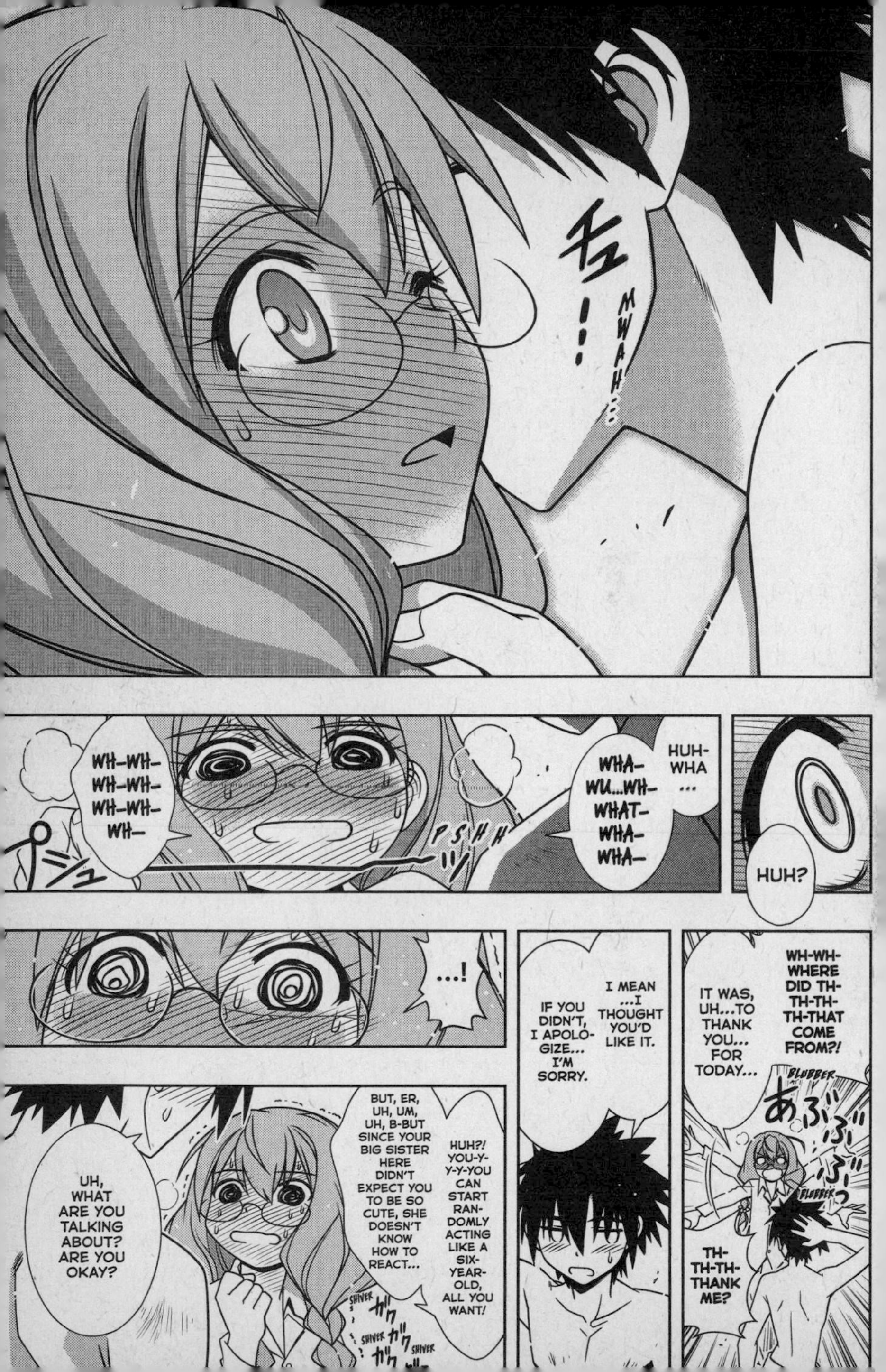
チュ
MWAH...
HUH?
HUH-WHA...
WHA-WU...WH-WHAT-WHA-WHA-
WH-WH-WH-WH-WH-WH-WH-
PSHH
WH-WH-WHERE DID TH-TH-TH-TH-THAT COME FROM?!
IT WAS, UH...TO THANK YOU... FOR TODAY...
BLUBBER
BLUBBER
TH-TH-TH-THANK ME?
I MEAN ...I THOUGHT YOU'D LIKE IT.
IF YOU DIDN'T, I APOLOGIZE... I'M SORRY.
...!
HUH?! YOU-Y-Y-Y-YOU CAN START RANDOMLY ACTING LIKE A SIX-YEAR-OLD, ALL YOU WANT!
BUT, ER, UH, UM, UH, B-BUT SINCE YOUR BIG SISTER HERE DIDN'T EXPECT YOU TO BE SO CUTE, SHE DOESN'T KNOW HOW TO REACT...
UH, WHAT ARE YOU TALKING ABOUT? ARE YOU OKAY?
SHIVER
SHIVER
SHIVER

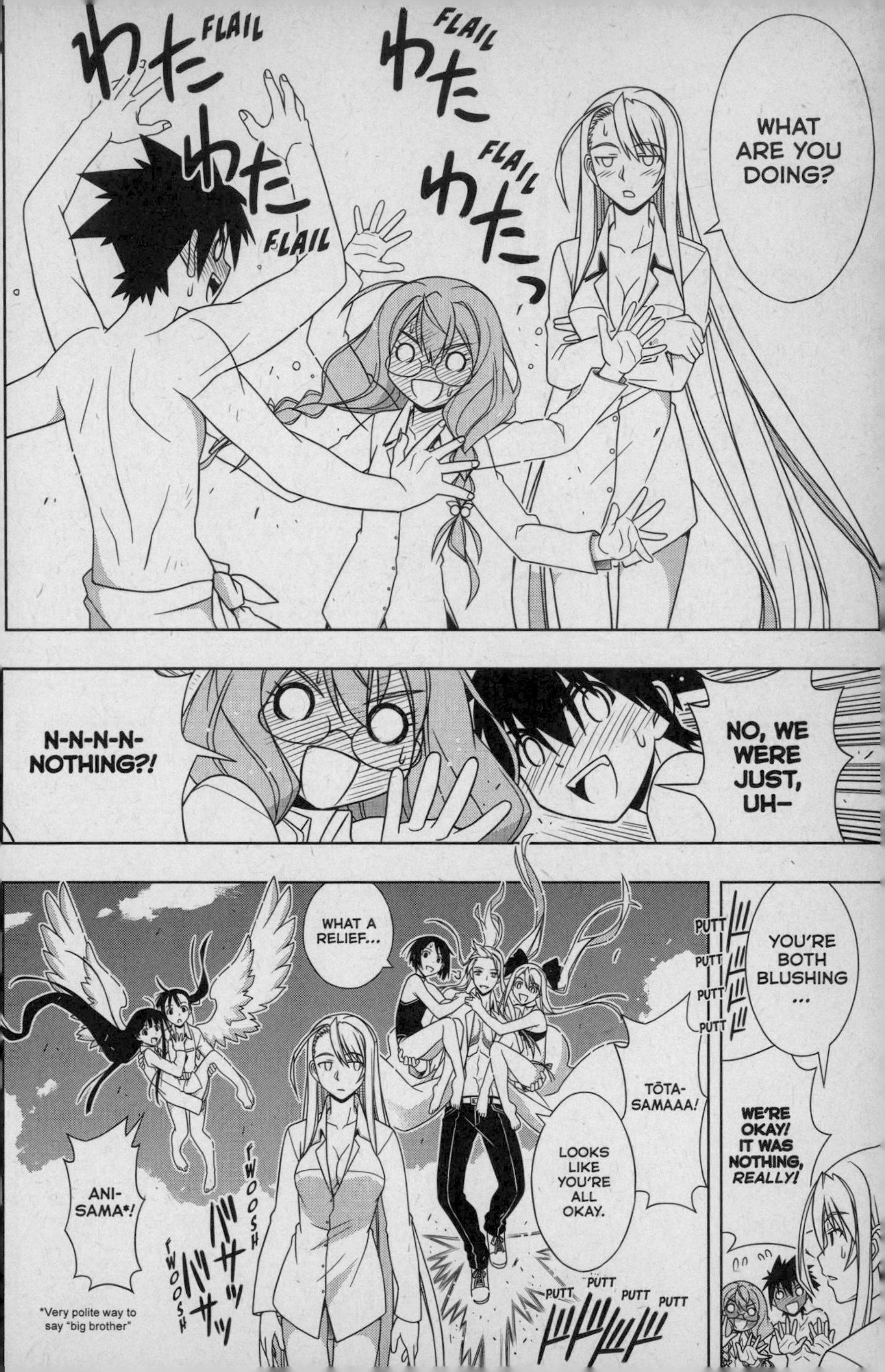
WHAT ARE YOU DOING?
わたわたっ
FLAIL
FLAIL
わたわた
FLAIL
FLAIL
NO, WE WERE JUST, UH–
N-N-N-N-NOTHING?!
YOU'RE BOTH BLUSHING ...
WE'RE OKAY! IT WAS NOTHING, *REALLY!*
PUTT PUTT PUTT PUTT
ドドドド
TŌTA-SAMAAA!
LOOKS LIKE YOU'RE ALL OKAY.
WHAT A RELIEF...
PUTT PUTT PUTT PUTT
ドドドド
FWOOSH
バサッ
FWOOSH
バサッ
ANI-SAMA*!

*Very polite way to say "big brother"

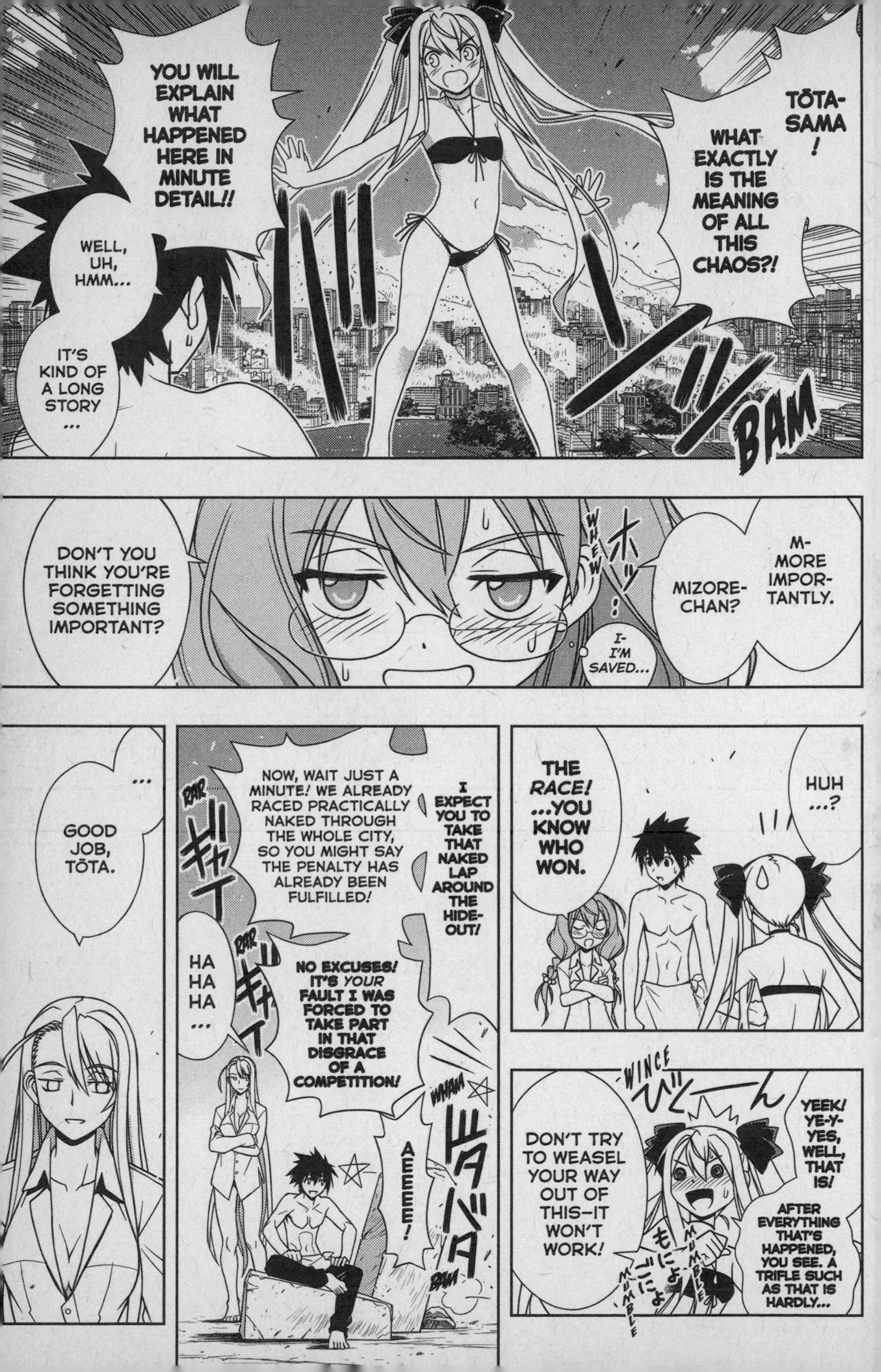
TŌTA-SAMA!
WHAT EXACTLY IS THE MEANING OF ALL THIS CHAOS?!
BAM
YOU WILL EXPLAIN WHAT HAPPENED HERE IN MINUTE DETAIL!!
WELL, UH, HMM...
IT'S KIND OF A LONG STORY...
M-MORE IMPORTANTLY.
MIZORE-CHAN?
WHEW
ホッ
I-I'M SAVED...
DON'T YOU THINK YOU'RE FORGETTING SOMETHING IMPORTANT?
HUH...?
THE *RACE!* ...YOU KNOW WHO WON.
WINCE
びくーん
YEEK! YE-Y-YES, WELL, THAT IS!
AFTER EVERYTHING THAT'S HAPPENED, YOU SEE. A TRIFLE SUCH AS THAT IS HARDLY...
MUMBLE
MUMBLE
DON'T TRY TO WEASEL YOUR WAY OUT OF THIS—IT WON'T WORK!
I EXPECT YOU TO TAKE THAT NAKED LAP AROUND THE HIDE-OUT!
NOW, WAIT JUST A MINUTE! WE ALREADY RACED PRACTICALLY NAKED THROUGH THE WHOLE CITY, SO YOU MIGHT SAY THE PENALTY HAS ALREADY BEEN FULFILLED!
RAR
RAR
NO EXCUSES! IT'S *YOUR* FAULT I WAS FORCED TO TAKE PART IN THAT DISGRACE OF A COMPETITION!
WHAM
ジタバタ
AEEEEE!
BAM
HA HA HA...
...
GOOD JOB, TŌTA.

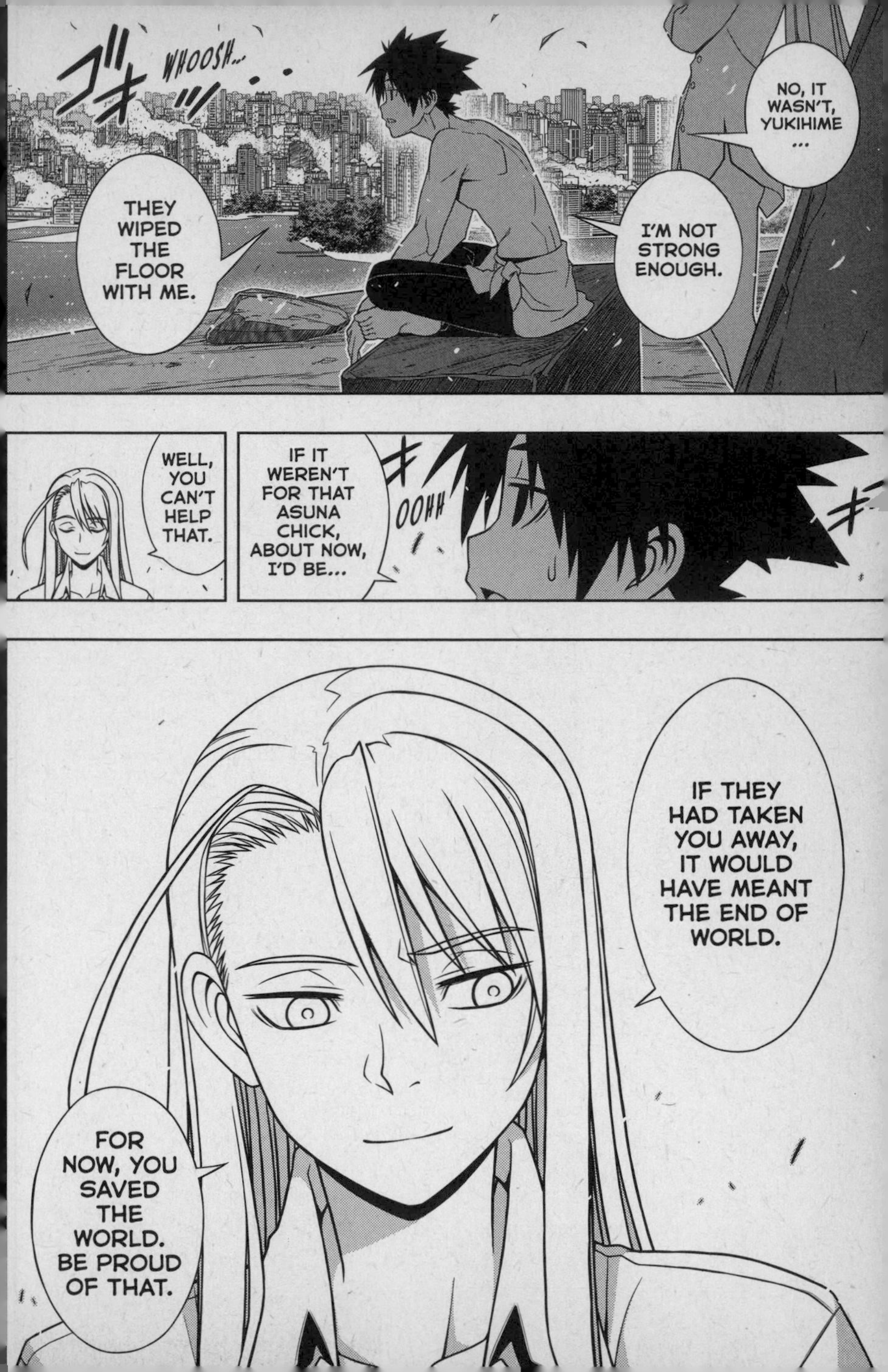
NO, IT WASN'T, YUKIHIME ...
I'M NOT STRONG ENOUGH.
WHOOSH...
THEY WIPED THE FLOOR WITH ME.
IF IT WEREN'T FOR THAT ASUNA CHICK, ABOUT NOW, I'D BE...
OOHH
WELL, YOU CAN'T HELP THAT.
IF THEY HAD TAKEN YOU AWAY, IT WOULD HAVE MEANT THE END OF WORLD.
FOR NOW, YOU SAVED THE WORLD. BE PROUD OF THAT.

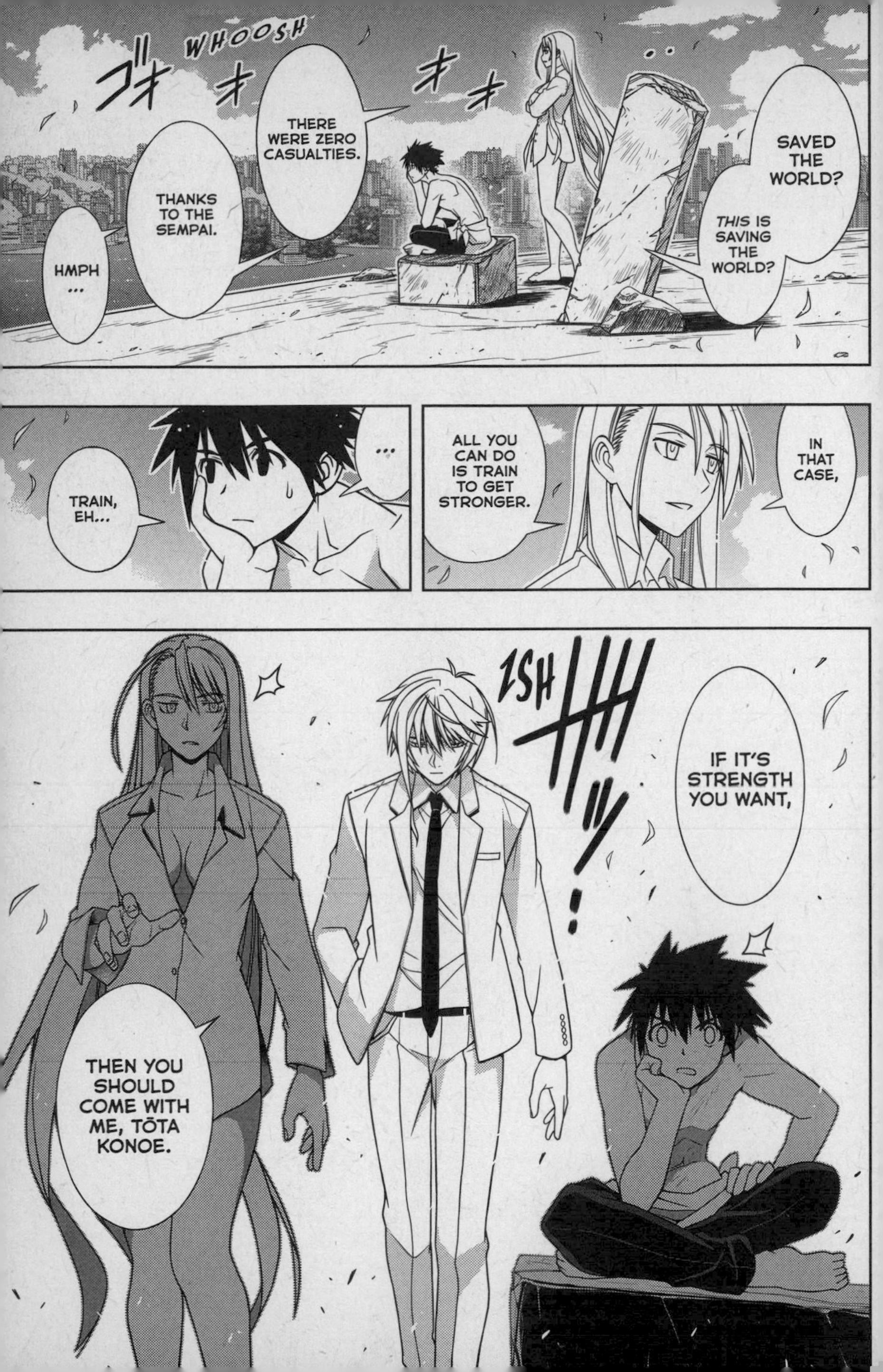
WHOOSH
SAVED THE WORLD?
THIS IS SAVING THE WORLD?
THERE WERE ZERO CASUALTIES.
THANKS TO THE SEMPAI.
HMPH ...
IN THAT CASE,
ALL YOU CAN DO IS TRAIN TO GET STRONGER.
...
TRAIN, EH...
IF IT'S STRENGTH YOU WANT,
ZSH
THEN YOU SHOULD COME WITH ME, TŌTA KONOE.

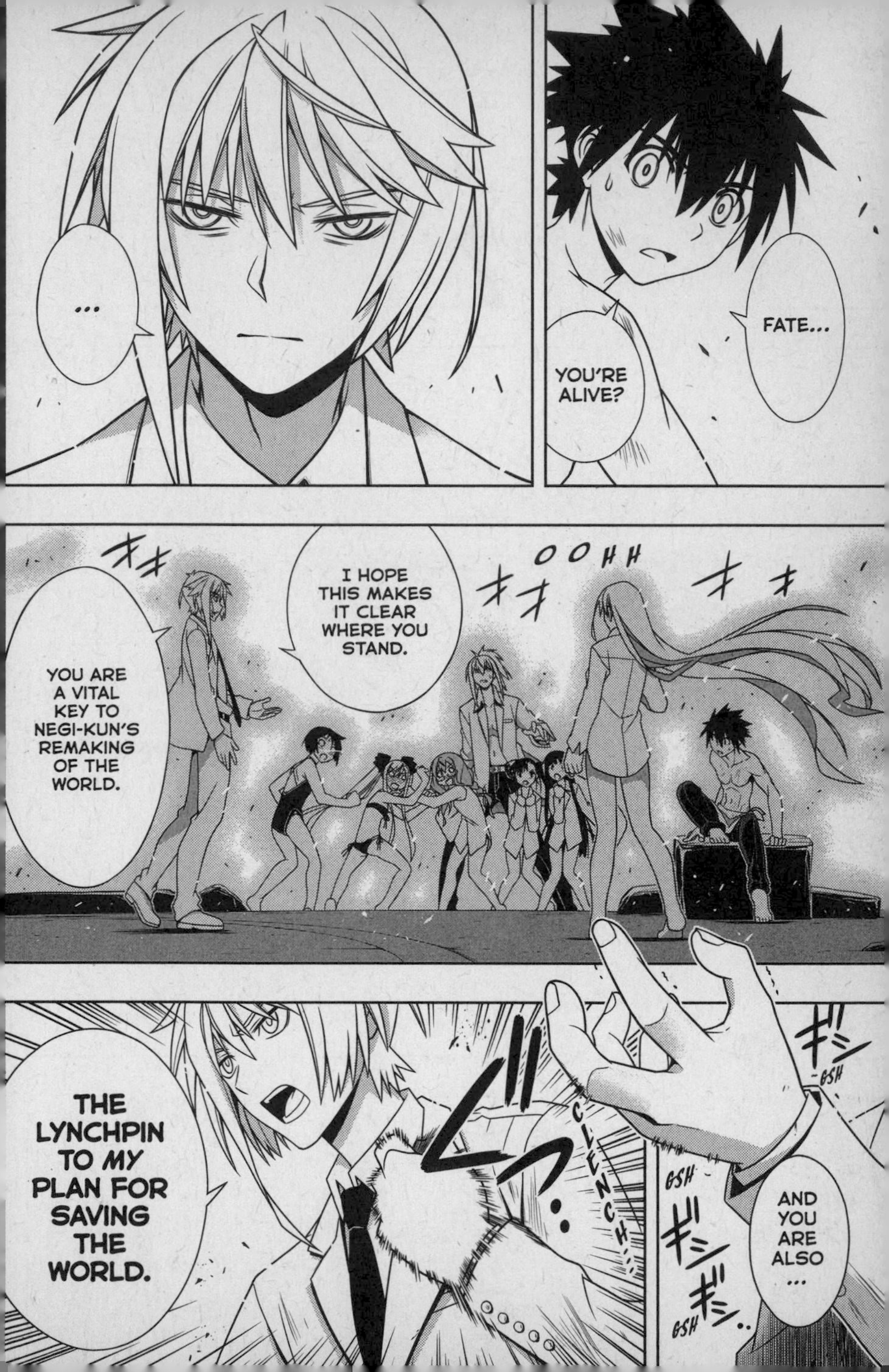
FATE...
YOU'RE ALIVE?
...
OOHH
I HOPE THIS MAKES IT CLEAR WHERE YOU STAND.
YOU ARE A VITAL KEY TO NEGI-KUN'S REMAKING OF THE WORLD.
GSH
GSH
GSH
AND YOU ARE ALSO...
CLENCH
THE LYNCHPIN TO MY PLAN FOR SAVING THE WORLD.

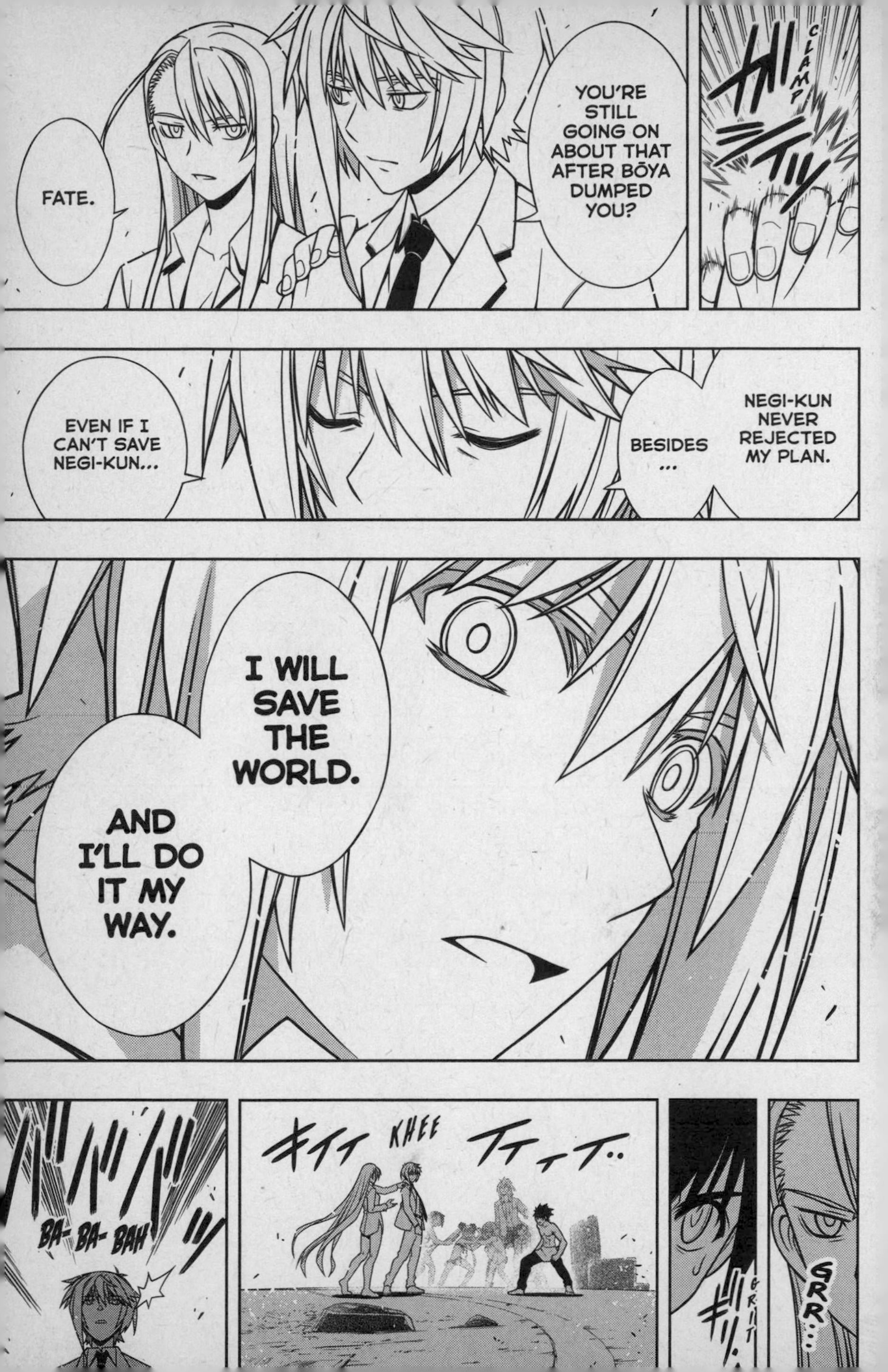
CLAMP
YOU'RE STILL GOING ON ABOUT THAT AFTER BŌYA DUMPED YOU?
FATE.
NEGI-KUN NEVER REJECTED MY PLAN.
BESIDES ...
EVEN IF I CAN'T SAVE NEGI-KUN...
I WILL SAVE THE WORLD.
AND I'LL DO IT MY WAY.
GRR...
GRIT
KHEE
BA-BA-BAH

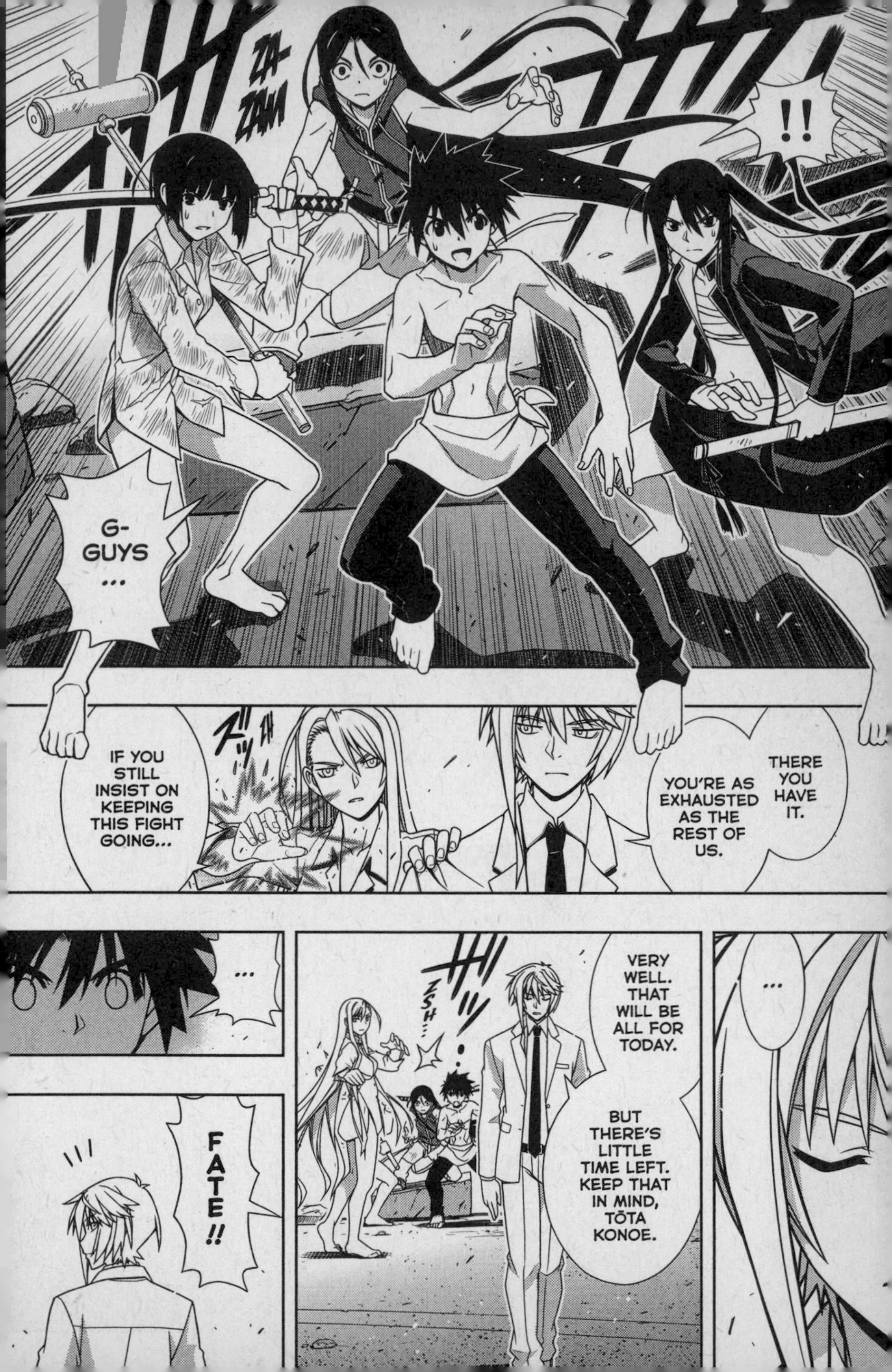

!!
ZA-ZAAA
G-GUYS...
THERE YOU HAVE IT.
YOU'RE AS EXHAUSTED AS THE REST OF US.
ZH
IF YOU STILL INSIST ON KEEPING THIS FIGHT GOING...
...
VERY WELL. THAT WILL BE ALL FOR TODAY.
ZSH!!
BUT THERE'S LITTLE TIME LEFT. KEEP THAT IN MIND, TŌTA KONOE.
...
FATE!!

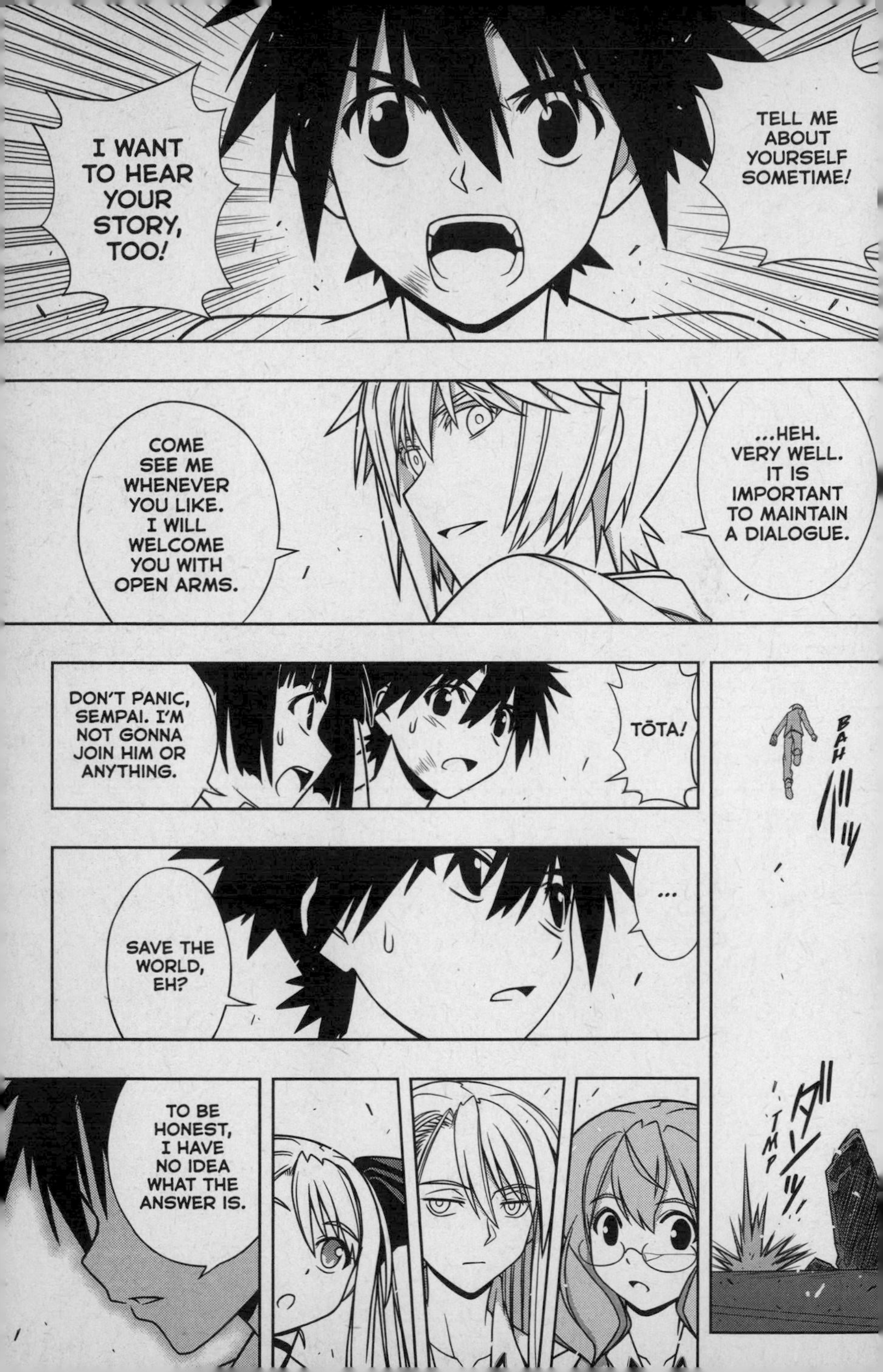
TELL ME ABOUT YOURSELF SOMETIME!
I WANT TO HEAR YOUR STORY, TOO!
...HEH. VERY WELL. IT IS IMPORTANT TO MAINTAIN A DIALOGUE.
COME SEE ME WHENEVER YOU LIKE. I WILL WELCOME YOU WITH OPEN ARMS.
BAH
TMP
TŌTA!
DON'T PANIC, SEMPAI. I'M NOT GONNA JOIN HIM OR ANYTHING.
...
SAVE THE WORLD, EH?
TO BE HONEST, I HAVE NO IDEA WHAT THE ANSWER IS.

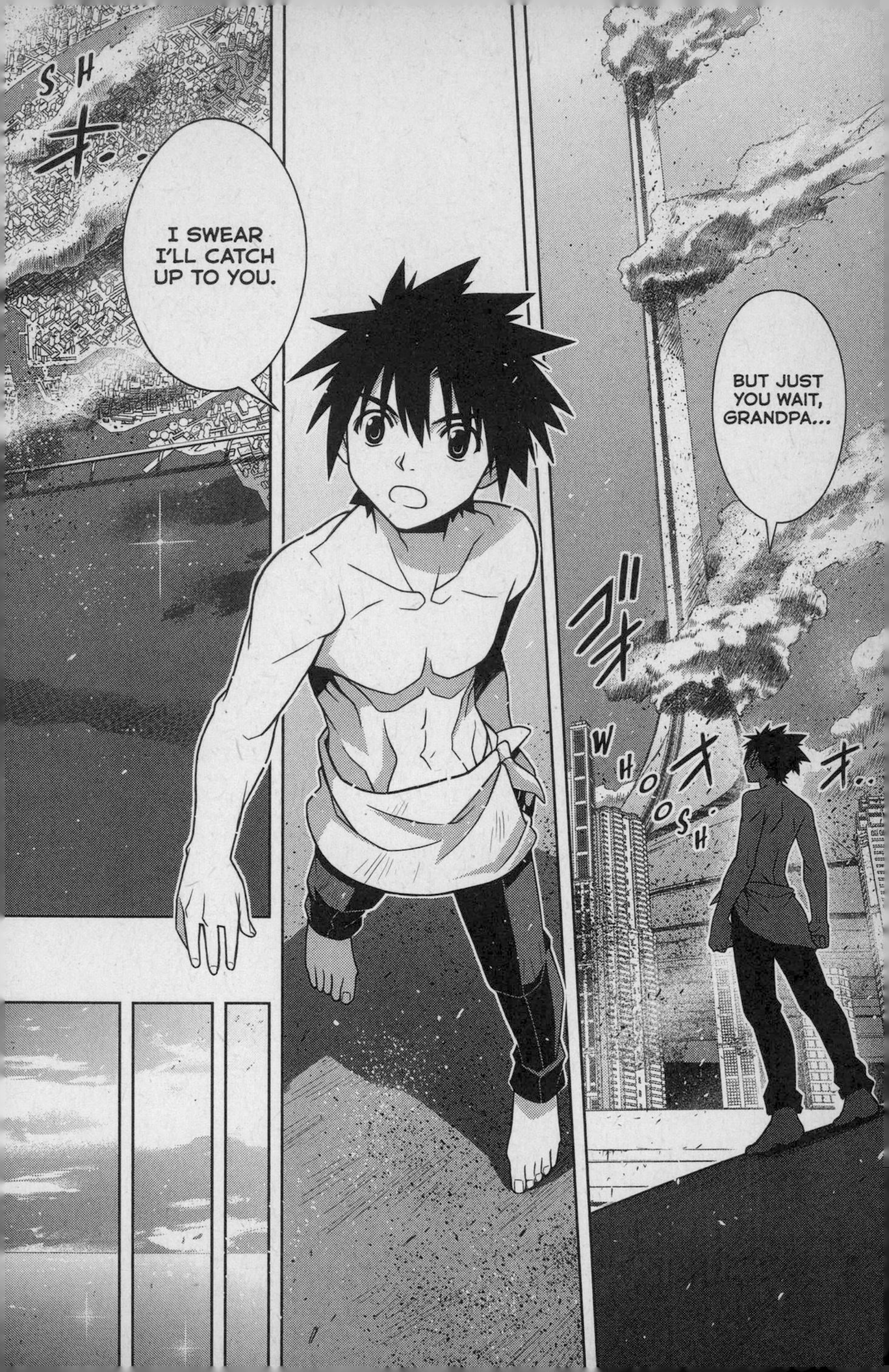
BUT JUST YOU WAIT, GRANDPA...
WHOOSH
I SWEAR I'LL CATCH UP TO YOU.
SH

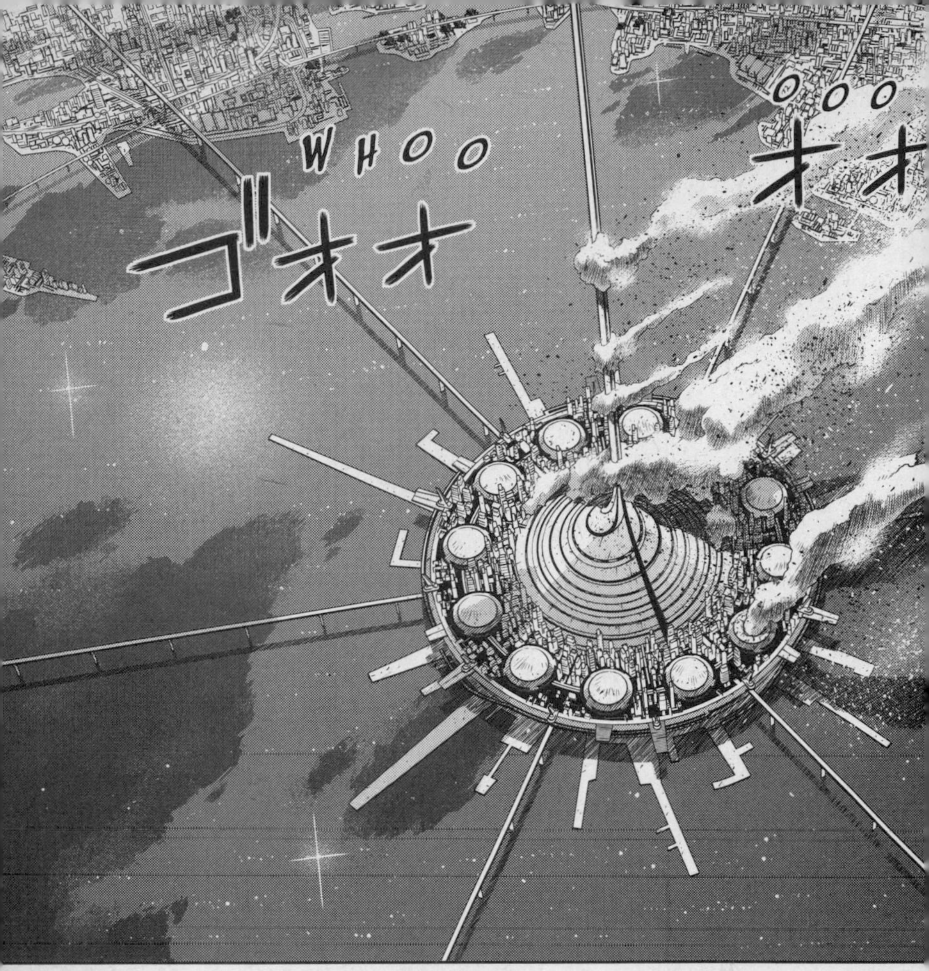
WHOO
ゴオオ
OOO
オオ

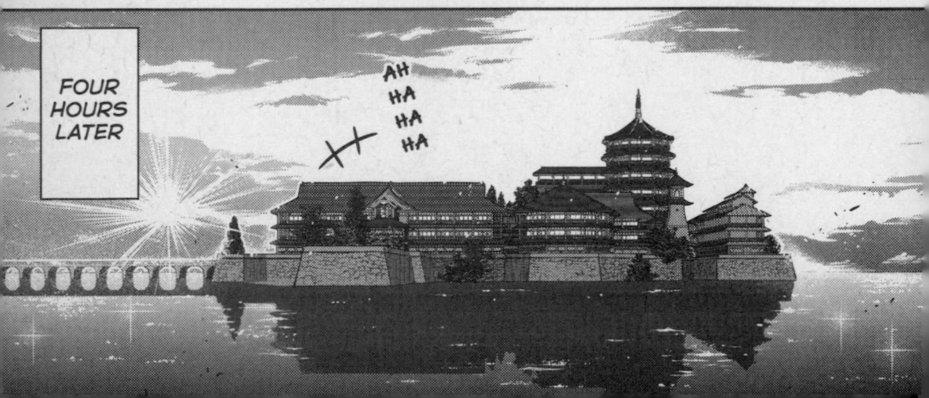
FOUR HOURS LATER
AH HA HA HA

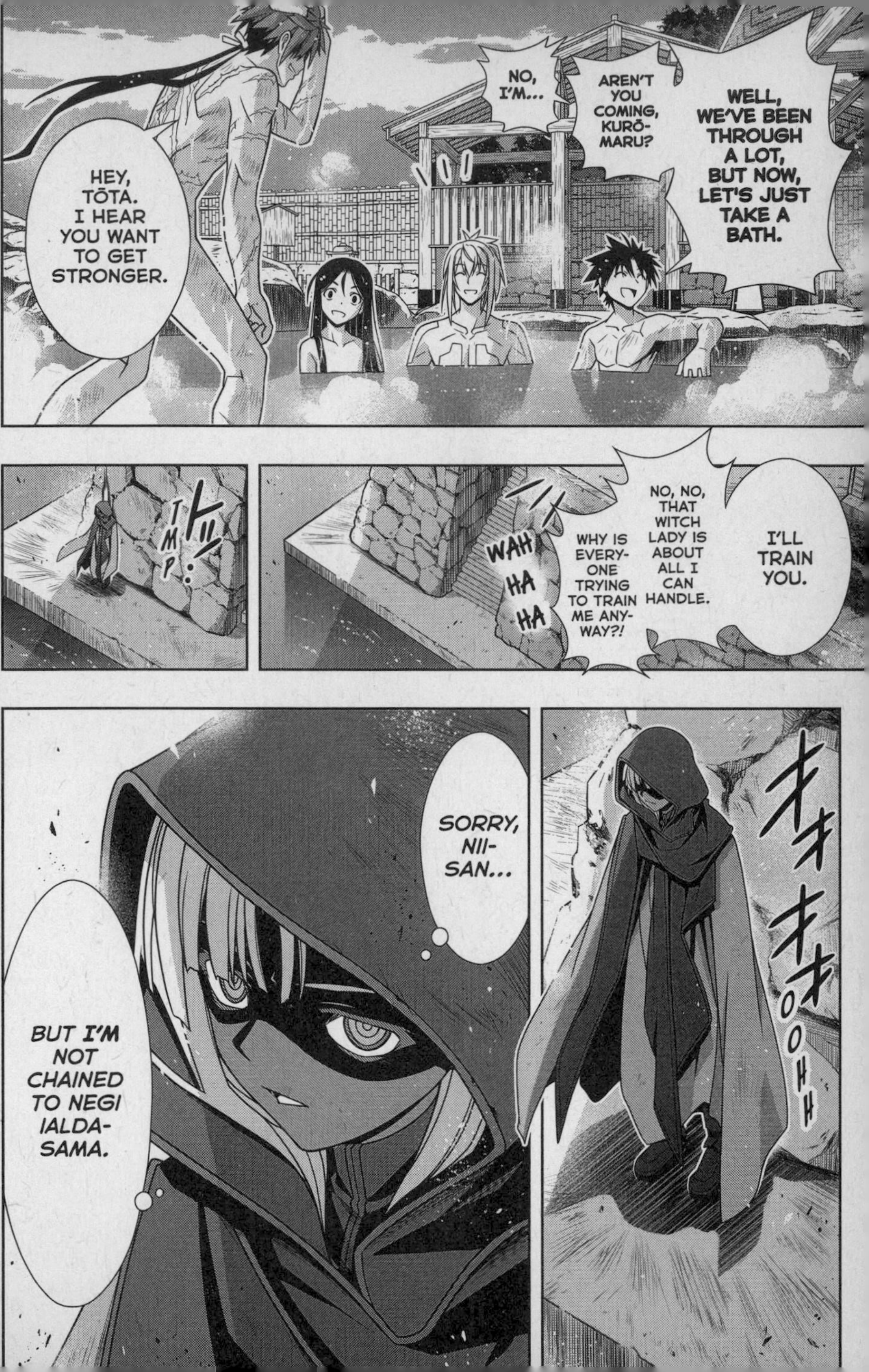
WELL, WE'VE BEEN THROUGH A LOT, BUT NOW, LET'S JUST TAKE A BATH.
AREN'T YOU COMING, KURŌ-MARU?
NO, I'M...
HEY, TŌTA. I HEAR YOU WANT TO GET STRONGER.
I'LL TRAIN YOU.
NO, NO, THAT WITCH LADY IS ABOUT ALL I CAN HANDLE.
WHY IS EVERY-ONE TRYING TO TRAIN ME ANY-WAY?!
WAH HA HA
TMP
OOOHH
SORRY, NII-SAN...
BUT I'M NOT CHAINED TO NEGI IALDA-SAMA.

悠久 UQ HOLDER!

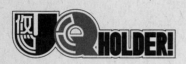

UQ HOLDER!

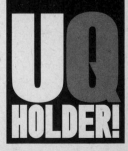

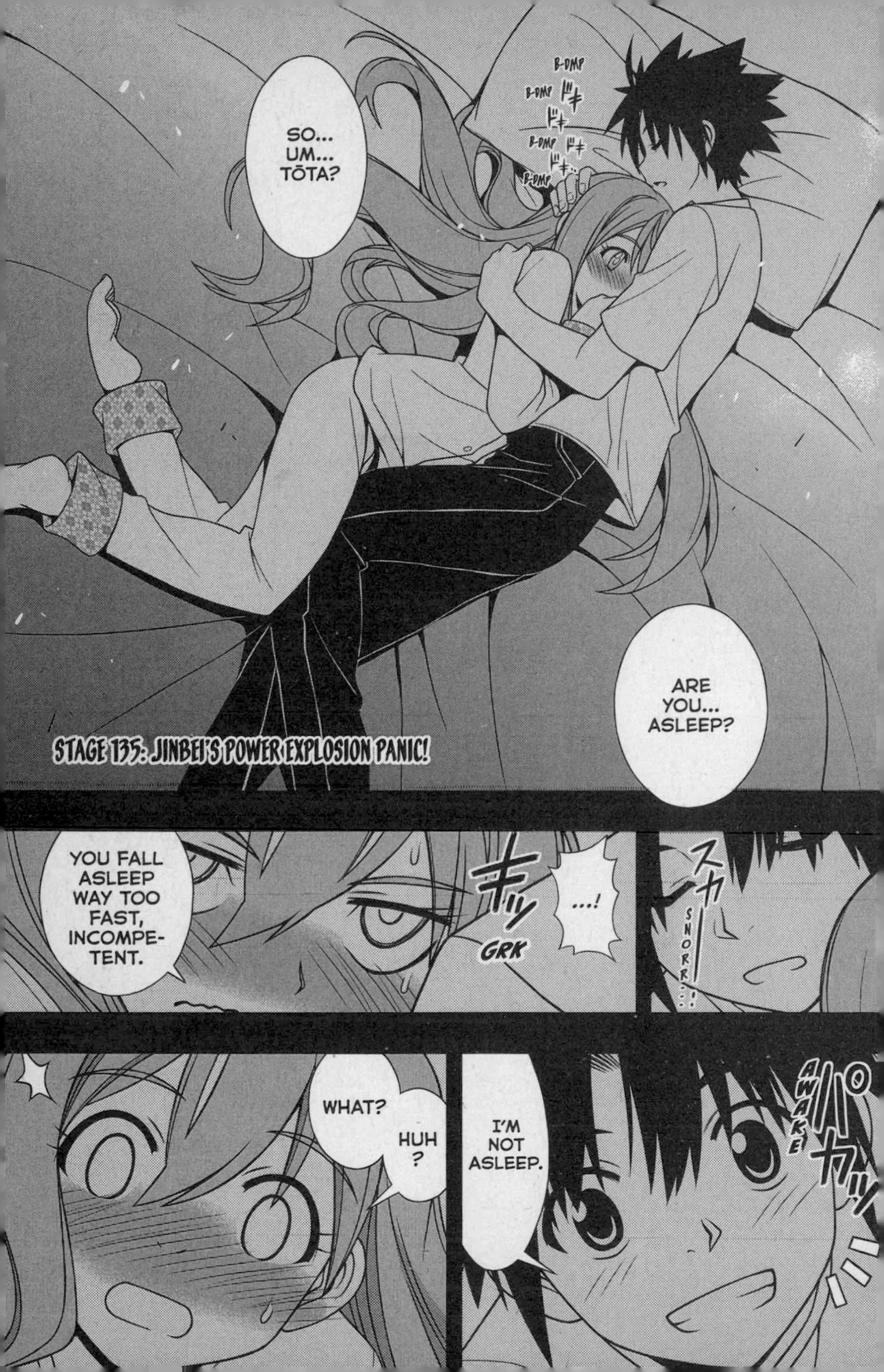
B-DMP
B-DMP
B-DMP
B-DMP
SO... UM... TŌTA?
ARE YOU... ASLEEP?
STAGE 135: JINBEI'S POWER EXPLOSION PANIC!
SNORR...!
...!
GRK
YOU FALL ASLEEP WAY TOO FAST, INCOMPE-TENT.
AWAKE
I'M NOT ASLEEP.
HUH?
WHAT?

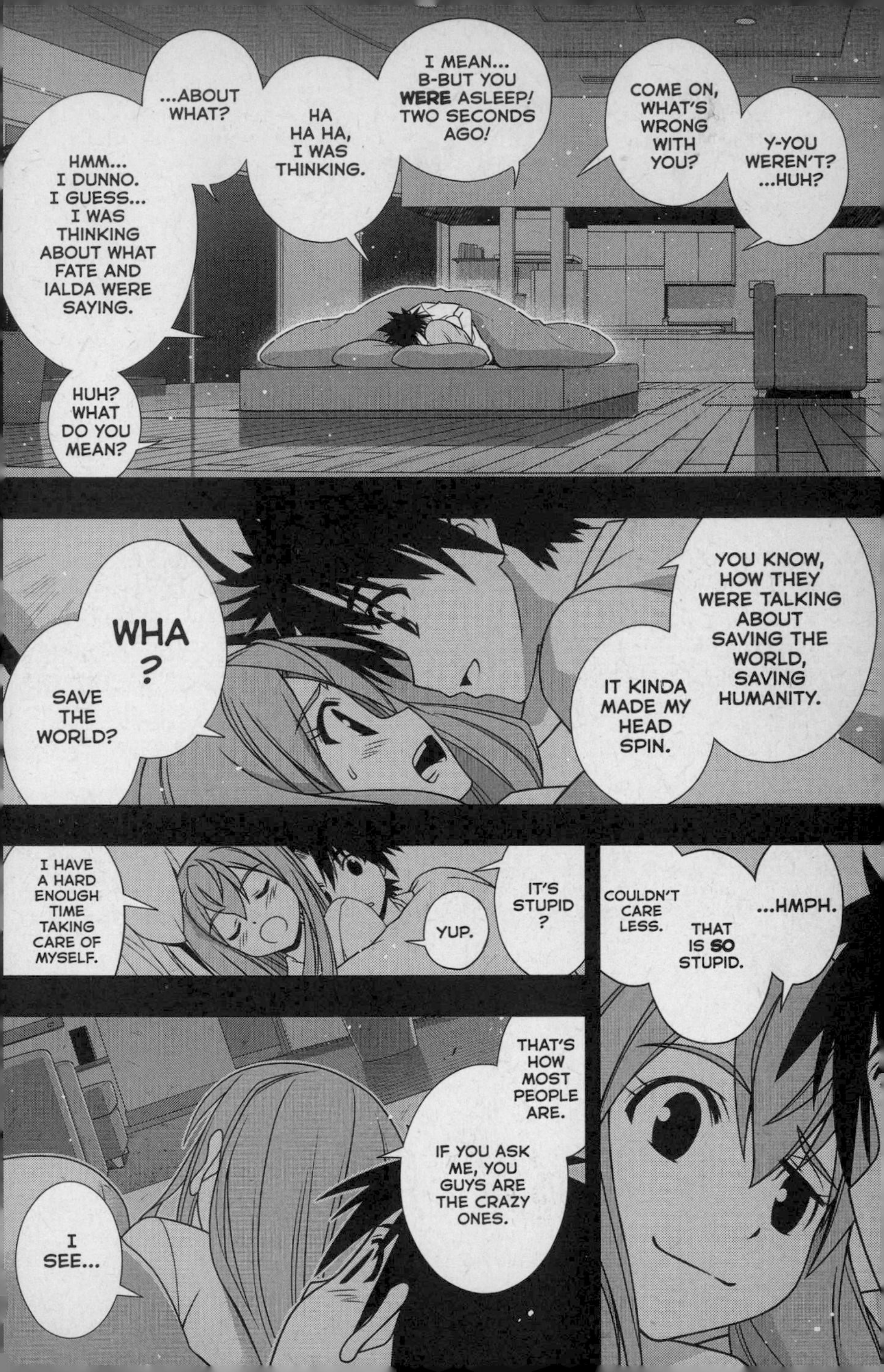
Y-YOU WEREN'T? ...HUH?
COME ON, WHAT'S WRONG WITH YOU?
I MEAN... B-BUT YOU **WERE** ASLEEP! TWO SECONDS AGO!
HA HA HA, I WAS THINKING.
...ABOUT WHAT?
HMM... I DUNNO. I GUESS... I WAS THINKING ABOUT WHAT FATE AND IALDA WERE SAYING.
HUH? WHAT DO YOU MEAN?
YOU KNOW, HOW THEY WERE TALKING ABOUT SAVING THE WORLD, SAVING HUMANITY.
IT KINDA MADE MY HEAD SPIN.
WHA? SAVE THE WORLD?
...HMPH.
THAT IS **SO** STUPID.
COULDN'T CARE LESS.
IT'S STUPID?
YUP.
I HAVE A HARD ENOUGH TIME TAKING CARE OF MYSELF.
THAT'S HOW MOST PEOPLE ARE.
IF YOU ASK ME, YOU GUYS ARE THE CRAZY ONES.
I SEE...

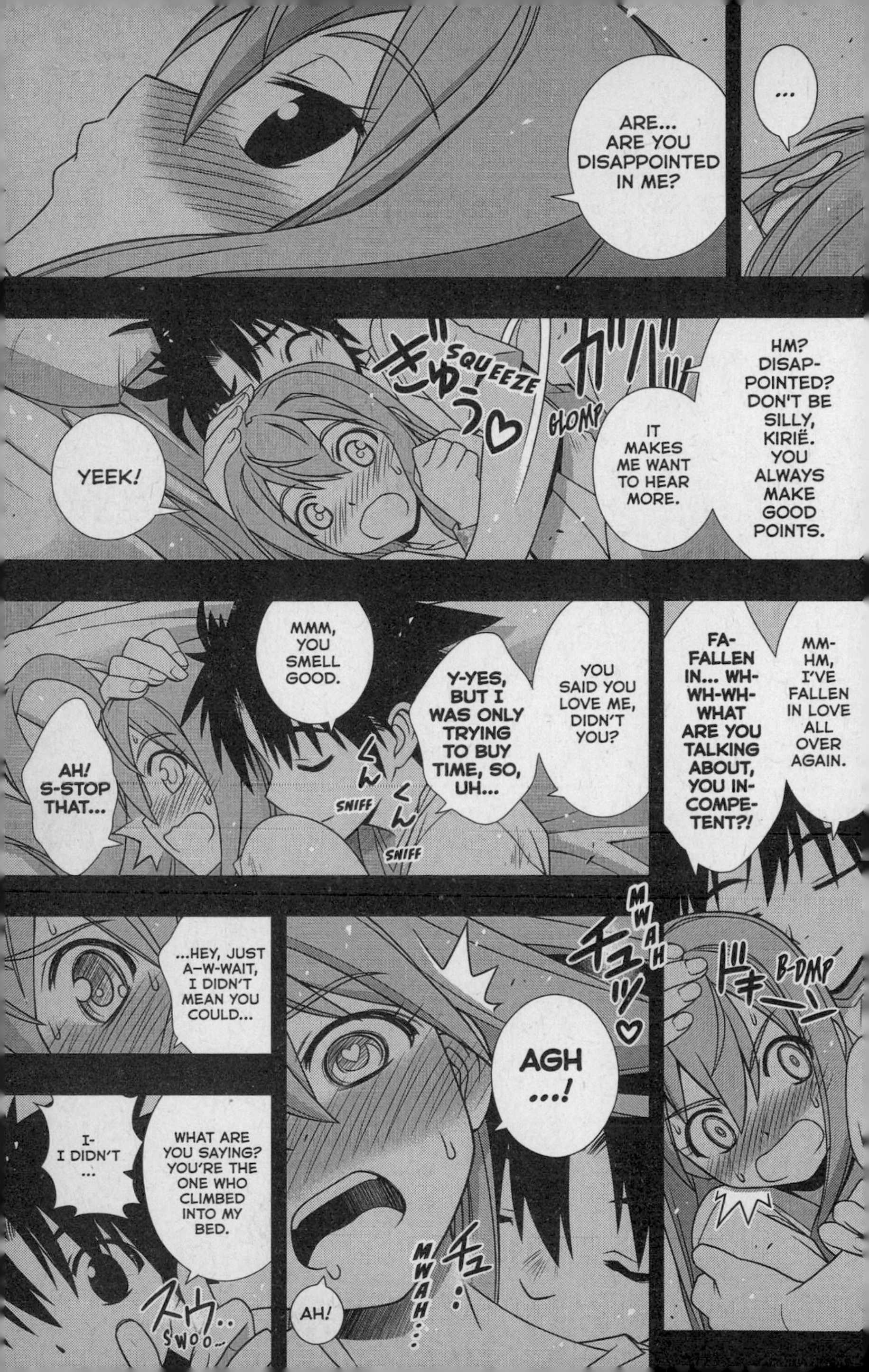
...
ARE... ARE YOU DISAPPOINTED IN ME?
HM? DISAP-POINTED? DON'T BE SILLY, KIRIË. YOU ALWAYS MAKE GOOD POINTS.
IT MAKES ME WANT TO HEAR MORE.
GLOMP
SQUEEZE
YEEK!
MM-HM, I'VE FALLEN IN LOVE ALL OVER AGAIN.
FA-FALLEN IN... WH-WH-WH-WHAT ARE YOU TALKING ABOUT, YOU IN-COMPE-TENT?!
YOU SAID YOU LOVE ME, DIDN'T YOU?
Y-YES, BUT I WAS ONLY TRYING TO BUY TIME, SO, UH...
MMM, YOU SMELL GOOD.
SNIFF
SNIFF
AH! S-STOP THAT...
B-DMP
MWAH
AGH ...!
MWAH...
AH!
...HEY, JUST A-W-WAIT, I DIDN'T MEAN YOU COULD...
WHAT ARE YOU SAYING? YOU'RE THE ONE WHO CLIMBED INTO MY BED.
I- I DIDN'T ...
SWOO...

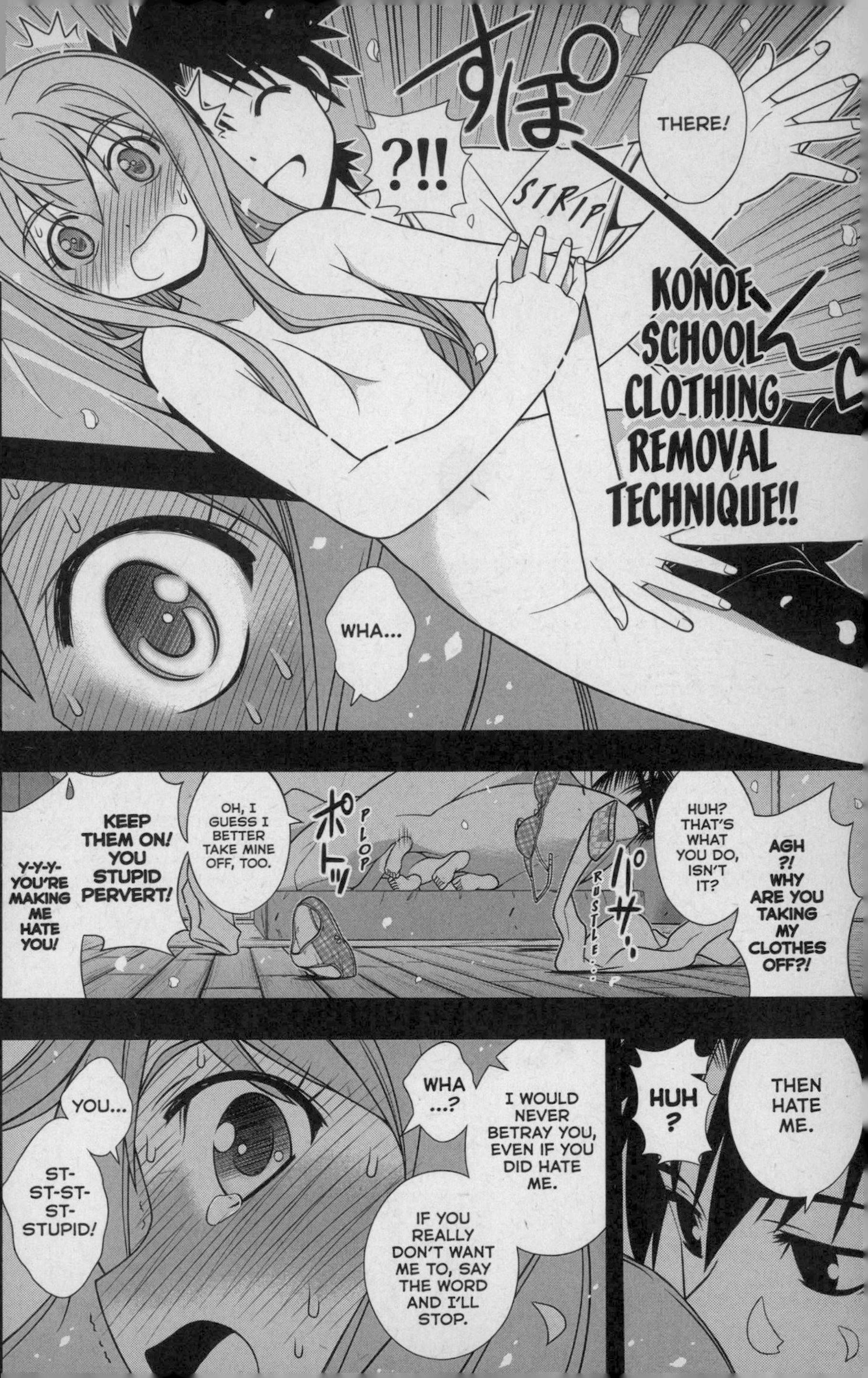

THERE!
すぽ
STRIP
?!!
KONOE SCHOOL CLOTHING REMOVAL TECHNIQUE!!
WHA...
AGH?! WHY ARE YOU TAKING MY CLOTHES OFF?!
HUH? THAT'S WHAT YOU DO, ISN'T IT?
パサ
RUSTLE...
OH, I GUESS I BETTER TAKE MINE OFF, TOO.
ポトッ
PLOP
KEEP THEM ON! YOU STUPID PERVERT!
Y-Y-Y-YOU'RE MAKING ME HATE YOU!
THEN HATE ME.
HUH?
I WOULD NEVER BETRAY YOU, EVEN IF YOU DID HATE ME.
WHA ...?
IF YOU REALLY DON'T WANT ME TO, SAY THE WORD AND I'LL STOP.
YOU...
ST-ST-ST-ST-STUPID!

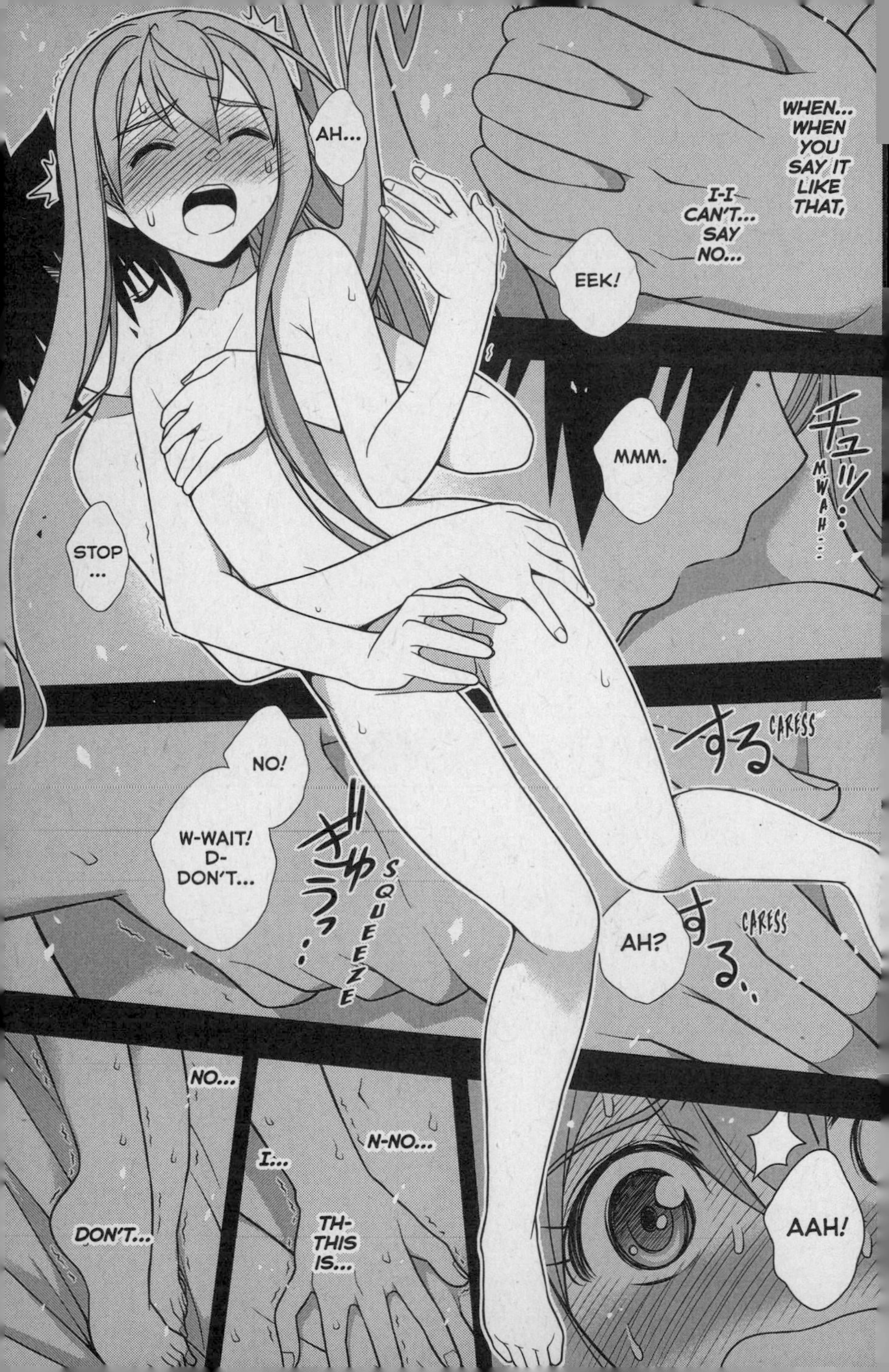

WHEN... WHEN YOU SAY IT LIKE THAT,
I-I CAN'T... SAY NO...
EEK!
AH...
チュッ.. MWAH...
MMM.
STOP...
する CARESS
する.. CARESS
AH?
ぎゅうっ.. SQUEEZE
NO!
W-WAIT! D-DON'T...
AAH!
N-NO...
I...
TH-THIS IS...
NO...
DON'T...

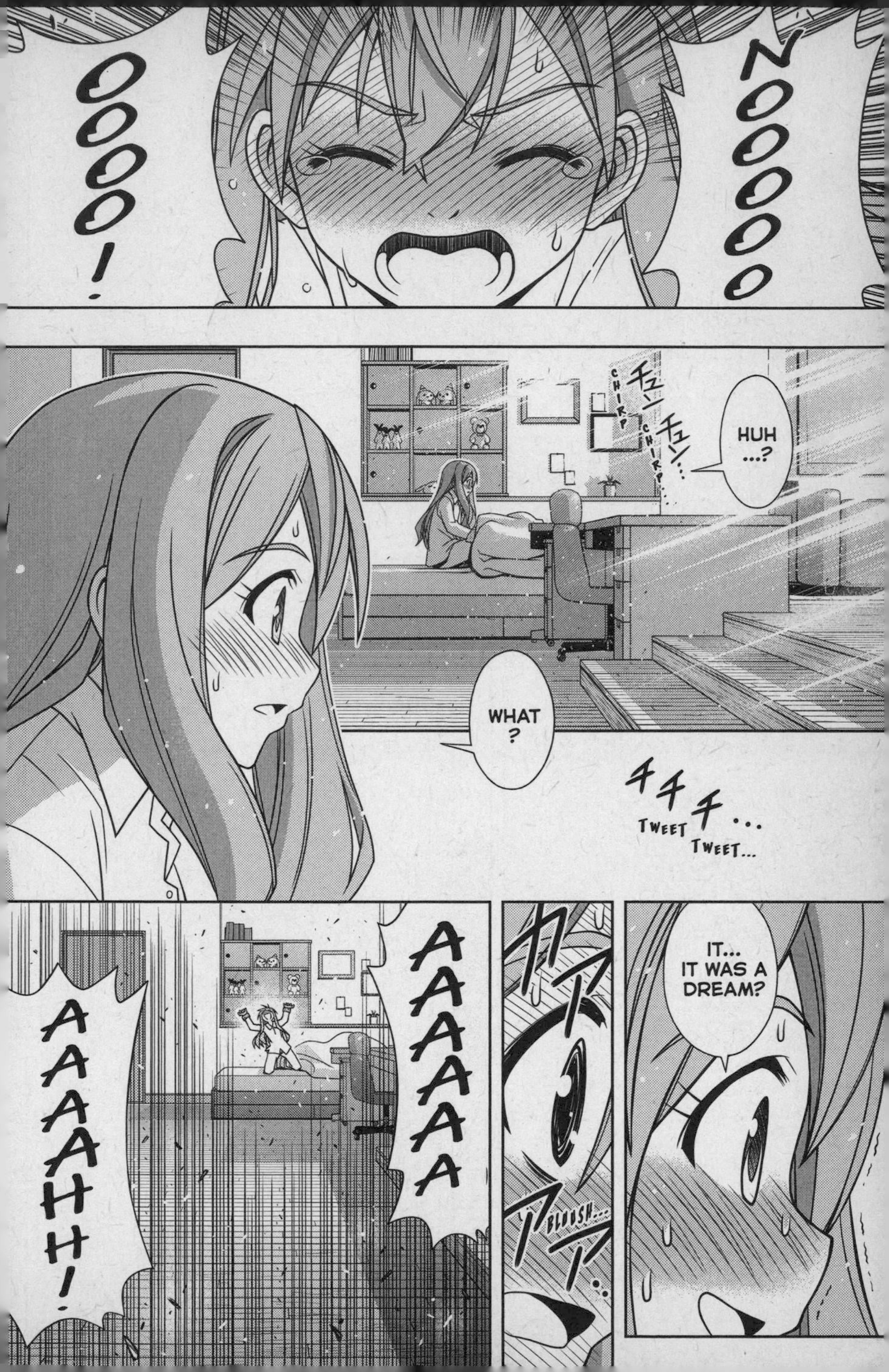
NOOOOOO
OOOOO!
チュン CHIRP
チュン CHIRP...
HUH ...?
WHAT ?
チチチ...
TWEET TWEET...
IT... IT WAS A DREAM?
BLUSH...
AAAAAA
AAAAHH!

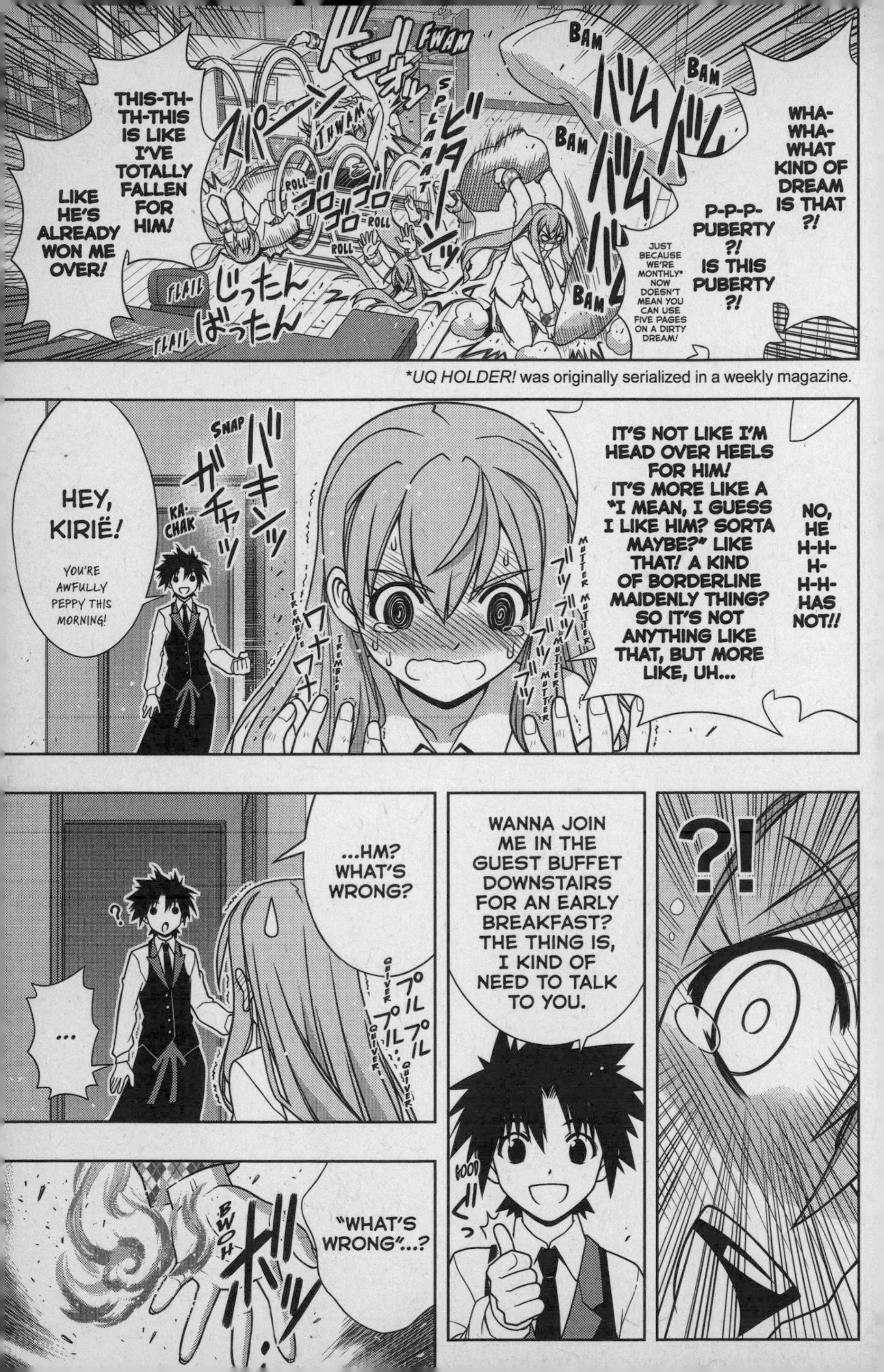
WHA-WHA-WHAT KIND OF DREAM IS THAT?!
P-P-P-PUBERTY?! IS THIS PUBERTY?!
JUST BECAUSE WE'RE MONTHLY* NOW DOESN'T MEAN YOU CAN USE FIVE PAGES ON A DIRTY DREAM!
BAM
BAM
BAM
BAM
SPLAAAAT
FWAM
THWAM
ROLL
ROLL
ROLL
THIS-TH-TH-THIS IS LIKE I'VE TOTALLY FALLEN FOR HIM!
LIKE HE'S ALREADY WON ME OVER!
FLAIL
FLAIL
じったん ばったん
NO, HE H-H-H-H-H-HAS NOT!!
IT'S NOT LIKE I'M HEAD OVER HEELS FOR HIM! IT'S MORE LIKE A "I MEAN, I GUESS I LIKE HIM? SORTA MAYBE?" LIKE THAT! A KIND OF BORDERLINE MAIDENLY THING? SO IT'S NOT ANYTHING LIKE THAT, BUT MORE LIKE, UH...
MUTTER MUTTER
MUTTER MUTTER
TREMBLE
TREMBLE
SNAP
KA-CHAK
HEY, KIRIË!
YOU'RE AWFULLY PEPPY THIS MORNING!
?!
WANNA JOIN ME IN THE GUEST BUFFET DOWNSTAIRS FOR AN EARLY BREAKFAST? THE THING IS, I KIND OF NEED TO TALK TO YOU.
GOOD
...HM? WHAT'S WRONG?
QUIVER
QUIVER
QUIVER
...
"WHAT'S WRONG"...?
BWOH

*UQ HOLDER! was originally serialized in a weekly magazine.

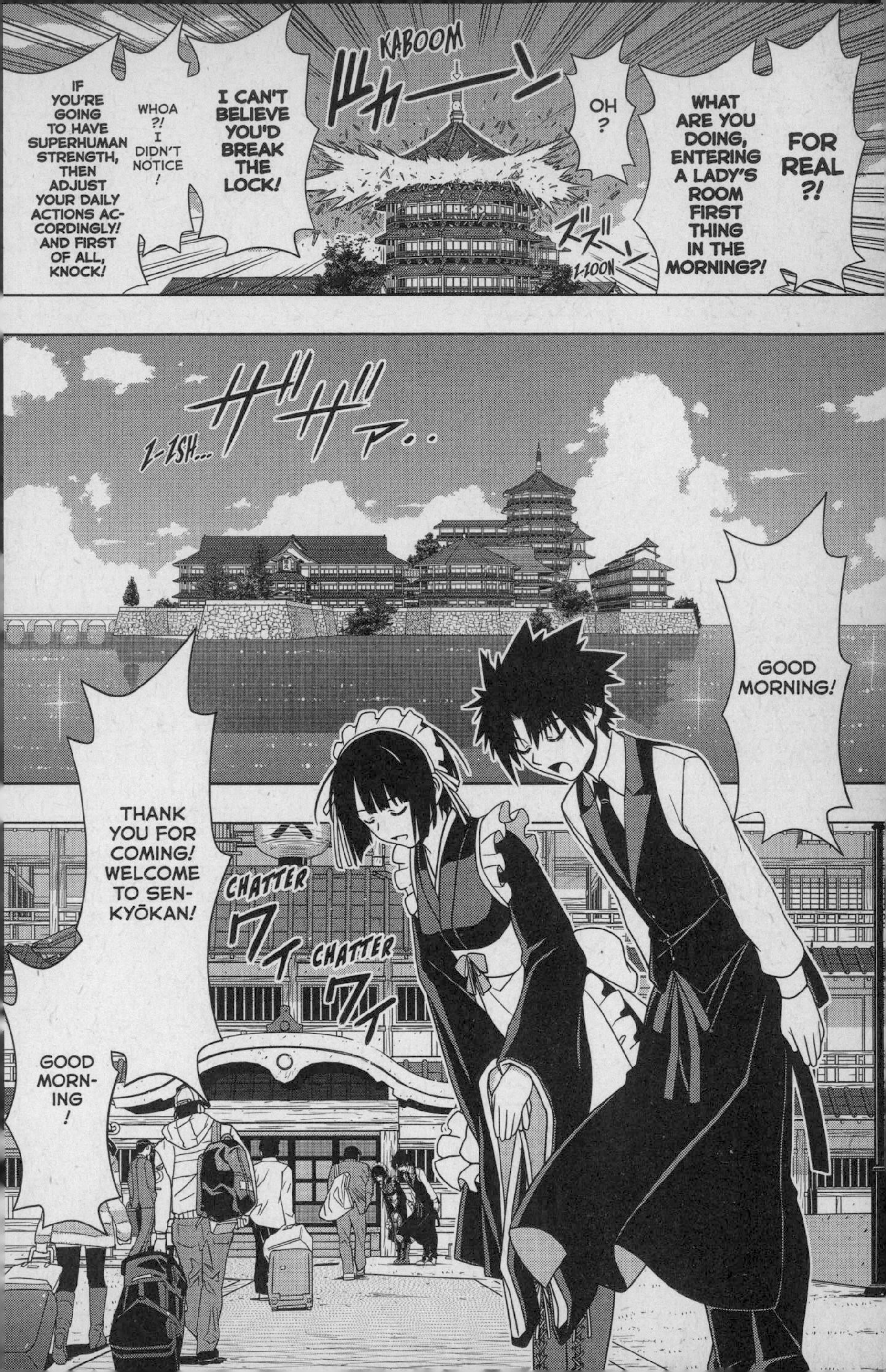
FOR REAL?!
WHAT ARE YOU DOING, ENTERING A LADY'S ROOM FIRST THING IN THE MORNING?!
OH?
KABOOM
Z-ZOON
I CAN'T BELIEVE YOU'D BREAK THE LOCK!
WHOA?! I DIDN'T NOTICE!
IF YOU'RE GOING TO HAVE SUPERHUMAN STRENGTH, THEN ADJUST YOUR DAILY ACTIONS AC-CORDINGLY! AND FIRST OF ALL, KNOCK!
Z-ZSH...
GOOD MORNING!
THANK YOU FOR COMING! WELCOME TO SEN-KYŌKAN!
CHATTER
CHATTER
GOOD MORN-ING!

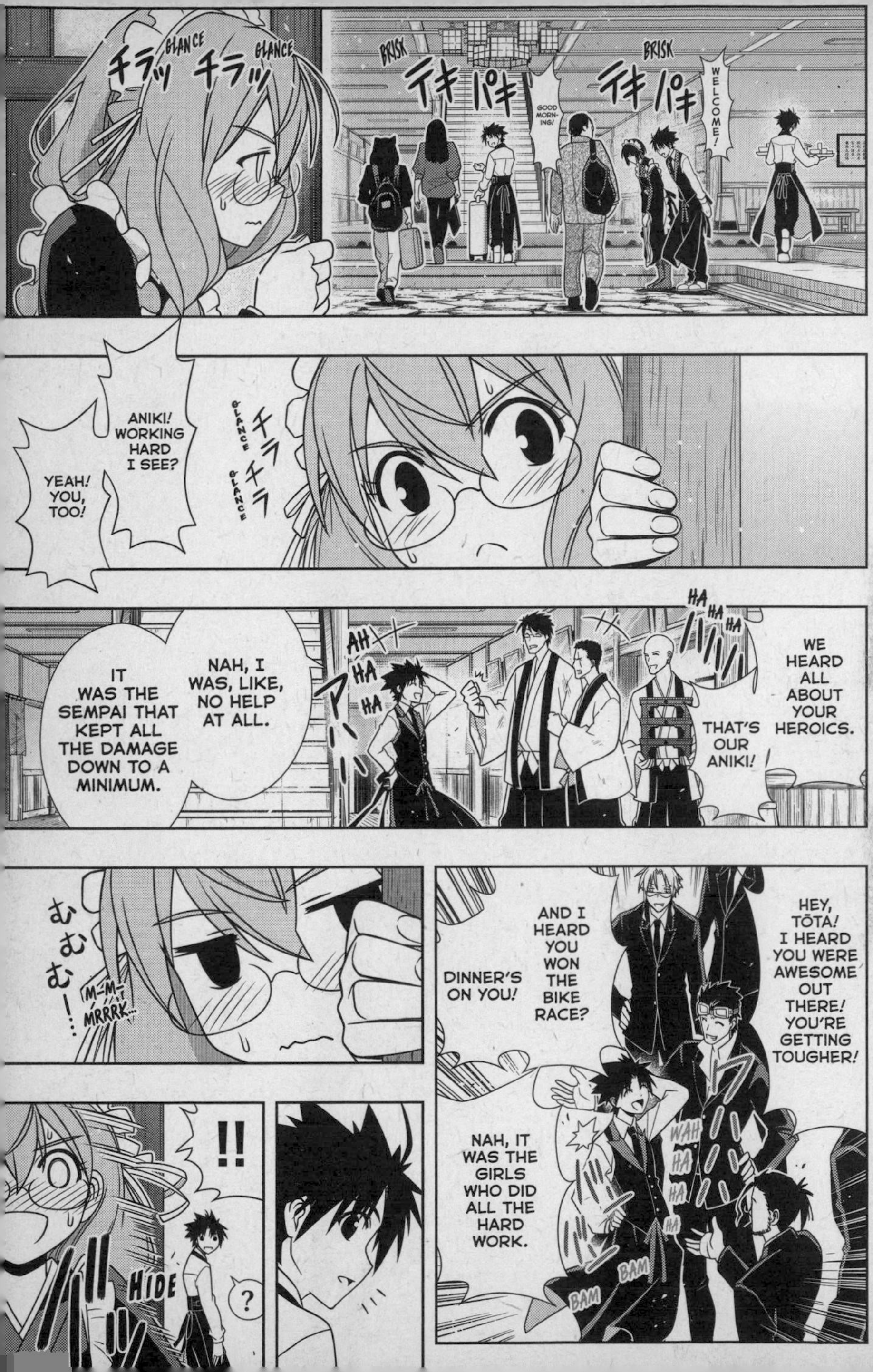

BRISK
BRISK
WELCOME!
GOOD MORNING!
チラッ GLANCE
チラッ GLANCE
ANIKI! WORKING HARD I SEE?
YEAH! YOU, TOO!
GLANCE GLANCE
WE HEARD ALL ABOUT YOUR HEROICS.
THAT'S OUR ANIKI!
HA HA HA
AH HA HA
NAH, I WAS, LIKE, NO HELP AT ALL.
IT WAS THE SEMPAI THAT KEPT ALL THE DAMAGE DOWN TO A MINIMUM.
HEY, TŌTA! I HEARD YOU WERE AWESOME OUT THERE! YOU'RE GETTING TOUGHER!
AND I HEARD YOU WON THE BIKE RACE?
DINNER'S ON YOU!
NAH, IT WAS THE GIRLS WHO DID ALL THE HARD WORK.
WAH HA HA HA
BAM BAM BAM
むむむ…!
M-M-MRRRK…
!!
HIDE
?

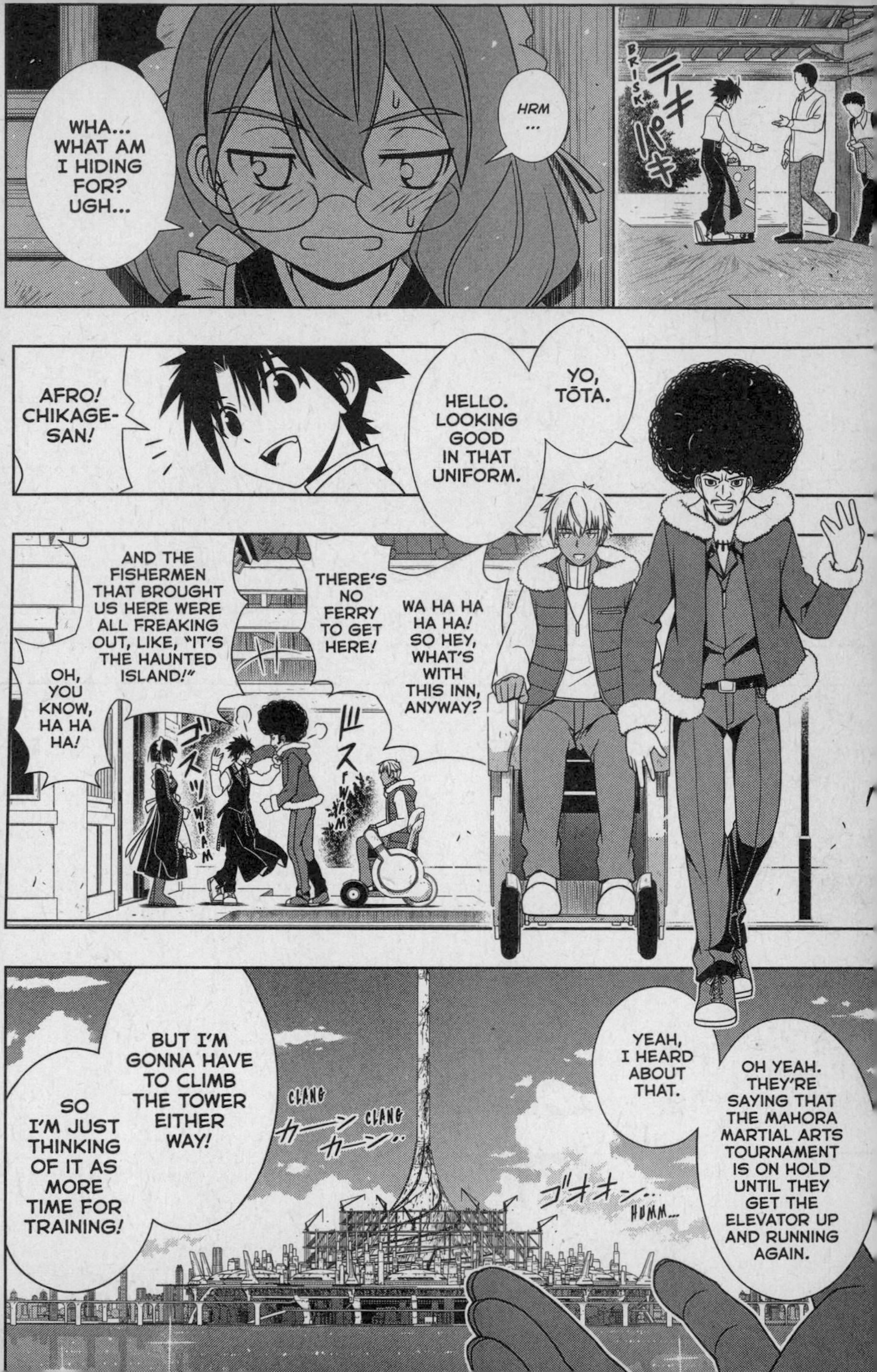
テキパキ
BRISK
HRM ...
WHA... WHAT AM I HIDING FOR? UGH...
YO, TŌTA.
HELLO. LOOKING GOOD IN THAT UNIFORM.
AFRO! CHIKAGE-SAN!
WA HA HA HA HA! SO HEY, WHAT'S WITH THIS INN, ANYWAY?
THERE'S NO FERRY TO GET HERE!
AND THE FISHERMEN THAT BROUGHT US HERE WERE ALL FREAKING OUT, LIKE, "IT'S THE HAUNTED ISLAND!"
OH, YOU KNOW, HA HA HA!
ドスッ
FWAM
ゴスッ
WHAM
OH YEAH. THEY'RE SAYING THAT THE MAHORA MARTIAL ARTS TOURNAMENT IS ON HOLD UNTIL THEY GET THE ELEVATOR UP AND RUNNING AGAIN.
YEAH, I HEARD ABOUT THAT.
ゴオオーン...
HUMM...
カーン カーン
CLANG CLANG
BUT I'M GONNA HAVE TO CLIMB THE TOWER EITHER WAY!
SO I'M JUST THINKING OF IT AS MORE TIME FOR TRAINING!

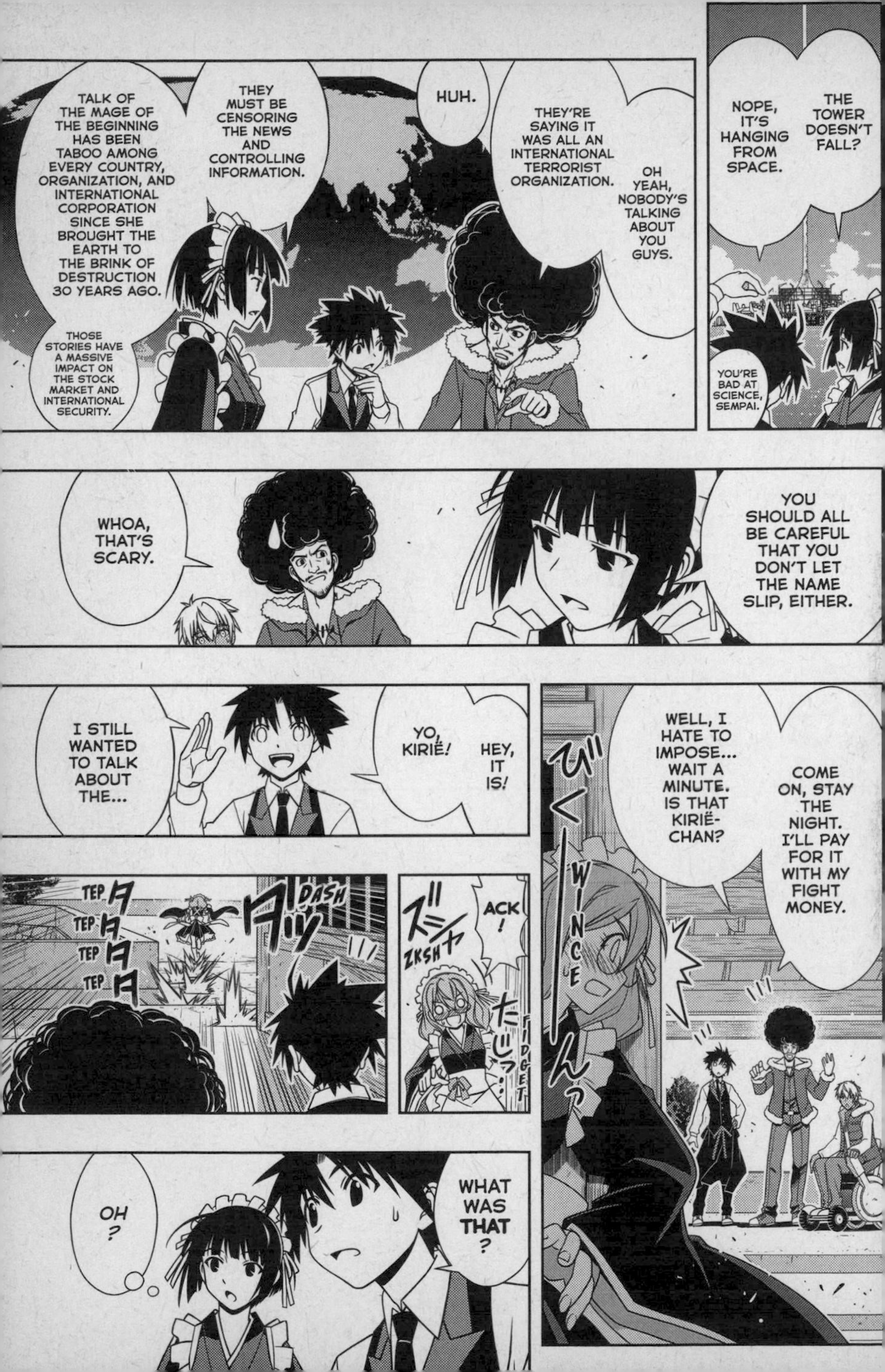

THE TOWER DOESN'T FALL?
NOPE, IT'S HANGING FROM SPACE.
YOU'RE BAD AT SCIENCE, SEMPAI.
OH YEAH, NOBODY'S TALKING ABOUT YOU GUYS.
THEY'RE SAYING IT WAS ALL AN INTERNATIONAL TERRORIST ORGANIZATION.
HUH.
THEY MUST BE CENSORING THE NEWS AND CONTROLLING INFORMATION.
TALK OF THE MAGE OF THE BEGINNING HAS BEEN TABOO AMONG EVERY COUNTRY, ORGANIZATION, AND INTERNATIONAL CORPORATION SINCE SHE BROUGHT THE EARTH TO THE BRINK OF DESTRUCTION 30 YEARS AGO.
THOSE STORIES HAVE A MASSIVE IMPACT ON THE STOCK MARKET AND INTERNATIONAL SECURITY.
YOU SHOULD ALL BE CAREFUL THAT YOU DON'T LET THE NAME SLIP, EITHER.
WHOA, THAT'S SCARY.
COME ON, STAY THE NIGHT. I'LL PAY FOR IT WITH MY FIGHT MONEY.
WELL, I HATE TO IMPOSE... WAIT A MINUTE. IS THAT KIRIÉ-CHAN?
びくーんっ
WINCE
HEY, IT IS!
YO, KIRIÉ!
I STILL WANTED TO TALK ABOUT THE...
ACK!
ズザャ
ZKSH
たじっ
FIDGET
タッ
DASH
タタタタ
TEP
TEP
TEP
TEP
WHAT WAS THAT?
OH?

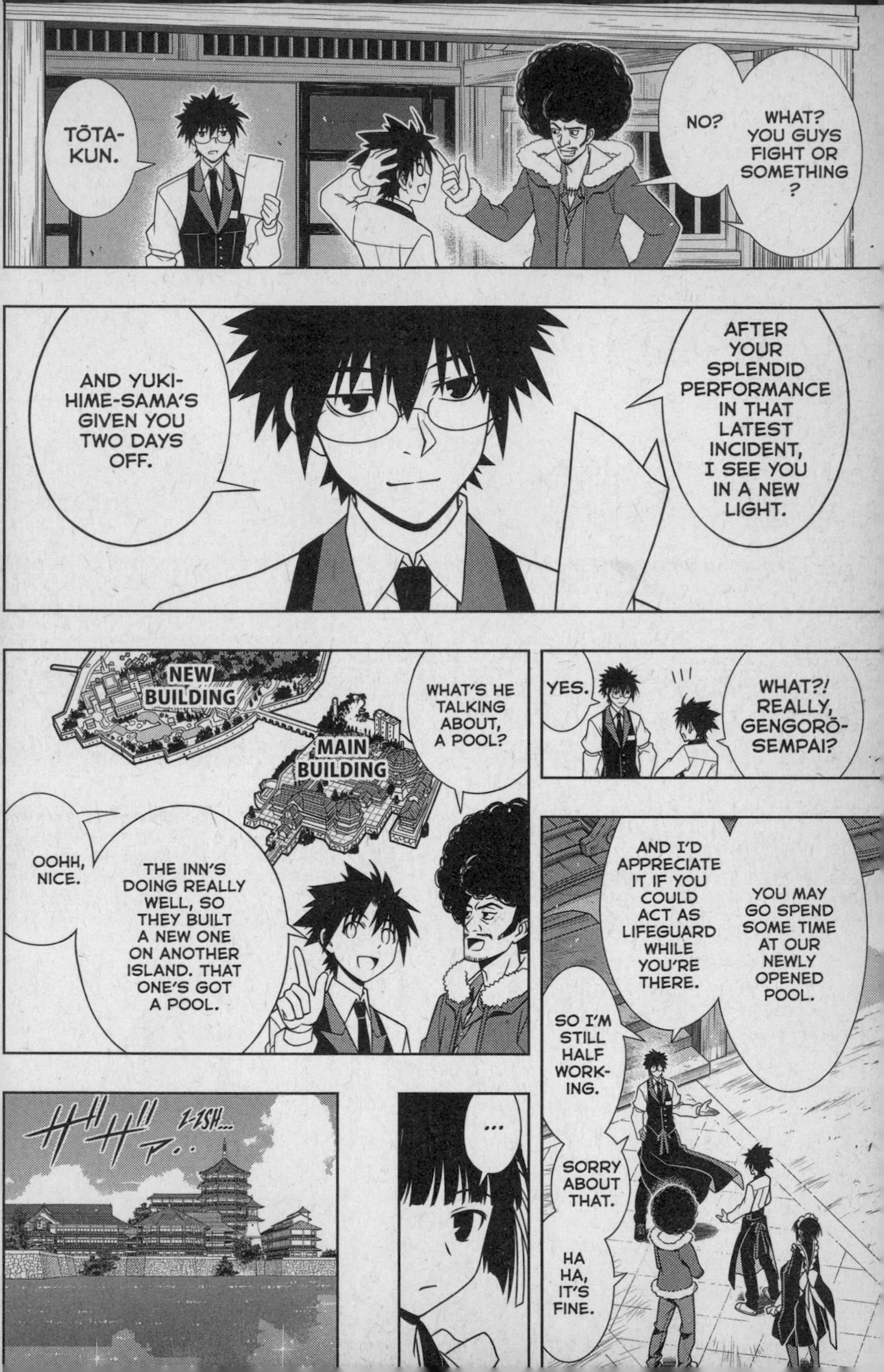
WHAT? YOU GUYS FIGHT OR SOMETHING?
NO?
TŌTA-KUN.
AFTER YOUR SPLENDID PERFORMANCE IN THAT LATEST INCIDENT, I SEE YOU IN A NEW LIGHT.
AND YUKI-HIME-SAMA'S GIVEN YOU TWO DAYS OFF.
WHAT?! REALLY, GENGORŌ-SEMPAI?
YES.
WHAT'S HE TALKING ABOUT, A POOL?
NEW BUILDING
MAIN BUILDING
THE INN'S DOING REALLY WELL, SO THEY BUILT A NEW ONE ON ANOTHER ISLAND. THAT ONE'S GOT A POOL.
OOHH, NICE.
YOU MAY GO SPEND SOME TIME AT OUR NEWLY OPENED POOL.
AND I'D APPRECIATE IT IF YOU COULD ACT AS LIFEGUARD WHILE YOU'RE THERE.
SO I'M STILL HALF WORKING.
SORRY ABOUT THAT.
HA HA, IT'S FINE.
...
Z-ZSH...

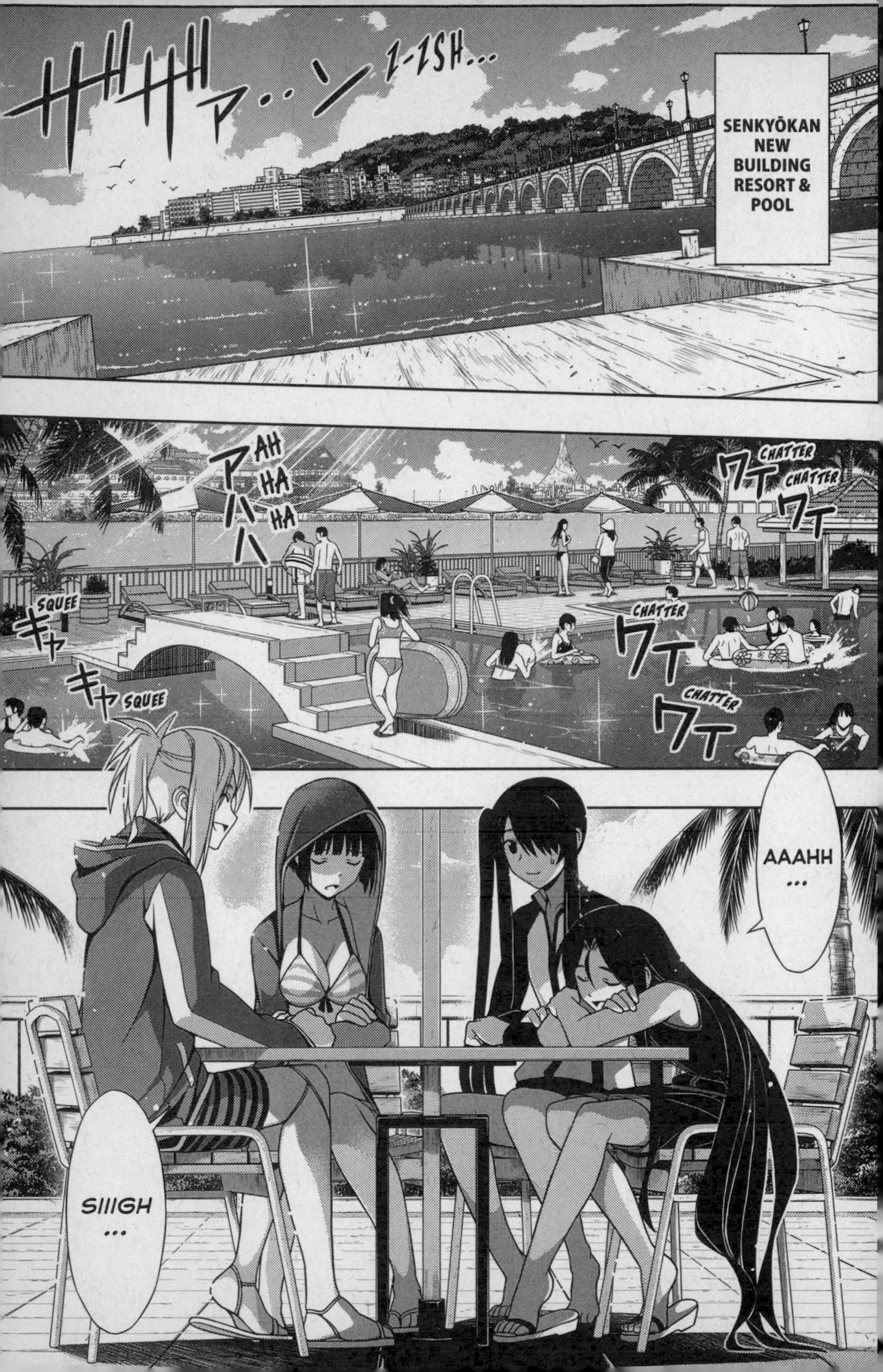
SENKYŌKAN NEW BUILDING RESORT & POOL
Z-ZSH...
CHATTER CHATTER
CHATTER
CHATTER
AH HA HA
SQUEE
SQUEE
AAAHH ...
SIIIGH ...

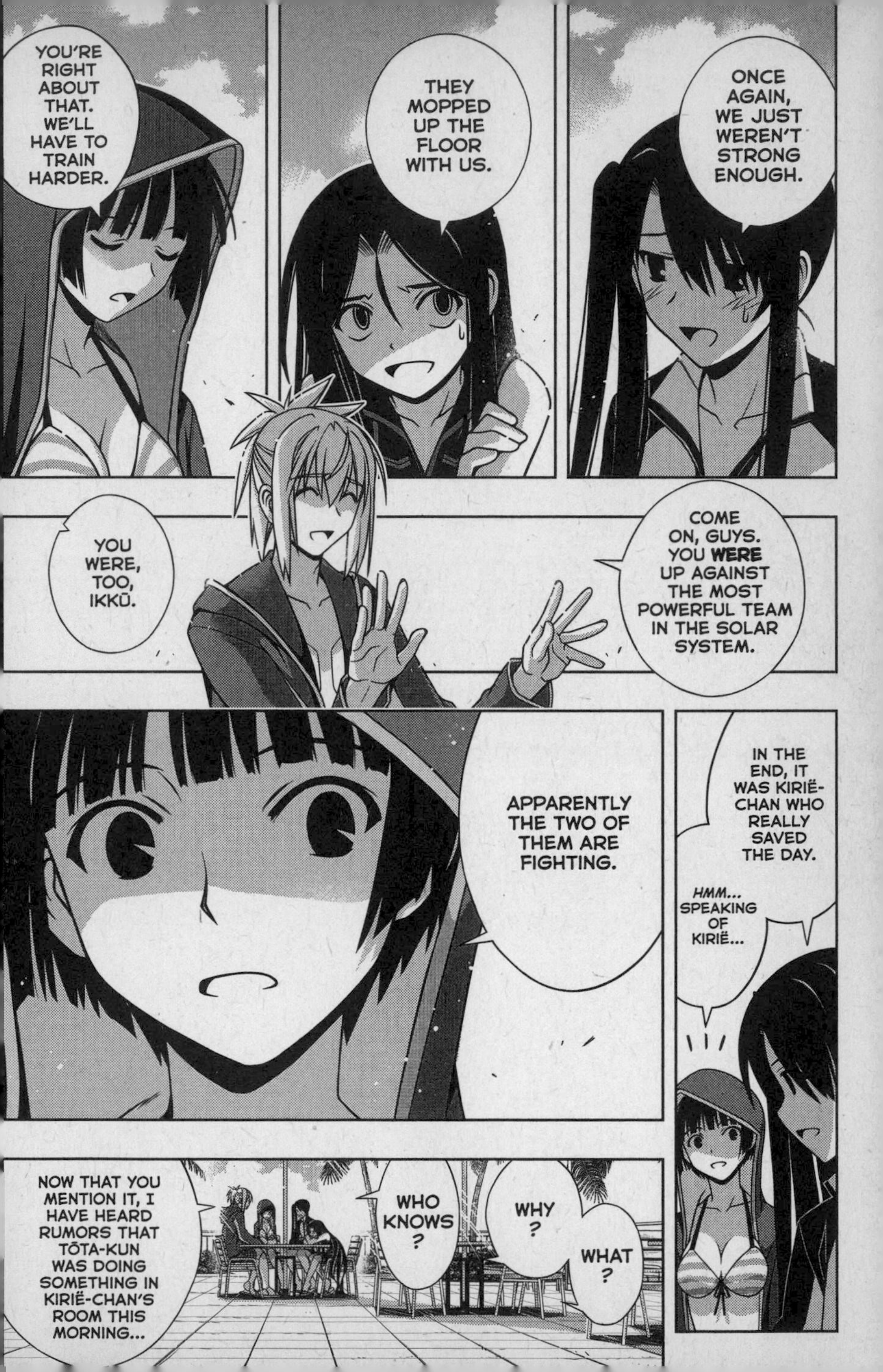
ONCE AGAIN, WE JUST WEREN'T STRONG ENOUGH.
THEY MOPPED UP THE FLOOR WITH US.
YOU'RE RIGHT ABOUT THAT. WE'LL HAVE TO TRAIN HARDER.
COME ON, GUYS. YOU **WERE** UP AGAINST THE MOST POWERFUL TEAM IN THE SOLAR SYSTEM.
YOU WERE, TOO, IKKŪ.
IN THE END, IT WAS KIRIË-CHAN WHO REALLY SAVED THE DAY.
HMM... SPEAKING OF KIRIË...
APPARENTLY THE TWO OF THEM ARE FIGHTING.
WHY?
WHAT?
WHO KNOWS?
NOW THAT YOU MENTION IT, I HAVE HEARD RUMORS THAT TŌTA-KUN WAS DOING SOMETHING IN KIRIË-CHAN'S ROOM THIS MORNING...

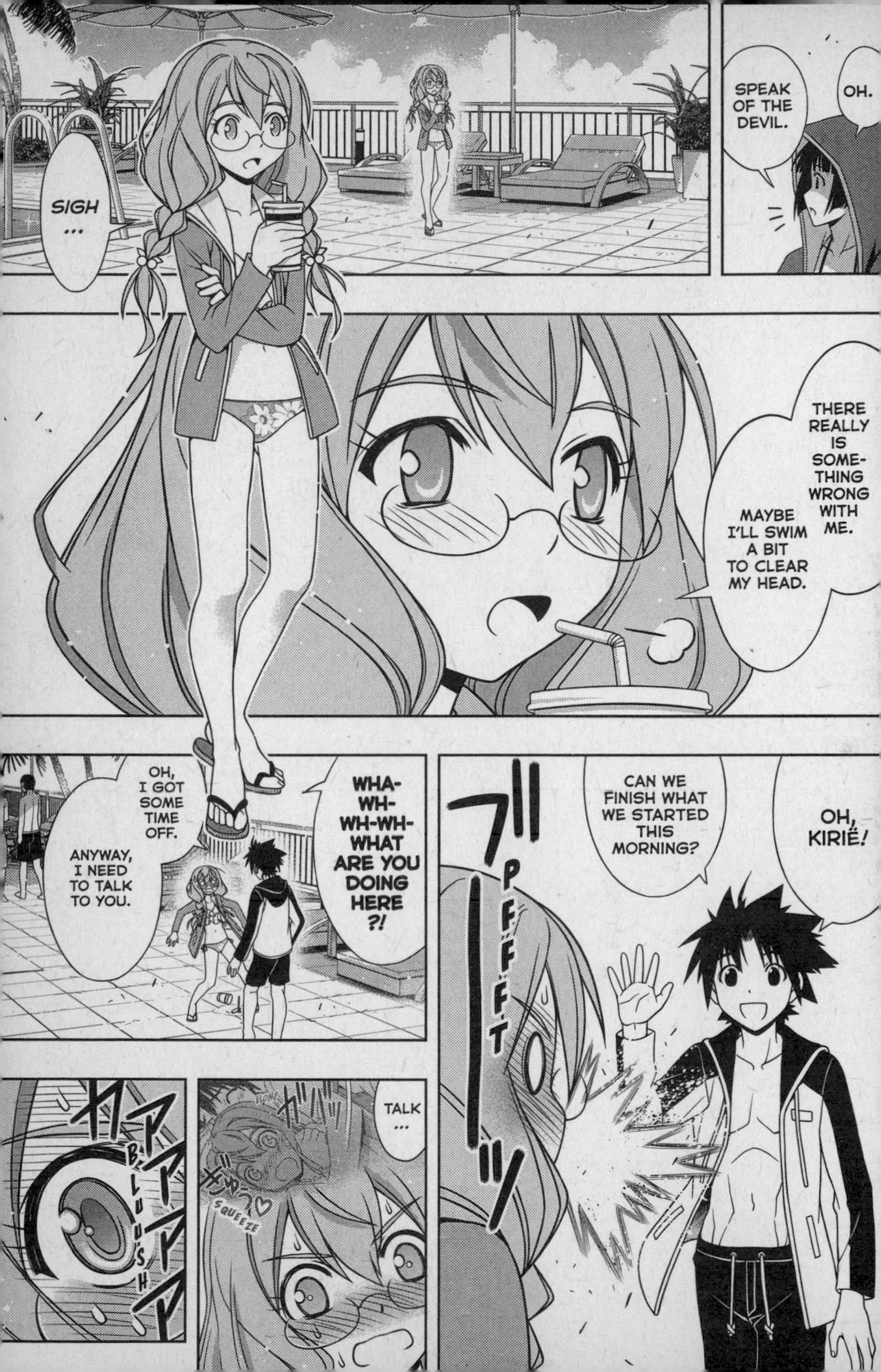
OH.
SPEAK OF THE DEVIL.
SIGH ...
THERE REALLY IS SOME-THING WRONG WITH ME.
MAYBE I'LL SWIM A BIT TO CLEAR MY HEAD.
OH, KIRIÉ!
CAN WE FINISH WHAT WE STARTED THIS MORNING?
PFFFT
WHA-WH-WH-WH-WHAT ARE YOU DOING HERE ?!
OH, I GOT SOME TIME OFF.
ANYWAY, I NEED TO TALK TO YOU.
TALK ...
SQUEEZE
BLUUSH

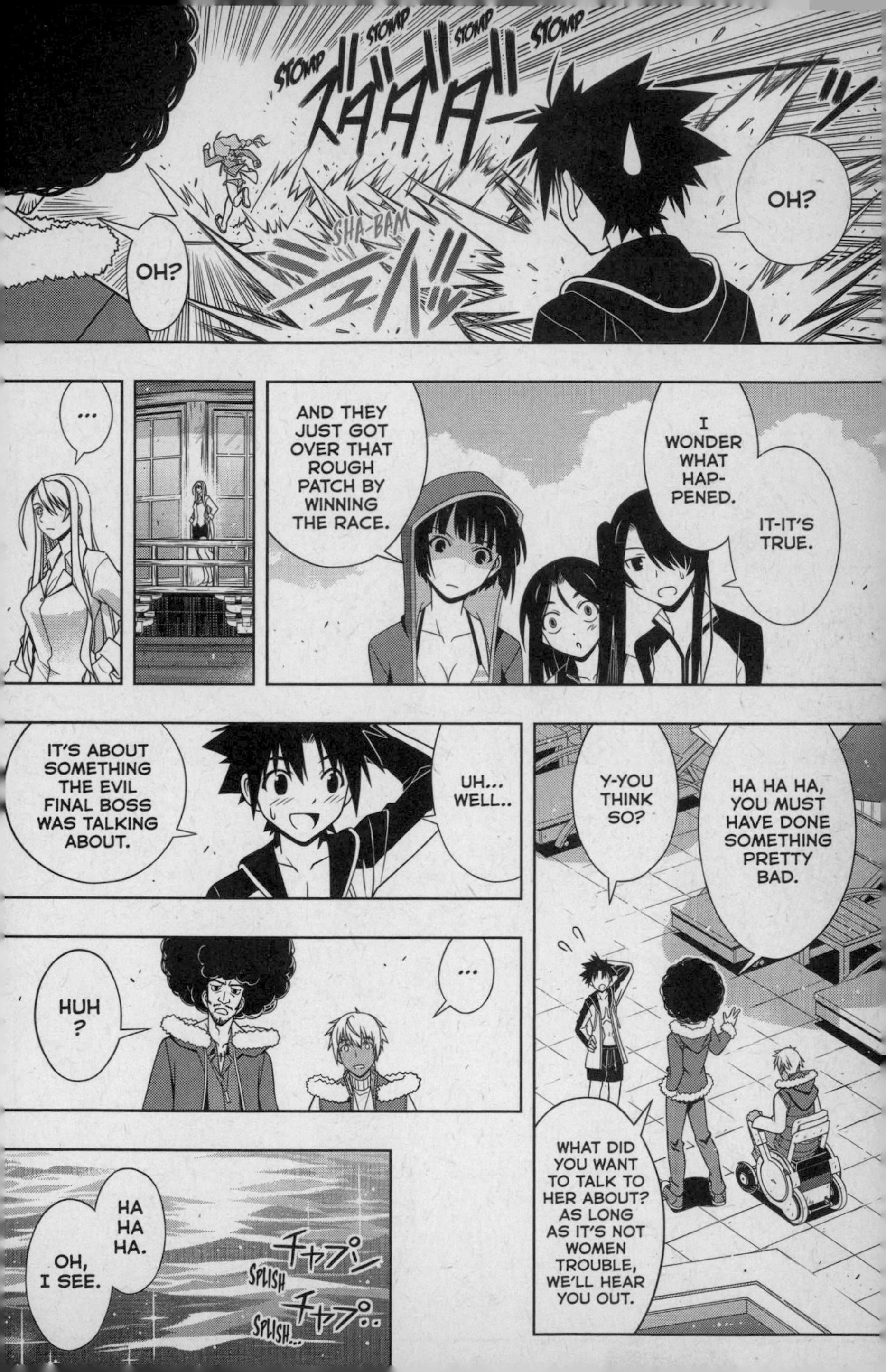
STOMP
STOMP
STOMP
STOMP
OH?
SHA-BAM
OH?
I WONDER WHAT HAP-PENED.
IT-IT'S TRUE.
AND THEY JUST GOT OVER THAT ROUGH PATCH BY WINNING THE RACE.
...
HA HA HA, YOU MUST HAVE DONE SOMETHING PRETTY BAD.
Y-YOU THINK SO?
WHAT DID YOU WANT TO TALK TO HER ABOUT? AS LONG AS IT'S NOT WOMEN TROUBLE, WE'LL HEAR YOU OUT.
UH... WELL..
IT'S ABOUT SOMETHING THE EVIL FINAL BOSS WAS TALKING ABOUT.
...
HUH ?
HA HA HA.
OH, I SEE.
SPLISH
SPLISH...

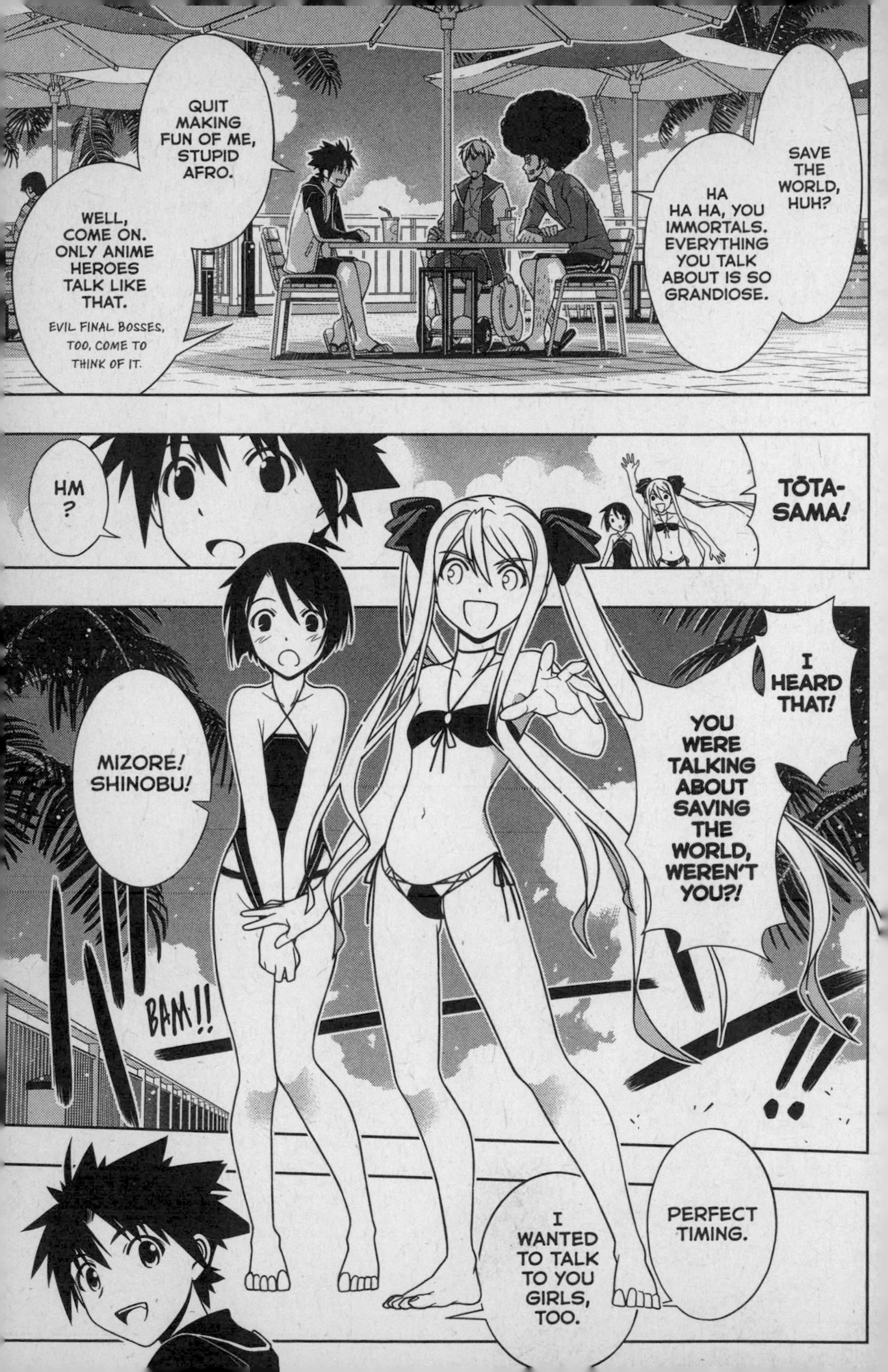

SAVE THE WORLD, HUH?
HA HA HA, YOU IMMORTALS. EVERYTHING YOU TALK ABOUT IS SO GRANDIOSE.
QUIT MAKING FUN OF ME, STUPID AFRO.
WELL, COME ON. ONLY ANIME HEROES TALK LIKE THAT.
EVIL FINAL BOSSES, TOO, COME TO THINK OF IT.
TŌTA-SAMA!
HM?
I HEARD THAT!
YOU WERE TALKING ABOUT SAVING THE WORLD, WEREN'T YOU?!
MIZORE! SHINOBU!
BAM!!
PERFECT TIMING.
I WANTED TO TALK TO YOU GIRLS, TOO.

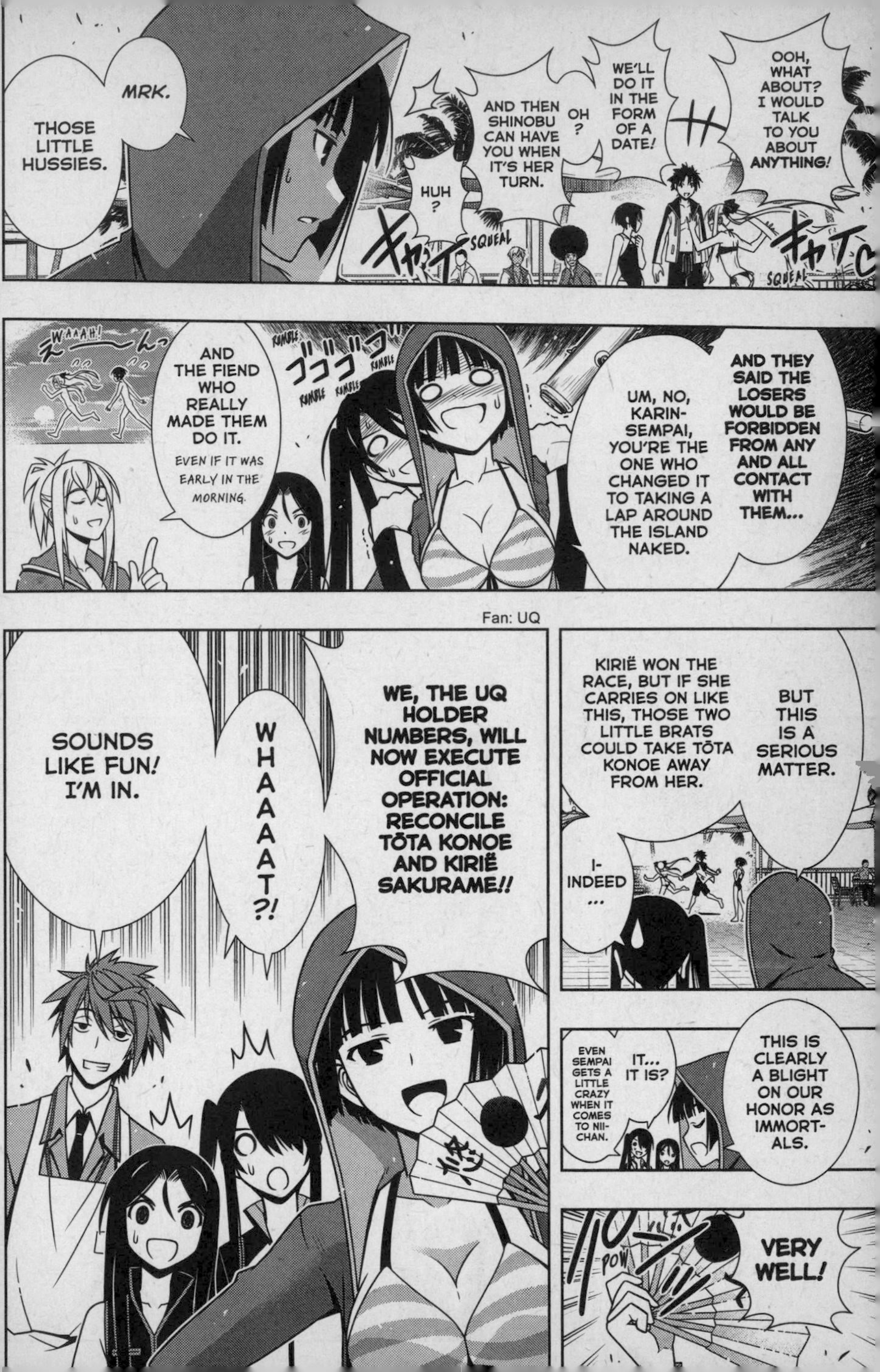
OOH, WHAT ABOUT? I WOULD TALK TO YOU ABOUT ANYTHING!
SQUEAL
WE'LL DO IT IN THE FORM OF A DATE!
OH ?
AND THEN SHINOBU CAN HAVE YOU WHEN IT'S HER TURN.
HUH ?
SQUEAL
MRK.
THOSE LITTLE HUSSIES.
AND THEY SAID THE LOSERS WOULD BE FORBIDDEN FROM ANY AND ALL CONTACT WITH THEM...
UM, NO, KARIN-SEMPAI, YOU'RE THE ONE WHO CHANGED IT TO TAKING A LAP AROUND THE ISLAND NAKED.
RUMBLE RUMBLE RUMBLE RUMBLE
AND THE FIEND WHO REALLY MADE THEM DO IT.
EVEN IF IT WAS EARLY IN THE MORNING.
W-AAAH!
Fan: UQ
BUT THIS IS A SERIOUS MATTER.
KIRIË WON THE RACE, BUT IF SHE CARRIES ON LIKE THIS, THOSE TWO LITTLE BRATS COULD TAKE TŌTA KONOE AWAY FROM HER.
I- INDEED ...
THIS IS CLEARLY A BLIGHT ON OUR HONOR AS IMMORT-ALS.
IT... IT IS?
EVEN SEMPAI GETS A LITTLE CRAZY WHEN IT COMES TO NII-CHAN.
VERY WELL!
POW
WE, THE UQ HOLDER NUMBERS, WILL NOW EXECUTE OFFICIAL OPERATION: RECONCILE TŌTA KONOE AND KIRIË SAKURAME!!
WHAAAAT?!
SOUNDS LIKE FUN! I'M IN.

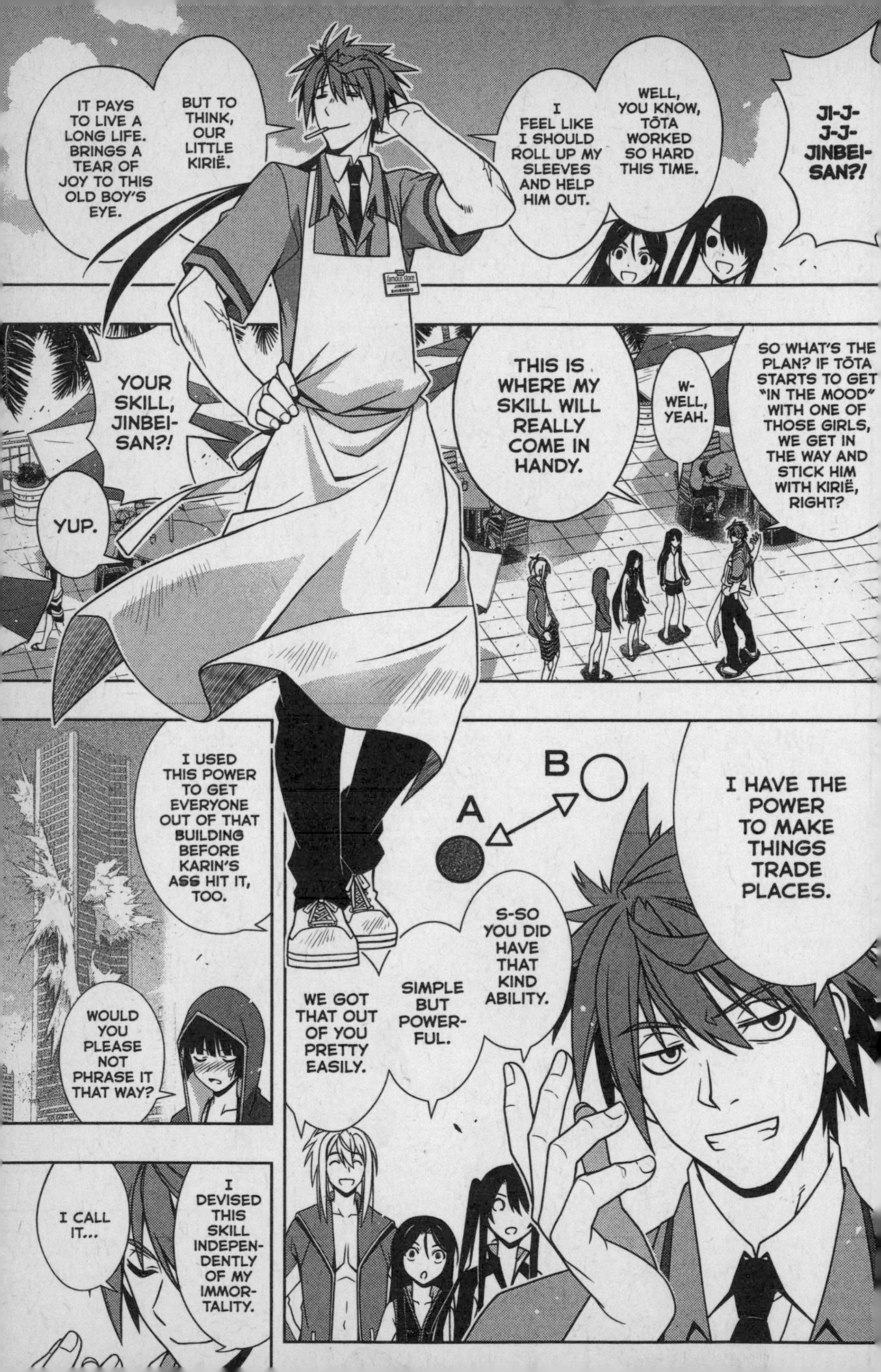
JI-J-J-J-JINBEI-SAN?!
WELL, YOU KNOW, TŌTA WORKED SO HARD THIS TIME.
I FEEL LIKE I SHOULD ROLL UP MY SLEEVES AND HELP HIM OUT.
BUT TO THINK, OUR LITTLE KIRIË.
IT PAYS TO LIVE A LONG LIFE. BRINGS A TEAR OF JOY TO THIS OLD BOY'S EYE.
famous store JINBEI SHISHIDO
SO WHAT'S THE PLAN? IF TŌTA STARTS TO GET "IN THE MOOD" WITH ONE OF THOSE GIRLS, WE GET IN THE WAY AND STICK HIM WITH KIRIË, RIGHT?
W-WELL, YEAH.
THIS IS WHERE MY SKILL WILL REALLY COME IN HANDY.
YOUR SKILL, JINBEI-SAN?!
YUP.
I HAVE THE POWER TO MAKE THINGS TRADE PLACES.
B
A
S-SO YOU DID HAVE THAT KIND ABILITY.
SIMPLE BUT POWERFUL.
WE GOT THAT OUT OF YOU PRETTY EASILY.
I USED THIS POWER TO GET EVERYONE OUT OF THAT BUILDING BEFORE KARIN'S ASS HIT IT, TOO.
WOULD YOU PLEASE NOT PHRASE IT THAT WAY?
I DEVISED THIS SKILL INDEPENDENTLY OF MY IMMORTALITY.
I CALL IT...

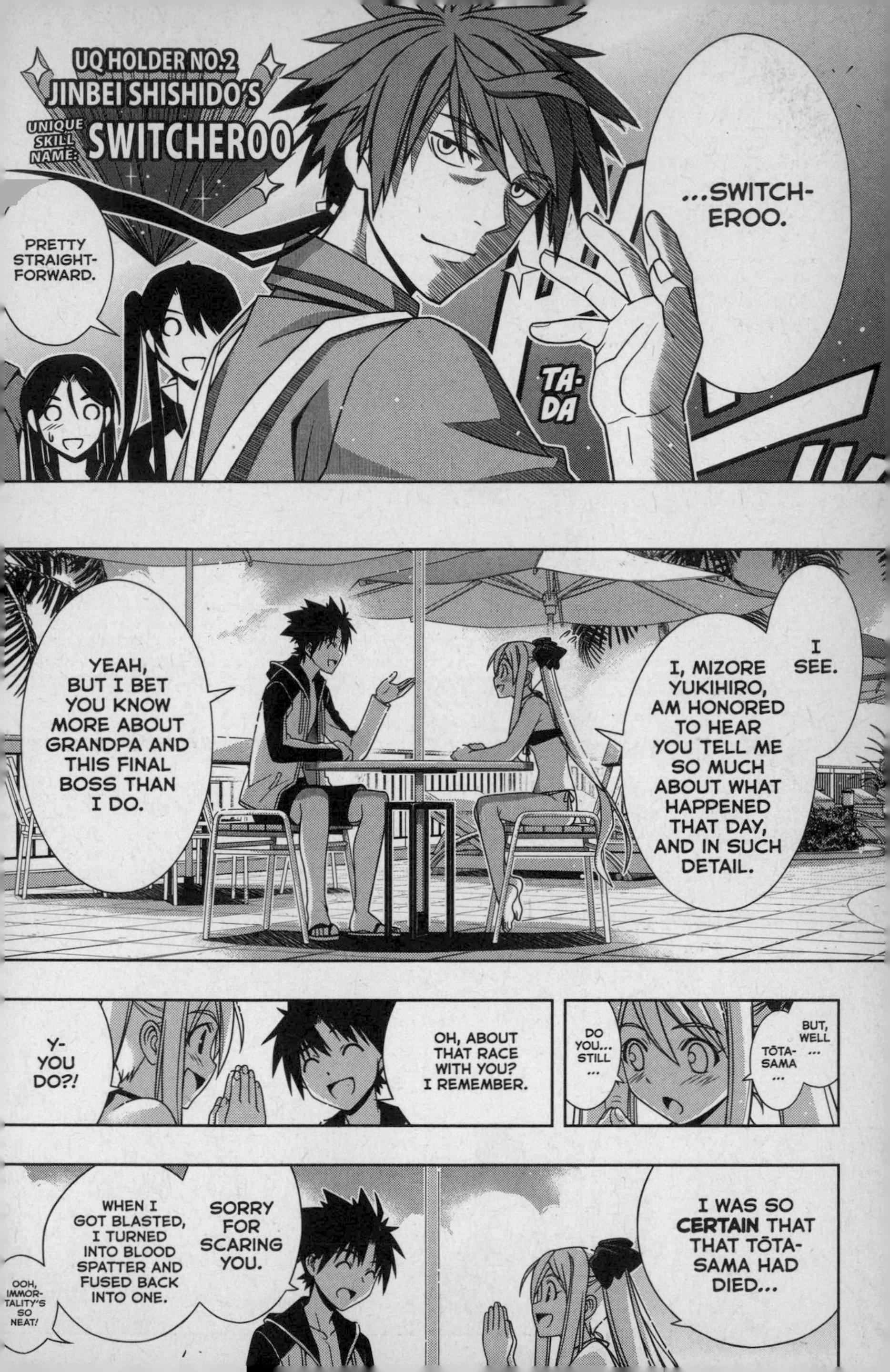

...SWITCH-EROO.
TA-DA
UQ HOLDER NO.2 JINBEI SHISHIDO'S
UNIQUE SKILL NAME: SWITCHEROO
PRETTY STRAIGHT-FORWARD.
I SEE.
I, MIZORE YUKIHIRO, AM HONORED TO HEAR YOU TELL ME SO MUCH ABOUT WHAT HAPPENED THAT DAY, AND IN SUCH DETAIL.
YEAH, BUT I BET YOU KNOW MORE ABOUT GRANDPA AND THIS FINAL BOSS THAN I DO.
BUT, WELL... TŌTA-SAMA...
DO YOU... STILL...
OH, ABOUT THAT RACE WITH YOU? I REMEMBER.
Y-YOU DO?!
I WAS SO **CERTAIN** THAT THAT TŌTA-SAMA HAD DIED...
SORRY FOR SCARING YOU.
WHEN I GOT BLASTED, I TURNED INTO BLOOD SPATTER AND FUSED BACK INTO ONE.
OOH, IMMORTALITY'S SO NEAT!

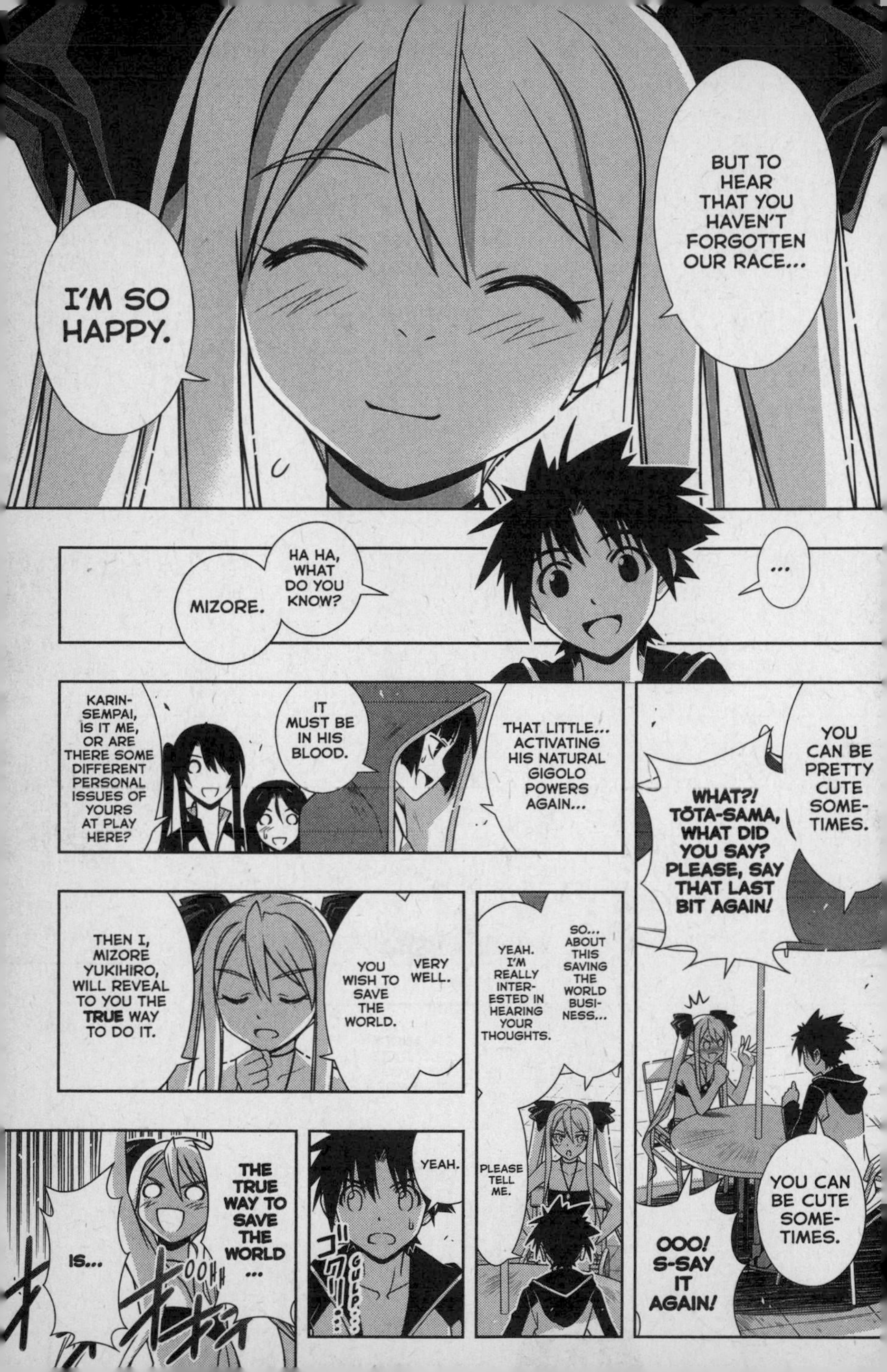

BUT TO HEAR THAT YOU HAVEN'T FORGOTTEN OUR RACE...
I'M SO HAPPY.
...
HA HA, WHAT DO YOU KNOW?
MIZORE.
YOU CAN BE PRETTY CUTE SOMETIMES.
WHAT?! TŌTA-SAMA, WHAT DID YOU SAY? PLEASE, SAY THAT LAST BIT AGAIN!
YOU CAN BE CUTE SOMETIMES.
OOO! S-SAY IT AGAIN!
THAT LITTLE... ACTIVATING HIS NATURAL GIGOLO POWERS AGAIN...
IT MUST BE IN HIS BLOOD.
KARIN-SEMPAI, IS IT ME, OR ARE THERE SOME DIFFERENT PERSONAL ISSUES OF YOURS AT PLAY HERE?
SO... ABOUT THIS SAVING THE WORLD BUSINESS...
YEAH. I'M REALLY INTERESTED IN HEARING YOUR THOUGHTS.
PLEASE TELL ME.
VERY WELL.
YOU WISH TO SAVE THE WORLD.
THEN I, MIZORE YUKIHIRO, WILL REVEAL TO YOU THE TRUE WAY TO DO IT.
YEAH.
GULP...
THE TRUE WAY TO SAVE THE WORLD...
IS...
OOHH

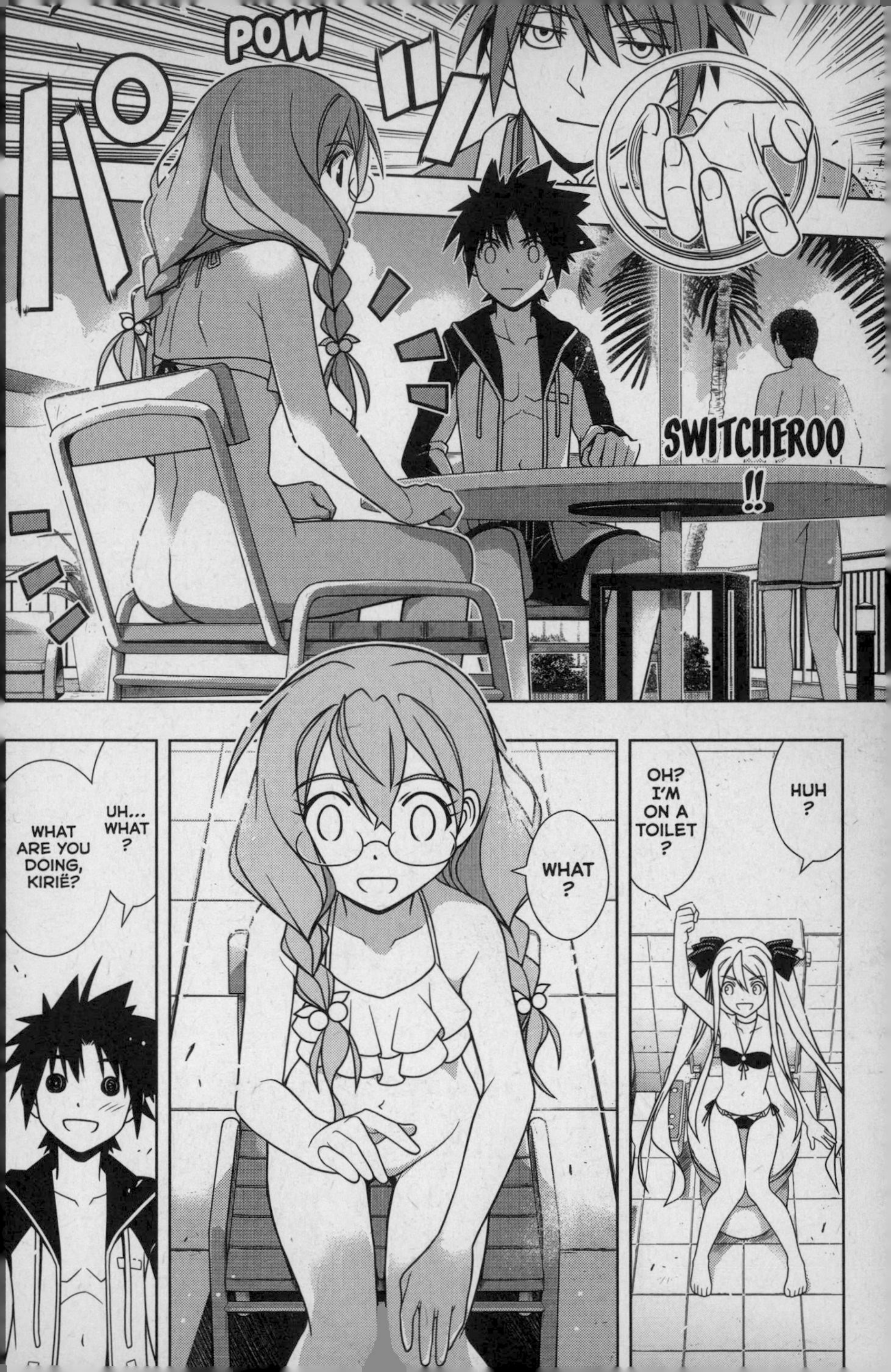
POW
SWITCHEROO !!
HUH ?
OH? I'M ON A TOILET ?
WHAT ?
UH... WHAT ?
WHAT ARE YOU DOING, KIRIË?

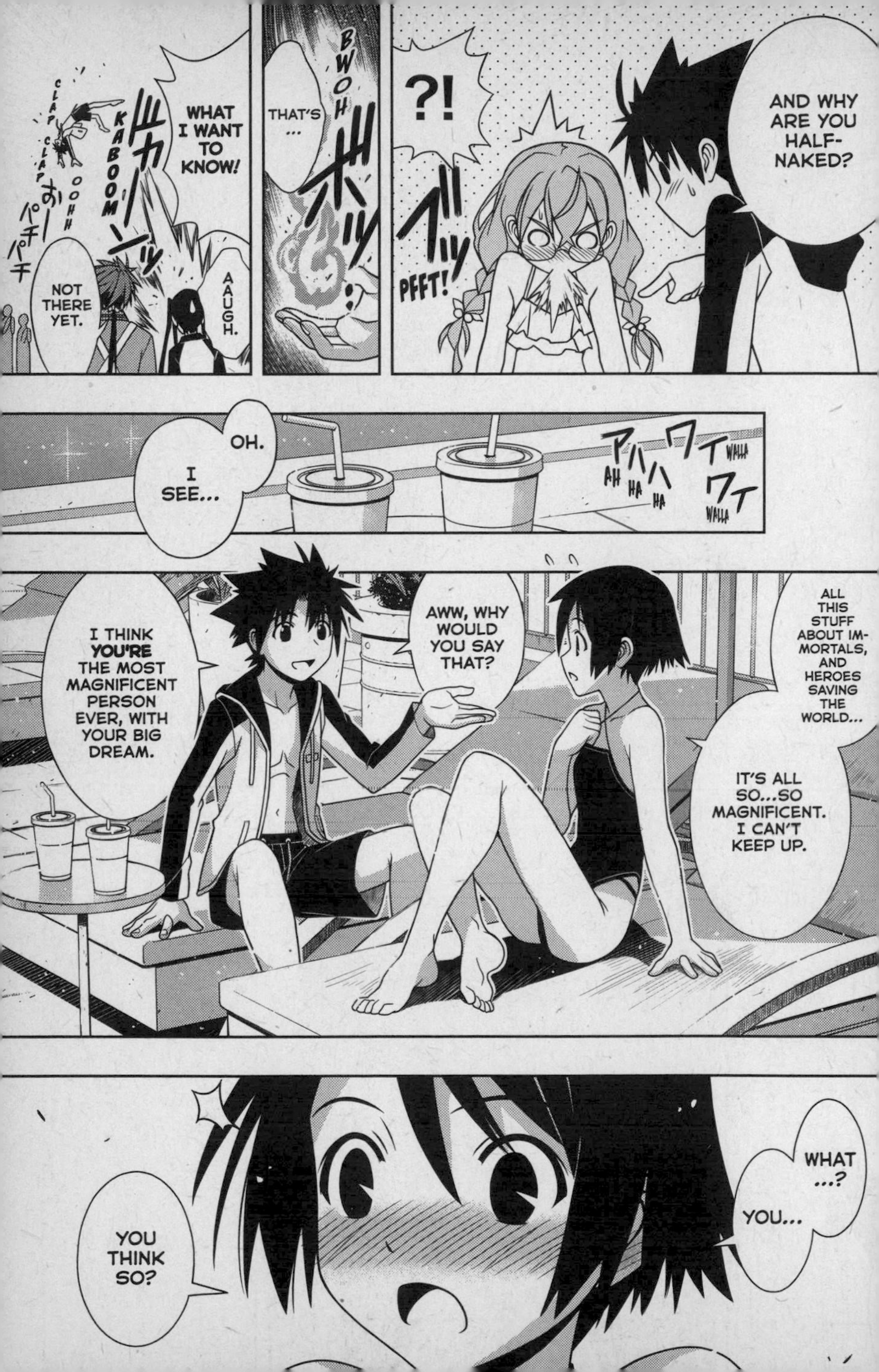
AND WHY ARE YOU HALF-NAKED?
?!
ブッ
PFFT!
THAT'S ...
ボッ
BWOH
WHAT I WANT TO KNOW!
ドカーン
KABOOM
AAUGH.
NOT THERE YET.
おー
OOHH
パチパチ
CLAP CLAP
ワイワイ
WALLA WALLA
アハハ
AH HA HA
OH.
I SEE...
ALL THIS STUFF ABOUT IMMORTALS, AND HEROES SAVING THE WORLD...
IT'S ALL SO...SO MAGNIFICENT. I CAN'T KEEP UP.
AWW, WHY WOULD YOU SAY THAT?
I THINK **YOU'RE** THE MOST MAGNIFICENT PERSON EVER, WITH YOUR BIG DREAM.
WHAT ...?
YOU...
YOU THINK SO?

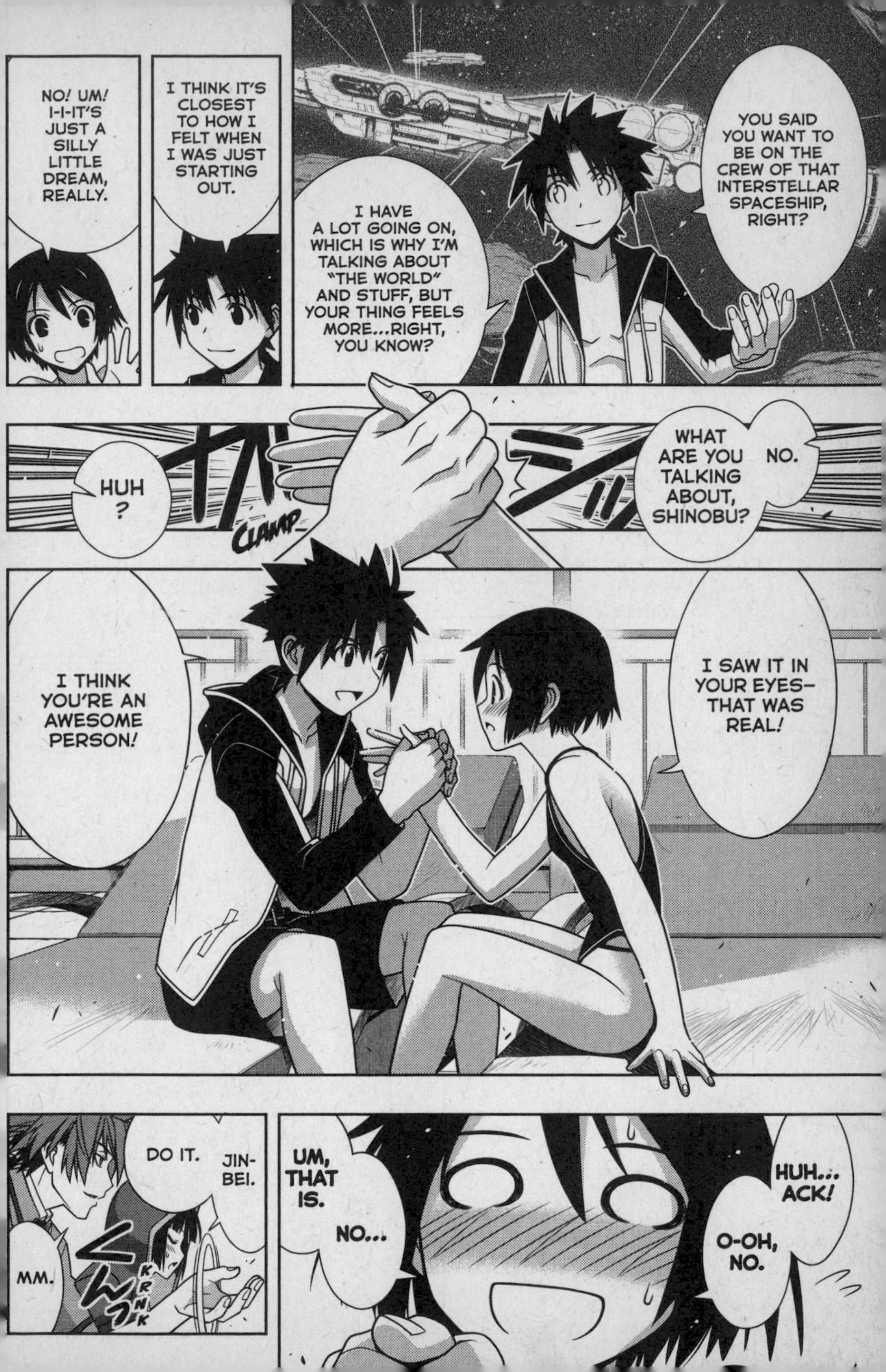
YOU SAID YOU WANT TO BE ON THE CREW OF THAT INTERSTELLAR SPACESHIP, RIGHT?
I HAVE A LOT GOING ON, WHICH IS WHY I'M TALKING ABOUT "THE WORLD" AND STUFF, BUT YOUR THING FEELS MORE...RIGHT, YOU KNOW?
I THINK IT'S CLOSEST TO HOW I FELT WHEN I WAS JUST STARTING OUT.
NO! UM! I-I-IT'S JUST A SILLY LITTLE DREAM, REALLY.
NO.
WHAT ARE YOU TALKING ABOUT, SHINOBU?
CLAMP
HUH ?
I SAW IT IN YOUR EYES— THAT WAS REAL!
I THINK YOU'RE AN AWESOME PERSON!
HUH... ACK!
O-OH, NO.
UM, THAT IS.
NO...
JIN-BEI.
DO IT.
KRNK
MM.

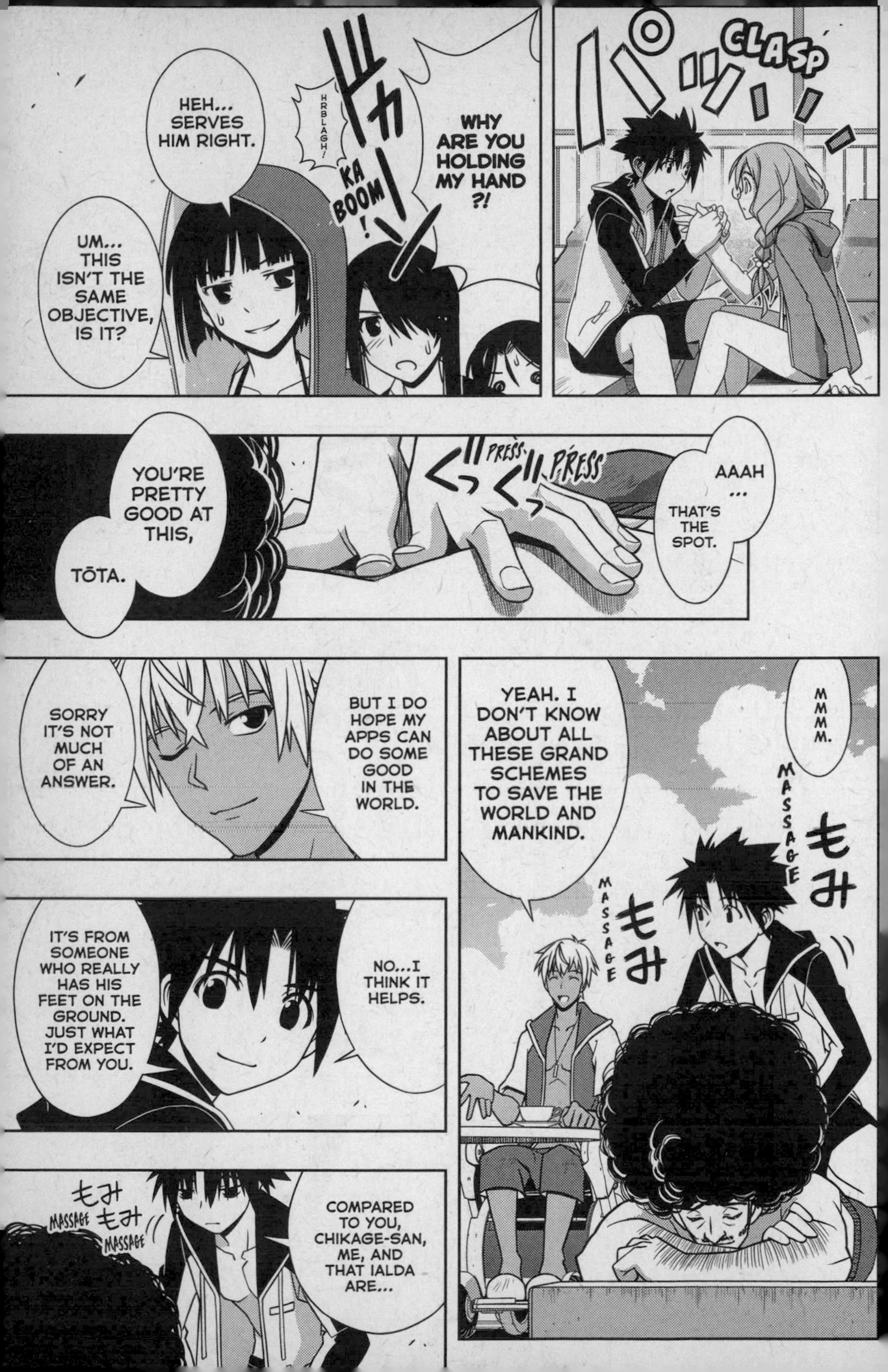
パッ
CLASP
WHY ARE YOU HOLDING MY HAND ?!
ドカ
KA BOOM!
HRBLAGH!
HEH... SERVES HIM RIGHT.
UM... THIS ISN'T THE SAME OBJECTIVE, IS IT?
AAAH ... THAT'S THE SPOT.
くっ PRESS
くっ PRESS
YOU'RE PRETTY GOOD AT THIS,
TŌTA.
MMMM.
もみ MASSAGE
もみ MASSAGE
YEAH. I DON'T KNOW ABOUT ALL THESE GRAND SCHEMES TO SAVE THE WORLD AND MANKIND.
BUT I DO HOPE MY APPS CAN DO SOME GOOD IN THE WORLD.
SORRY IT'S NOT MUCH OF AN ANSWER.
NO...I THINK IT HELPS.
IT'S FROM SOMEONE WHO REALLY HAS HIS FEET ON THE GROUND. JUST WHAT I'D EXPECT FROM YOU.
COMPARED TO YOU, CHIKAGE-SAN, ME, AND THAT IALDA ARE...
もみ MASSAGE
もみ MASSAGE

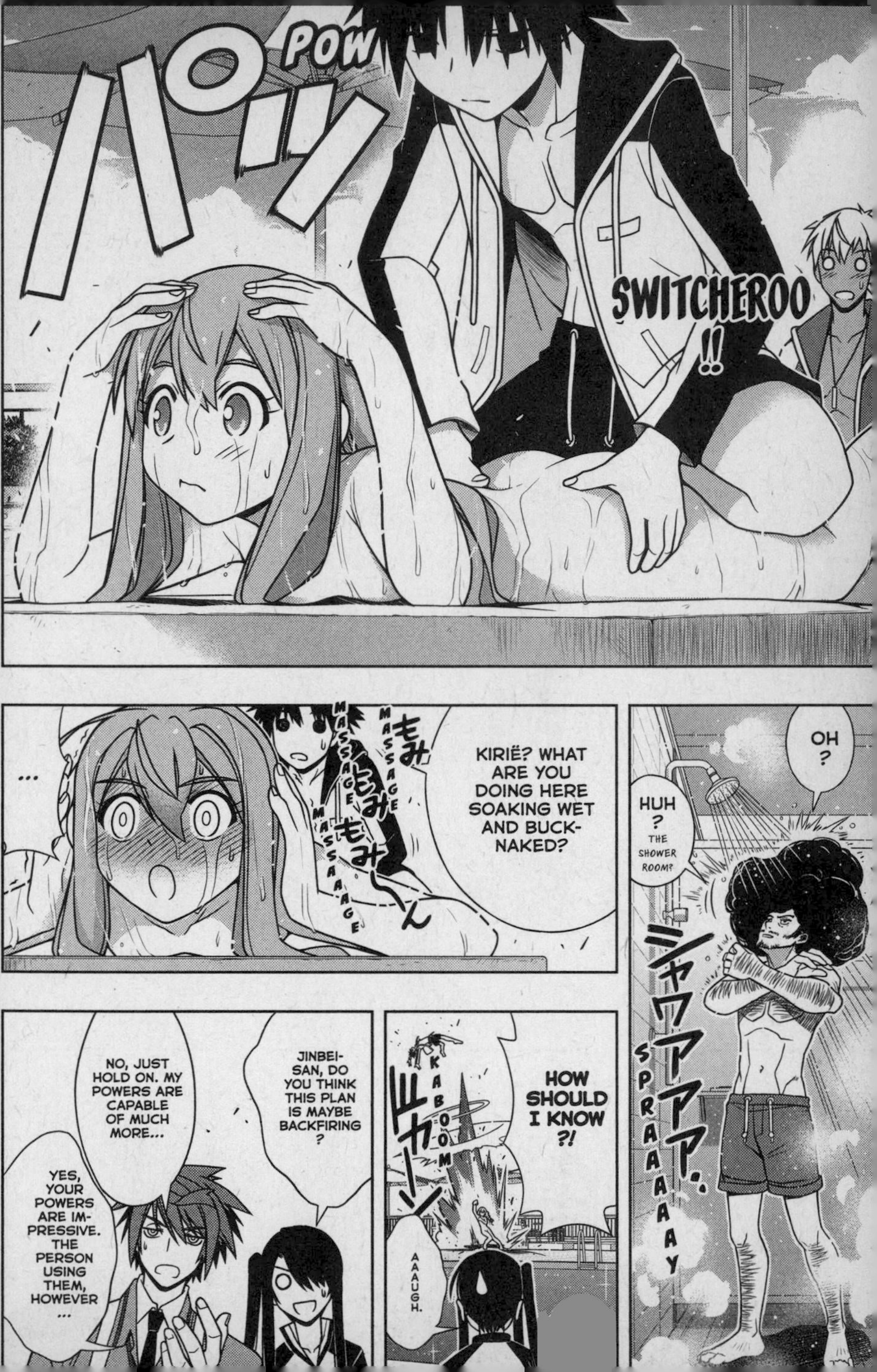
POW
SWITCHEROO!!
OH?
HUH? THE SHOWER ROOM?
SPRAAAAAAY
KIRIË? WHAT ARE YOU DOING HERE SOAKING WET AND BUCK-NAKED?
MASSAGE
MASSAGE
MASSAAGE
...
HOW SHOULD I KNOW?!
KABOOM
AAAUGH.
JINBEI-SAN, DO YOU THINK THIS PLAN IS MAYBE BACKFIRING?
NO, JUST HOLD ON. MY POWERS ARE CAPABLE OF MUCH MORE...
YES, YOUR POWERS ARE IMPRESSIVE. THE PERSON USING THEM, HOWEVER...

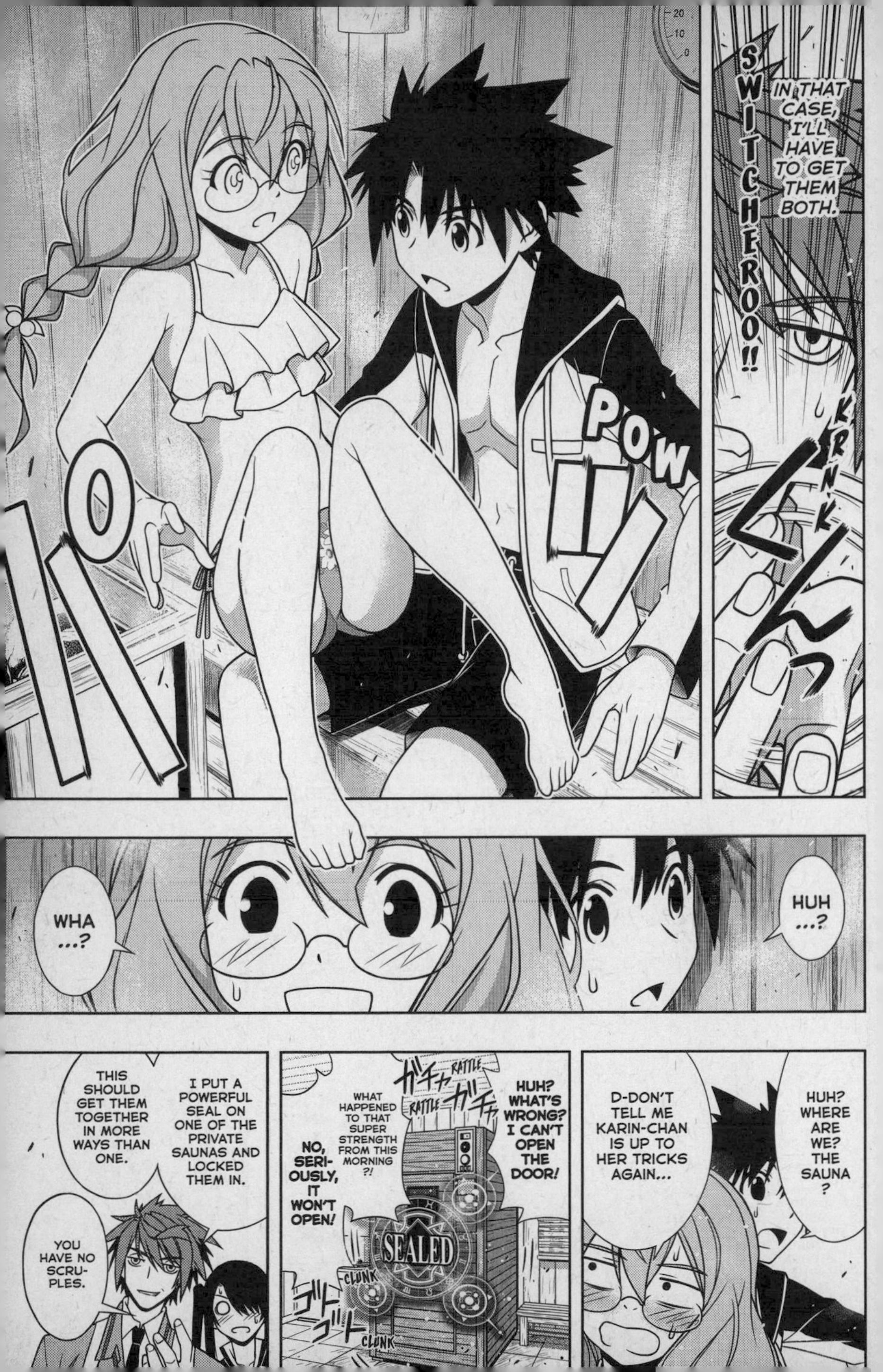
SWITCHEROO!!
IN THAT CASE, I'LL HAVE TO GET THEM BOTH.
KRNK
POW
HUH ...?
WHA ...?
HUH? WHERE ARE WE? THE SAUNA?
D-DON'T TELL ME KARIN-CHAN IS UP TO HER TRICKS AGAIN...
HUH? WHAT'S WRONG? I CAN'T OPEN THE DOOR!
RATTLE RATTLE
WHAT HAPPENED TO THAT SUPER STRENGTH FROM THIS MORNING?!
NO, SERIOUSLY, IT WON'T OPEN!
SEALED
CLUNK CLUNK
I PUT A POWERFUL SEAL ON ONE OF THE PRIVATE SAUNAS AND LOCKED THEM IN.
THIS SHOULD GET THEM TOGETHER IN MORE WAYS THAN ONE.
YOU HAVE NO SCRUPLES.

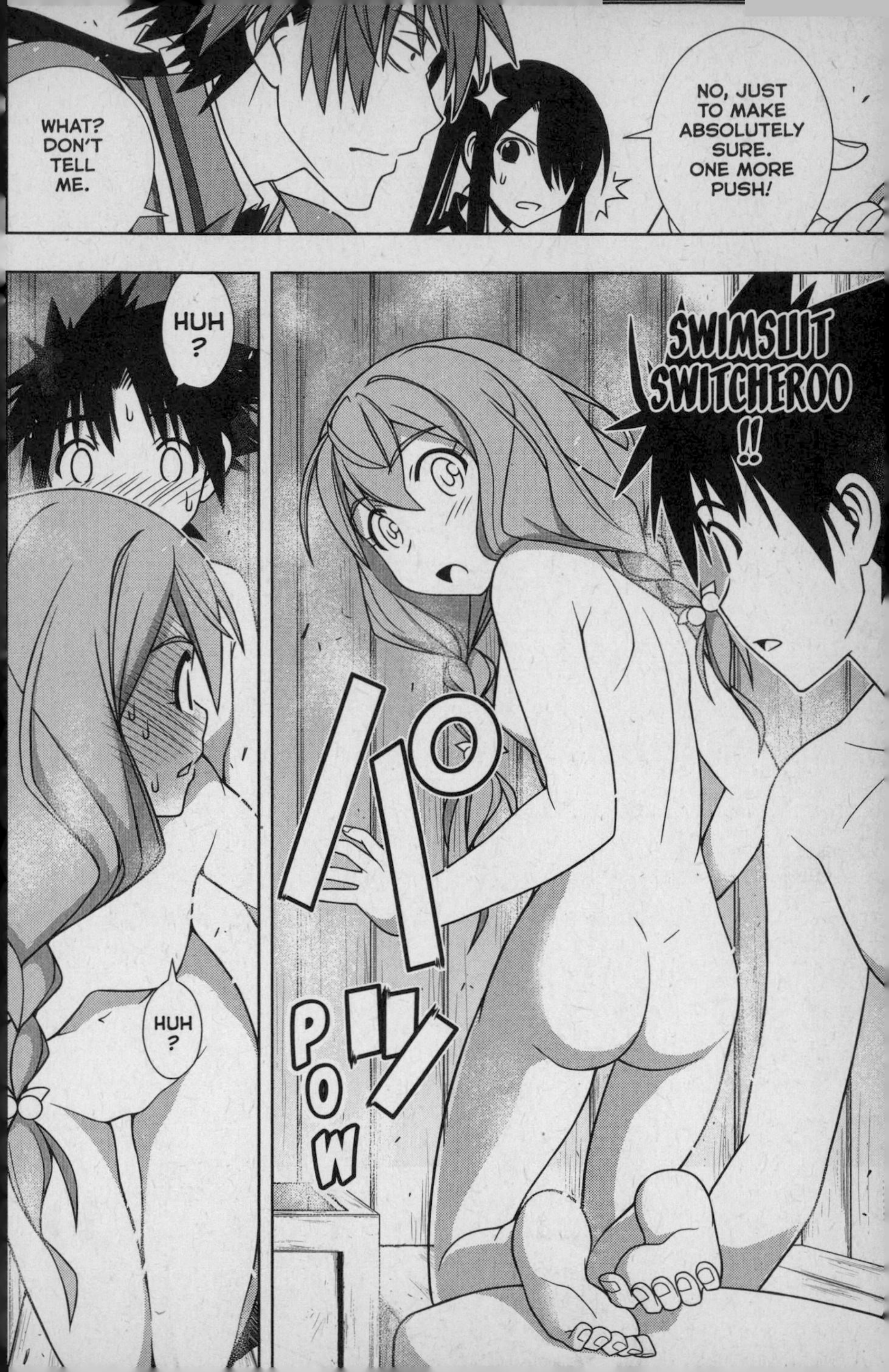
NO, JUST TO MAKE ABSOLUTELY SURE. ONE MORE PUSH!
WHAT? DON'T TELL ME.
SWIMSUIT SWITCHEROO !!
POW
HUH ?
HUH ?

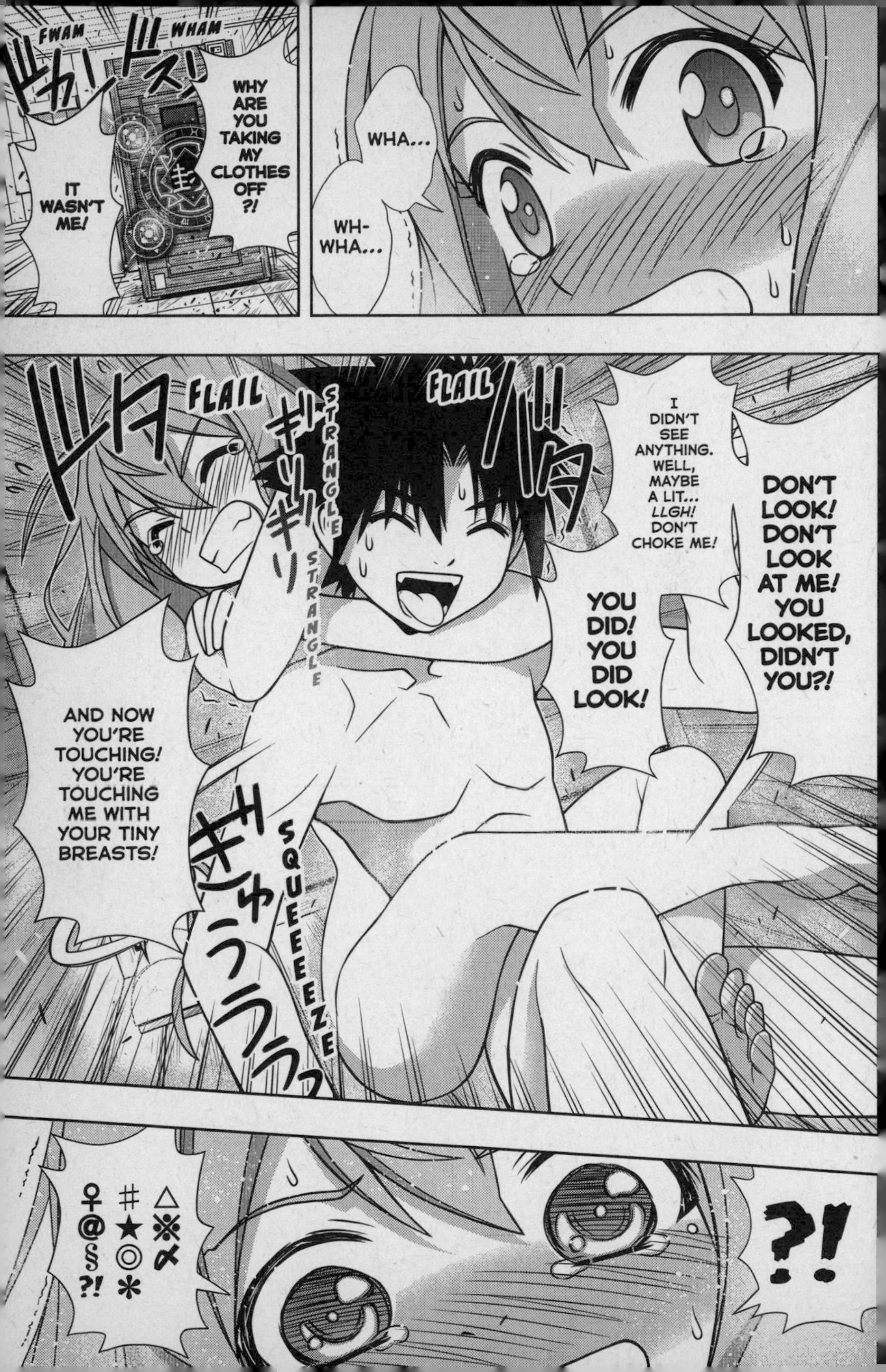

WHA...
WH- WHA...
FWAM WHAM
ドカ ドス
WHY ARE YOU TAKING MY CLOTHES OFF?!
IT WASN'T ME!
バタ
FLAIL
DON'T LOOK! DON'T LOOK AT ME! YOU LOOKED, DIDN'T YOU?!
I DIDN'T SEE ANYTHING. WELL, MAYBE A LIT... LLGH! DON'T CHOKE ME!
YOU DID! YOU DID LOOK!
ギリギリ
STRANGLE STRANGLE
ドタ
FLAIL
AND NOW YOU'RE TOUCHING! YOU'RE TOUCHING ME WITH YOUR TINY BREASTS!
ぎゅうううっ
SQUEEEEEZE
?!
△※〆#★◎*♀@§?!

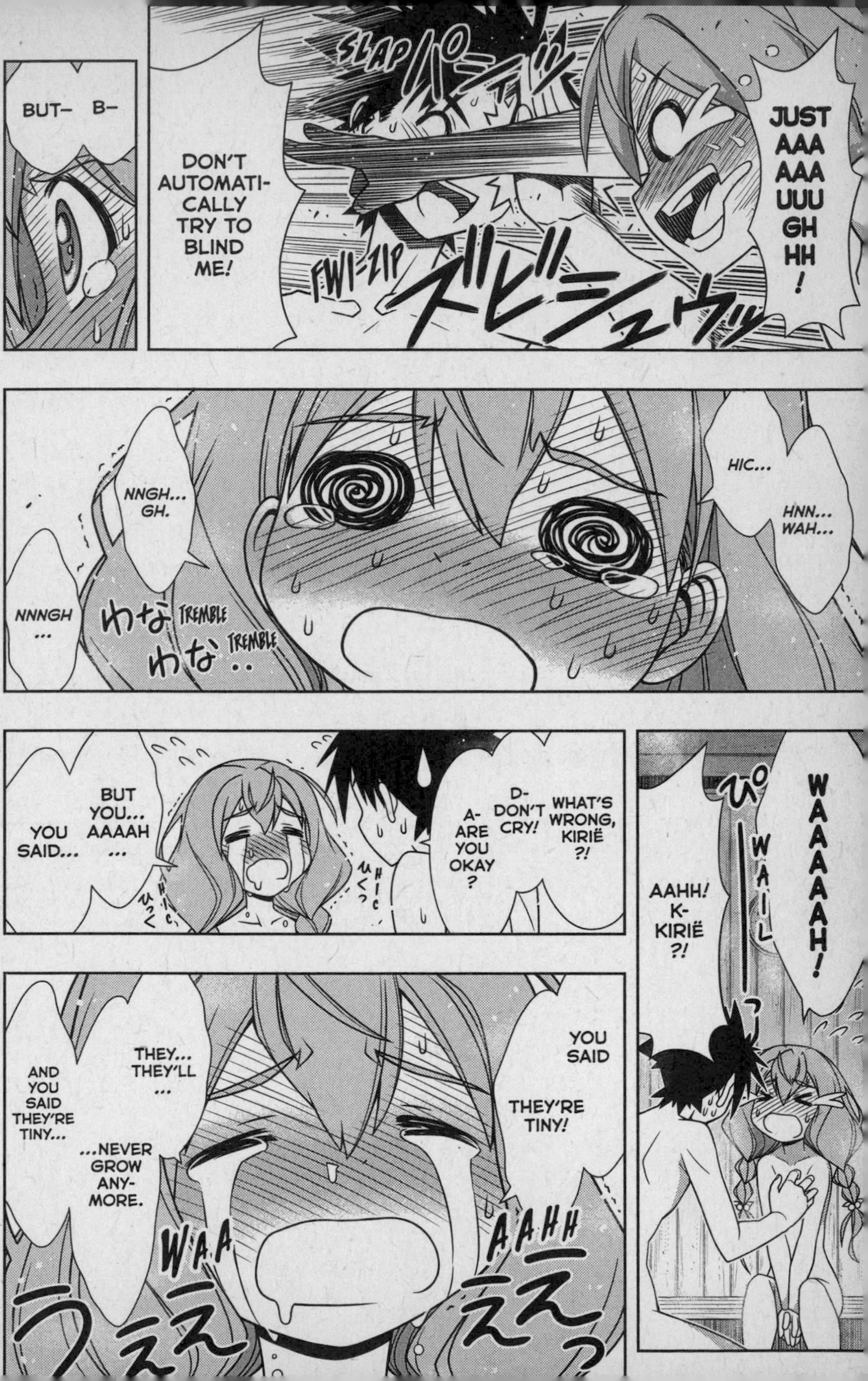

JUST AAAAAAUUUGHHH!
SLAP
DON'T AUTOMATICALLY TRY TO BLIND ME!
FWI-ZIP
BUT— B—
HIC...
HNN... WAH...
NNGH... GH.
NNNGH...
TREMBLE TREMBLE
WAAAAAAAH!
WAIL
AAHH! K-KIRIË?!
WHAT'S WRONG, KIRIË?!
D-DON'T CRY!
A-ARE YOU OKAY?
HIC
BUT YOU... AAAAH...
YOU SAID...
HIC
YOU SAID
THEY'RE TINY!
THEY... THEY'LL...
...NEVER GROW ANYMORE.
AND YOU SAID THEY'RE TINY...
WAA
AAHH

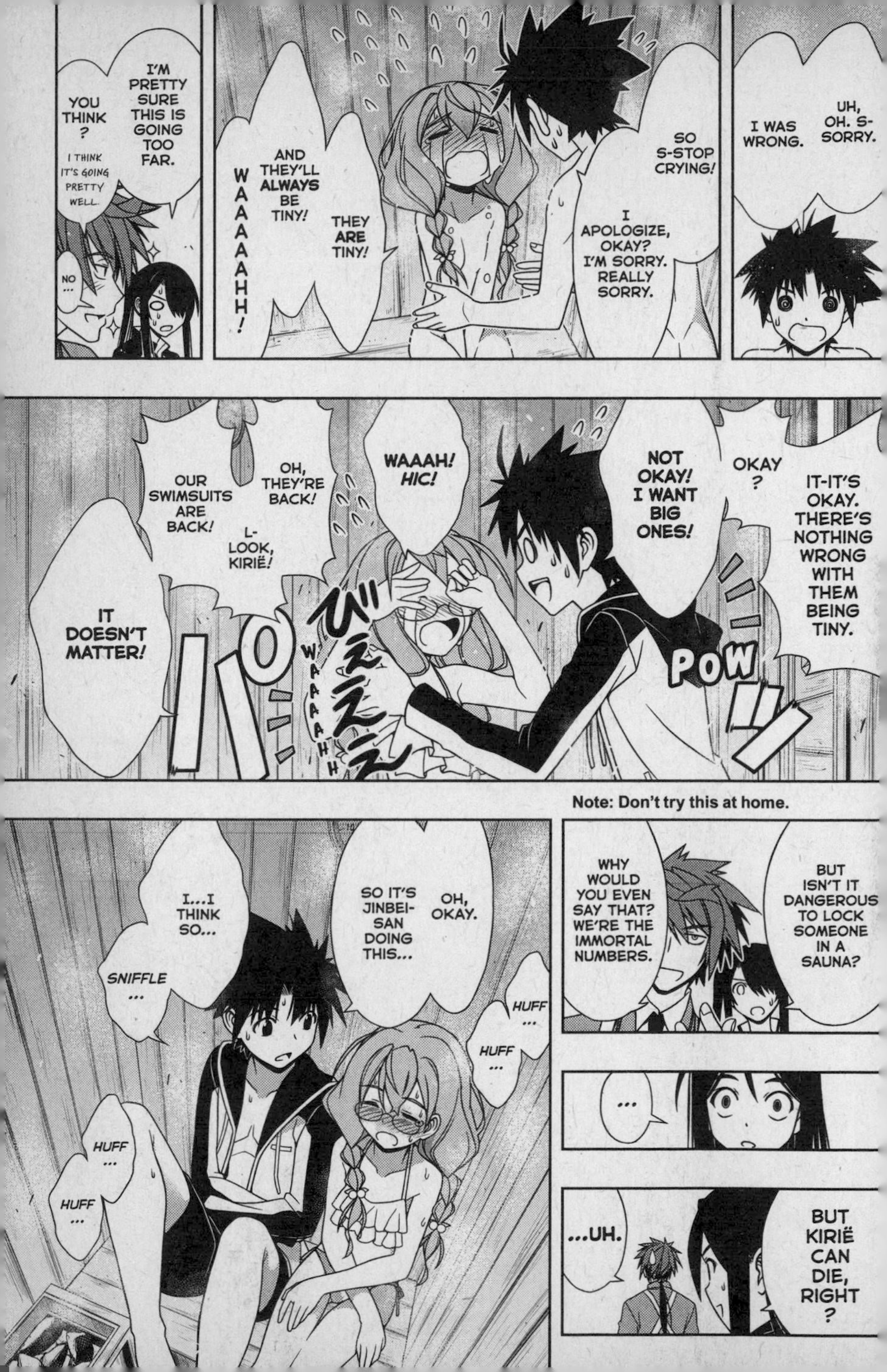
UH, OH. S-SORRY.
I WAS WRONG.
SO S-STOP CRYING!
I APOLOGIZE, OKAY? I'M SORRY. REALLY SORRY.
AND THEY'LL ALWAYS BE TINY!
THEY ARE TINY!
WAAAAAAHH!
I'M PRETTY SURE THIS IS GOING TOO FAR.
YOU THINK?
I THINK IT'S GOING PRETTY WELL.
NO...
IT-IT'S OKAY. THERE'S NOTHING WRONG WITH THEM BEING TINY.
OKAY?
NOT OKAY! I WANT BIG ONES!
POW
WAAAH! HIC!
OH, THEY'RE BACK!
L-LOOK, KIRIË!
OUR SWIMSUITS ARE BACK!
IT DOESN'T MATTER!
WAAAAAHH
Note: Don't try this at home.
OH, OKAY.
SO IT'S JINBEI-SAN DOING THIS...
I...I THINK SO...
SNIFFLE...
HUFF...
HUFF...
HUFF...
HUFF...
BUT ISN'T IT DANGEROUS TO LOCK SOMEONE IN A SAUNA?
WHY WOULD YOU EVEN SAY THAT? WE'RE THE IMMORTAL NUMBERS.
...
BUT KIRIË CAN DIE, RIGHT?
...UH.

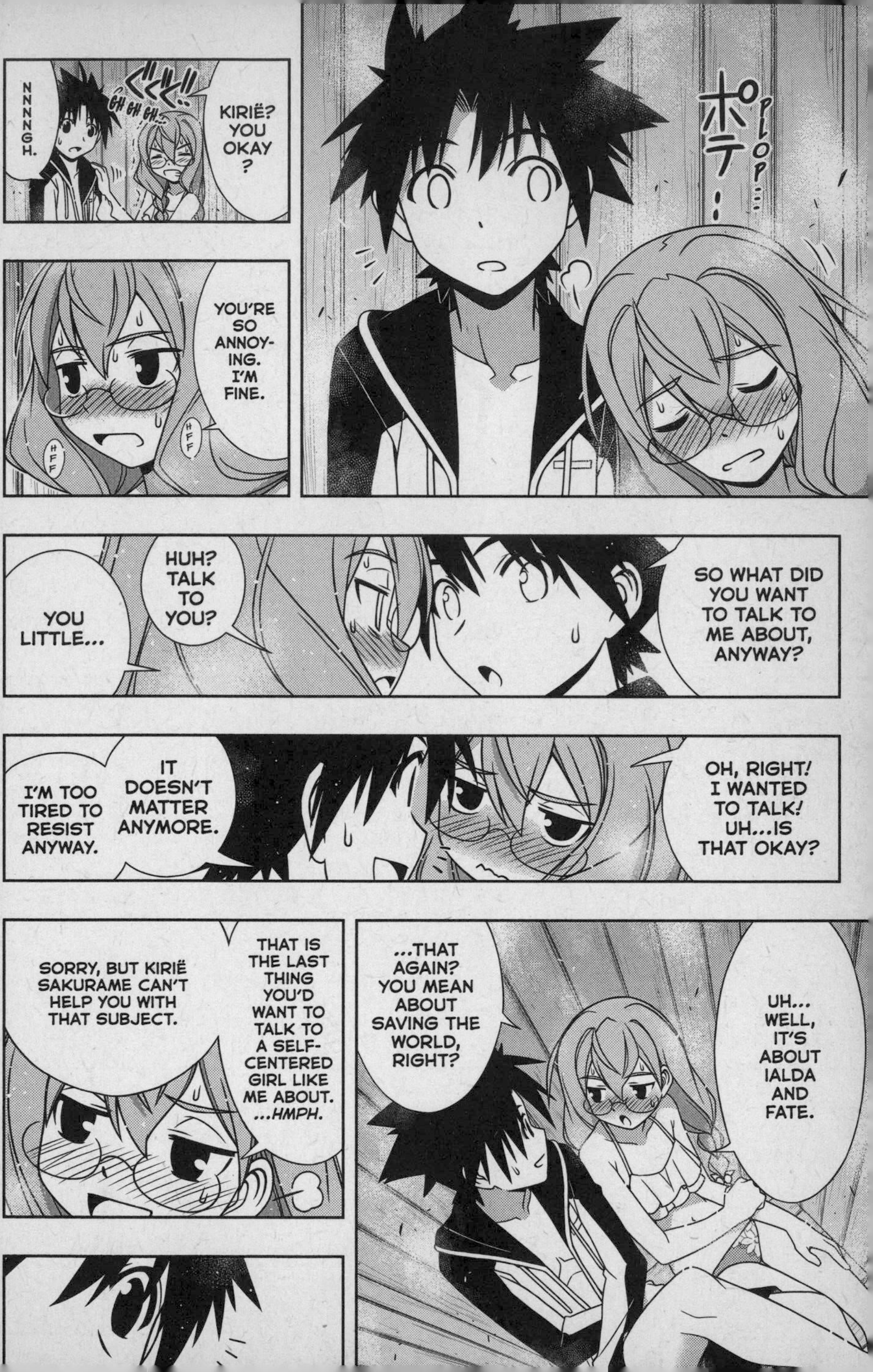
ポテ
PLOP...
KIRIË? YOU OKAY?
ぐぐぐ!!
GH GH GH...
NNNNGH.
YOU'RE SO ANNOY-ING. I'M FINE.
HFF
HFF
SO WHAT DID YOU WANT TO TALK TO ME ABOUT, ANYWAY?
HUH? TALK TO YOU?
YOU LITTLE...
OH, RIGHT! I WANTED TO TALK! UH...IS THAT OKAY?
IT DOESN'T MATTER ANYMORE.
I'M TOO TIRED TO RESIST ANYWAY.
UH... WELL, IT'S ABOUT IALDA AND FATE.
...THAT AGAIN? YOU MEAN ABOUT SAVING THE WORLD, RIGHT?
THAT IS THE LAST THING YOU'D WANT TO TALK TO A SELF-CENTERED GIRL LIKE ME ABOUT. ...HMPH.
SORRY, BUT KIRIË SAKURAME CAN'T HELP YOU WITH THAT SUBJECT.

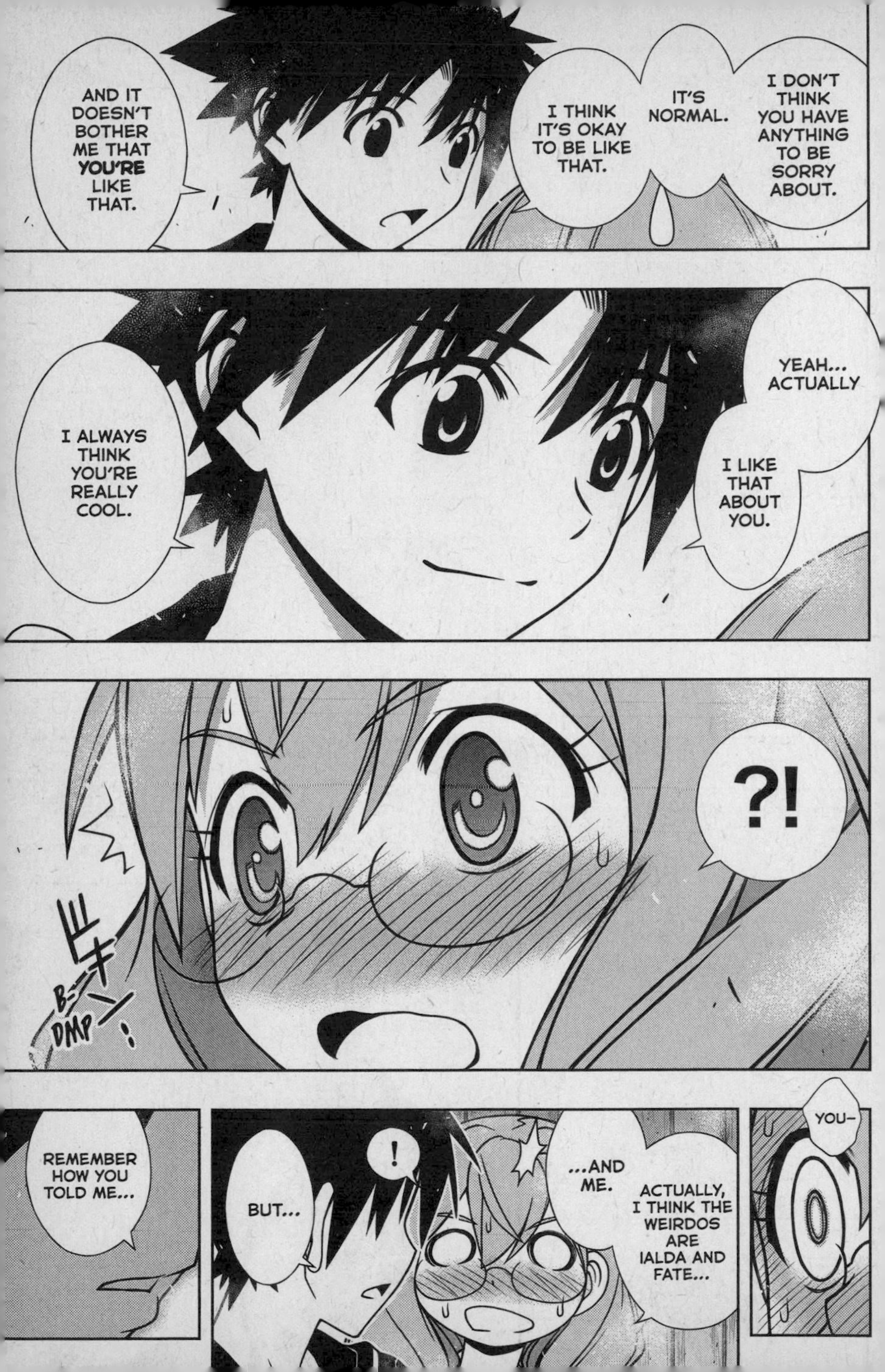
I DON'T THINK YOU HAVE ANYTHING TO BE SORRY ABOUT.
IT'S NORMAL.
I THINK IT'S OKAY TO BE LIKE THAT.
AND IT DOESN'T BOTHER ME THAT **YOU'RE** LIKE THAT.
YEAH... ACTUALLY
I LIKE THAT ABOUT YOU.
I ALWAYS THINK YOU'RE REALLY COOL.
?!
B-DMP
YOU–
ACTUALLY, I THINK THE WEIRDOS ARE IALDA AND FATE...
...AND ME.
!
BUT...
REMEMBER HOW YOU TOLD ME...

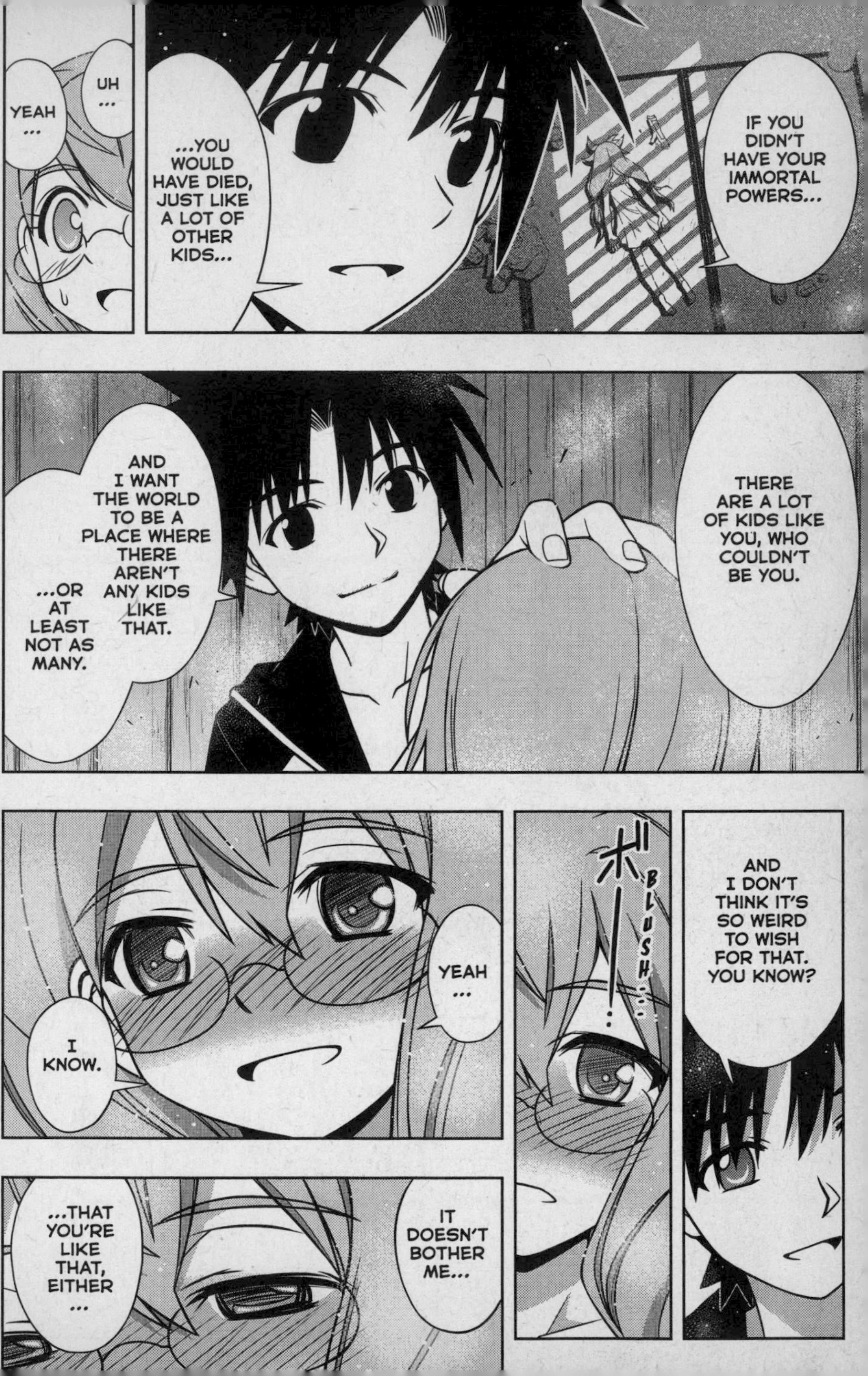
IF YOU DIDN'T HAVE YOUR IMMORTAL POWERS...
...YOU WOULD HAVE DIED, JUST LIKE A LOT OF OTHER KIDS...
UH ...
YEAH ...
THERE ARE A LOT OF KIDS LIKE YOU, WHO COULDN'T BE YOU.
AND I WANT THE WORLD TO BE A PLACE WHERE THERE AREN'T ANY KIDS LIKE THAT.
...OR AT LEAST NOT AS MANY.
AND I DON'T THINK IT'S SO WEIRD TO WISH FOR THAT. YOU KNOW?
ボー
BLUSH...!
YEAH ...
I KNOW.
IT DOESN'T BOTHER ME...
...THAT YOU'RE LIKE THAT, EITHER ...

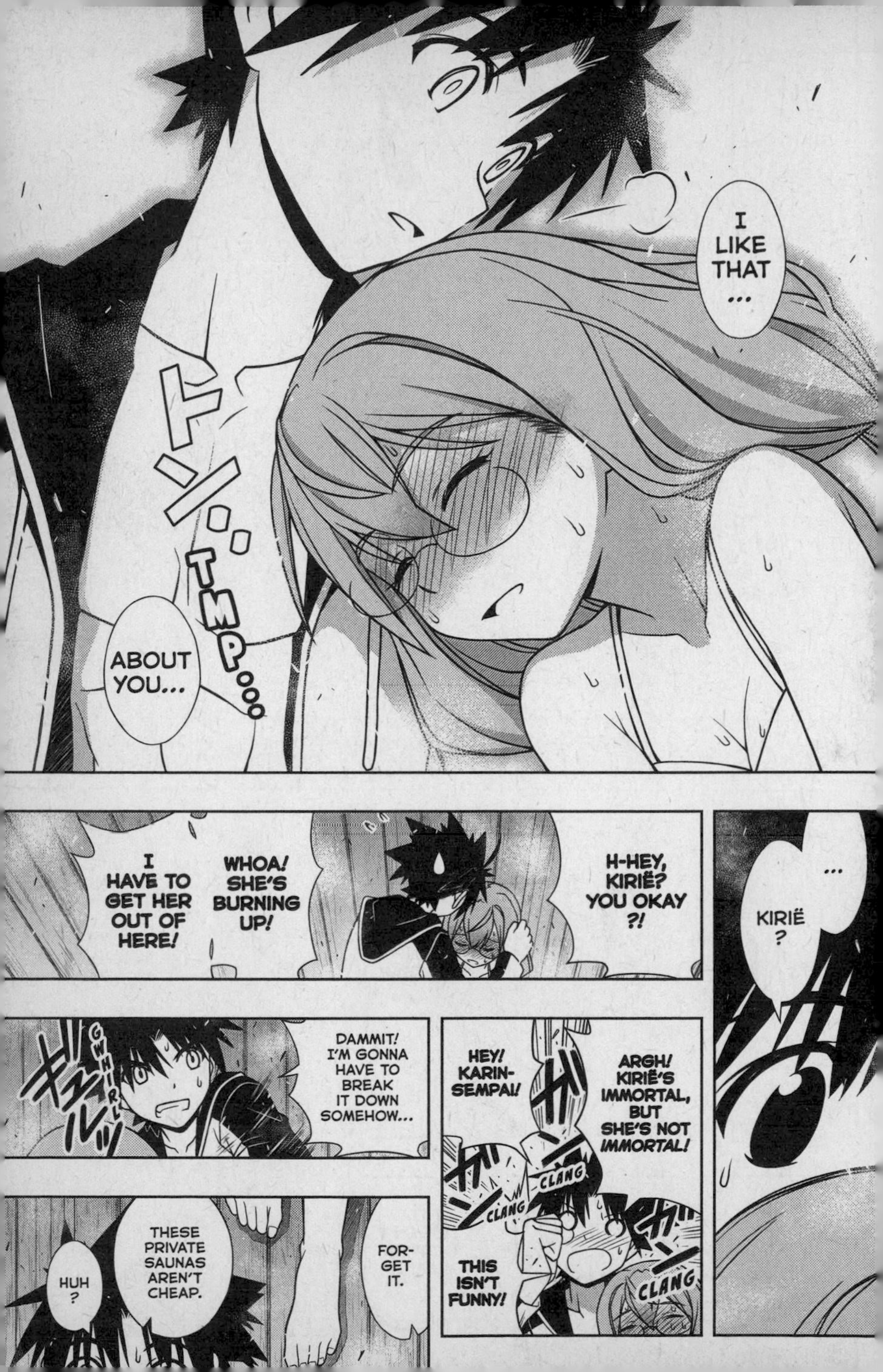
I LIKE THAT...
TMP...
ABOUT YOU...
... KIRIË?
H-HEY, KIRIË? YOU OKAY?!
WHOA! SHE'S BURNING UP!
I HAVE TO GET HER OUT OF HERE!
ARGH! KIRIË'S IMMORTAL, BUT SHE'S NOT *IMMORTAL!*
HEY! KARIN-SEMPAI!
CLANG
CLANG
CLANG
THIS ISN'T FUNNY!
DAMMIT! I'M GONNA HAVE TO BREAK IT DOWN SOMEHOW...
GWHIRL
FOR-GET IT.
THESE PRIVATE SAUNAS AREN'T CHEAP.
HUH?

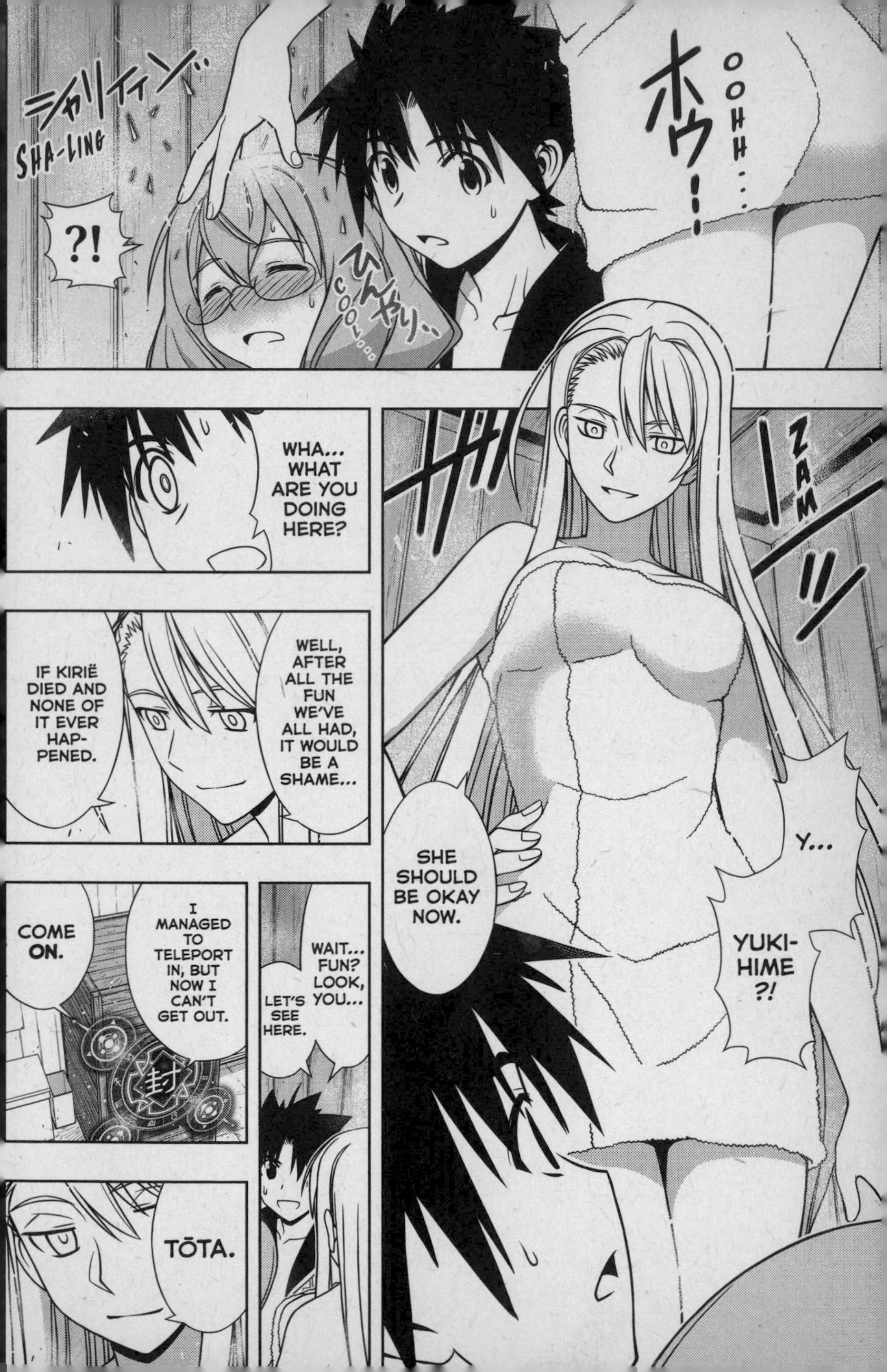
OOHH...
ホウー!!
ひんやり…
COOL...
SHA-LING
シャリィィン
?!
ZAM
Y...
YUKI-HIME?!
SHE SHOULD BE OKAY NOW.
WHA... WHAT ARE YOU DOING HERE?
WELL, AFTER ALL THE FUN WE'VE ALL HAD, IT WOULD BE A SHAME...
IF KIRIË DIED AND NONE OF IT EVER HAPPENED.
WAIT... FUN? LOOK, YOU...
LET'S SEE HERE.
I MANAGED TO TELEPORT IN, BUT NOW I CAN'T GET OUT.
COME ON.
TŌTA.

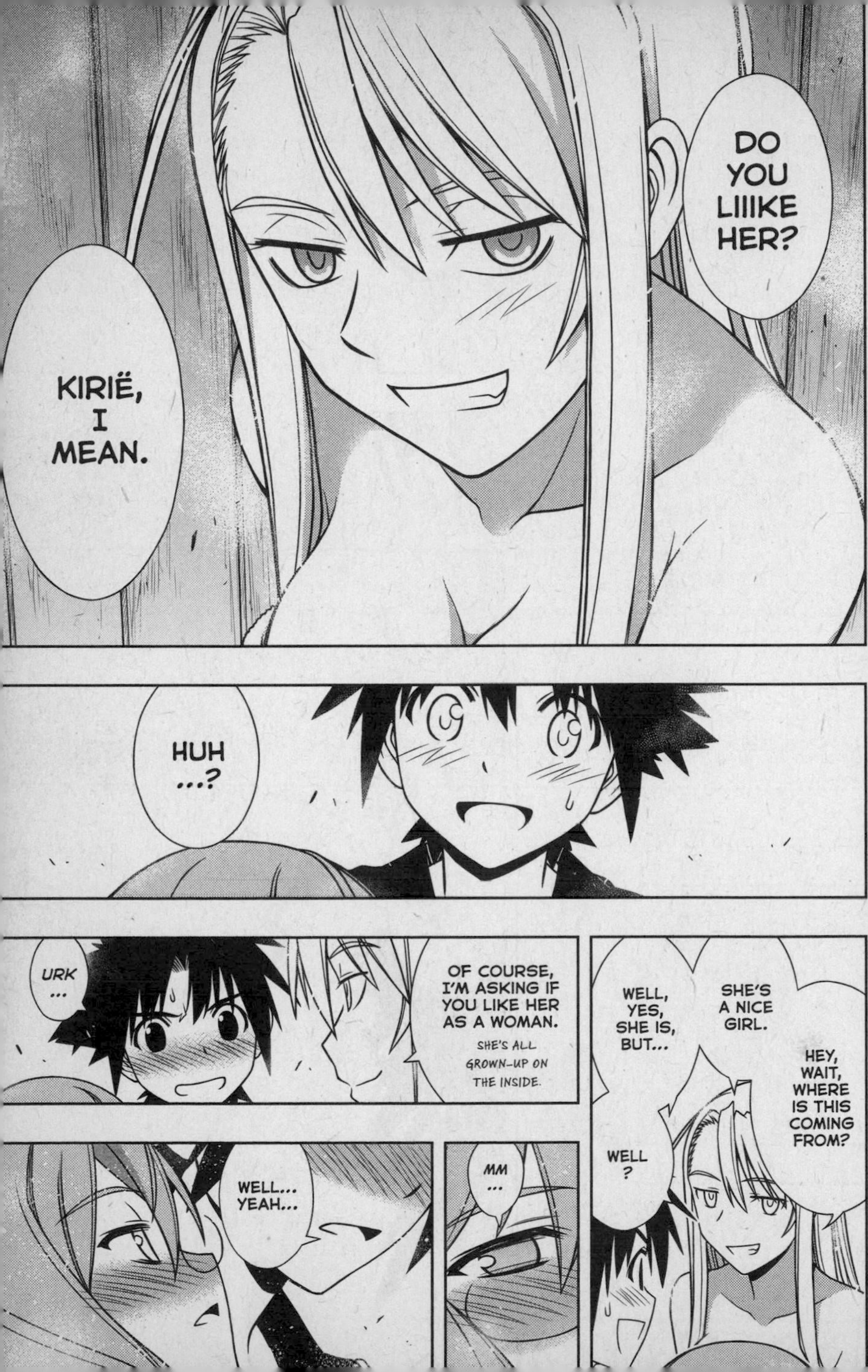
DO YOU LIIIKE HER?
KIRIË, I MEAN.
HUH ...?
SHE'S A NICE GIRL.
WELL, YES, SHE IS, BUT...
HEY, WAIT, WHERE IS THIS COMING FROM?
WELL ?
OF COURSE, I'M ASKING IF YOU LIKE HER AS A WOMAN.
SHE'S ALL GROWN-UP ON THE INSIDE.
URK ...
MM ...
WELL... YEAH...

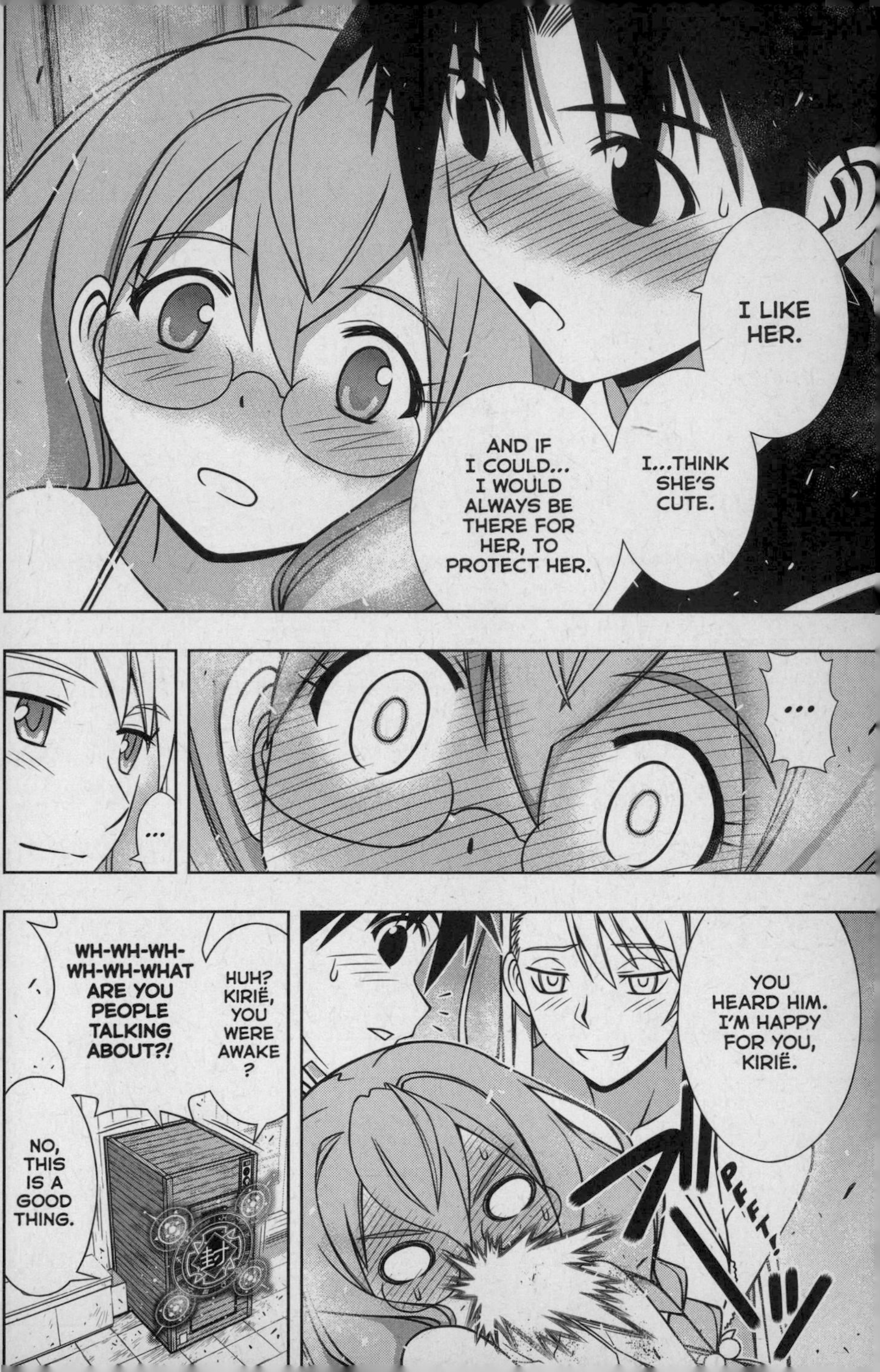
I LIKE HER.
I...THINK SHE'S CUTE.
AND IF I COULD... I WOULD ALWAYS BE THERE FOR HER, TO PROTECT HER.
...
...
YOU HEARD HIM. I'M HAPPY FOR YOU, KIRIË.
QEEET!
HUH? KIRIË, YOU WERE AWAKE?
WH-WH-WH-WH-WH-WHAT ARE YOU PEOPLE TALKING ABOUT?!
NO, THIS IS A GOOD THING.

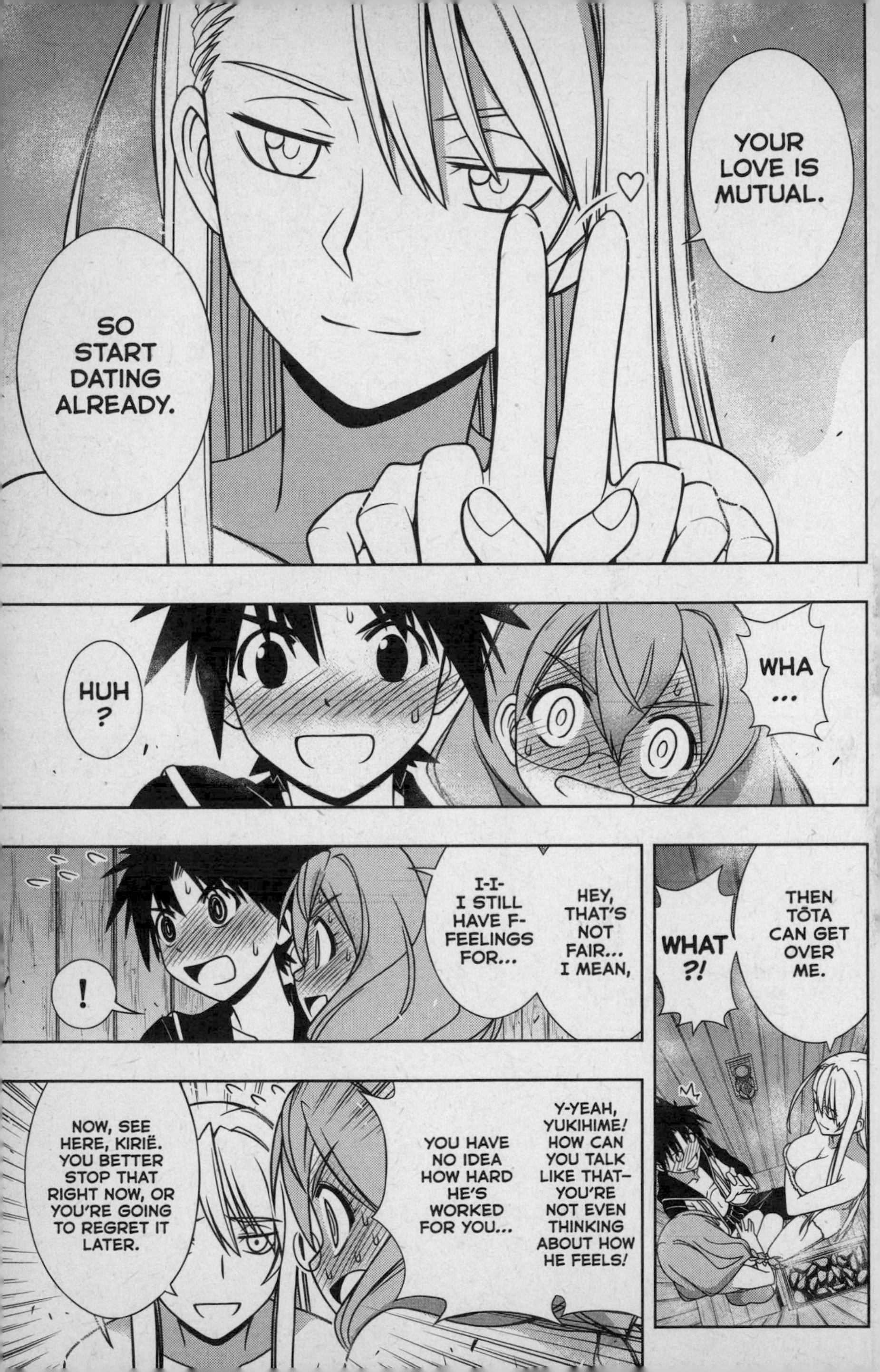
YOUR LOVE IS MUTUAL.
SO START DATING ALREADY.
WHA...
HUH?
THEN TŌTA CAN GET OVER ME.
WHAT?!
HEY, THAT'S NOT FAIR... I MEAN,
I-I- I STILL HAVE F-FEELINGS FOR...
!
Y-YEAH, YUKIHIME! HOW CAN YOU TALK LIKE THAT—YOU'RE NOT EVEN THINKING ABOUT HOW HE FEELS!
YOU HAVE NO IDEA HOW HARD HE'S WORKED FOR YOU...
NOW, SEE HERE, KIRIË. YOU BETTER STOP THAT RIGHT NOW, OR YOU'RE GOING TO REGRET IT LATER.

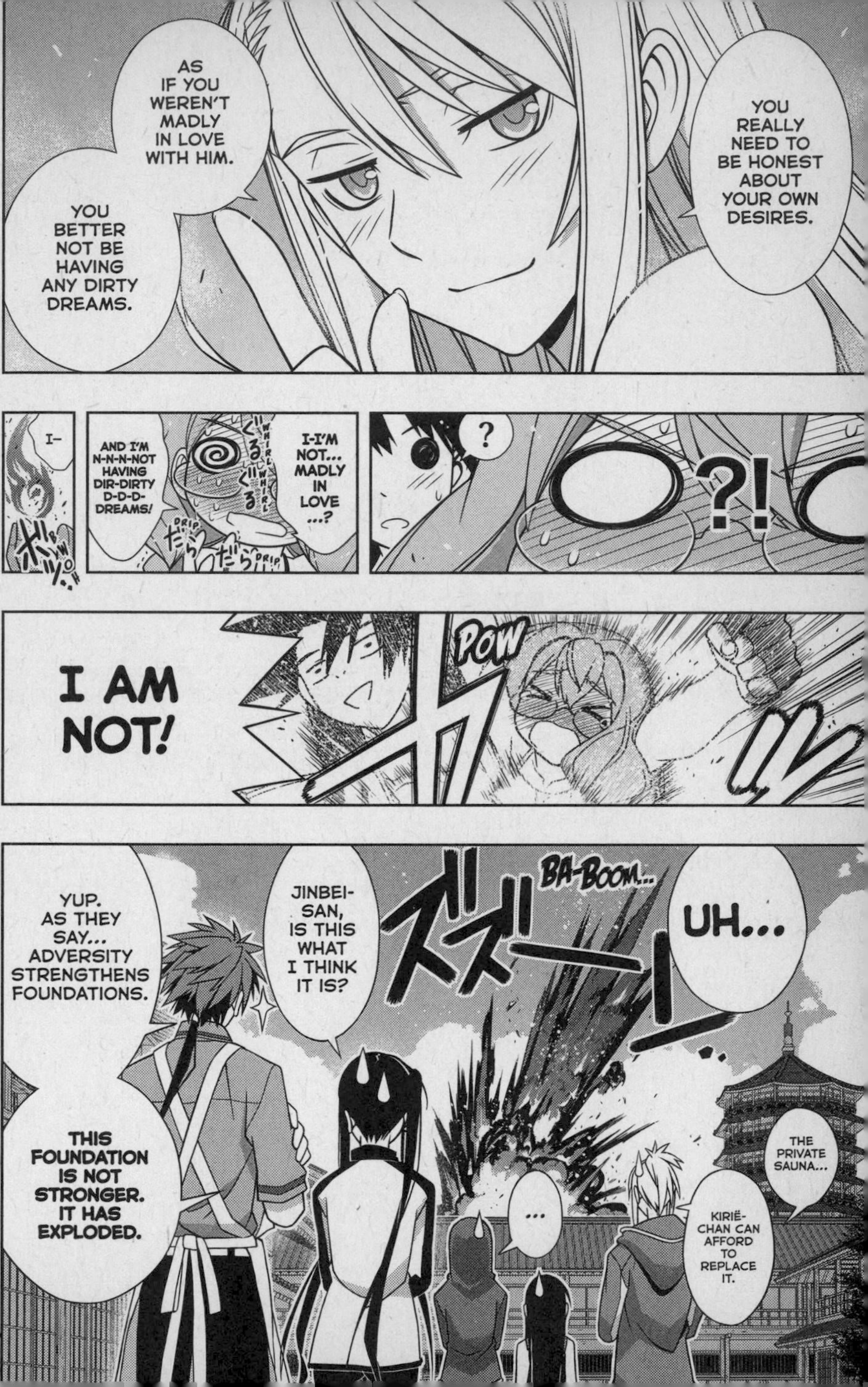
YOU REALLY NEED TO BE HONEST ABOUT YOUR OWN DESIRES.
AS IF YOU WEREN'T MADLY IN LOVE WITH HIM.
YOU BETTER NOT BE HAVING ANY DIRTY DREAMS.
?!
?
I-I'M NOT... MADLY IN LOVE ...?
WHIRL WHIRL
AND I'M N-N-N-NOT HAVING DIR-DIRTY D-D-D-DREAMS!
DRIP DRIP
I–
POW
I AM NOT!
BA-BOOM...
UH...
JINBEI-SAN, IS THIS WHAT I THINK IT IS?
YUP. AS THEY SAY... ADVERSITY STRENGTHENS FOUNDATIONS.
THE PRIVATE SAUNA...
KIRIË-CHAN CAN AFFORD TO REPLACE IT.
...
THIS FOUNDATION IS NOT STRONGER. IT HAS EXPLODED.

UQ HOLDER!

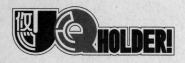

UQ HOLDER!

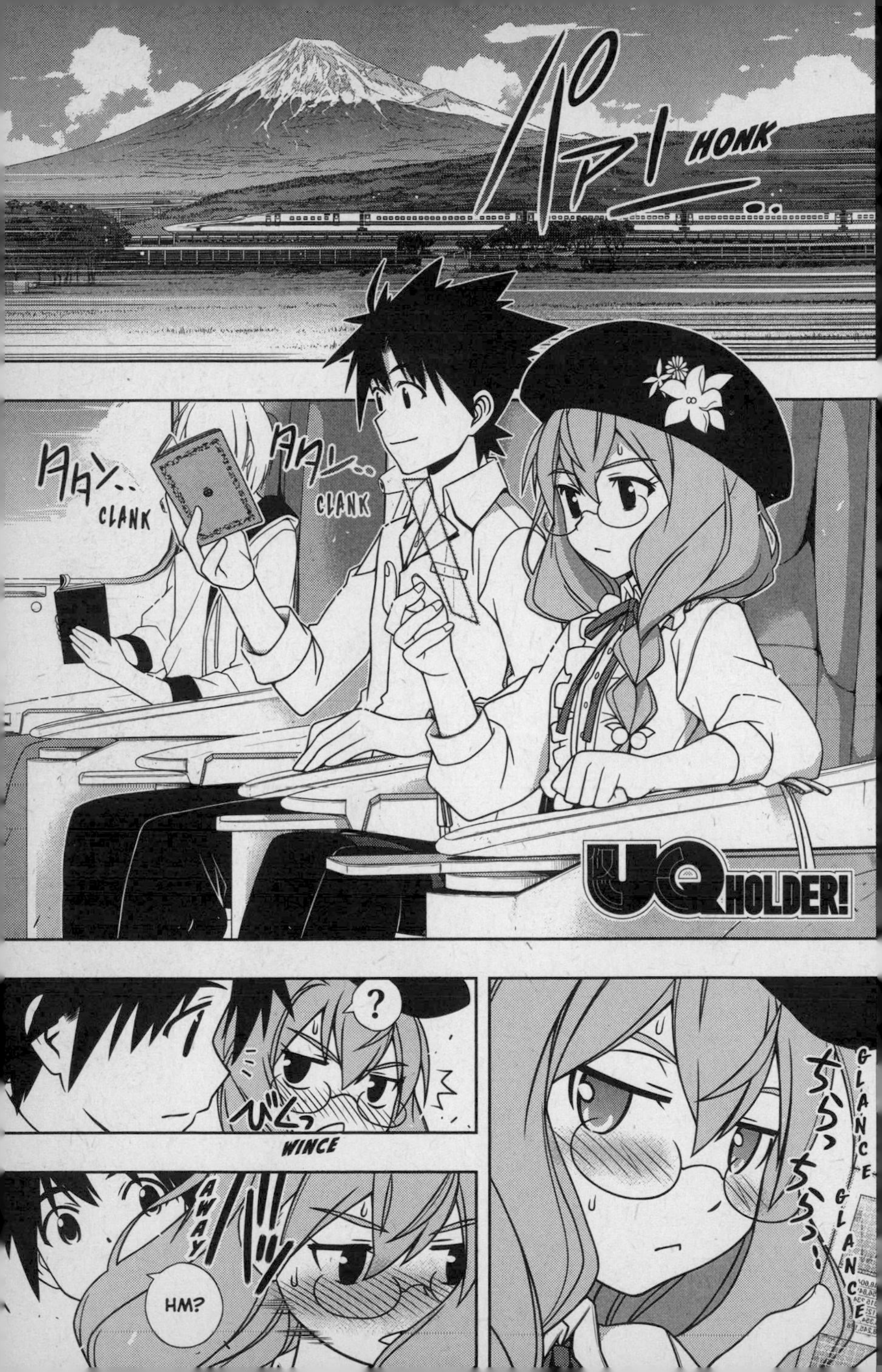
パァー
HONK
カタン..
CLANK
カタン..
CLANK
UQ HOLDER!
ちらっ ちらっ
GLANCE GLANCE
?
びくっ
WINCE
AWAY
HM?

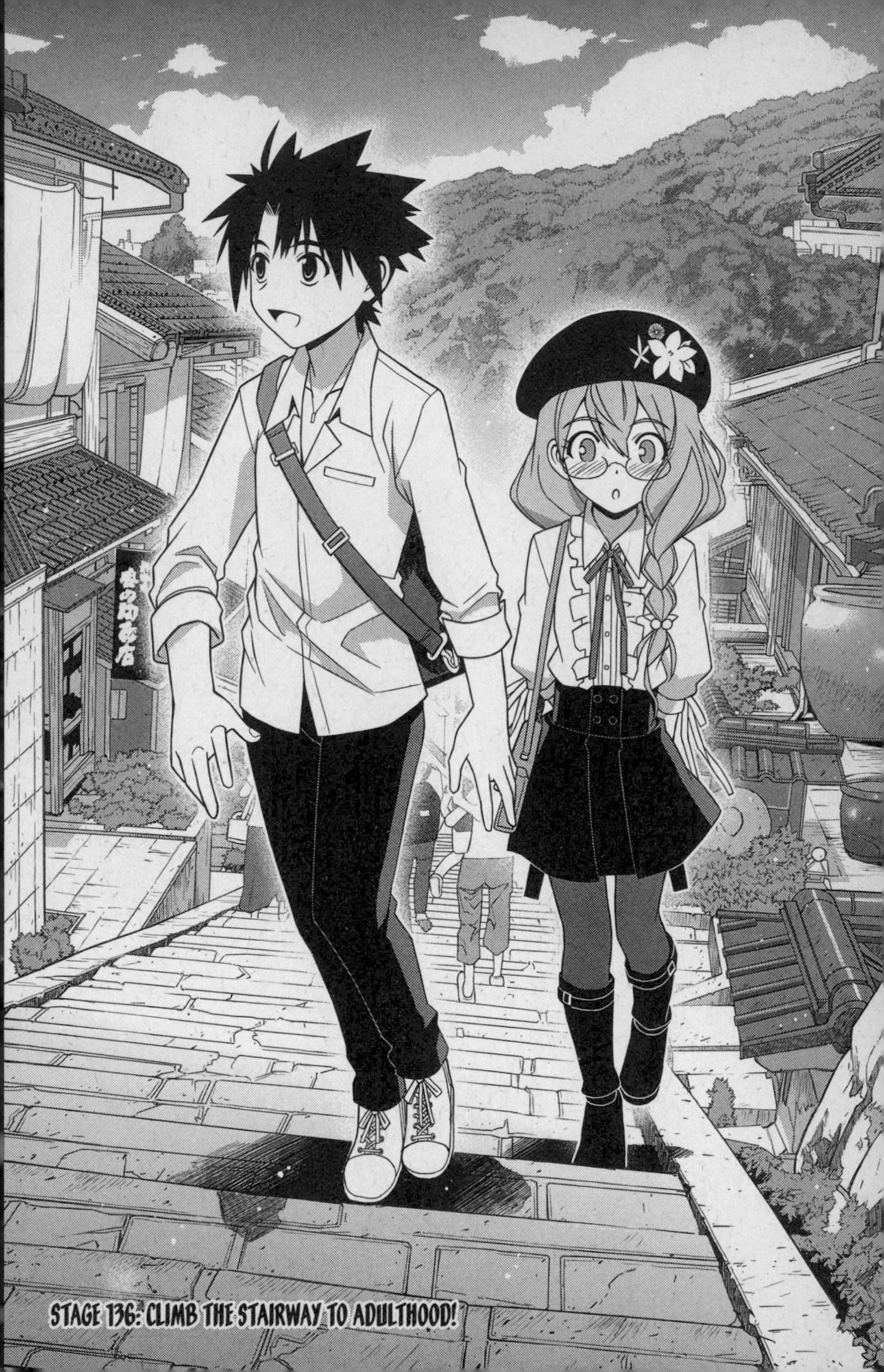
STAGE 136: CLIMB THE STAIRWAY TO ADULTHOOD!

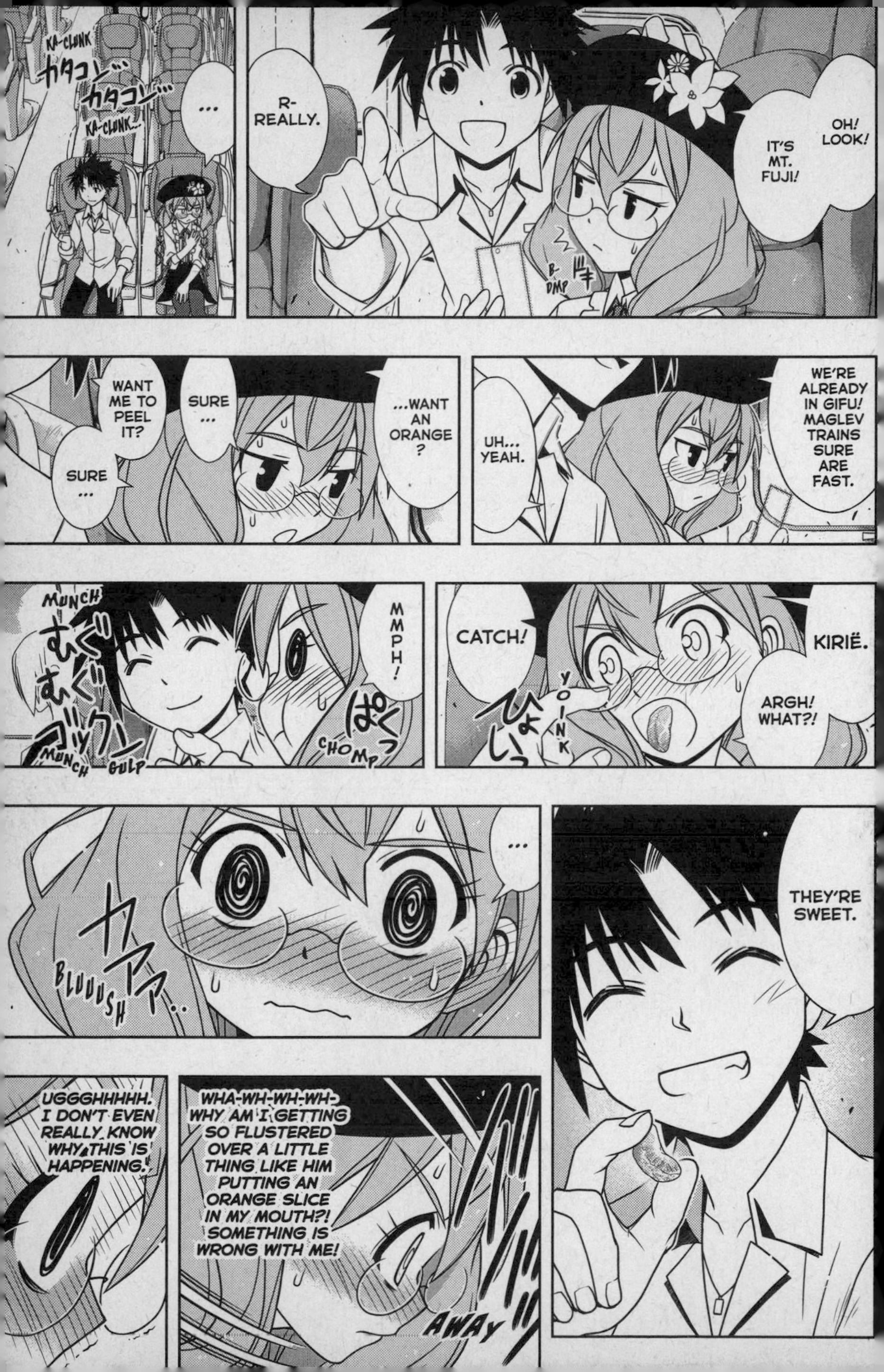
OH! LOOK!
IT'S MT. FUJI!
R-REALLY.
B-DMP
...
KA-CLUNK
KA-CLUNK...
WE'RE ALREADY IN GIFU! MAGLEV TRAINS SURE ARE FAST.
UH... YEAH.
...WANT AN ORANGE?
SURE...
WANT ME TO PEEL IT?
SURE...
KIRIË.
ARGH! WHAT?!
CATCH!
YOINK
MMPH!
CHOMP
MUNCH
MUNCH
GULP
THEY'RE SWEET.
...
BLUUUSH
WHA-WH-WH-WH-WHY AM I GETTING SO FLUSTERED OVER A LITTLE THING LIKE HIM PUTTING AN ORANGE SLICE IN MY MOUTH?! SOMETHING IS WRONG WITH ME!
AWAY
UGGGHHHHH. I DON'T EVEN REALLY KNOW WHY THIS IS HAPPENING.

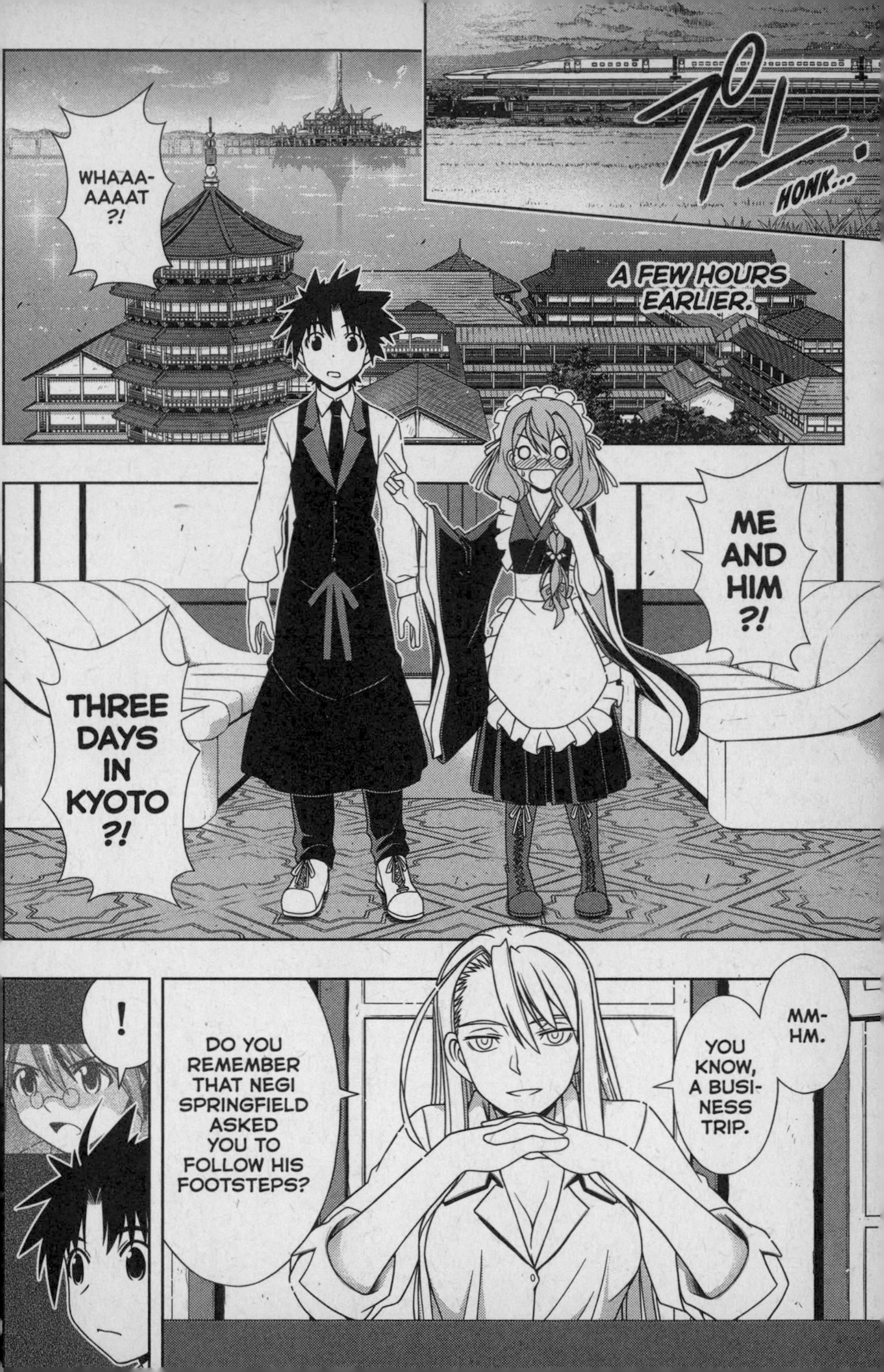
HONK…
WHAAAA-AAAAT ?!
A FEW HOURS EARLIER.
ME AND HIM ?!
THREE DAYS IN KYOTO ?!
MM-HM.
YOU KNOW, A BUSI-NESS TRIP.
DO YOU REMEMBER THAT NEGI SPRINGFIELD ASKED YOU TO FOLLOW HIS FOOTSTEPS?
!

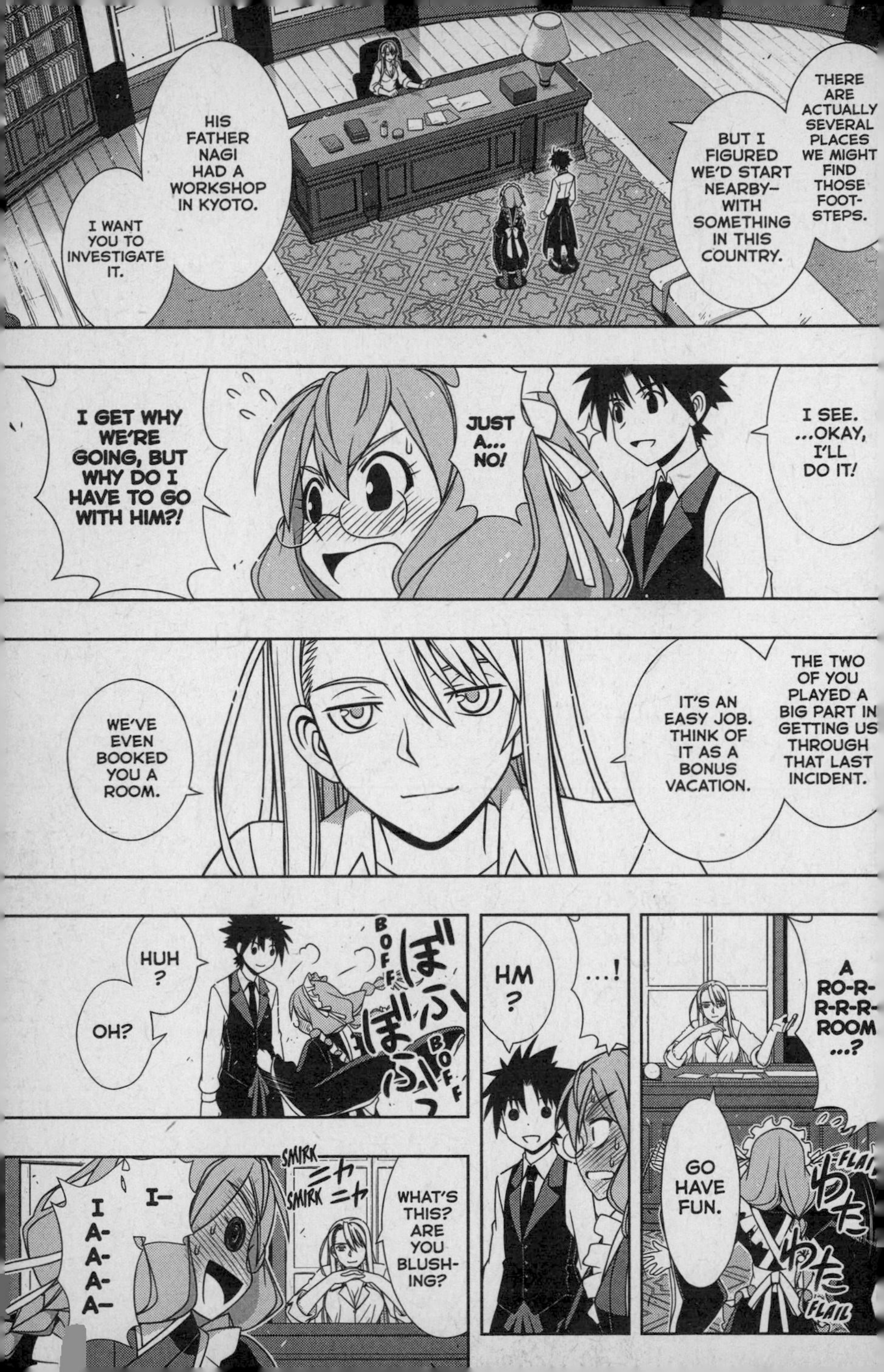
THERE ARE ACTUALLY SEVERAL PLACES WE MIGHT FIND THOSE FOOT-STEPS.
BUT I FIGURED WE'D START NEARBY—WITH SOMETHING IN THIS COUNTRY.
HIS FATHER NAGI HAD A WORKSHOP IN KYOTO.
I WANT YOU TO INVESTIGATE IT.
I SEE. ...OKAY, I'LL DO IT!
JUST A... NO!
I GET WHY WE'RE GOING, BUT WHY DO I HAVE TO GO WITH HIM?!
THE TWO OF YOU PLAYED A BIG PART IN GETTING US THROUGH THAT LAST INCIDENT.
IT'S AN EASY JOB. THINK OF IT AS A BONUS VACATION.
WE'VE EVEN BOOKED YOU A ROOM.
A RO-R-R-R-R-ROOM...?
GO HAVE FUN.
わた FLAIL
わた FLAIL
...!
HM?
ぼふ BOFF
ぼふ BOFF
HUH?
OH?
ニヤ SMIRK
ニヤ SMIRK
WHAT'S THIS? ARE YOU BLUSHING?
I—
I A-A-A-A—

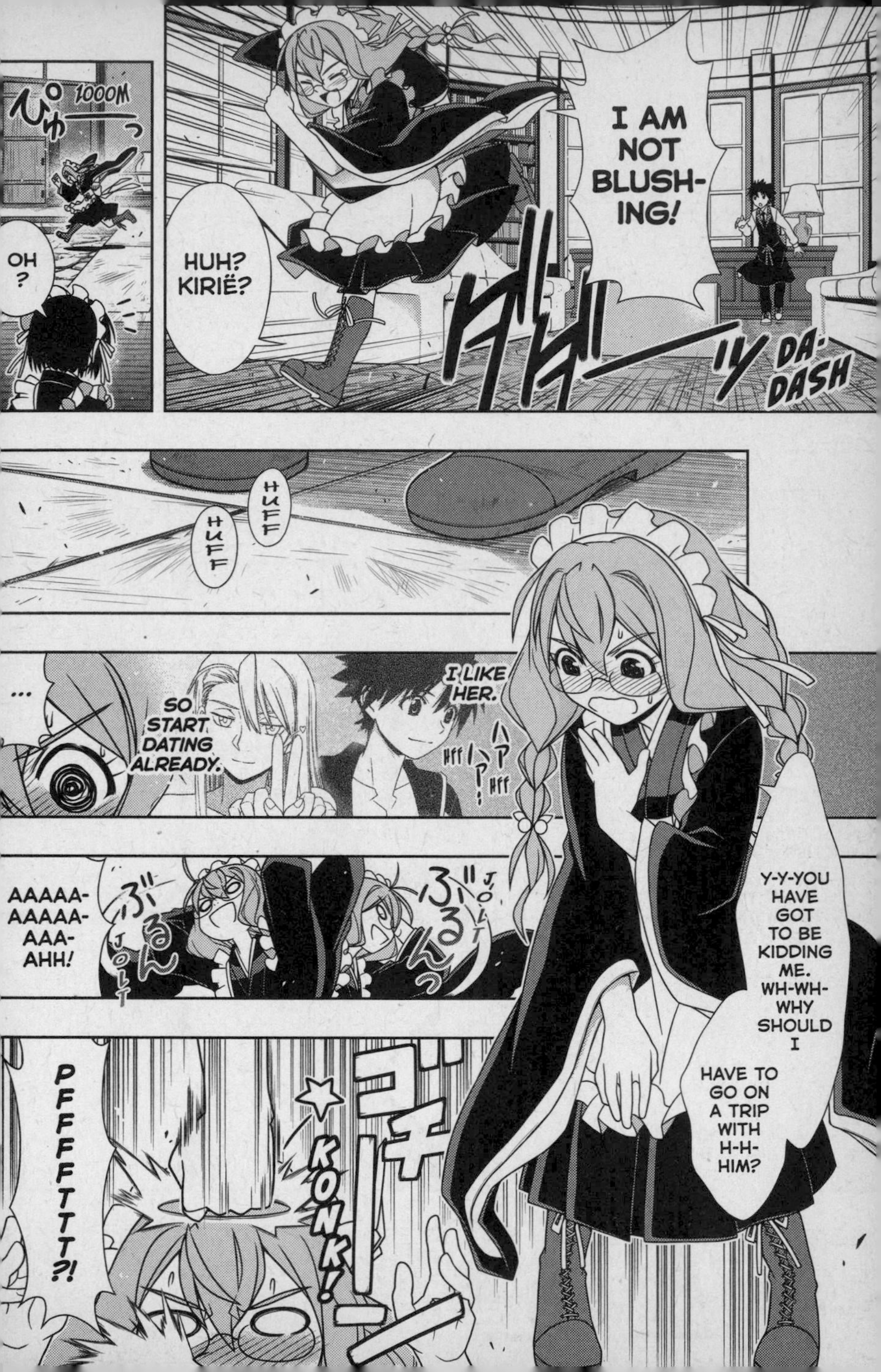
I AM NOT BLUSHING!
DA-DASH
HUH? KIRIË?
1000M
OH?
HUFF
HUFF
Y-Y-YOU HAVE GOT TO BE KIDDING ME. WH-WH-WHY SHOULD I
HAVE TO GO ON A TRIP WITH H-H-HIM?
I LIKE HER.
HFF HFF
SO START DATING ALREADY.
...
JOLT
JOLT
AAAAA-AAAAA-AAA-AHH!
KONK!
PFFFFTTTT?!

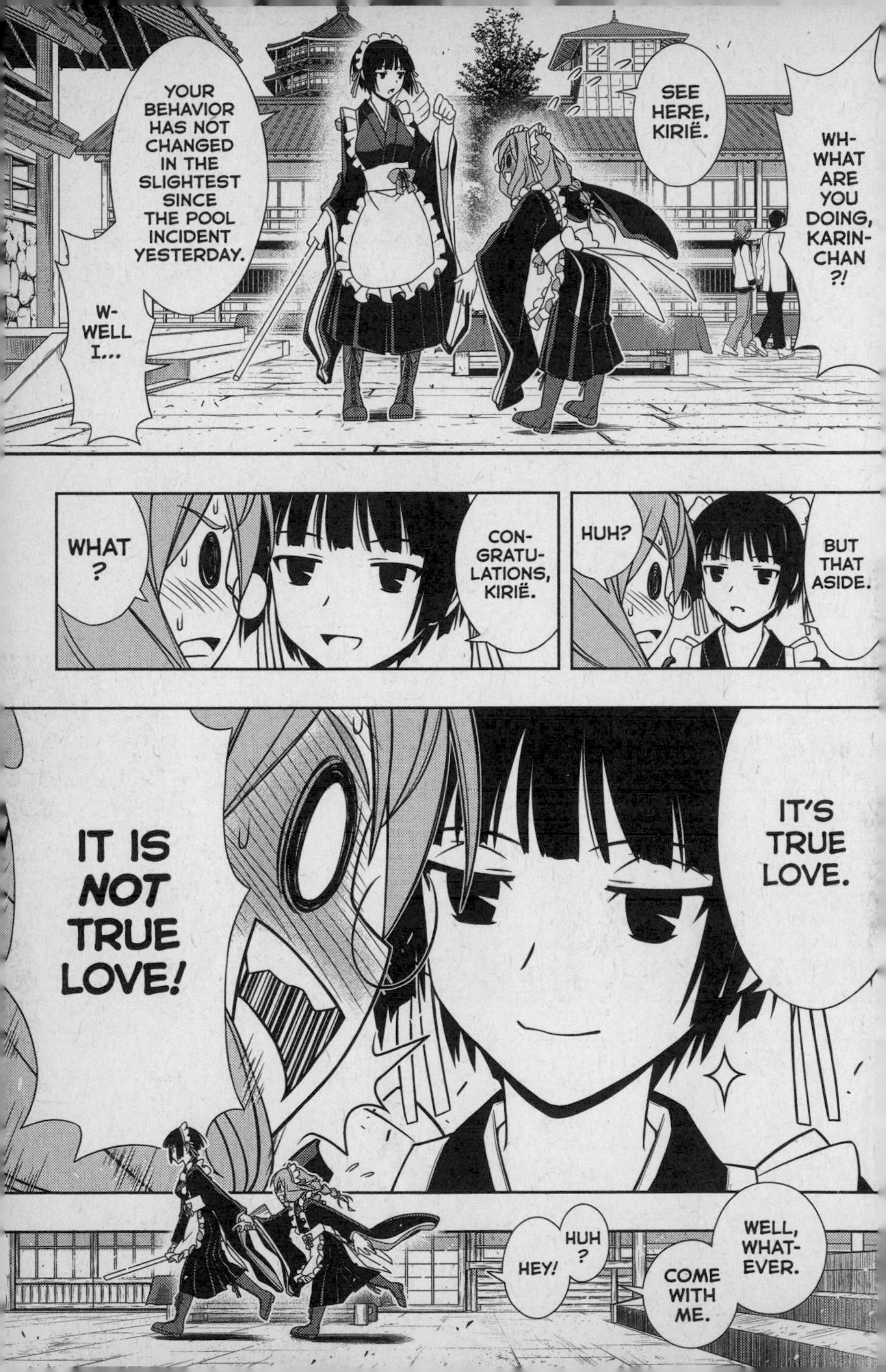
WH-WHAT ARE YOU DOING, KARIN-CHAN?!
SEE HERE, KIRIË.
YOUR BEHAVIOR HAS NOT CHANGED IN THE SLIGHTEST SINCE THE POOL INCIDENT YESTERDAY.
W-WELL I...
BUT THAT ASIDE.
HUH?
CON-GRATU-LATIONS, KIRIË.
WHAT?
IT'S TRUE LOVE.
IT IS *NOT* TRUE LOVE!
WELL, WHAT-EVER.
COME WITH ME.
HUH?
HEY!

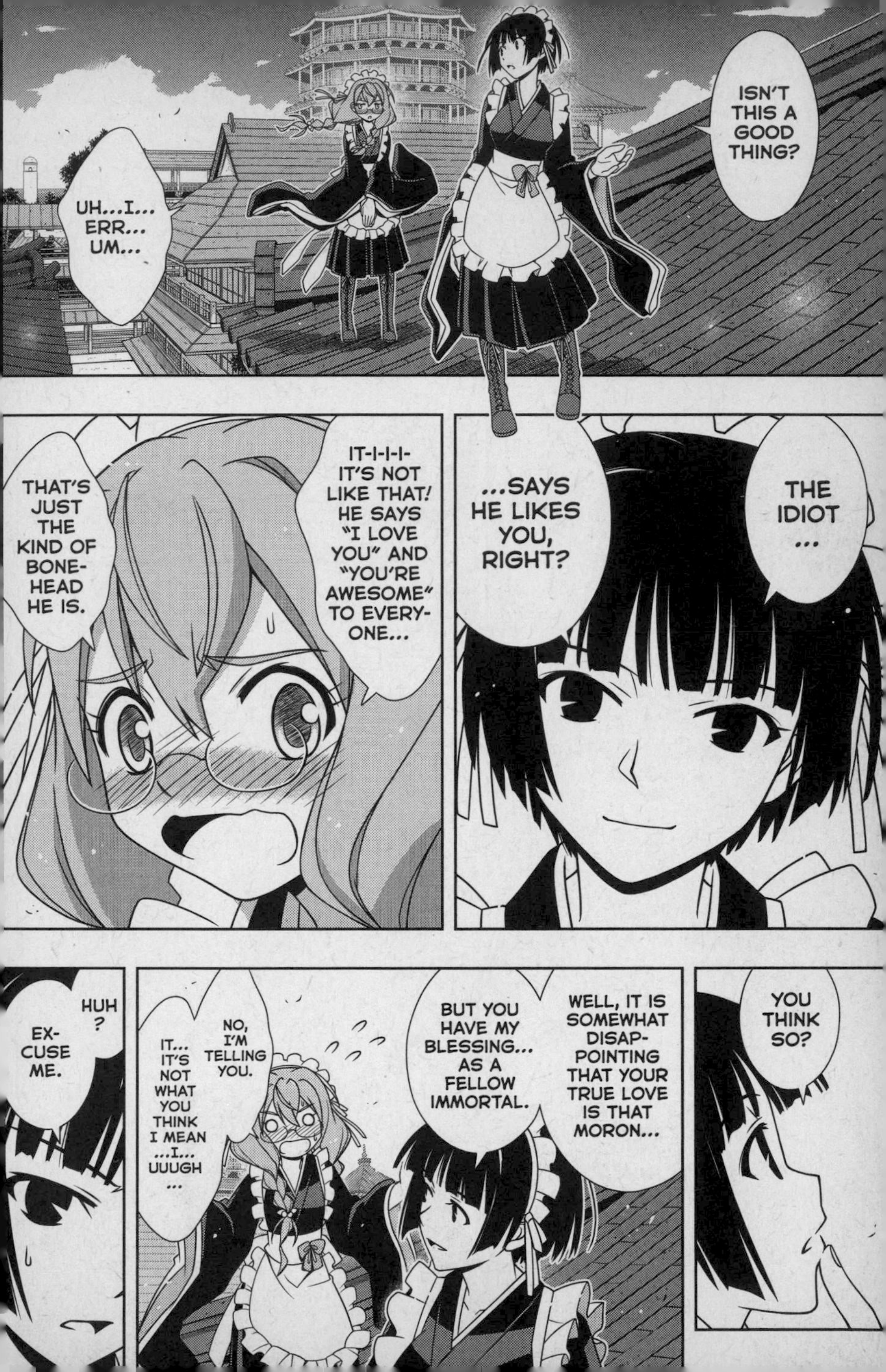
ISN'T THIS A GOOD THING?
UH...I... ERR... UM...
THE IDIOT ...
...SAYS HE LIKES YOU, RIGHT?
IT-I-I-I- IT'S NOT LIKE THAT! HE SAYS "I LOVE YOU" AND "YOU'RE AWESOME" TO EVERY-ONE...
THAT'S JUST THE KIND OF BONE-HEAD HE IS.
YOU THINK SO?
WELL, IT IS SOMEWHAT DISAP-POINTING THAT YOUR TRUE LOVE IS THAT MORON...
BUT YOU HAVE MY BLESSING... AS A FELLOW IMMORTAL.
NO, I'M TELLING YOU.
IT... IT'S NOT WHAT YOU THINK I MEAN ...I... UUUGH ...
HUH ?
EX-CUSE ME.

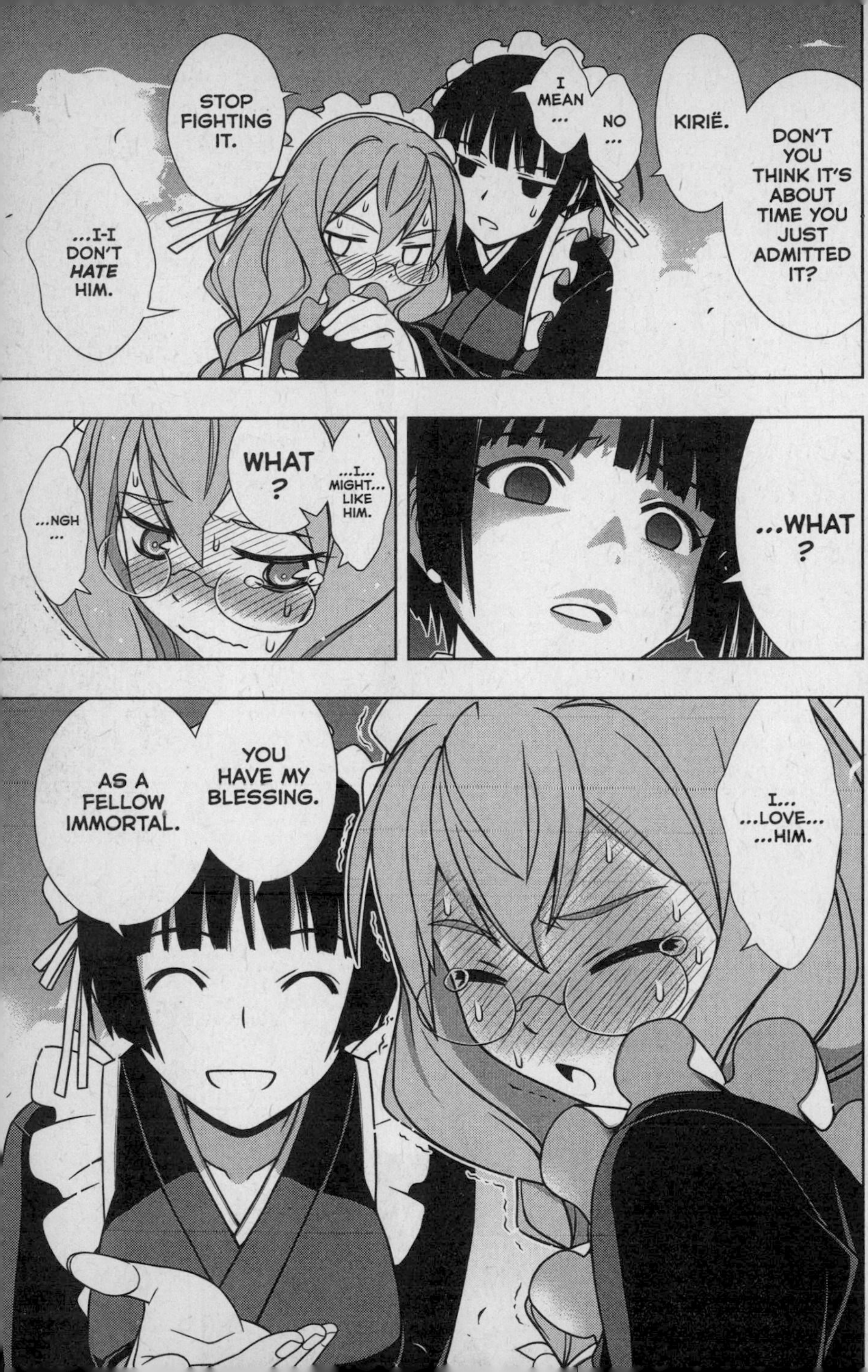
KIRIË.
DON'T YOU THINK IT'S ABOUT TIME YOU JUST ADMITTED IT?
NO ...
I MEAN ...
STOP FIGHTING IT.
...I-I DON'T *HATE* HIM.
...WHAT?
...I... MIGHT... LIKE HIM.
WHAT?
...NGH ...
I... ...LOVE... ...HIM.
YOU HAVE MY BLESSING.
AS A FELLOW IMMORTAL.

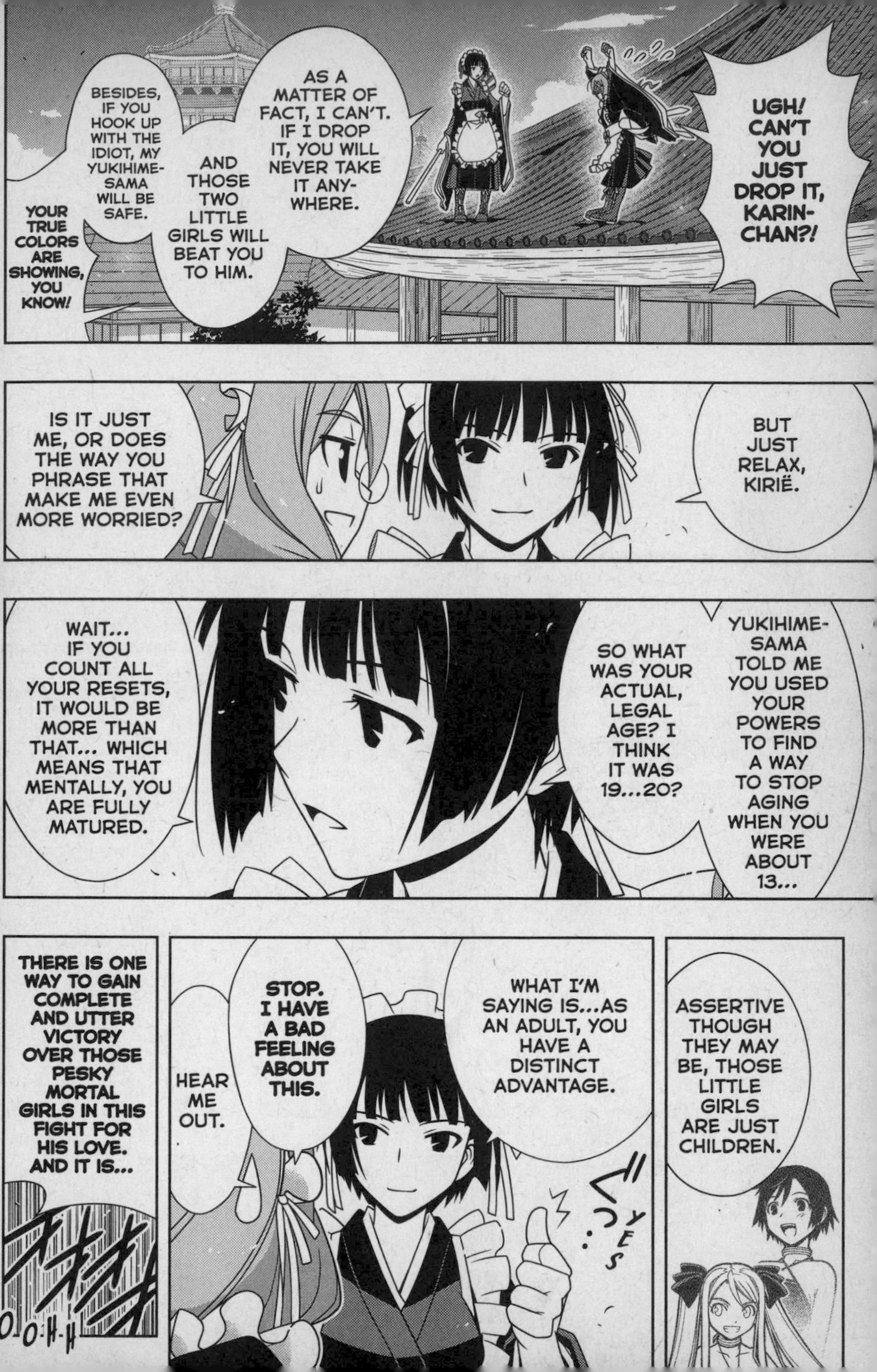
UGH! CAN'T YOU JUST DROP IT, KARIN-CHAN?!
AS A MATTER OF FACT, I CAN'T. IF I DROP IT, YOU WILL NEVER TAKE IT ANYWHERE.
AND THOSE TWO LITTLE GIRLS WILL BEAT YOU TO HIM.
BESIDES, IF YOU HOOK UP WITH THE IDIOT, MY YUKIHIME-SAMA WILL BE SAFE.
YOUR TRUE COLORS ARE SHOWING, YOU KNOW!
BUT JUST RELAX, KIRIË.
IS IT JUST ME, OR DOES THE WAY YOU PHRASE THAT MAKE ME EVEN MORE WORRIED?
YUKIHIME-SAMA TOLD ME YOU USED YOUR POWERS TO FIND A WAY TO STOP AGING WHEN YOU WERE ABOUT 13...
SO WHAT WAS YOUR ACTUAL, LEGAL AGE? I THINK IT WAS 19...20?
WAIT... IF YOU COUNT ALL YOUR RESETS, IT WOULD BE MORE THAN THAT... WHICH MEANS THAT MENTALLY, YOU ARE FULLY MATURED.
ASSERTIVE THOUGH THEY MAY BE, THOSE LITTLE GIRLS ARE JUST CHILDREN.
WHAT I'M SAYING IS...AS AN ADULT, YOU HAVE A DISTINCT ADVANTAGE.
YES
STOP. I HAVE A BAD FEELING ABOUT THIS.
HEAR ME OUT.
THERE IS ONE WAY TO GAIN COMPLETE AND UTTER VICTORY OVER THOSE PESKY MORTAL GIRLS IN THIS FIGHT FOR HIS LOVE. AND IT IS...
O-O-H-H

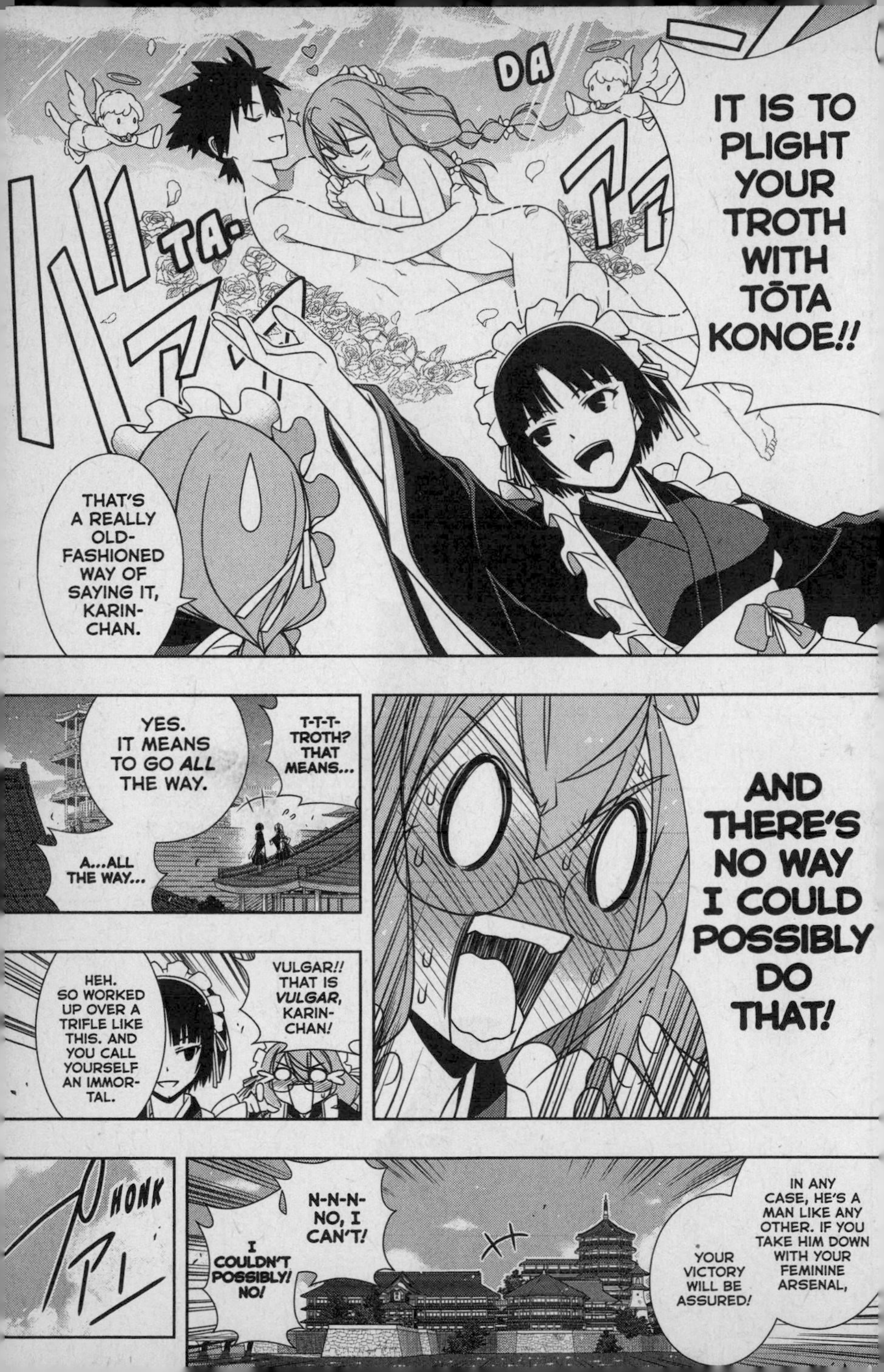
DA
IT IS TO PLIGHT YOUR TROTH WITH TŌTA KONOE!!
TA-
THAT'S A REALLY OLD-FASHIONED WAY OF SAYING IT, KARIN-CHAN.
AND THERE'S NO WAY I COULD POSSIBLY DO THAT!
T-T-T-TROTH? THAT MEANS...
YES. IT MEANS TO GO ALL THE WAY.
A...ALL THE WAY...
VULGAR!! THAT IS VULGAR, KARIN-CHAN!
HEH. SO WORKED UP OVER A TRIFLE LIKE THIS. AND YOU CALL YOURSELF AN IMMORTAL.
IN ANY CASE, HE'S A MAN LIKE ANY OTHER. IF YOU TAKE HIM DOWN WITH YOUR FEMININE ARSENAL,
YOUR VICTORY WILL BE ASSURED!
N-N-N-NO, I CAN'T!
I COULDN'T POSSIBLY! NO!
HONK

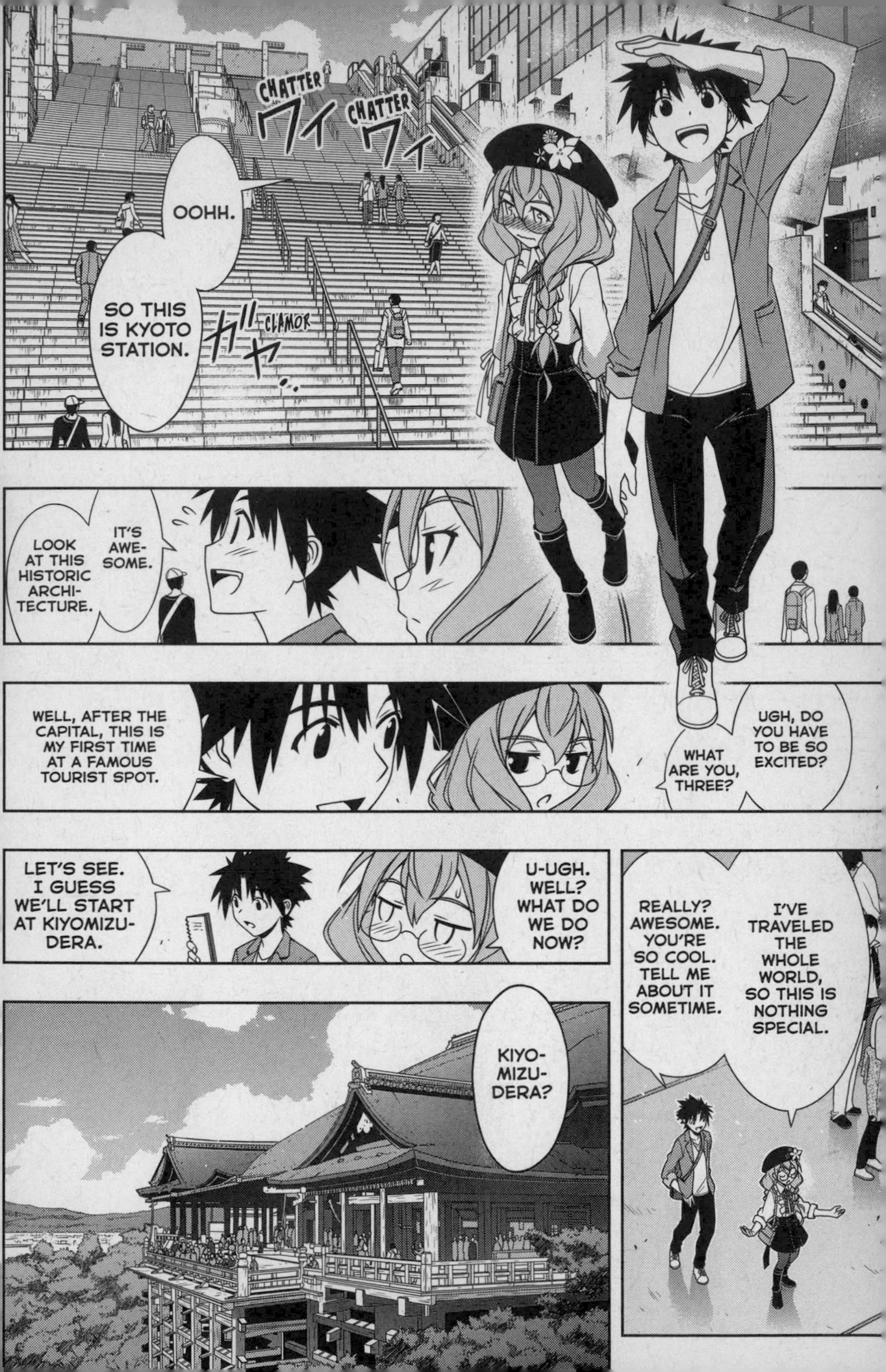
CHATTER
ワイ
CHATTER
ワイ
OOHH.
SO THIS IS KYOTO STATION.
ガヤ
CLAMOR
IT'S AWESOME.
LOOK AT THIS HISTORIC ARCHITECTURE.
UGH, DO YOU HAVE TO BE SO EXCITED?
WHAT ARE YOU, THREE?
WELL, AFTER THE CAPITAL, THIS IS MY FIRST TIME AT A FAMOUS TOURIST SPOT.
I'VE TRAVELED THE WHOLE WORLD, SO THIS IS NOTHING SPECIAL.
REALLY? AWESOME. YOU'RE SO COOL. TELL ME ABOUT IT SOMETIME.
U-UGH. WELL? WHAT DO WE DO NOW?
LET'S SEE. I GUESS WE'LL START AT KIYOMIZUDERA.
KIYOMIZUDERA?

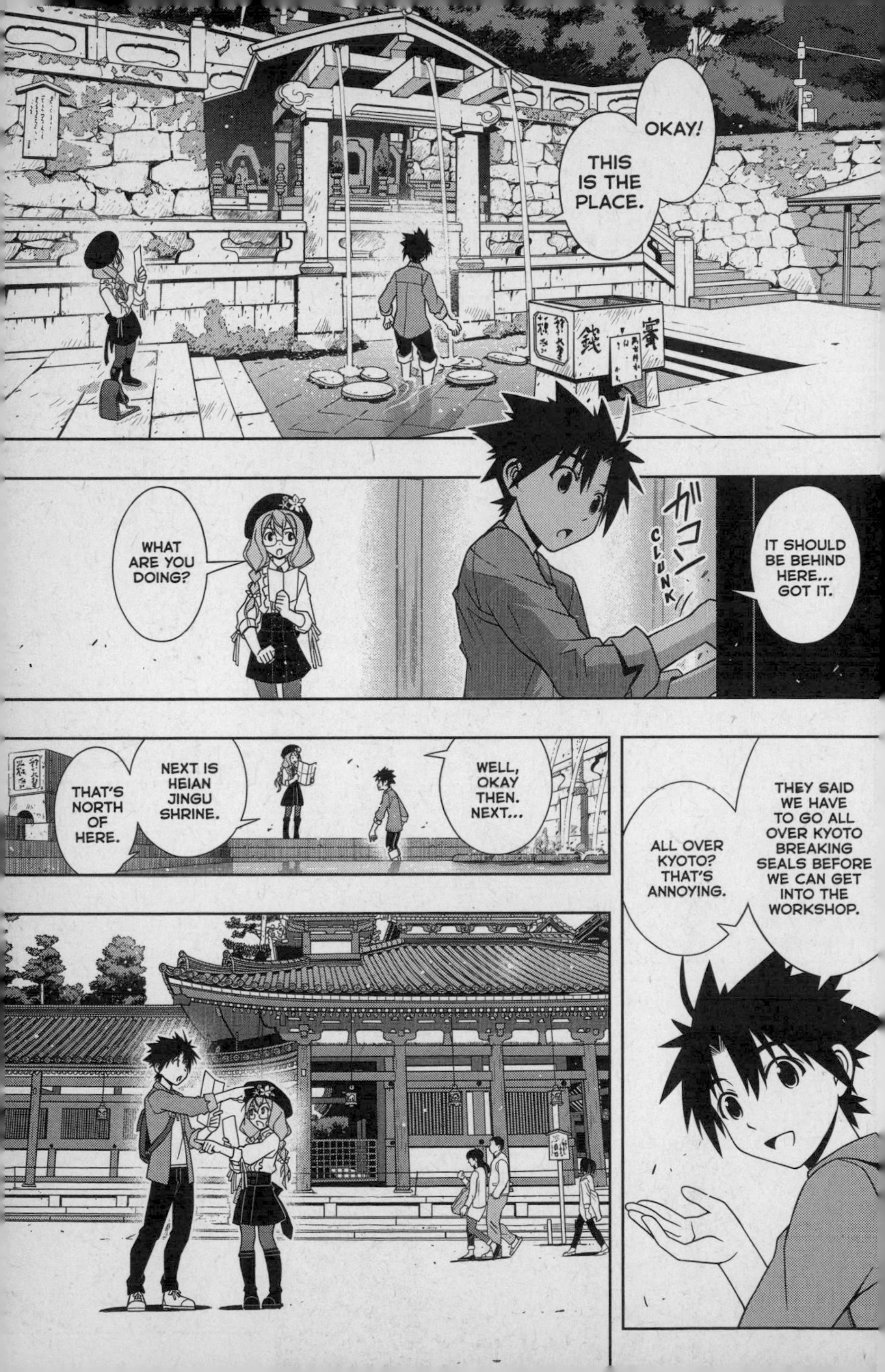
OKAY!
THIS IS THE PLACE.
賽銭
IT SHOULD BE BEHIND HERE... GOT IT.
ガコン
CLUNK
WHAT ARE YOU DOING?
THEY SAID WE HAVE TO GO ALL OVER KYOTO BREAKING SEALS BEFORE WE CAN GET INTO THE WORKSHOP.
ALL OVER KYOTO? THAT'S ANNOYING.
WELL, OKAY THEN. NEXT...
NEXT IS HEIAN JINGU SHRINE.
THAT'S NORTH OF HERE.

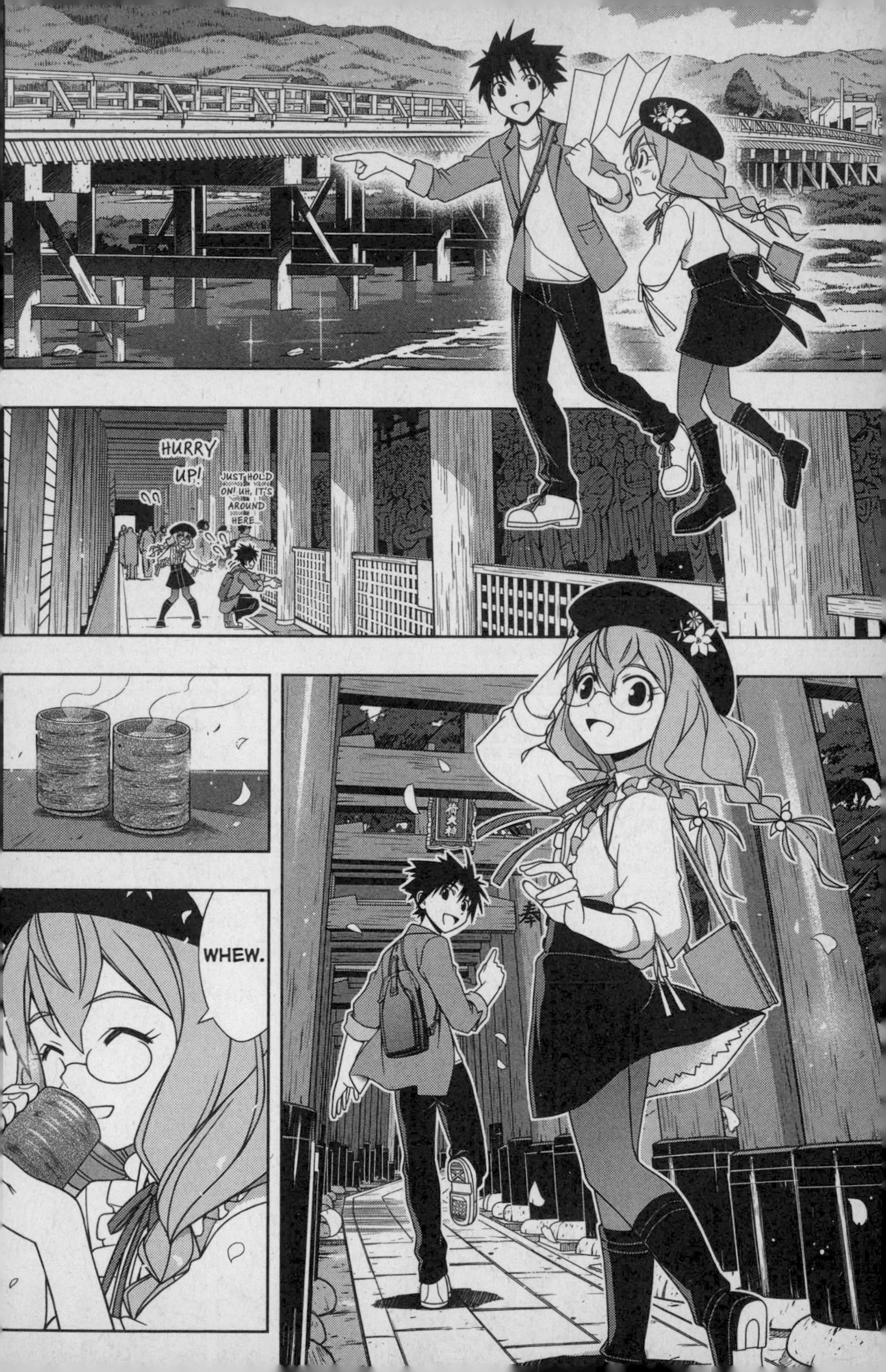
HURRY UP!
JUST HOLD ON! UH, IT'S AROUND HERE...
WHEW.

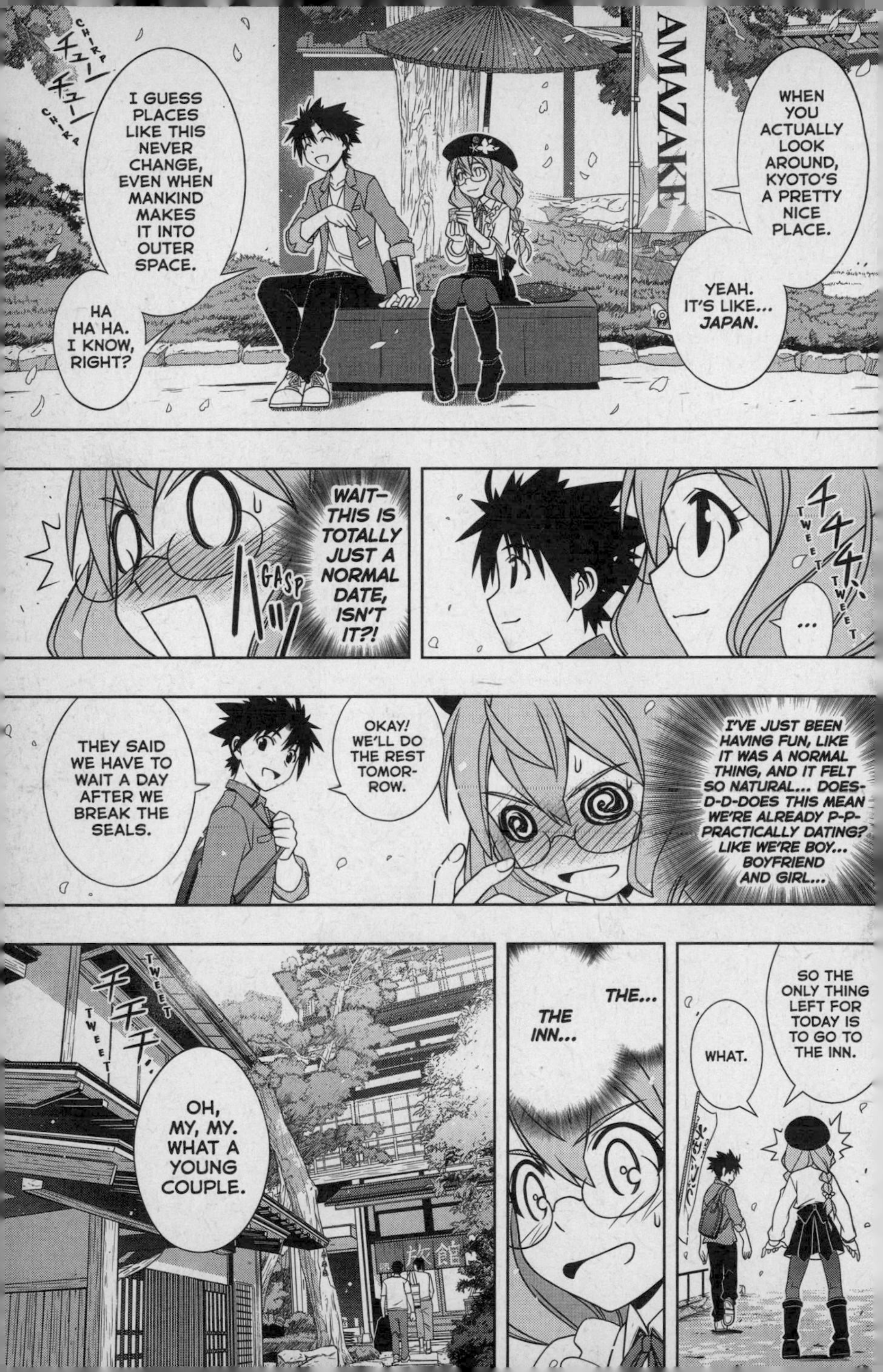
AMAZAKE
WHEN YOU ACTUALLY LOOK AROUND, KYOTO'S A PRETTY NICE PLACE.
YEAH. IT'S LIKE... JAPAN.
CHIRP CHIRP
I GUESS PLACES LIKE THIS NEVER CHANGE, EVEN WHEN MANKIND MAKES IT INTO OUTER SPACE.
HA HA HA. I KNOW, RIGHT?
TWEET TWEET
...
WAIT— THIS IS TOTALLY JUST A NORMAL DATE, ISN'T IT?!
GASP
I'VE JUST BEEN HAVING FUN, LIKE IT WAS A NORMAL THING, AND IT FELT SO NATURAL... DOES-D-D-DOES THIS MEAN WE'RE ALREADY P-P-PRACTICALLY DATING? LIKE WE'RE BOY... BOYFRIEND AND GIRL...
OKAY! WE'LL DO THE REST TOMORROW.
THEY SAID WE HAVE TO WAIT A DAY AFTER WE BREAK THE SEALS.
SO THE ONLY THING LEFT FOR TODAY IS TO GO TO THE INN.
WHAT.
THE...
THE INN...
TWEET TWEET
OH, MY, MY. WHAT A YOUNG COUPLE.

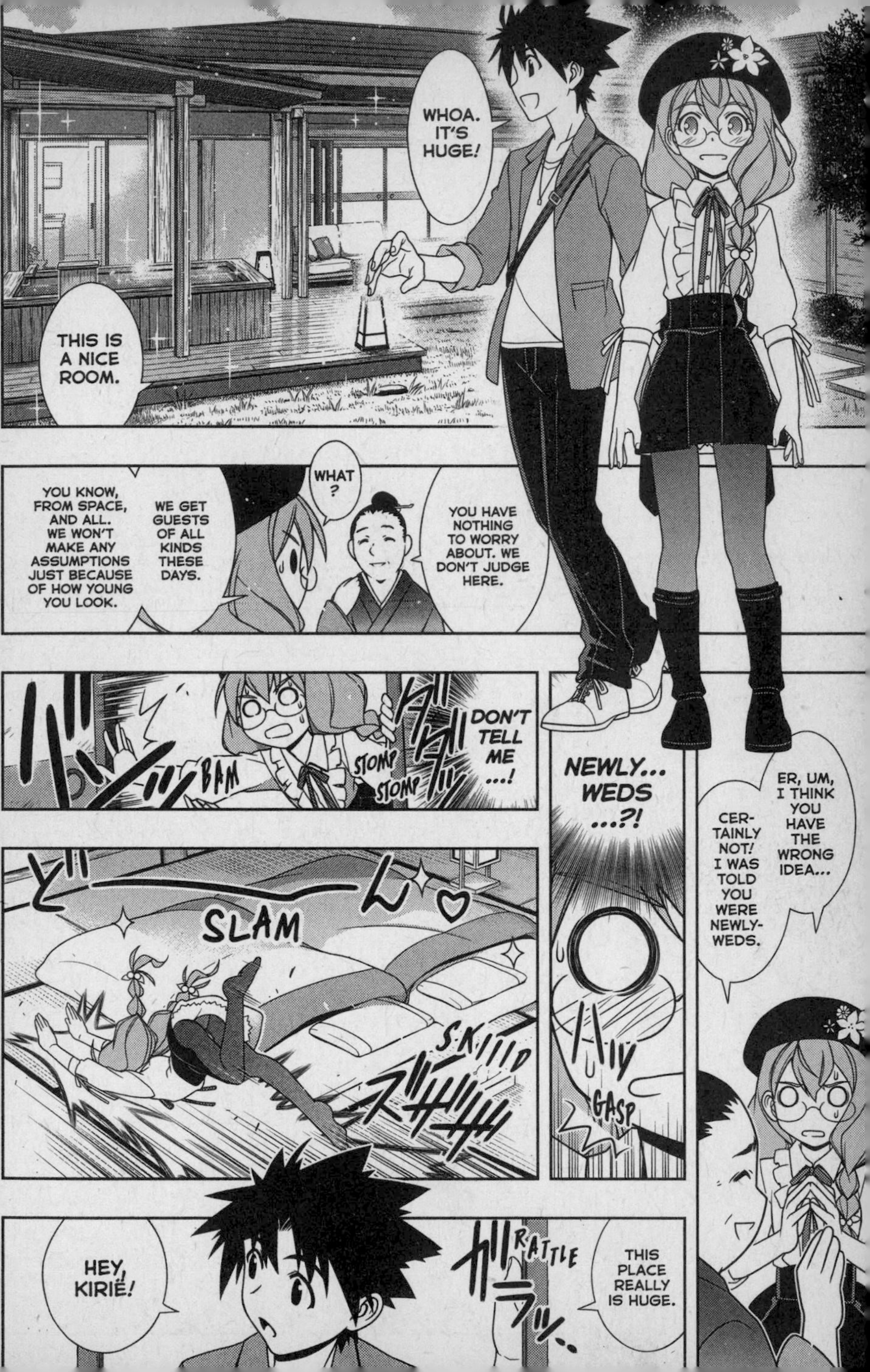

WHOA. IT'S HUGE!
THIS IS A NICE ROOM.
YOU HAVE NOTHING TO WORRY ABOUT. WE DON'T JUDGE HERE.
WHAT?
WE GET GUESTS OF ALL KINDS THESE DAYS.
YOU KNOW, FROM SPACE, AND ALL. WE WON'T MAKE ANY ASSUMPTIONS JUST BECAUSE OF HOW YOUNG YOU LOOK.
ER, UM, I THINK YOU HAVE THE WRONG IDEA...
CER- TAINLY NOT! I WAS TOLD YOU WERE NEWLY- WEDS.
NEWLY... WEDS ...?!
GASP
DON'T TELL ME ...!
STOMP
STOMP
BAM
SLAM
SKIIID
THIS PLACE REALLY IS HUGE.
RATTLE
HEY, KIRIË!

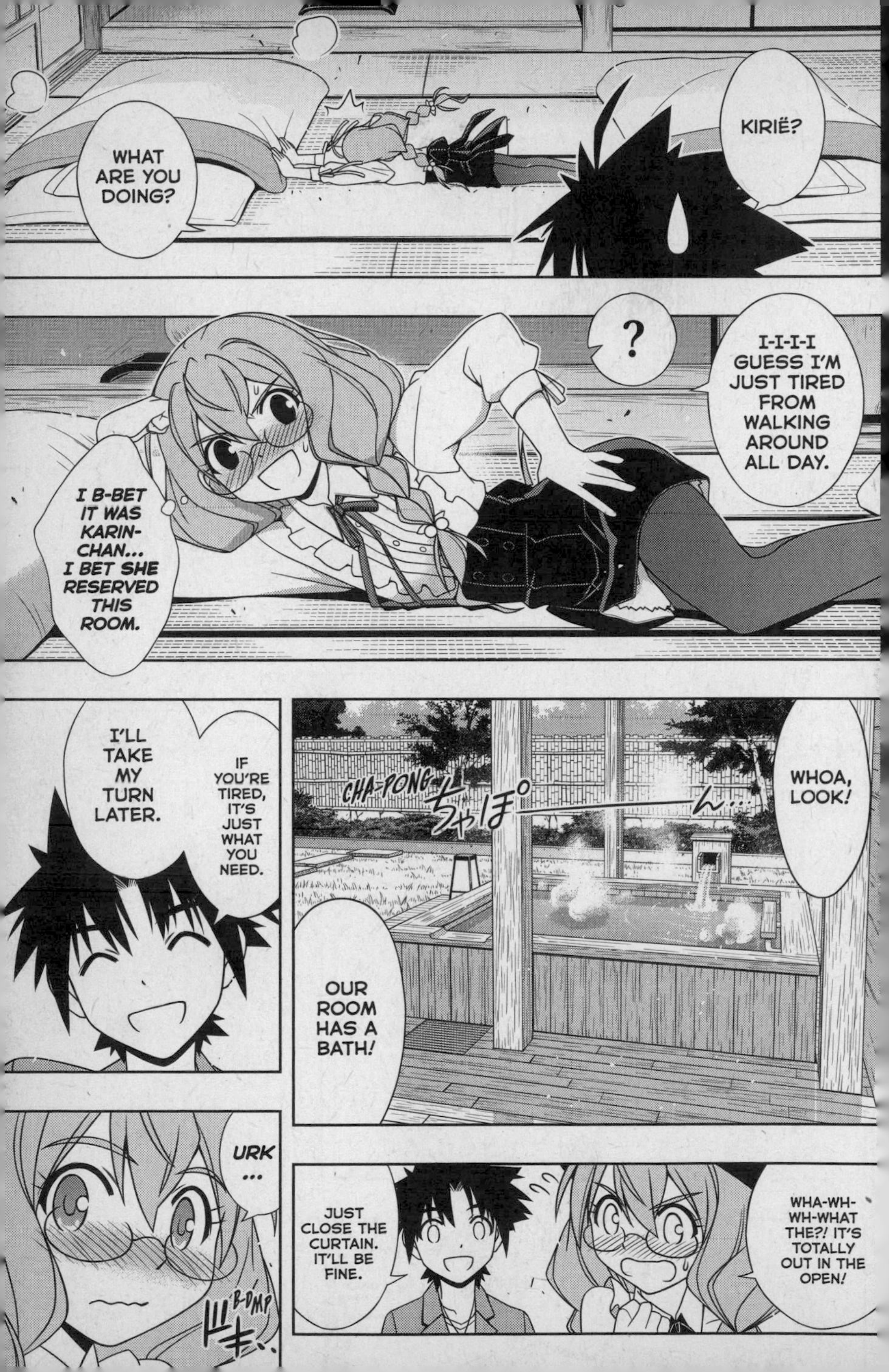
KIRIË?
WHAT ARE YOU DOING?
I-I-I-I GUESS I'M JUST TIRED FROM WALKING AROUND ALL DAY.
?
I B-BET IT WAS KARIN-CHAN... I BET SHE RESERVED THIS ROOM.
WHOA, LOOK!
CHA-PONG ちゃぽーーーん...
OUR ROOM HAS A BATH!
IF YOU'RE TIRED, IT'S JUST WHAT YOU NEED.
I'LL TAKE MY TURN LATER.
WHA-WH-WH-WHAT THE?! IT'S TOTALLY OUT IN THE OPEN!
JUST CLOSE THE CURTAIN. IT'LL BE FINE.
URK ...
B-DMP ドキ

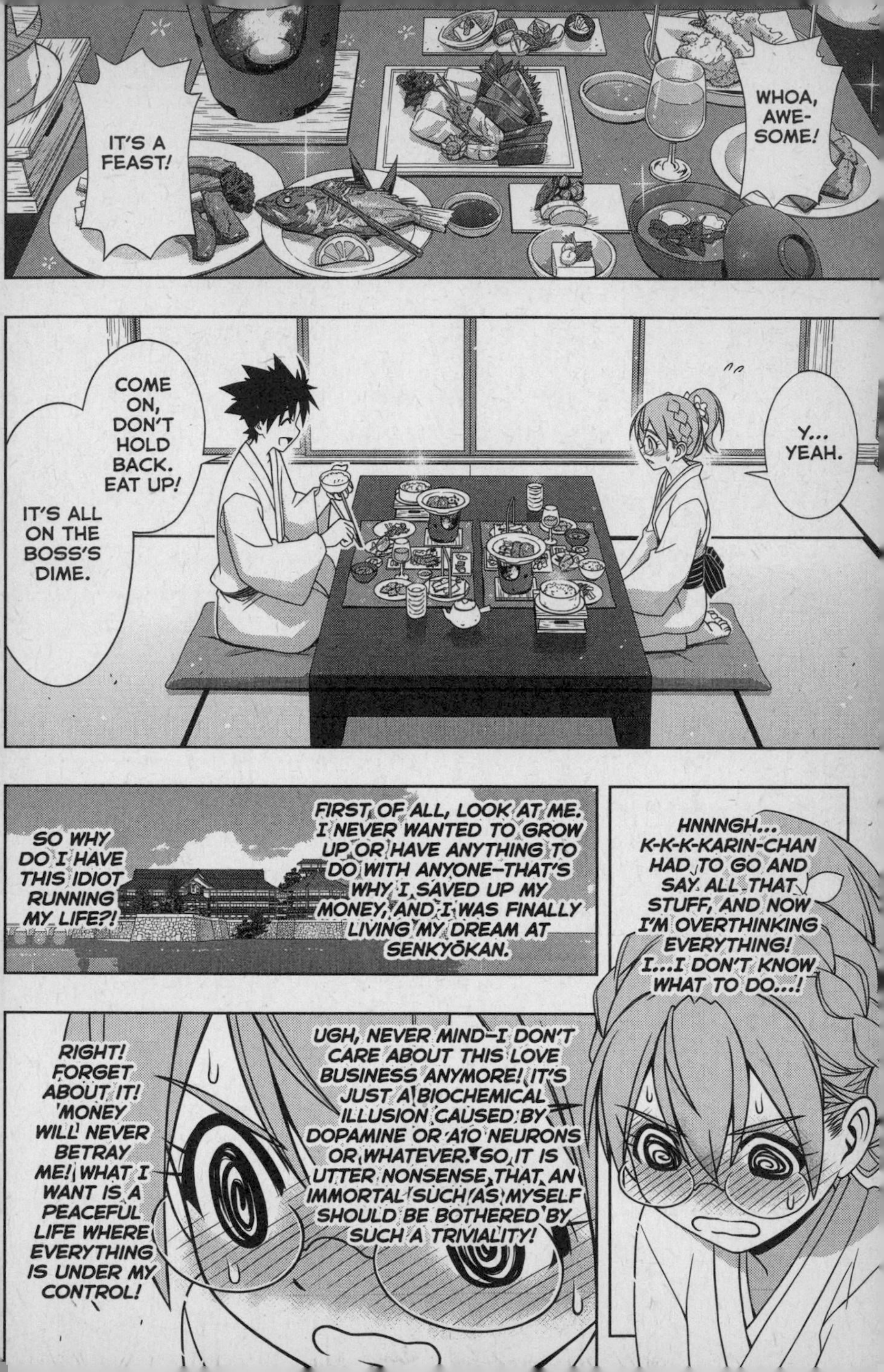

WHOA, AWE-SOME!
IT'S A FEAST!
COME ON, DON'T HOLD BACK. EAT UP!
IT'S ALL ON THE BOSS'S DIME.
Y... YEAH.
HNNNGH... K-K-K-KARIN-CHAN HAD TO GO AND SAY ALL THAT STUFF, AND NOW I'M OVERTHINKING EVERYTHING! I...I DON'T KNOW WHAT TO DO...!
FIRST OF ALL, LOOK AT ME. I NEVER WANTED TO GROW UP OR HAVE ANYTHING TO DO WITH ANYONE—THAT'S WHY I SAVED UP MY MONEY, AND I WAS FINALLY LIVING MY DREAM AT SENKYŌKAN.
SO WHY DO I HAVE THIS IDIOT RUNNING MY LIFE?!
UGH, NEVER MIND—I DON'T CARE ABOUT THIS LOVE BUSINESS ANYMORE! IT'S JUST A BIOCHEMICAL ILLUSION CAUSED BY DOPAMINE OR A10 NEURONS OR WHATEVER. SO IT IS UTTER NONSENSE THAT AN IMMORTAL SUCH AS MYSELF SHOULD BE BOTHERED BY SUCH A TRIVIALITY!
RIGHT! FORGET ABOUT IT! MONEY WILL NEVER BETRAY ME! WHAT I WANT IS A PEACEFUL LIFE WHERE EVERYTHING IS UNDER MY CONTROL!

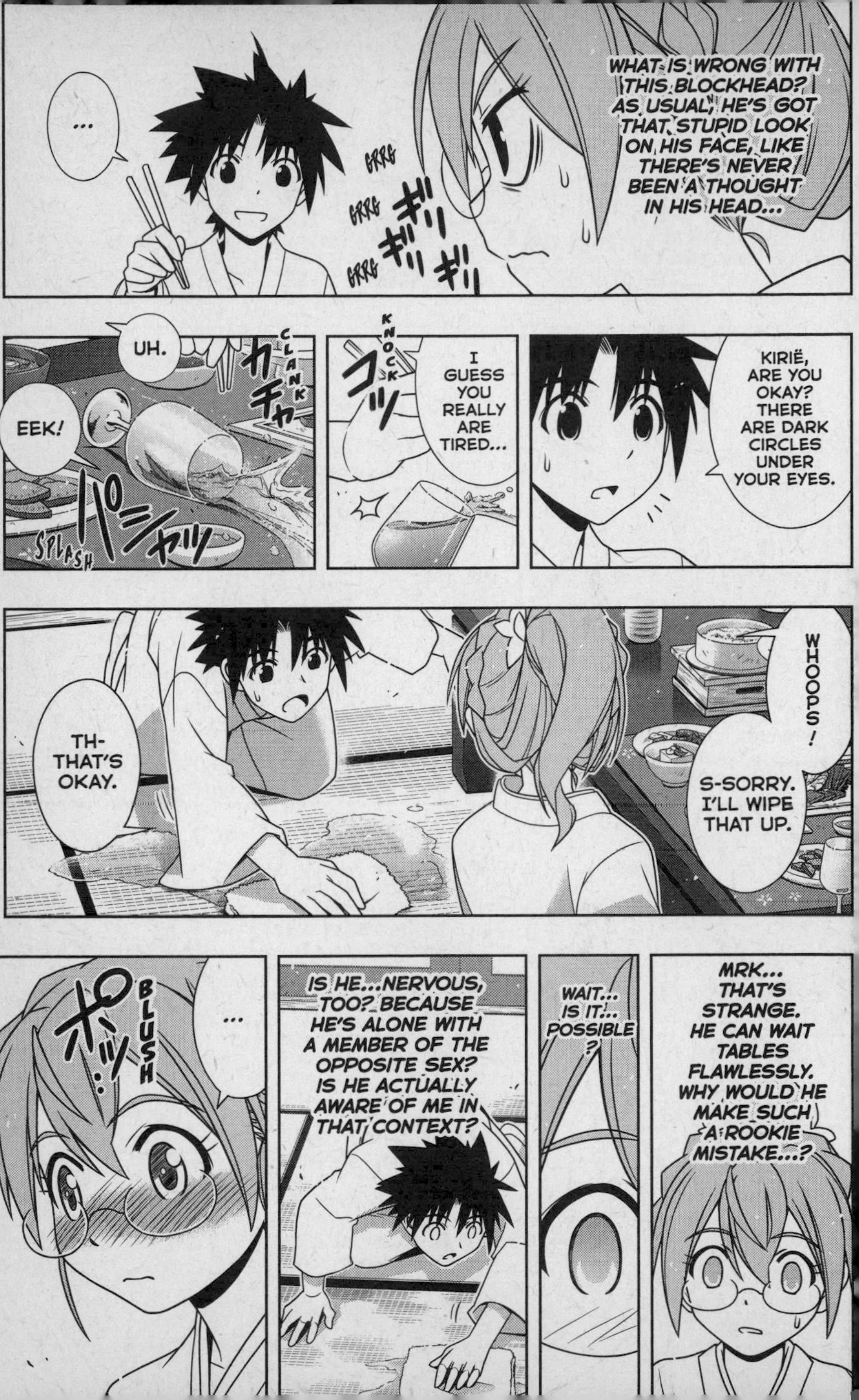
WHAT IS WRONG WITH THIS BLOCKHEAD? AS USUAL, HE'S GOT THAT STUPID LOOK ON HIS FACE, LIKE THERE'S NEVER BEEN A THOUGHT IN HIS HEAD...
GRRG
GRRG
GRRG
...
KIRIË, ARE YOU OKAY? THERE ARE DARK CIRCLES UNDER YOUR EYES.
I GUESS YOU REALLY ARE TIRED...
KNOCK
UH.
CLANK
EEK!
SPLASH
WHOOPS!
S-SORRY. I'LL WIPE THAT UP.
TH-THAT'S OKAY.
MRK... THAT'S STRANGE. HE CAN WAIT TABLES FLAWLESSLY. WHY WOULD HE MAKE SUCH A ROOKIE MISTAKE...?
WAIT... IS IT... POSSIBLE?
IS HE...NERVOUS, TOO? BECAUSE HE'S ALONE WITH A MEMBER OF THE OPPOSITE SEX? IS HE ACTUALLY AWARE OF ME IN THAT CONTEXT?
...
BLUSH

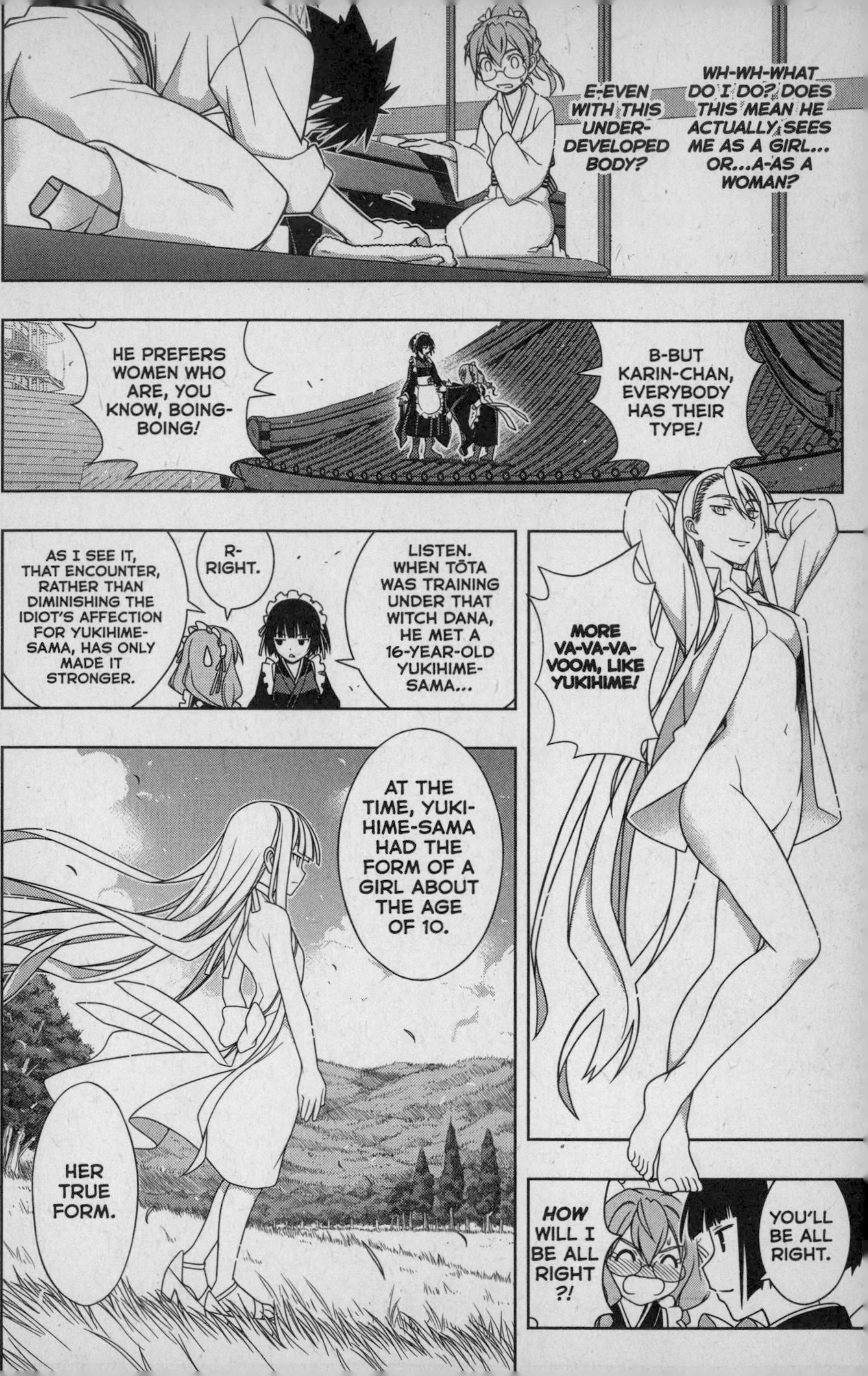
WH-WH-WHAT DO I DO? DOES THIS MEAN HE ACTUALLY SEES ME AS A GIRL... OR...A-AS A WOMAN?
E-EVEN WITH THIS UNDER-DEVELOPED BODY?
B-BUT KARIN-CHAN, EVERYBODY HAS THEIR TYPE!
HE PREFERS WOMEN WHO ARE, YOU KNOW, BOING-BOING!
MORE VA-VA-VA-VOOM, LIKE YUKIHIME!
YOU'LL BE ALL RIGHT.
HOW WILL I BE ALL RIGHT?!
LISTEN. WHEN TŌTA WAS TRAINING UNDER THAT WITCH DANA, HE MET A 16-YEAR-OLD YUKIHIME-SAMA...
R-RIGHT.
AS I SEE IT, THAT ENCOUNTER, RATHER THAN DIMINISHING THE IDIOT'S AFFECTION FOR YUKIHIME-SAMA, HAS ONLY MADE IT STRONGER.
AT THE TIME, YUKI-HIME-SAMA HAD THE FORM OF A GIRL ABOUT THE AGE OF 10.
HER TRUE FORM.

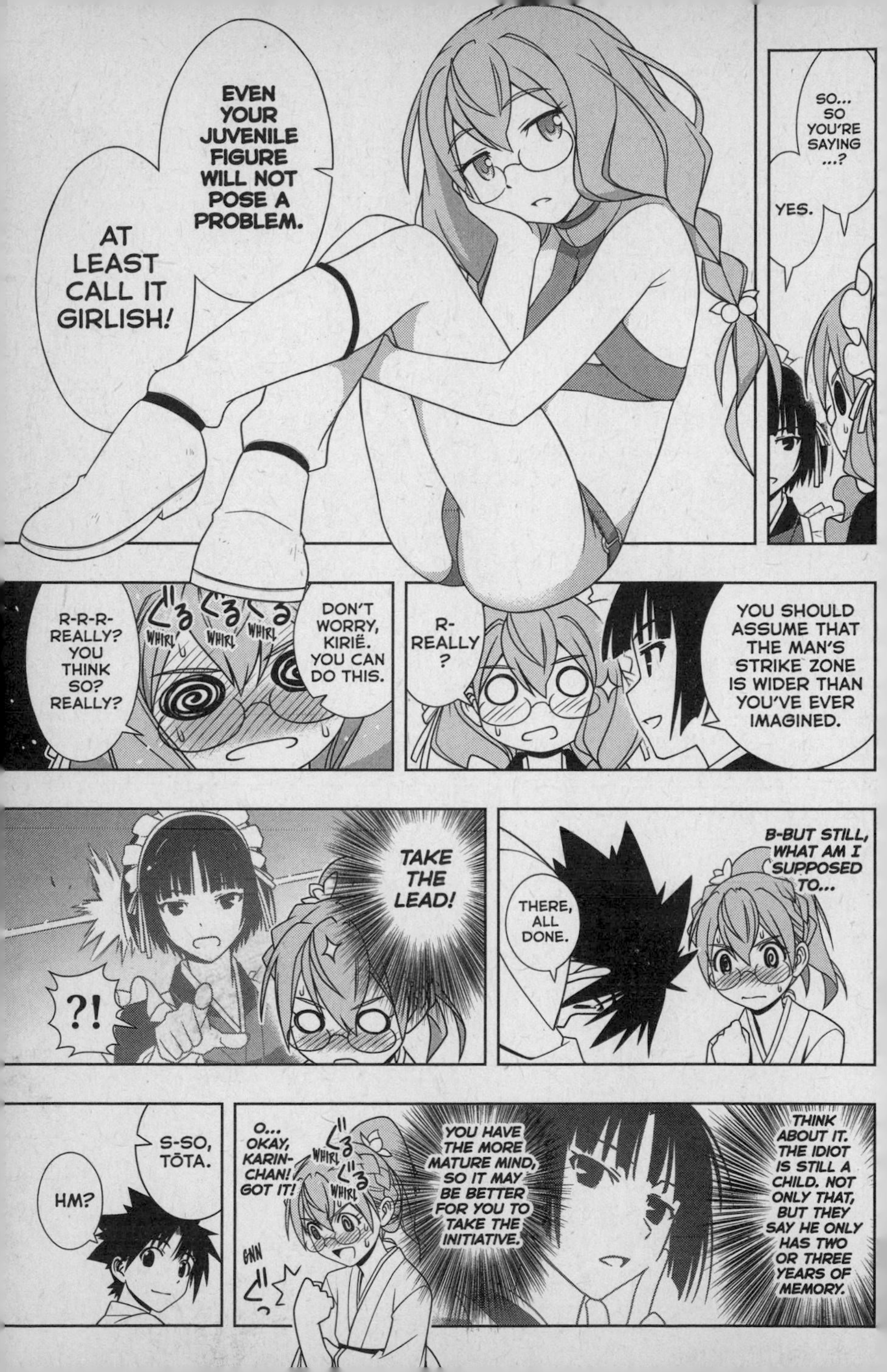
SO... SO YOU'RE SAYING ...?
YES.
EVEN YOUR JUVENILE FIGURE WILL NOT POSE A PROBLEM.
AT LEAST CALL IT GIRLISH!
YOU SHOULD ASSUME THAT THE MAN'S STRIKE ZONE IS WIDER THAN YOU'VE EVER IMAGINED.
R-REALLY?
DON'T WORRY, KIRIË. YOU CAN DO THIS.
ぐるぐるぐる
WHIRL WHIRL WHIRL
R-R-R-REALLY? YOU THINK SO? REALLY?
B-BUT STILL, WHAT AM I SUPPOSED TO...
THERE, ALL DONE.
TAKE THE LEAD!
?!
THINK ABOUT IT. THE IDIOT IS STILL A CHILD. NOT ONLY THAT, BUT THEY SAY HE ONLY HAS TWO OR THREE YEARS OF MEMORY.
YOU HAVE THE MORE MATURE MIND, SO IT MAY BE BETTER FOR YOU TO TAKE THE INITIATIVE.
ぐる WHIRL ぐる WHIRL
O... OKAY, KARIN-CHAN! GOT IT!
GNN ぐ
S-SO, TŌTA.
HM?

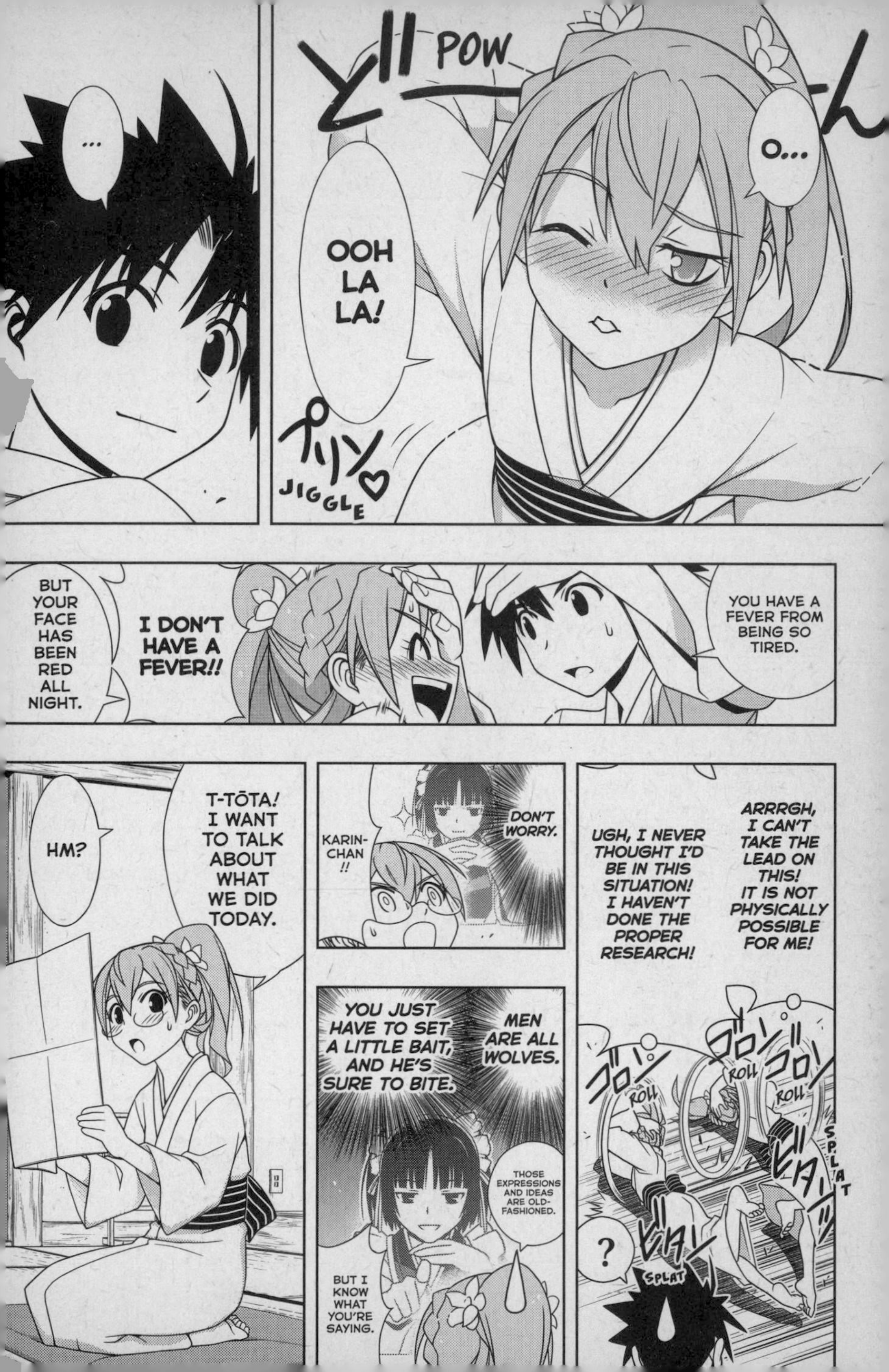
POW
O...
OOH LA LA!
JIGGLE
...
YOU HAVE A FEVER FROM BEING SO TIRED.
I DON'T HAVE A FEVER!!
BUT YOUR FACE HAS BEEN RED ALL NIGHT.
ARRRGH, I CAN'T TAKE THE LEAD ON THIS! IT IS NOT PHYSICALLY POSSIBLE FOR ME!
UGH, I NEVER THOUGHT I'D BE IN THIS SITUATION! I HAVEN'T DONE THE PROPER RESEARCH!
ROLL
ROLL
ROLL
SPLAT
SPLAT
?
DON'T WORRY.
KARIN-CHAN!!
MEN ARE ALL WOLVES.
YOU JUST HAVE TO SET A LITTLE BAIT, AND HE'S SURE TO BITE.
THOSE EXPRESSIONS AND IDEAS ARE OLD-FASHIONED.
BUT I KNOW WHAT YOU'RE SAYING.
T-TŌTA! I WANT TO TALK ABOUT WHAT WE DID TODAY.
HM?

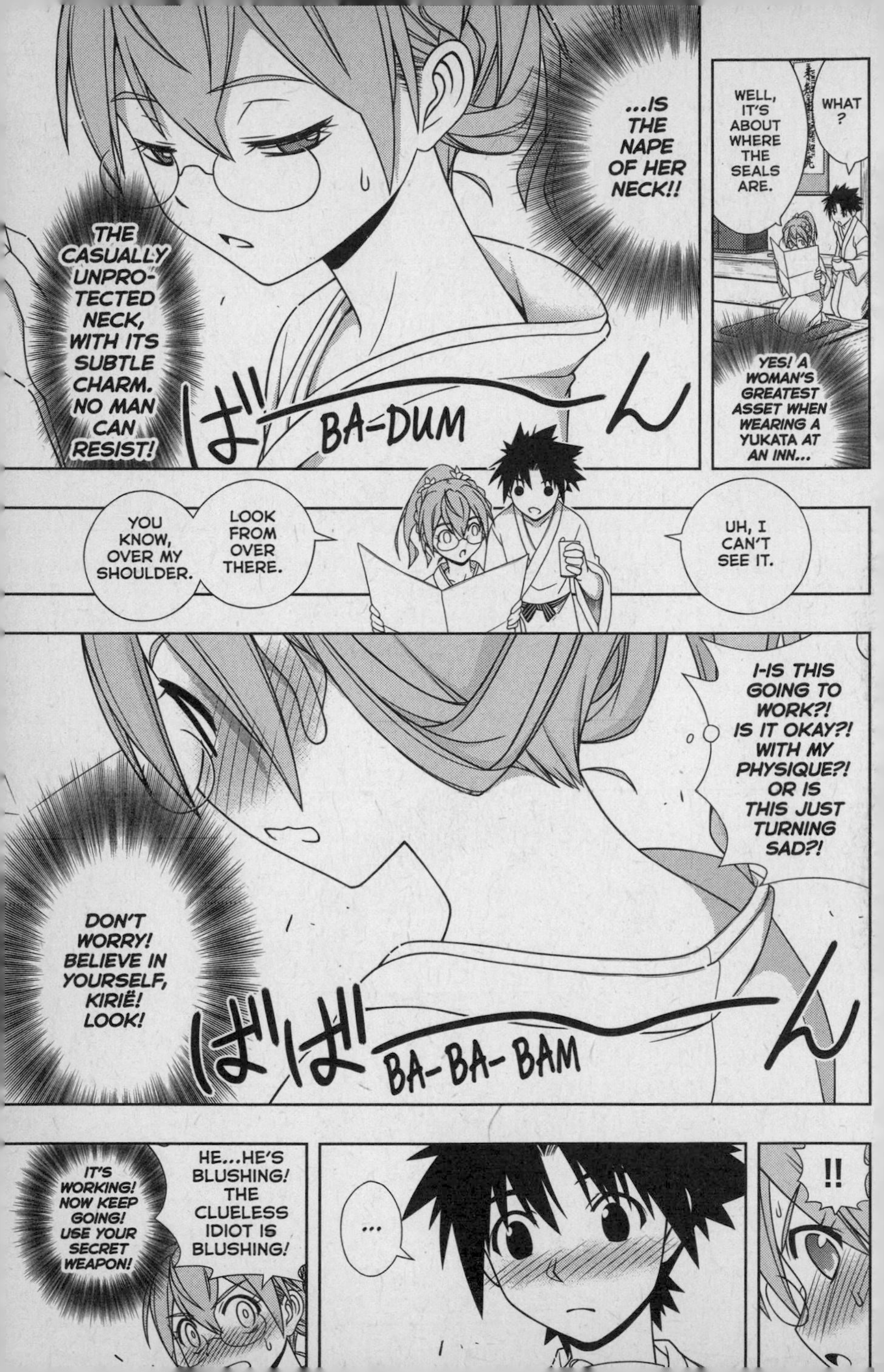
WHAT?
WELL, IT'S ABOUT WHERE THE SEALS ARE.
YES! A WOMAN'S GREATEST ASSET WHEN WEARING A YUKATA AT AN INN...
...IS THE NAPE OF HER NECK!!
THE CASUALLY UNPROTECTED NECK, WITH ITS SUBTLE CHARM. NO MAN CAN RESIST!
ば!ーん
BA-DUM
UH, I CAN'T SEE IT.
LOOK FROM OVER THERE.
YOU KNOW, OVER MY SHOULDER.
I-IS THIS GOING TO WORK?! IS IT OKAY?! WITH MY PHYSIQUE?! OR IS THIS JUST TURNING SAD?!
DON'T WORRY! BELIEVE IN YOURSELF, KIRIË! LOOK!
ば!ば!ーん
BA-BA-BAM
!!
...
HE...HE'S BLUSHING! THE CLUELESS IDIOT IS BLUSHING!
IT'S WORKING! NOW KEEP GOING! USE YOUR SECRET WEAPON!

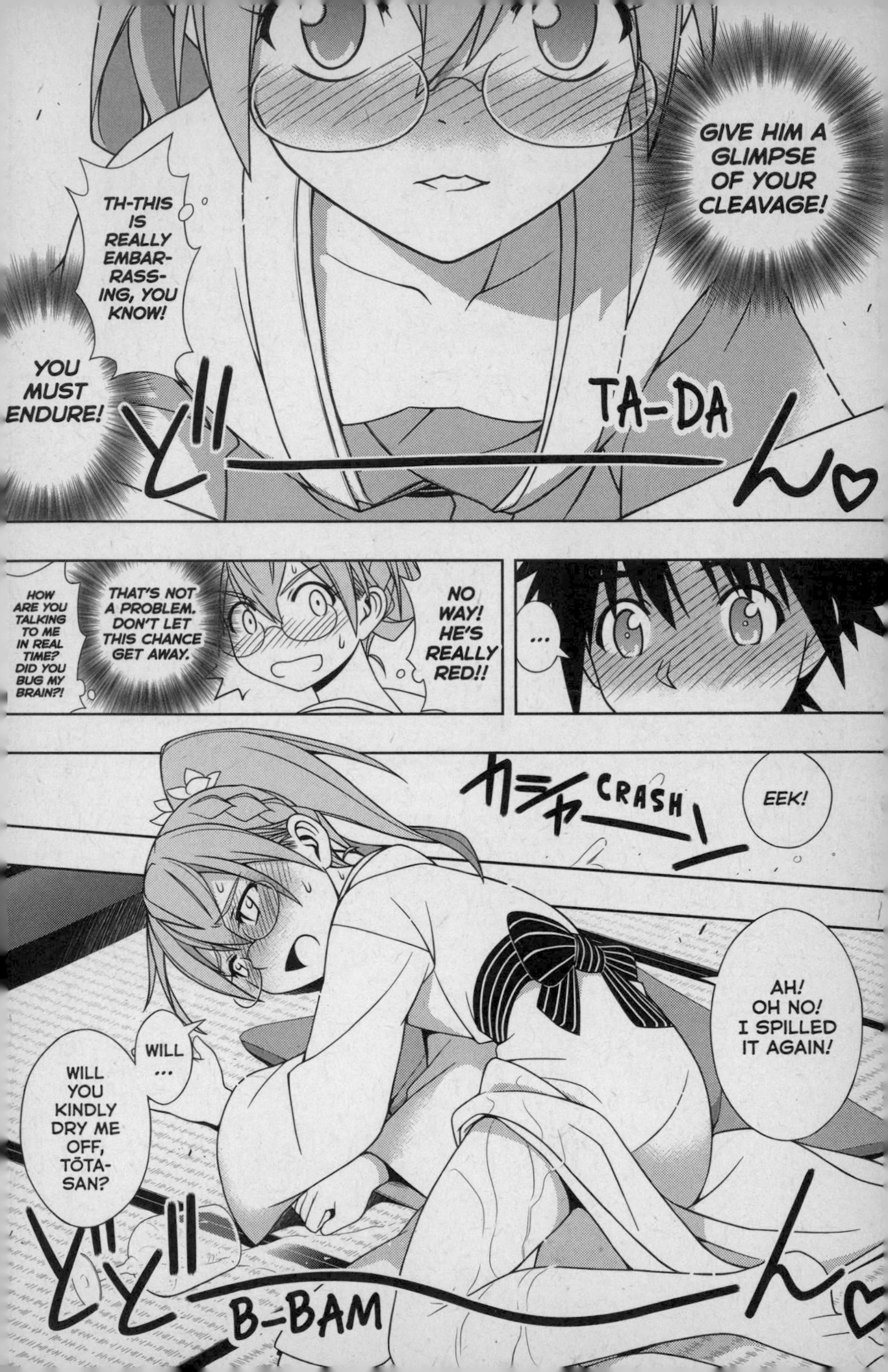
GIVE HIM A GLIMPSE OF YOUR CLEAVAGE!
TA-DA
TH-THIS IS REALLY EMBARRASSING, YOU KNOW!
YOU MUST ENDURE!
...
NO WAY! HE'S REALLY RED!!
THAT'S NOT A PROBLEM. DON'T LET THIS CHANCE GET AWAY.
HOW ARE YOU TALKING TO ME IN REAL TIME? DID YOU BUG MY BRAIN?!
EEK!
CRASH
AH! OH NO! I SPILLED IT AGAIN!
WILL...
WILL YOU KINDLY DRY ME OFF, TŌTA-SAN?
B-BAM

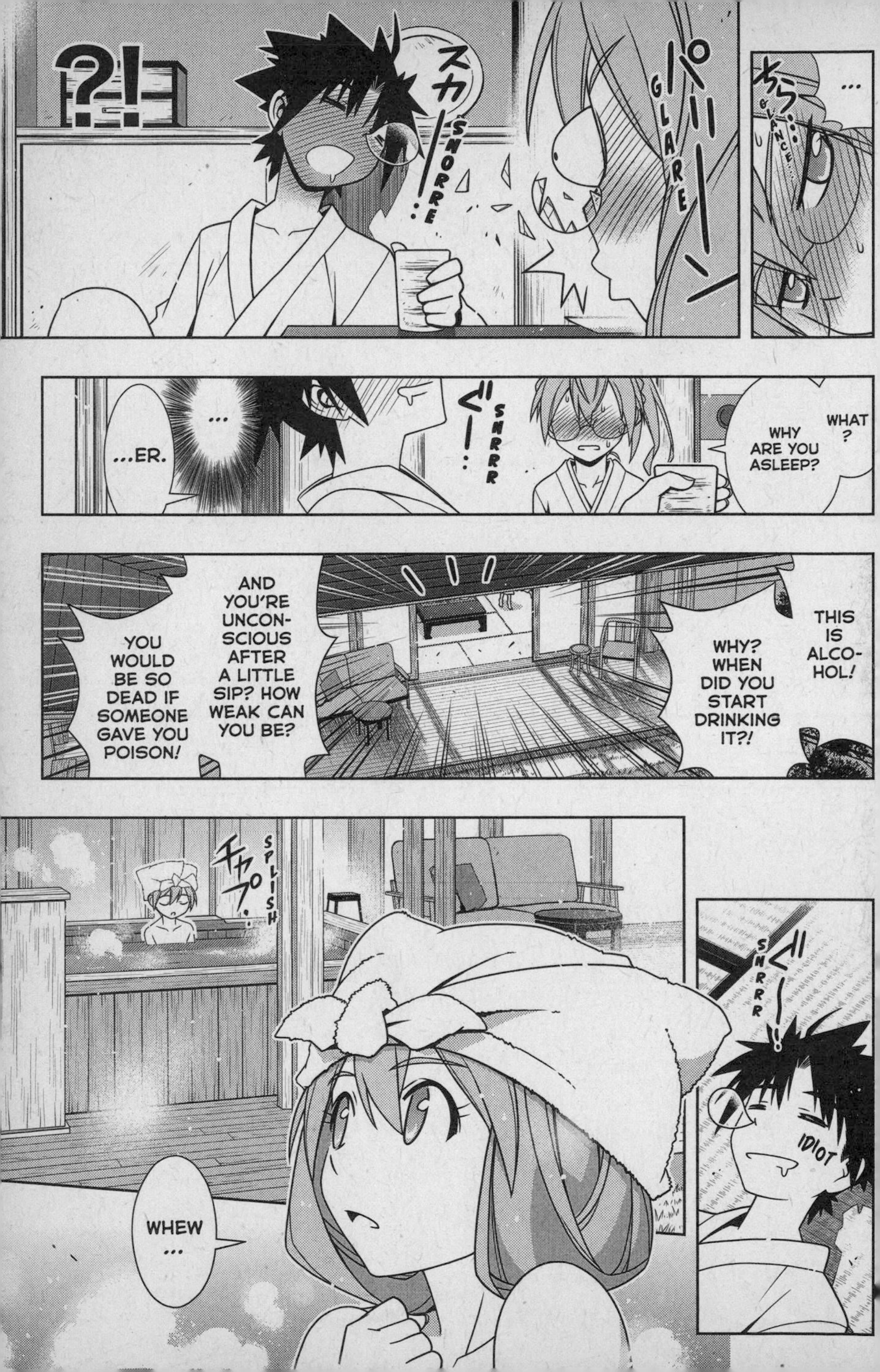
ちら…
GLANCE…
…
パーー
GLARE
スカー
SNORRE
?!
WHAT?
WHY ARE YOU ASLEEP?
ぐー
SNRRR
…
…ER.
THIS IS ALCOHOL!
WHY? WHEN DID YOU START DRINKING IT?!
AND YOU'RE UNCONSCIOUS AFTER A LITTLE SIP? HOW WEAK CAN YOU BE?
YOU WOULD BE SO DEAD IF SOMEONE GAVE YOU POISON!
ぐー
SNRRR
IDIOT
チャプ
SPLISH
WHEW …

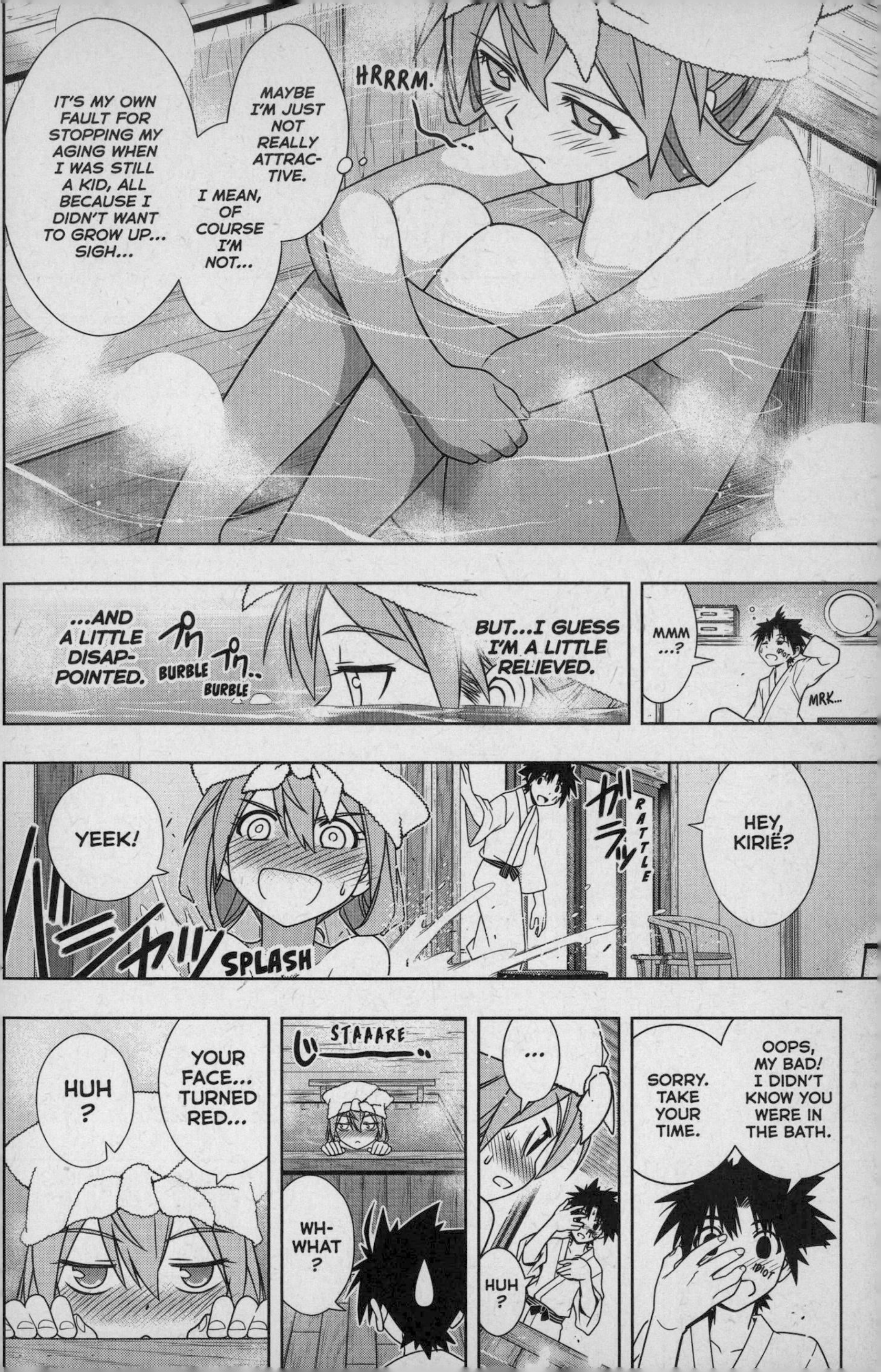
HRRRM.
MAYBE I'M JUST NOT REALLY ATTRACTIVE.
I MEAN, OF COURSE I'M NOT...
IT'S MY OWN FAULT FOR STOPPING MY AGING WHEN I WAS STILL A KID, ALL BECAUSE I DIDN'T WANT TO GROW UP... SIGH...
MMM ...?
MRK...
BUT...I GUESS I'M A LITTLE RELIEVED.
...AND A LITTLE DISAPPOINTED.
BURBLE
BURBLE
HEY, KIRIË?
RATTLE
YEEK!
SPLASH
OOPS, MY BAD! I DIDN'T KNOW YOU WERE IN THE BATH.
SORRY. TAKE YOUR TIME.
IDIOT
...
HUH ?
STAAARE
WH- WHAT ?
YOUR FACE... TURNED RED...
HUH ?

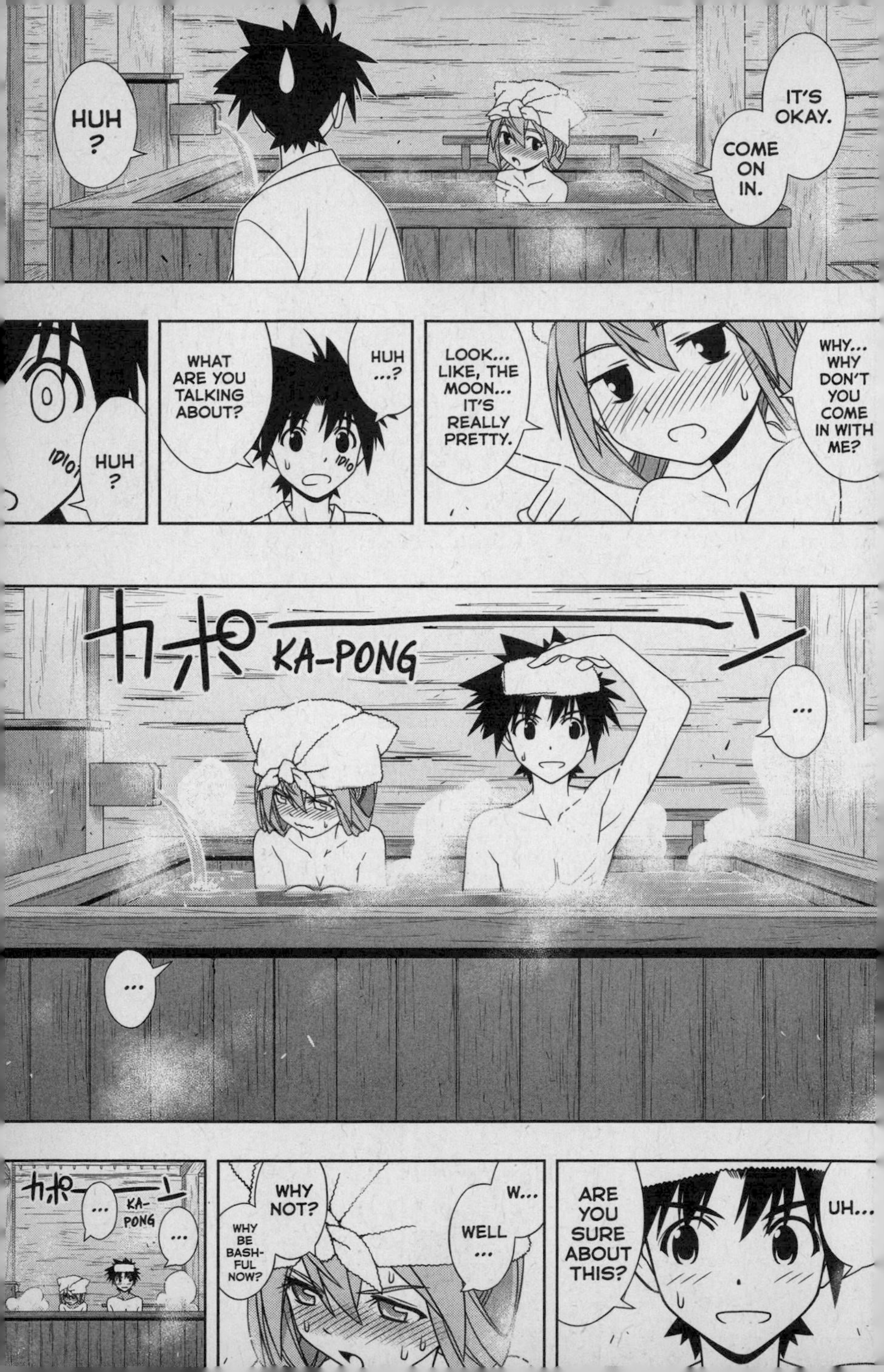
IT'S OKAY.
COME ON IN.
HUH ?
WHY... WHY DON'T YOU COME IN WITH ME?
LOOK... LIKE, THE MOON... IT'S REALLY PRETTY.
HUH ...?
WHAT ARE YOU TALKING ABOUT?
IDIO
HUH ?
IDIOT
カポ——ン
KA-PONG
...
...
UH...
ARE YOU SURE ABOUT THIS?
W... WELL ...
WHY NOT?
WHY BE BASHFUL NOW?
カポ——ン
KA-PONG
...
...

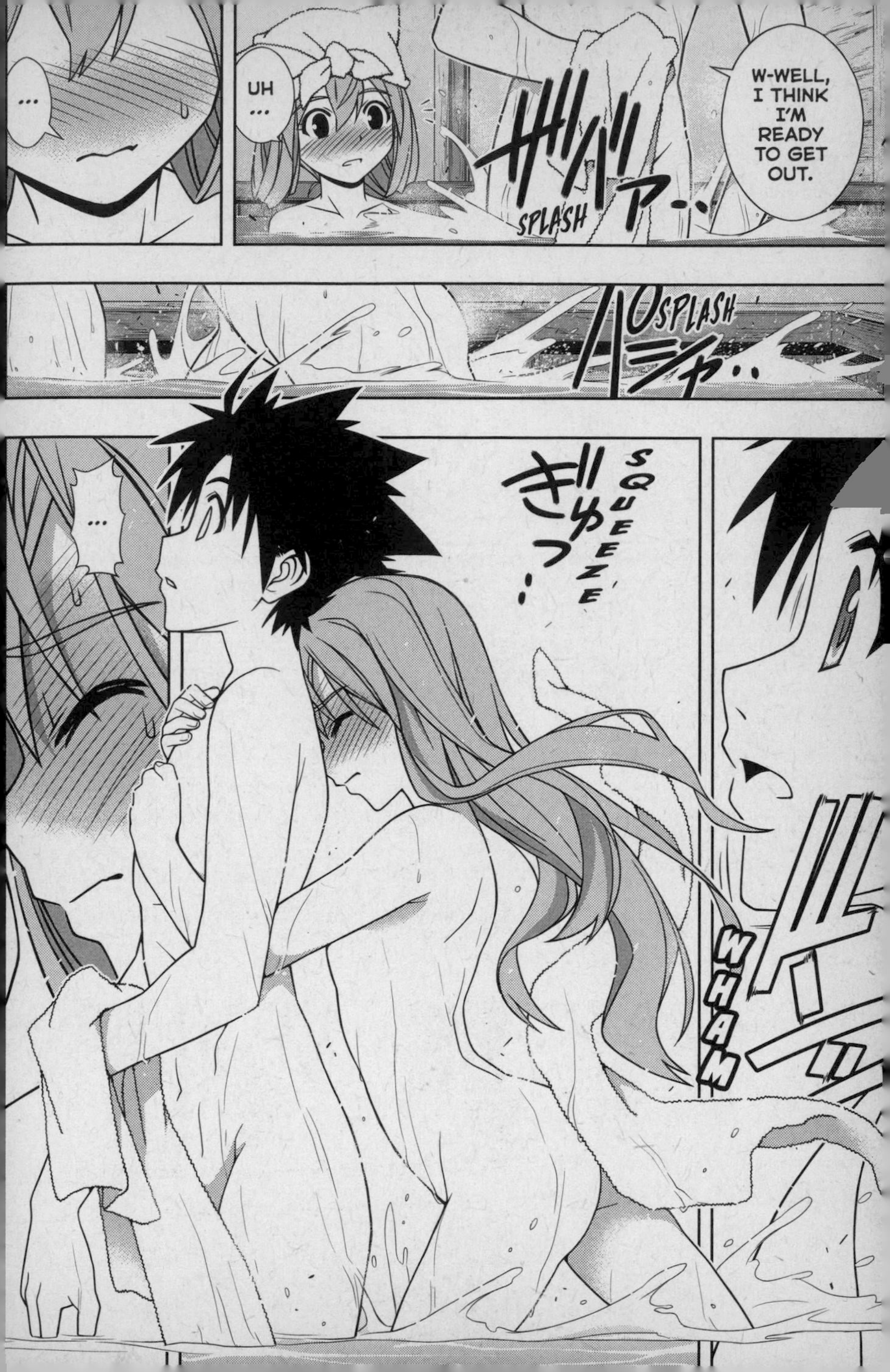
W-WELL, I THINK I'M READY TO GET OUT.
ザバァ..
SPLASH
UH ...
...
バシャ..
SPLASH
WHAM
きゅっ..
SQUEEZE
...

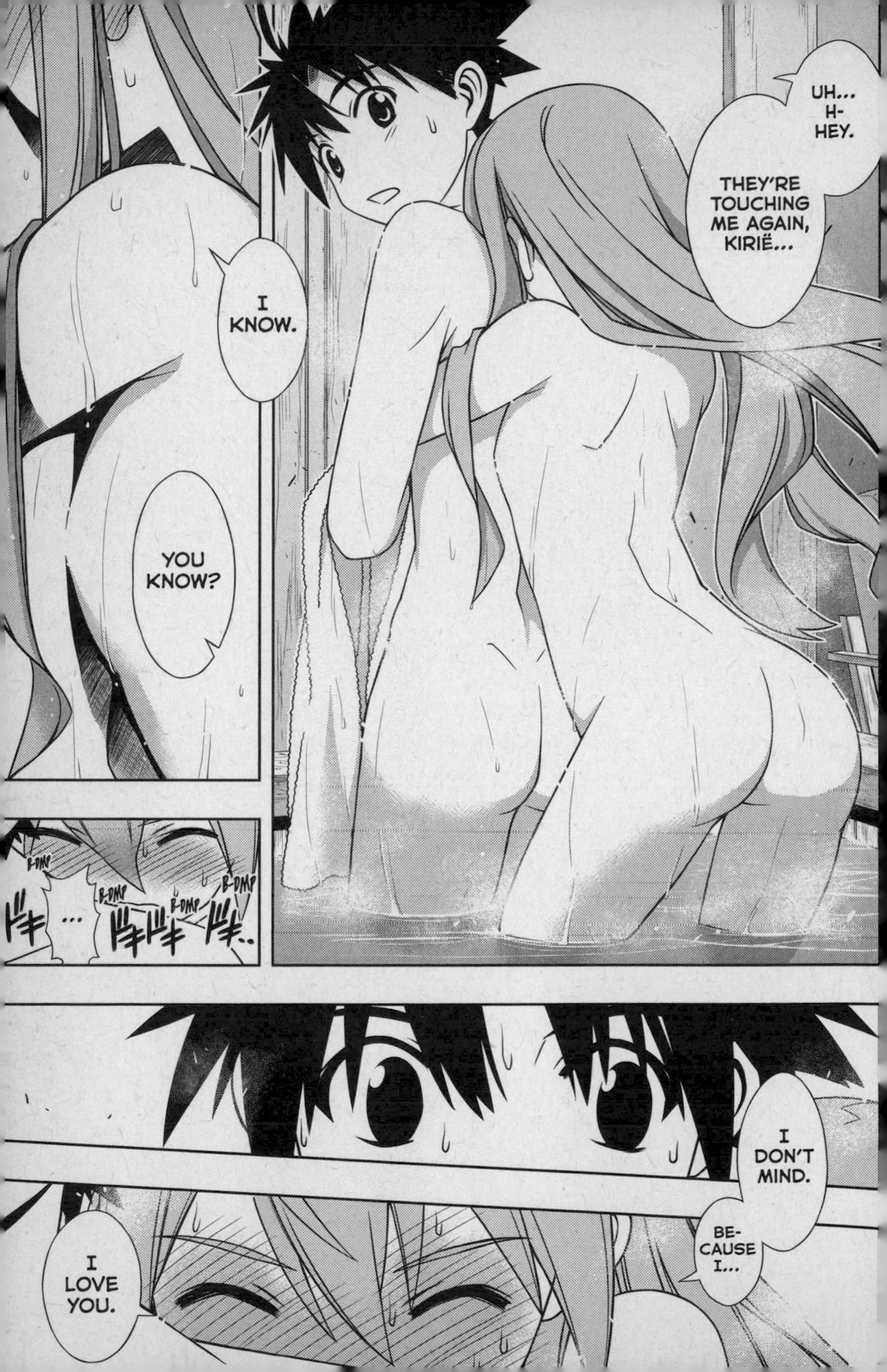
UH... H- HEY.
THEY'RE TOUCHING ME AGAIN, KIRIË...
I KNOW.
YOU KNOW?
B-DMP
B-DMP
B-DMP
B-DMP
...
I DON'T MIND.
BE-CAUSE I...
I LOVE YOU.

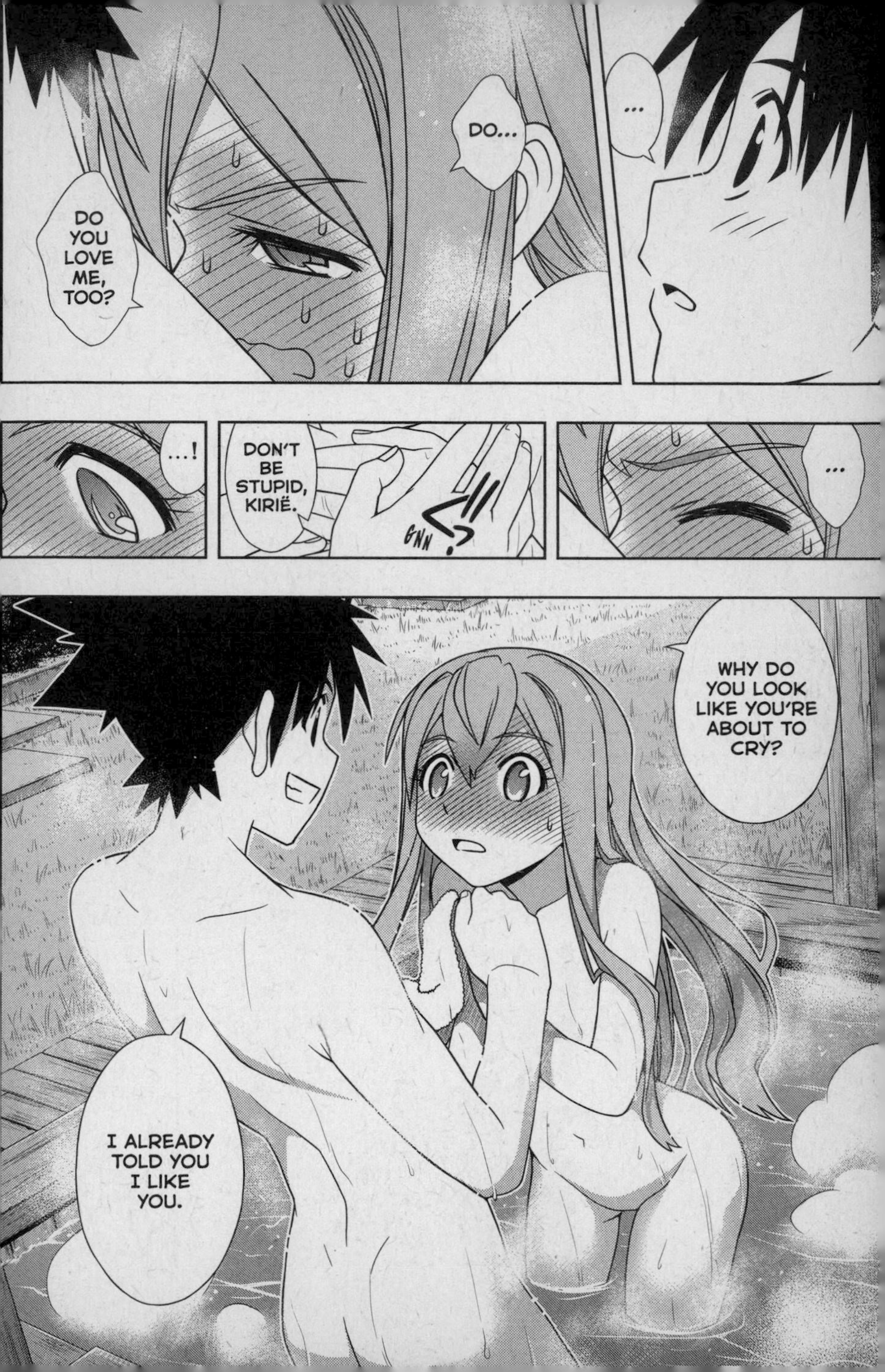
...
DO...
DO YOU LOVE ME, TOO?
...
DON'T BE STUPID, KIRIË.
GNN
...!
WHY DO YOU LOOK LIKE YOU'RE ABOUT TO CRY?
I ALREADY TOLD YOU I LIKE YOU.

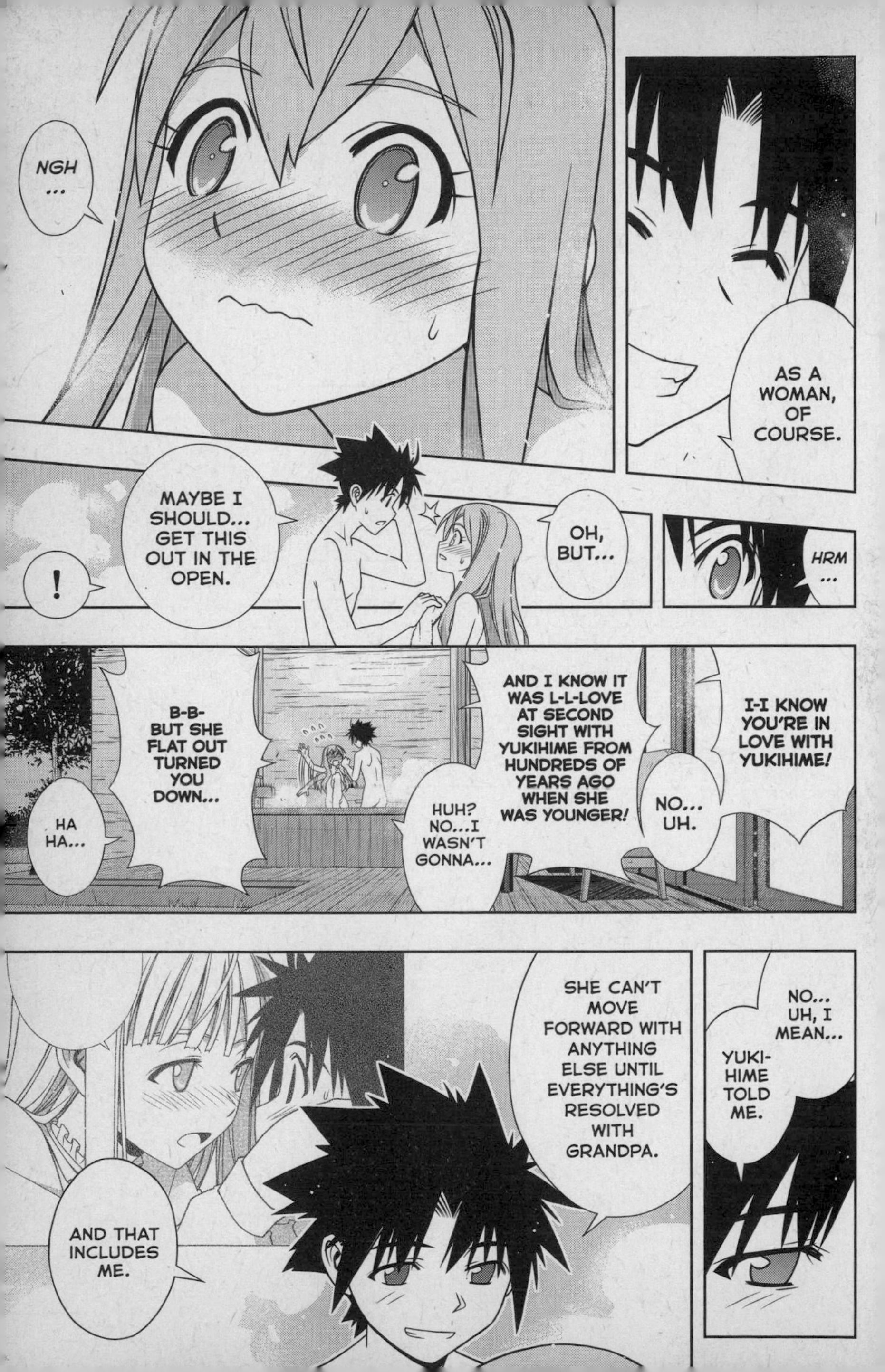
AS A WOMAN, OF COURSE.
NGH ...
HRM ...
OH, BUT...
MAYBE I SHOULD... GET THIS OUT IN THE OPEN.
!
I-I KNOW YOU'RE IN LOVE WITH YUKIHIME!
NO... UH.
AND I KNOW IT WAS L-L-LOVE AT SECOND SIGHT WITH YUKIHIME FROM HUNDREDS OF YEARS AGO WHEN SHE WAS YOUNGER!
HUH? NO...I WASN'T GONNA...
B-B- BUT SHE FLAT OUT TURNED YOU DOWN...
HA HA...
NO... UH, I MEAN...
YUKI-HIME TOLD ME.
SHE CAN'T MOVE FORWARD WITH ANYTHING ELSE UNTIL EVERYTHING'S RESOLVED WITH GRANDPA.
AND THAT INCLUDES ME.

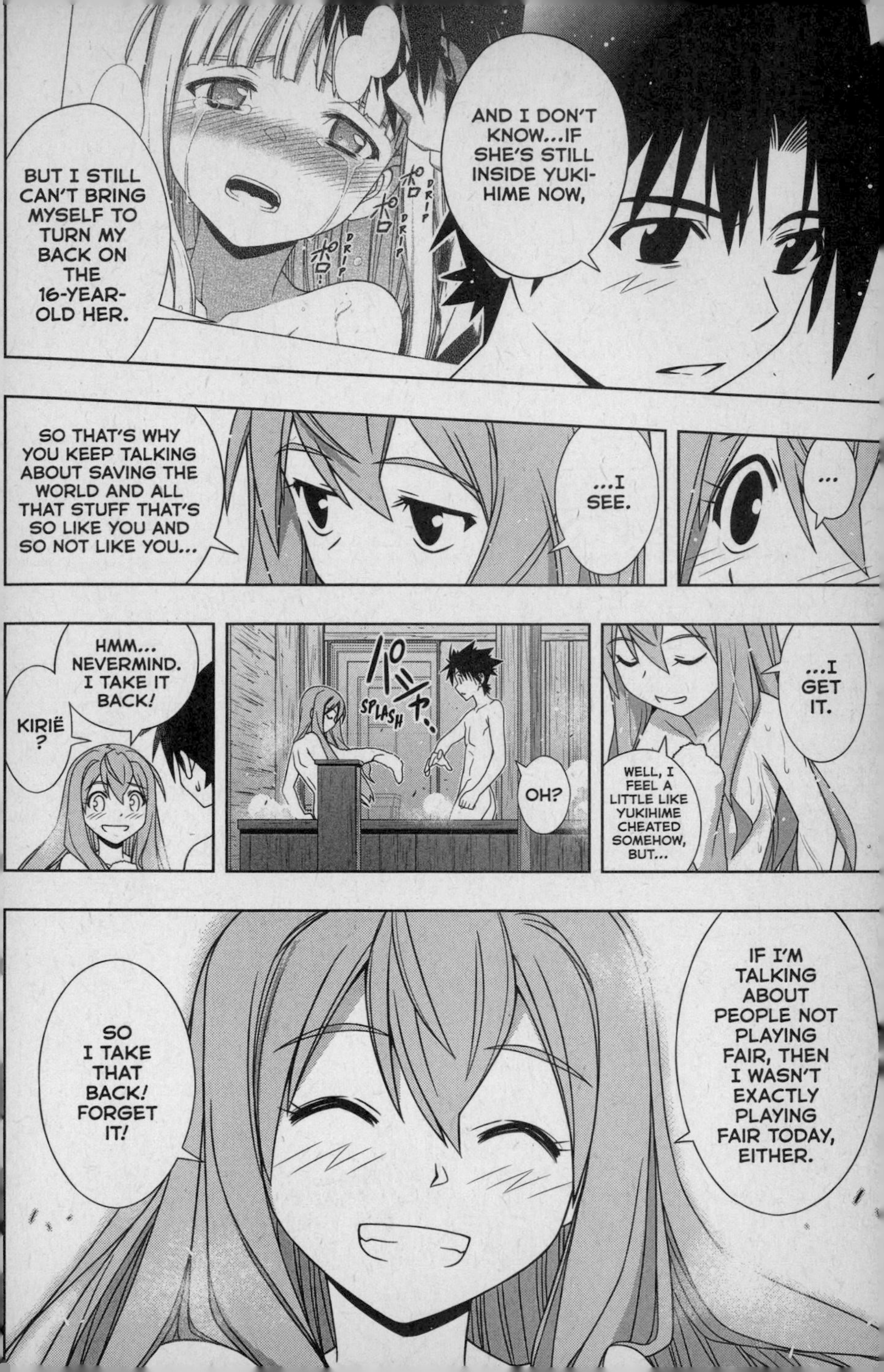

AND I DON'T KNOW...IF SHE'S STILL INSIDE YUKI-HIME NOW,
ポロ ポロ ポロ DRIP DRIP DRIP
BUT I STILL CAN'T BRING MYSELF TO TURN MY BACK ON THE 16-YEAR-OLD HER.
...
...I SEE.
SO THAT'S WHY YOU KEEP TALKING ABOUT SAVING THE WORLD AND ALL THAT STUFF THAT'S SO LIKE YOU AND SO NOT LIKE YOU...
...I GET IT.
WELL, I FEEL A LITTLE LIKE YUKIHIME CHEATED SOMEHOW, BUT...
パシャ... SPLASH
OH?
HMM... NEVERMIND. I TAKE IT BACK!
KIRIË?
IF I'M TALKING ABOUT PEOPLE NOT PLAYING FAIR, THEN I WASN'T EXACTLY PLAYING FAIR TODAY, EITHER.
SO I TAKE THAT BACK! FORGET IT!

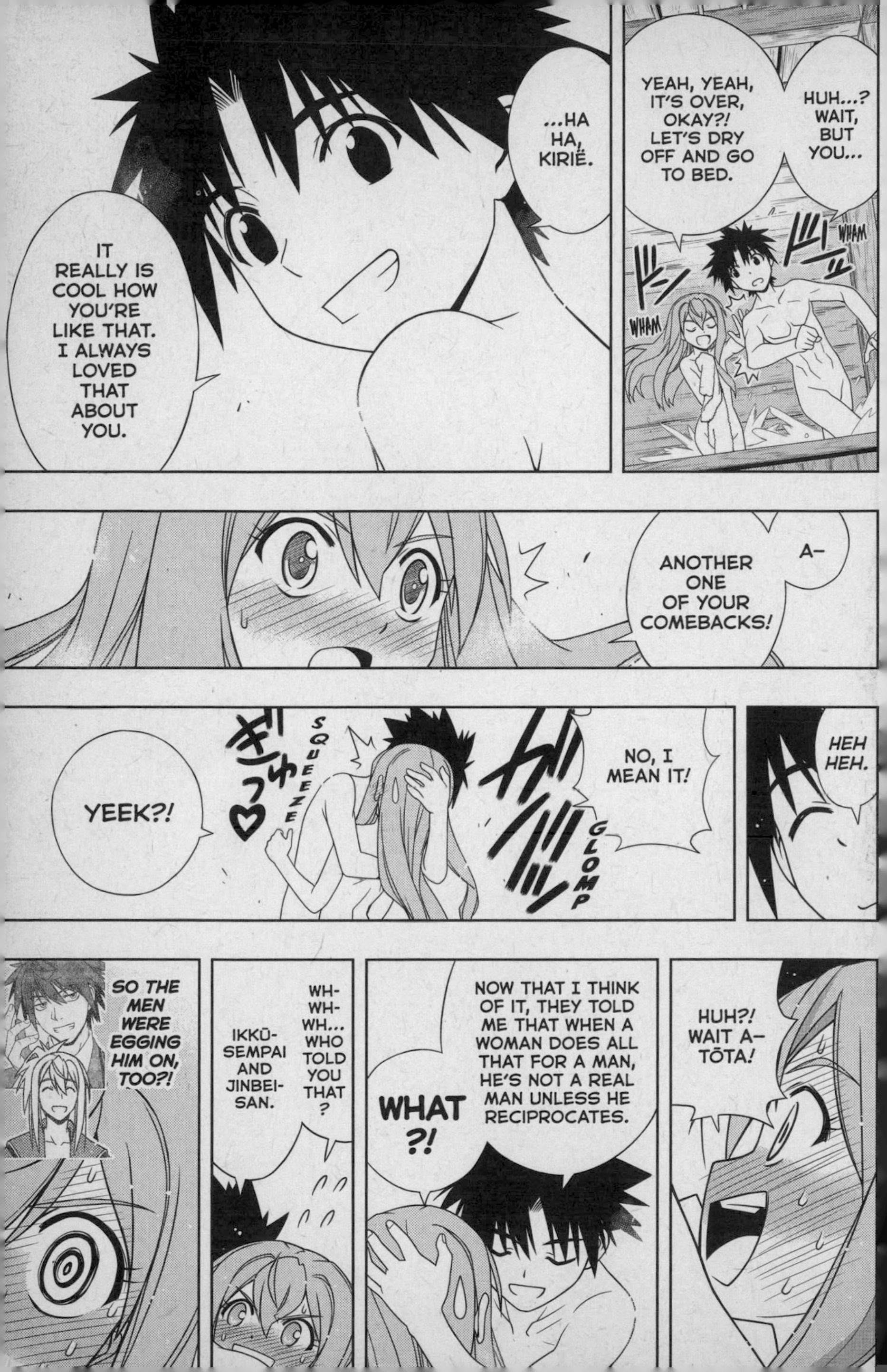
HUH...? WAIT, BUT YOU...
YEAH, YEAH, IT'S OVER, OKAY?! LET'S DRY OFF AND GO TO BED.
WHAM
WHAM
...HA HA, KIRIË.
IT REALLY IS COOL HOW YOU'RE LIKE THAT. I ALWAYS LOVED THAT ABOUT YOU.
A–
ANOTHER ONE OF YOUR COMEBACKS!
HEH HEH.
NO, I MEAN IT!
GLOMP
SQUEEZE
YEEK?!
HUH?! WAIT A– TŌTA!
NOW THAT I THINK OF IT, THEY TOLD ME THAT WHEN A WOMAN DOES ALL THAT FOR A MAN, HE'S NOT A REAL MAN UNLESS HE RECIPROCATES.
WHAT?!
WH-WH-WH... WHO TOLD YOU THAT?
IKKŪ-SEMPAI AND JINBEI-SAN.
SO THE MEN WERE EGGING HIM ON, TOO?!

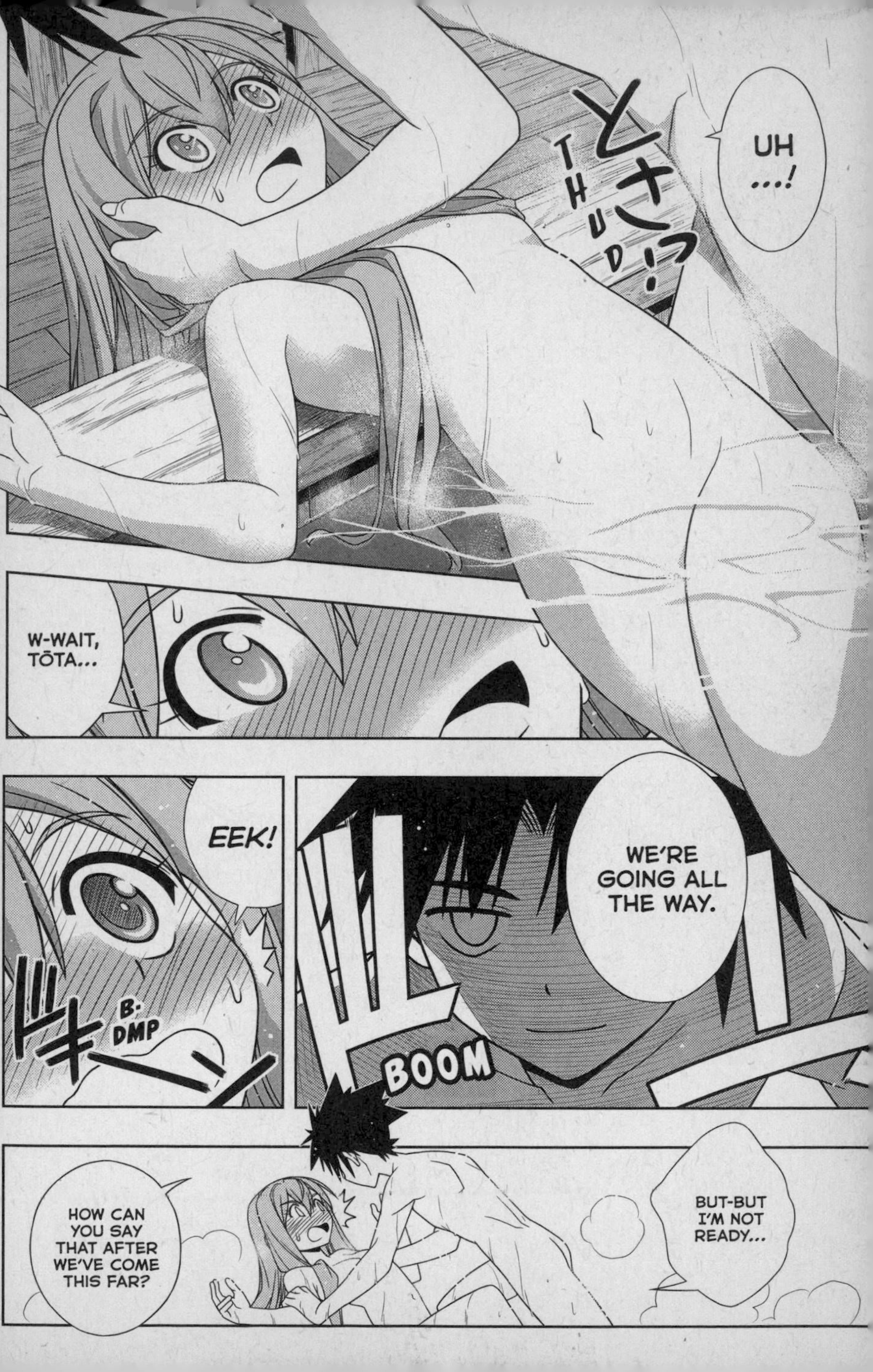

UH ...!
とさっ!
THUD
W-WAIT, TŌTA...
WE'RE GOING ALL THE WAY.
BOOM
EEK!
B-DMP
BUT-BUT I'M NOT READY...
HOW CAN YOU SAY THAT AFTER WE'VE COME THIS FAR?

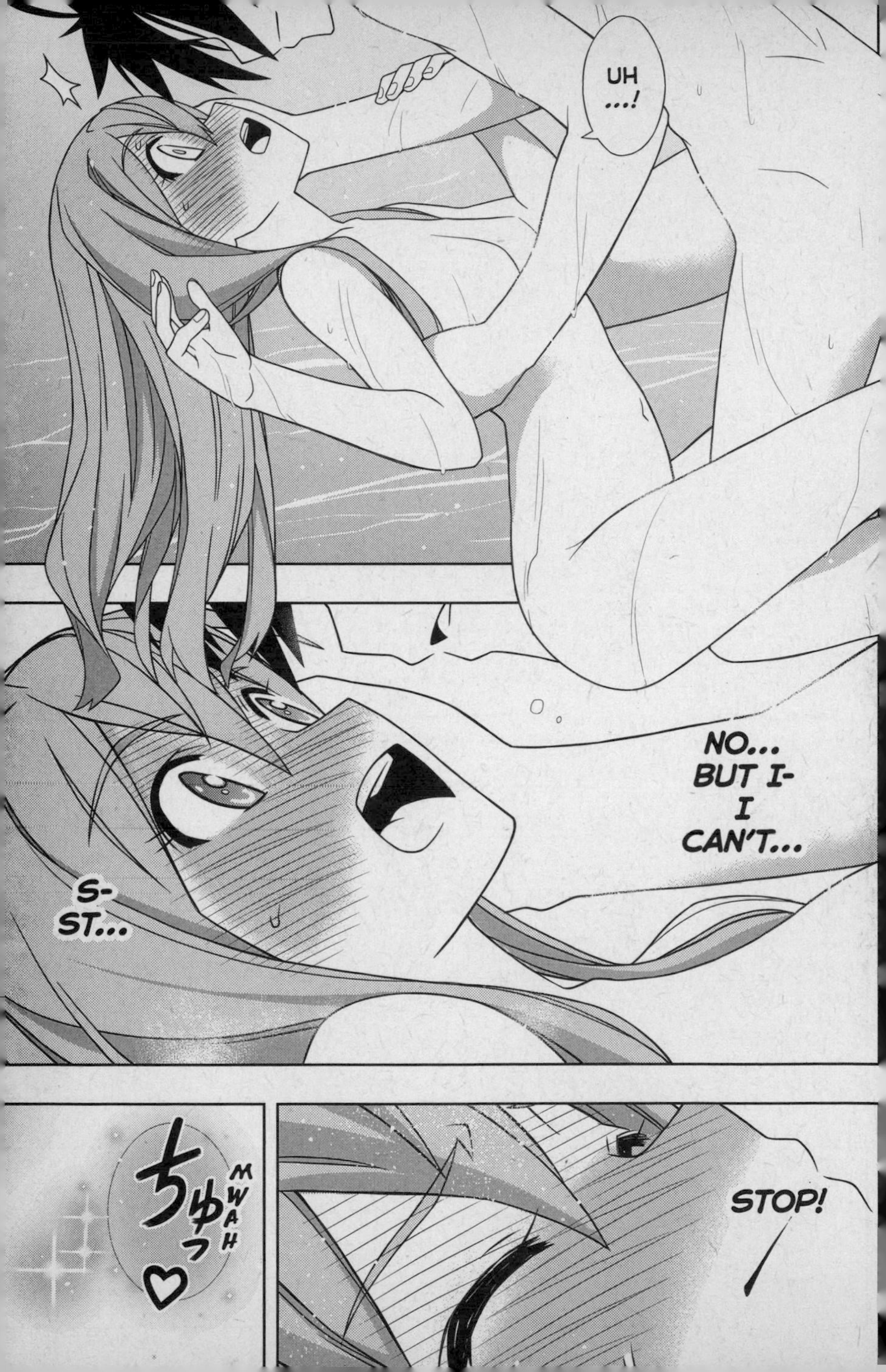
UH ...!
NO... BUT I- I CAN'T...
S- ST...
STOP!
ちゅっ♡
MWAH

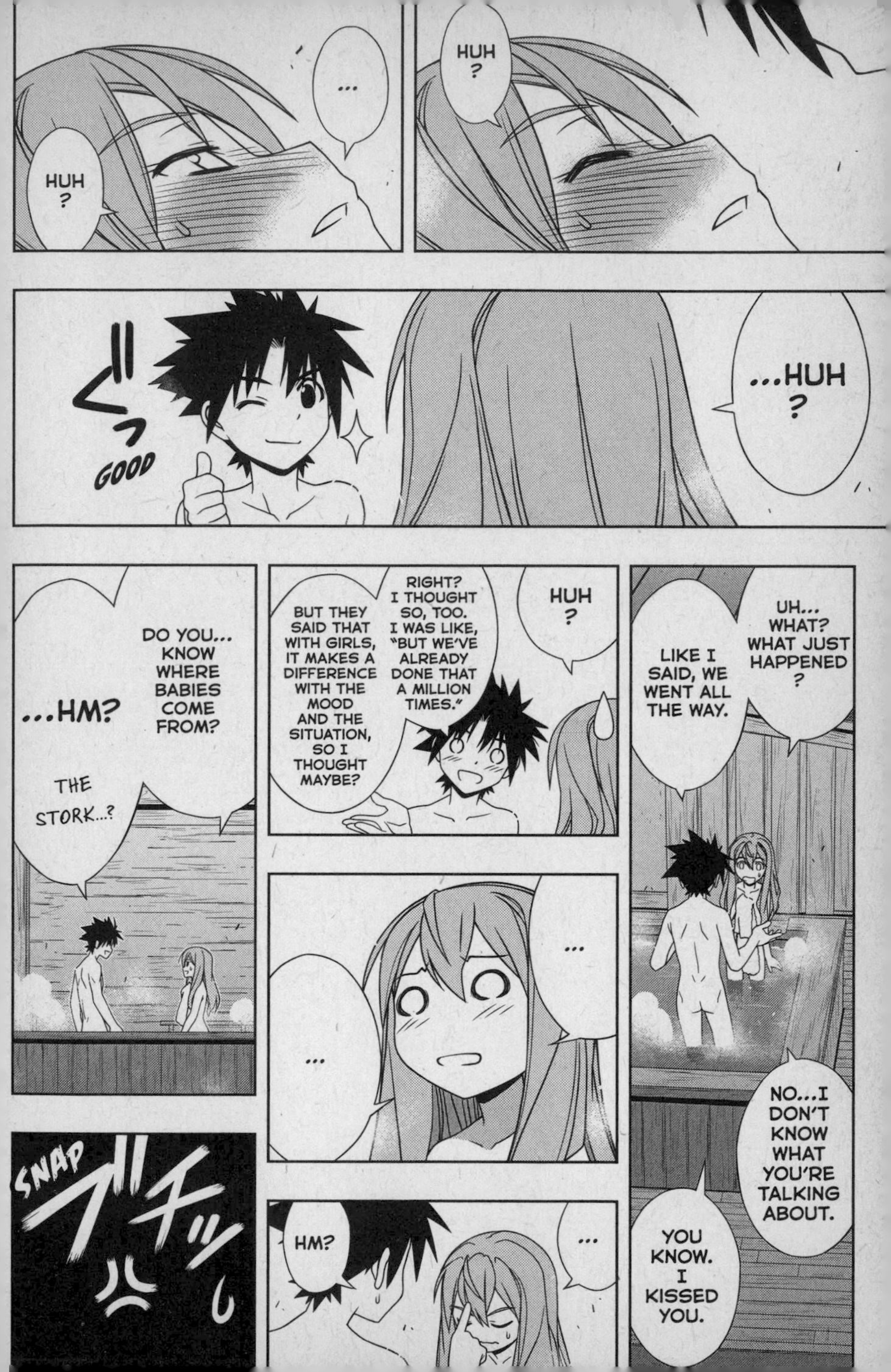
HUH ?
...
HUH ?
...HUH ?
GOOD
UH... WHAT? WHAT JUST HAPPENED ?
LIKE I SAID, WE WENT ALL THE WAY.
NO...I DON'T KNOW WHAT YOU'RE TALKING ABOUT.
YOU KNOW. I KISSED YOU.
HUH ?
RIGHT? I THOUGHT SO, TOO. I WAS LIKE, "BUT WE'VE ALREADY DONE THAT A MILLION TIMES."
BUT THEY SAID THAT WITH GIRLS, IT MAKES A DIFFERENCE WITH THE MOOD AND THE SITUATION, SO I THOUGHT MAYBE?
...
...
...
HM?
DO YOU... KNOW WHERE BABIES COME FROM?
...HM?
THE STORK...?
SNAP

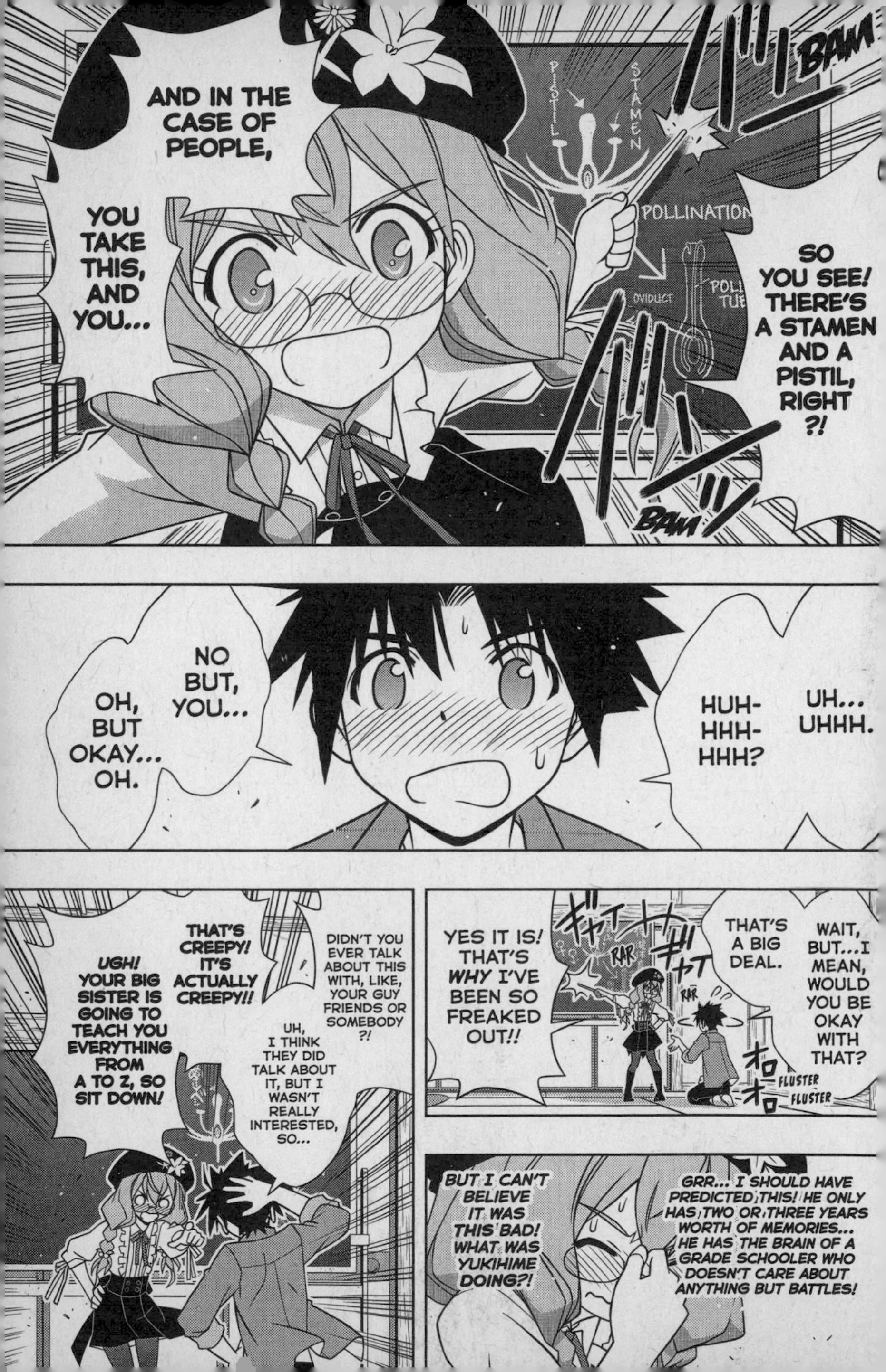
SO YOU SEE! THERE'S A STAMEN AND A PISTIL, RIGHT?!
BAM
PISTIL
STAMEN
POLLINATION
OVIDUCT
AND IN THE CASE OF PEOPLE,
YOU TAKE THIS, AND YOU...
BAM
UH... UHHH.
HUH-HHH-HHH?
NO BUT, YOU...
OH, BUT OKAY... OH.
WAIT, BUT...I MEAN, WOULD YOU BE OKAY WITH THAT?
THAT'S A BIG DEAL.
YES IT IS! THAT'S *WHY* I'VE BEEN SO FREAKED OUT!!
RAR
RAR
FLUSTER FLUSTER
GRR... I SHOULD HAVE PREDICTED THIS! HE ONLY HAS TWO OR THREE YEARS WORTH OF MEMORIES... HE HAS THE BRAIN OF A GRADE SCHOOLER WHO DOESN'T CARE ABOUT ANYTHING BUT BATTLES!
BUT I CAN'T BELIEVE IT WAS THIS BAD! WHAT WAS YUKIHIME DOING?!
DIDN'T YOU EVER TALK ABOUT THIS WITH, LIKE, YOUR GUY FRIENDS OR SOMEBODY?!
UH, I THINK THEY DID TALK ABOUT IT, BUT I WASN'T REALLY INTERESTED, SO...
THAT'S CREEPY! IT'S ACTUALLY CREEPY!!
UGH! YOUR BIG SISTER IS GOING TO TEACH YOU EVERYTHING FROM A TO Z, SO SIT DOWN!

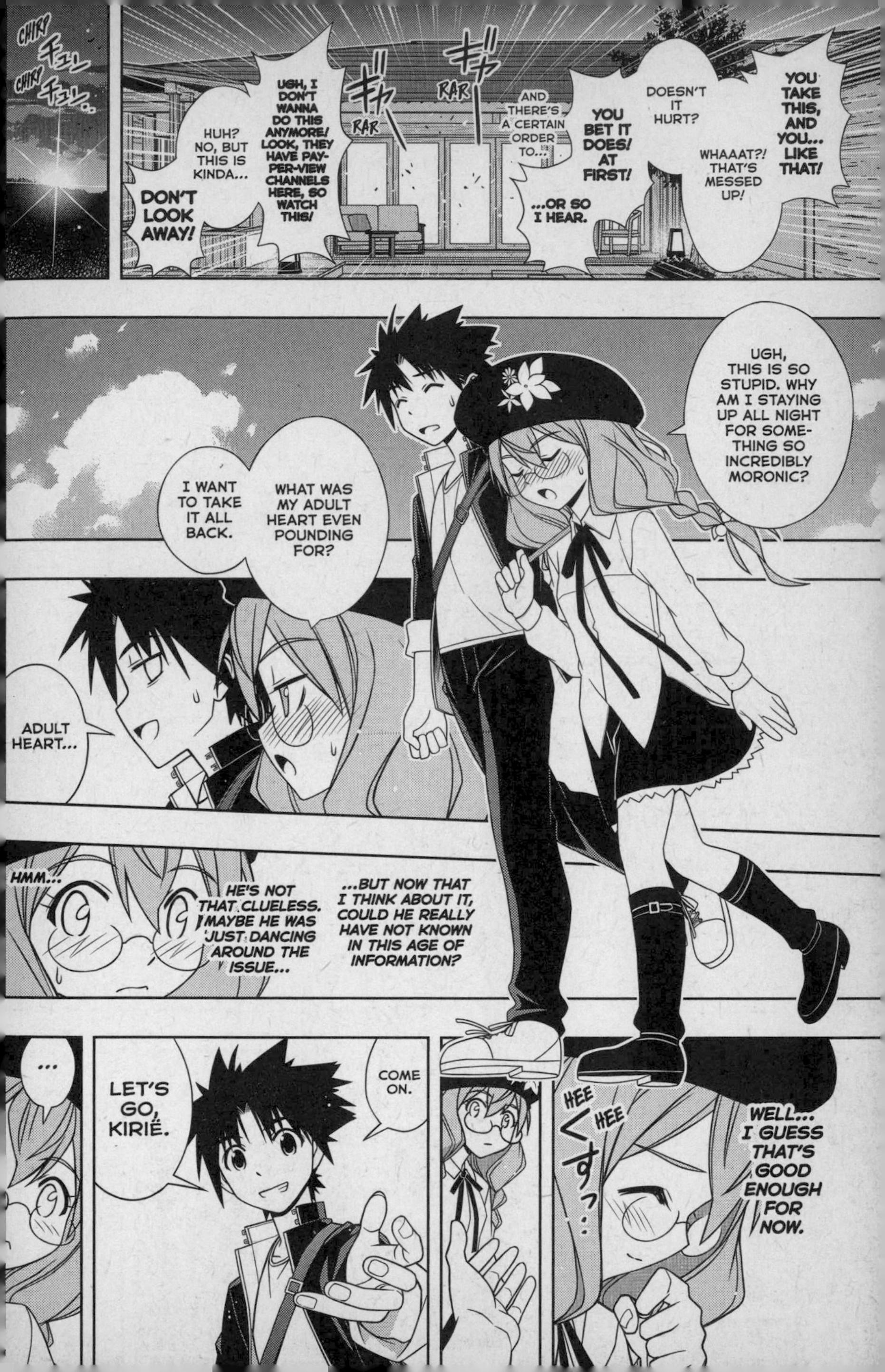
YOU TAKE THIS, AND YOU... LIKE THAT!
WHAAAT?! THAT'S MESSED UP!
DOESN'T IT HURT?
YOU BET IT DOES! AT FIRST!
...OR SO I HEAR.
AND THERE'S A CERTAIN ORDER TO...
RAR
RAR
UGH, I DON'T WANNA DO THIS ANYMORE! LOOK, THEY HAVE PAY-PER-VIEW CHANNELS HERE, SO WATCH THIS!
HUH? NO, BUT THIS IS KINDA...
DON'T LOOK AWAY!
CHIRP
CHIRP
UGH, THIS IS SO STUPID. WHY AM I STAYING UP ALL NIGHT FOR SOMETHING SO INCREDIBLY MORONIC?
WHAT WAS MY ADULT HEART EVEN POUNDING FOR?
I WANT TO TAKE IT ALL BACK.
ADULT HEART...
...BUT NOW THAT I THINK ABOUT IT, COULD HE REALLY HAVE NOT KNOWN IN THIS AGE OF INFORMATION?
HE'S NOT THAT CLUELESS. MAYBE HE WAS JUST DANCING AROUND THE ISSUE...
HMM...
WELL... I GUESS THAT'S GOOD ENOUGH FOR NOW.
HEE HEE
くすっ
COME ON.
LET'S GO, KIRIË.
...

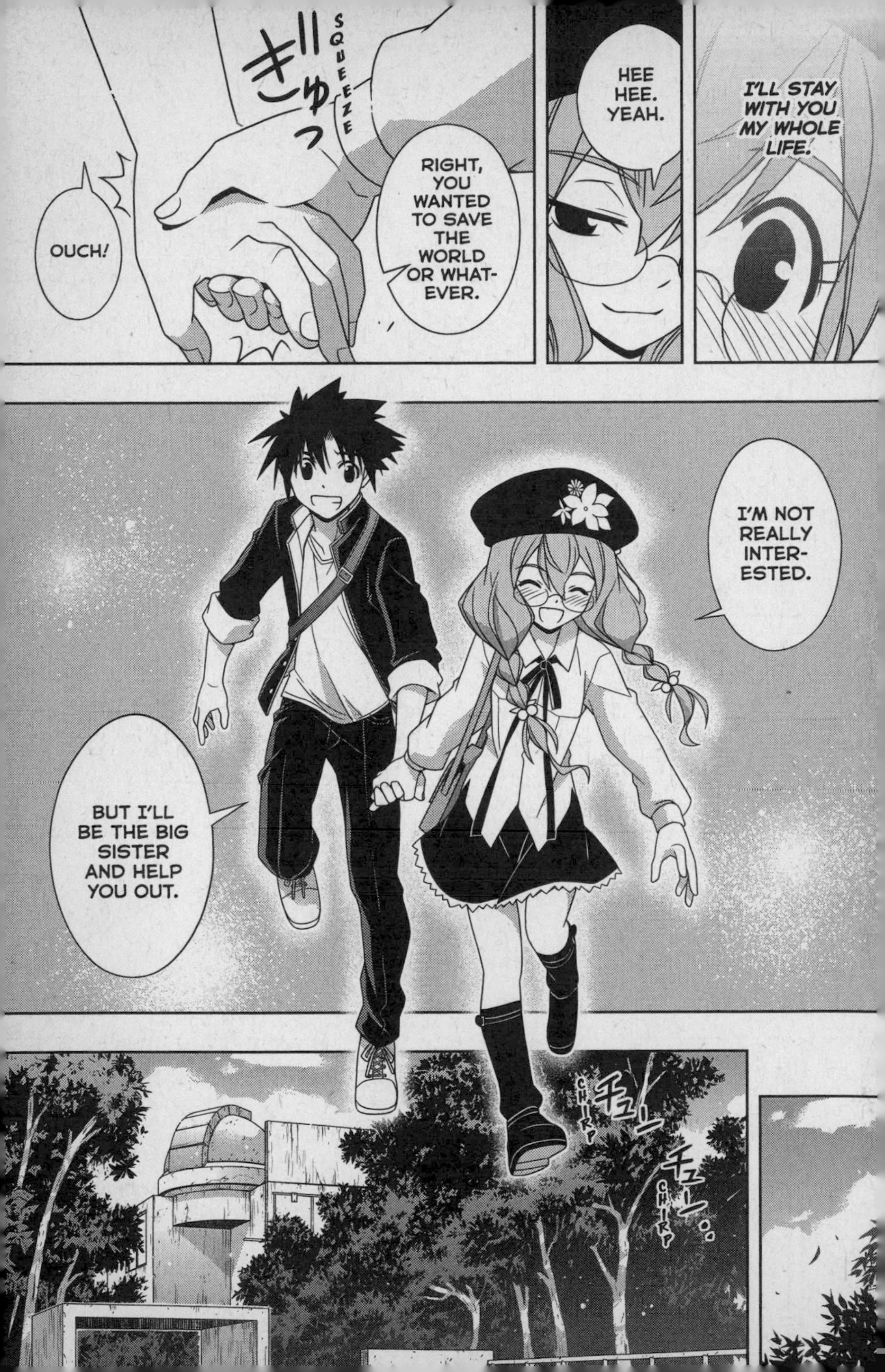
I'LL STAY WITH YOU MY WHOLE LIFE!
HEE HEE. YEAH.
きゅっ
SQUEEZE
RIGHT, YOU WANTED TO SAVE THE WORLD OR WHATEVER.
OUCH!
I'M NOT REALLY INTER-ESTED.
BUT I'LL BE THE BIG SISTER AND HELP YOU OUT.
チュー
CHIRP
チュー。。
CHIRP

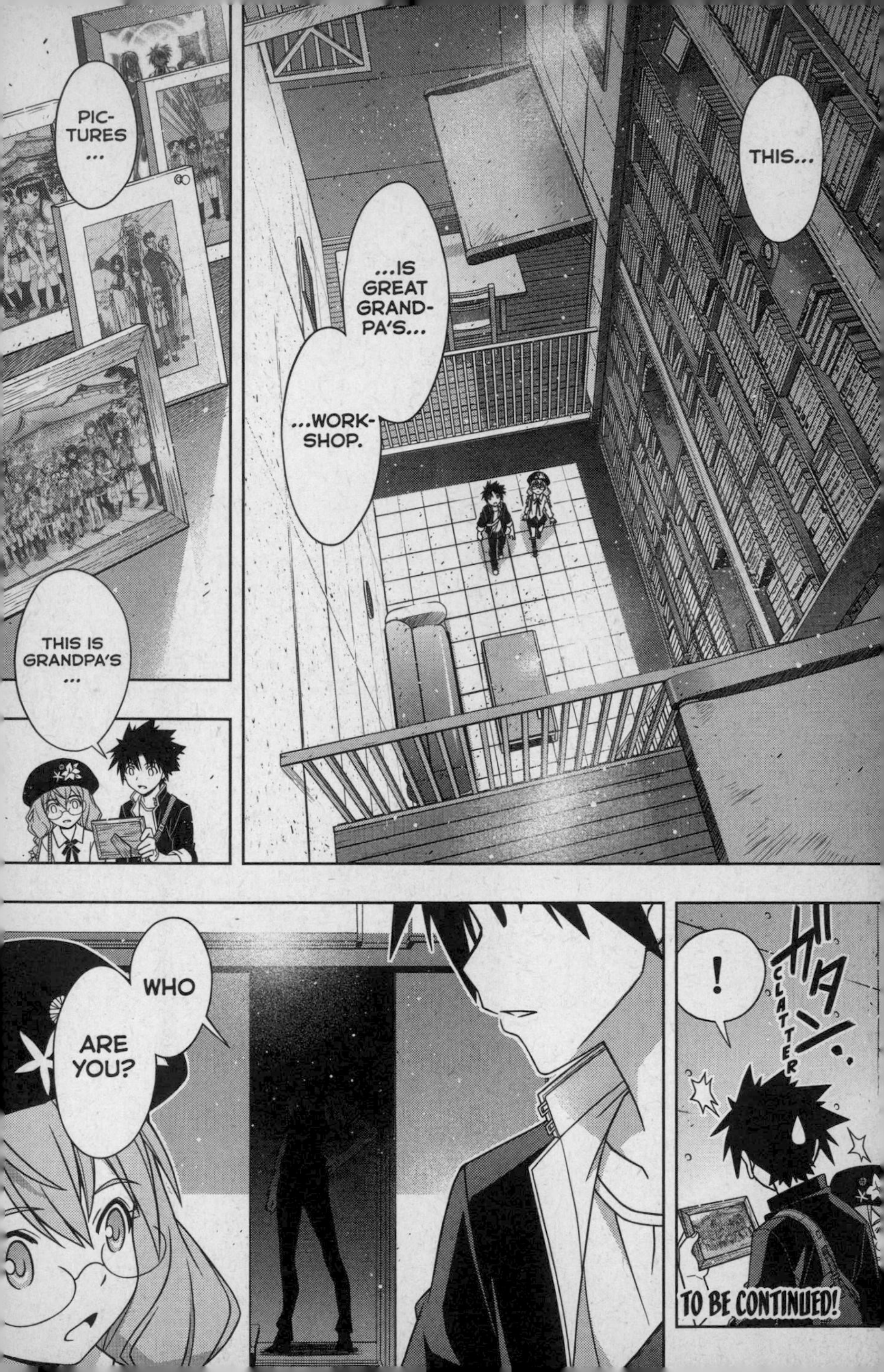
THIS...
...IS GREAT GRANDPA'S...
...WORK-SHOP.
PIC-TURES ...
THIS IS GRANDPA'S ...
!
CLATTER
TO BE CONTINUED!
WHO ARE YOU?

UQ HOLDER!

STAFF

Ken Akamatsu
Takashi Takemoto
Kenichi Nakamura
Keiichi Yamashita
Yuri Sasaki
Madoka Akanuma

Thanks to Ran Ayanaga

UQ HOLDER!

BONUS EXTRA! THE ROAD TO A COMPLETED MANUSCRIPT!

AKAMATSU STUDIO'S ART HAS EVOLVED GREATLY SINCE THE DAYS OF *NEGIMA!* NOW WE WILL DISCOVER THE PROCESS USED IN MAKING ITS SEQUEL *UQ HOLDER!!*

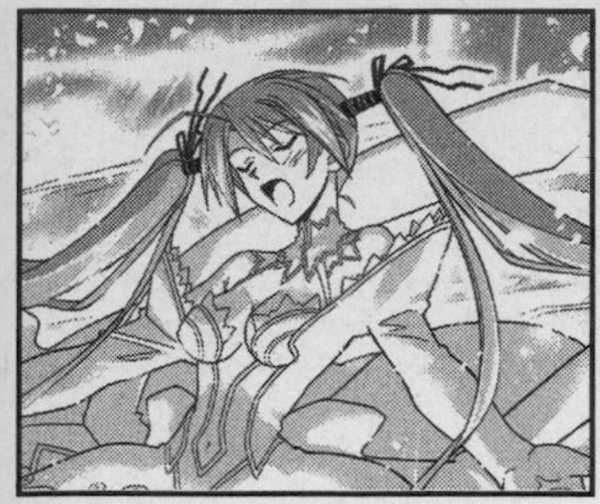

Above is a CG panel from *Negima!*. When it was made, the computer graphics were printed on paper, then revised and corrected by hand, and pasted onto the final manuscript. So the series was actually rather low-tech.

1 WORK PROCESS

The biggest change between this series and the last is that this one is all digital. Computer graphics were used to create *Negima*!, but most of the manga was made using the old-fashioned analog techniques of ink, paper, and screen tone. (Maybe that's more surprising than the switch to digital?) Digital makes it easier to correct mistakes, allows for a wider range of expression, and creates a more beautiful end product. Have you all noticed the difference?

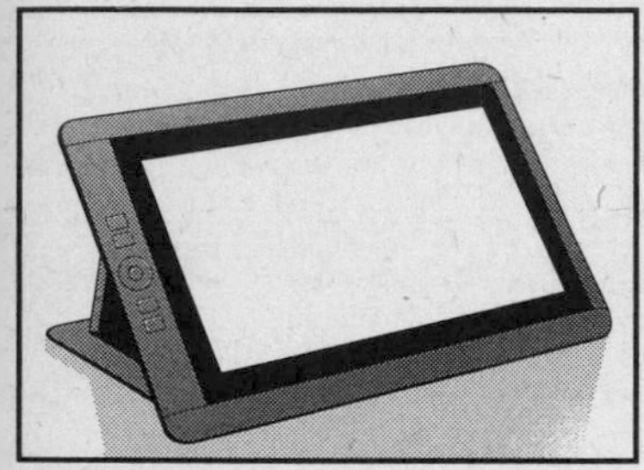

Work is done on LCD tablets. The sizes depend on the staff members' preference, and ranges from 13-24 inches.

2 WORK ENVIRONMENT

Because the work is done digitally, everything from the rough draft to the addition of tone is done on the computer. The program used is Comic Studio*. Some of you may be thinking "Still?", but with the work style at Akamatsu Studio, they have yet to find a need for anything more advanced. Furthermore, because the manuscript can be transferred electronically, more of the staff are working from home.

*Marketed as Manga Studio in the US, this program's latest version was released in 2007.

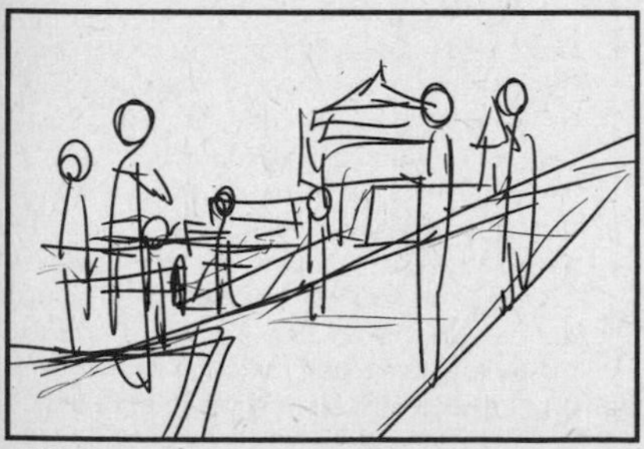

This is the *name* for the two-page spread six pages into Stage 97.
All that's needed is the concept for the picture, so it can be drawn very simply.

3 *NAME*

The "*name*" (storyboard) is like an even rougher version of a rough draft. We will be using the chapter title page from Stage 97 as our example here, so there are no panel divisions. Normally, a *name* is used to work out the flow of the story, placement of panels, etc.

4 ROUGH BACKGROUND

Normally, the rough draft is the next step after the *name*, but in the case of this image, the background and character placement were so complex that an exception was made, and a background was created to help prepare the rough draft. The background artist creates a background based on the concept shown in the *name*, and for this picture, it was used to determine character positions and size in a rough draft. Nevertheless, there's no need to be this meticulous unless a panel is exceptionally complex, so normally this step is not part of the process.

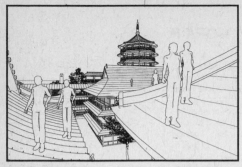

A completed rough draft background. This is just a temporary version used to help draw the characters. Incidentally, the humanoid polygon models are used as reference for proportions..

5 ROUGH DRAFT

The division of labor is very specific at Akamatsu Studio, with different people assigned to characters, backgrounds, touch-up, etc., so the rough draft, which will serve as their blueprint, is extremely important. The draft is drawn in detail so that the entire staff can share the same idea of what the completed version should look like. Every member of the staff, whether they work at the studio or remotely, uses this blueprint to create a single, unified piece of art.
This time, there is a rough background to work with, and the characters are drawn to fit on top of it.

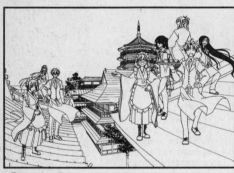

This is the finished rough draft.
It's so detailed, it's almost like a completed drawing.

6 BACKGROUND LINE ART PRODUCTION

Next, the background line art is drawn for the final version. The layout won't be any different from the rough background, but the roof on the right is a model for use in wide shots, so it's easy to see just how incomplete it is in a closeup. Let's just go ahead and replace that with a more detailed model. This is actually the first time the roof has been seen so closely, therefore a new model will be created for it. Incidentally, this process takes place during the rough draft in the previous step.

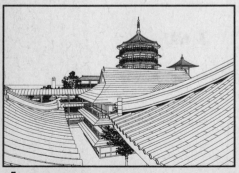

The completed background line art. The missing details of the rooftop have been filled in. Incidentally, the 3D software used is Lightwave 3D, which allows for easy polygon editing.

This is the background line art combined with the shadow art. The thickness of the shadows will be adjusted in touch-up. It's impressive to see the tree in the front casting a shadow on the ground.

7 SHADOW PRODUCTION

This isn't done with smaller panels, but in a big panel like this, with an especially conspicuous background, shadows are sometimes created using 3D software. But while creating them in 3D is fast and precise, it doesn't always go as planned, and shadows don't always fall in the desired locations. Therefore, a background touch-up artist may go over it again and make corrections based on this shadow image. This is the final step in the 3D background process.

A background that has been edited by hand. The inorganic feel is gone, and it has more presence and realism overall. The trees have been drawn over, too, creating a better balance.

8 BACKGROUND DETAILS

This is where the touch-up artist comes in. Once the background line art is created in 3D, the line thickness in an untouched version is too uniform, resulting in a bland, inorganic look, so textures, stains, etc. are drawn in by hand. Natural objects like plants are overwhelmingly more suited to be drawn by hand, so these are touched up at this stage.

A completed background. There's a sense of depth and breadth in this space. The shapes of the clouds have been calculated to create the best balance when the characters have been put in place.

9 BACKGROUND TOUCH-UP

Once the background has been edited, color and highlights are added with screen tone. In this particular panel, the background has prominence, but the characters are the real stars, and we don't want them to be overshadowed. Notice that the buildings in the back have been given a lighter color. This not only helps the characters stand out, but also creates a sense of perspective and makes the space feel wider.

10 CHARACTER LINE ART PRODUCTION

This is the finished character line art. *UQ HOLDER!* doesn't use as much tone as *Negima!*, so the lines must be that much more precise. This particular drawing even has some beta inked in by Akamatsu-sensei himself.

Now the characters will be drawn to be superimposed onto the background. Of course, Akamatsu-sensei is in charge of the character line art. Every single line, even the difficult curves from the hair blowing in the wind, is drawn in beautiful flowing strokes. However, an assistant will take care of some of the characters' weapons and props, as well as the details on their clothing, so they will be drawn in at the touch-up stage.

11 CHARACTER *BETA*

Characters with beta. The beta brings the picture together, and the characters start to feel alive.

The *beta* (areas filled in solid black ink) is added to the completed line drawing. When *beta* is added to hair and clothes, the characters instantly come to life, don't they? It seems simple at a glance, but the appearance of the image will change drastically based on the balance of black and white, so it's a very important process. Back in the *Negima!* days, one mistake could cause revision headaches, but working digitally makes revisions simple, and it's easy to try out all kinds of patterns. Convenient, wouldn't you say?

12 CHARACTER TOUCH-UP

Characters complete with tone. At Stage 97, there were almost no tone shadows, so only the colors in hair and clothing are expressed with tone.

Tone is added to the characters. With *Negima!*, detailed shadows were added with tone, but that practice was deliberately scaled back for *UQ HOLDER!* This was done intentionally to create a sharp, clean style distinctive of shonen manga. But now, as the story begins to sync up with *Negima!*, more tone shadows are being added, and the art is starting to look closer to *Negima!*. The difference is subtle, but have any of you noticed it? We will explain more about this later.

13 COMPOSITION & FINE TUNING

The characters are added to the completed background. With a digital manuscript, this is easily accomplished with a simple copy and paste. In the *Negima!* days, the characters were drawn on a separate sheet of paper. They had to be cut out with a utility knife and literally pasted onto the background. This was a high-pressure job that allowed no margin of error. Incidentally, because of this cut and paste technique, Akamatsu-sensei's manuscripts were famous for being thick and heavy (ha ha).

Once the characters are added to the image, shadows are added at their feet and minor adjustments are made to their positions. Thus the characters become a real part of the scene.

---

14 COMPLETION

FINALLY THE MANUSCRIPT IS FINISHED!

Finally, specks of dust, light, etc. are added to create a sense of movement, like of the atmosphere or the wind. Once those little details are finished, the manuscript is finally complete. For this panel, the same artist was in charge of touching-up the background and the characters, but even so, four people, including Akamatsu-sensei, were involved in completing this picture. This is the lengthy process to create a manuscript. A lot of planning and attention to detail go into these manuscripts, so we hope you enjoy those aspects in addition to the story.

Below is the completed image. The final product has an exquisite balance that makes the characters pop while still giving the background a sense of depth and breadth.

A DEEPER DIVE!
REVEALING THE DETAILS OF THE PROCESS!

Let's further explore the artistry and intricacy that are also integral to the production process described so far.

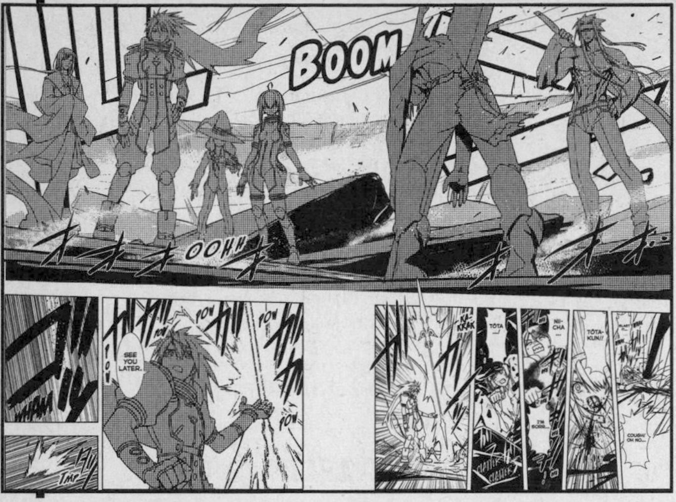
BOOM
SEE YOU LATER...

POINT 1 DETAILED ROUGH DRAFTS

This is the rough draft of a scene from Stage 133, which you'll find in this volume. Even though this is a rough version, there is enough tone that at first glance, you might think it's a completed manuscript. This draft assures that each member of the staff, in their different roles, works with a consistent image of what the finished version will be.

POINT 2 BEAUTIFUL PEN STROKES

The art is already detailed in the rough draft stage, but then Akamatsu-sensei takes his pen to it and cleans it up into an even more beautiful drawing. The soft, flowing, gentle strokes, bring out the characters' charm.

POINT 3 PERFECTIONISM IN TOUCH-UP

This series specifically scaled back the use of tone to make it more of a shonen manga style, but as the story syncs with *Negima!*, the art is being brought closer to the preceding series as well. It brings another level of nostalgia to the manga.

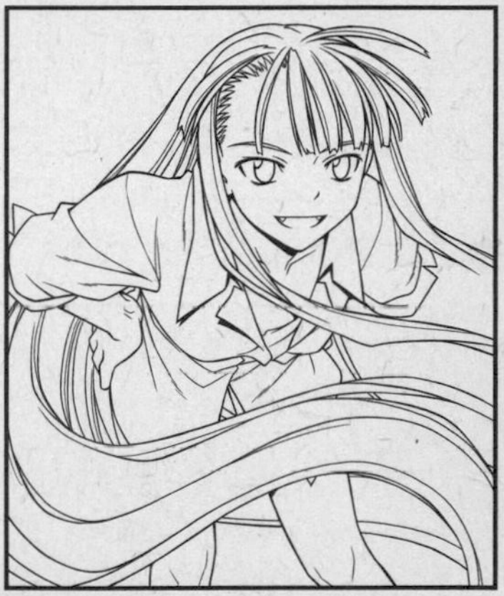

↑ Pen strokes polished even further through digital technology.

↓ Stage 62 without tone shadows (left) and Stage 130 with tone shadows (right).

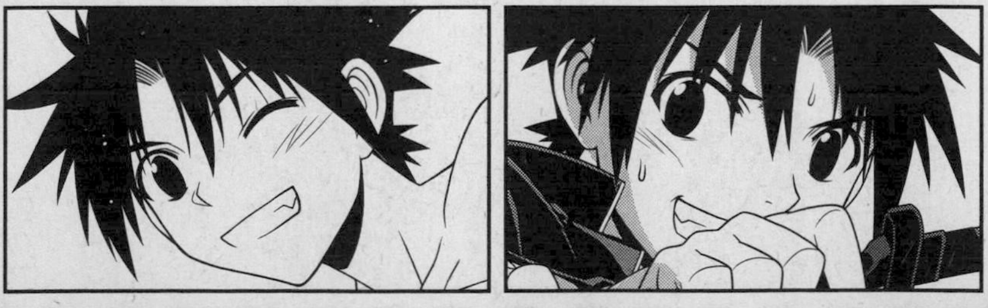

Japan's most powerful spirit medium delves into the ghost world's greatest mysteries!

Story by Kyo Shirodaira, famed author of mystery fiction and creator of *Spiral*, *Blast of Tempest*, and *The Record of a Fallen Vampire*.

Both touched by spirits called yôkai, Kotoko and Kurô have gained unique superhuman powers. But to gain her powers Kotoko has given up an eye and a leg, and Kurô's personal life is in shambles. So when Kotoko suggests they team up to deal with renegades from the spirit world, Kurô doesn't have many other choices, but Kotoko might just have a few ulterior motives...

IN/SPECTRE

STORY BY KYO SHIRODAIRA
ART BY CHASHIBA KATASE

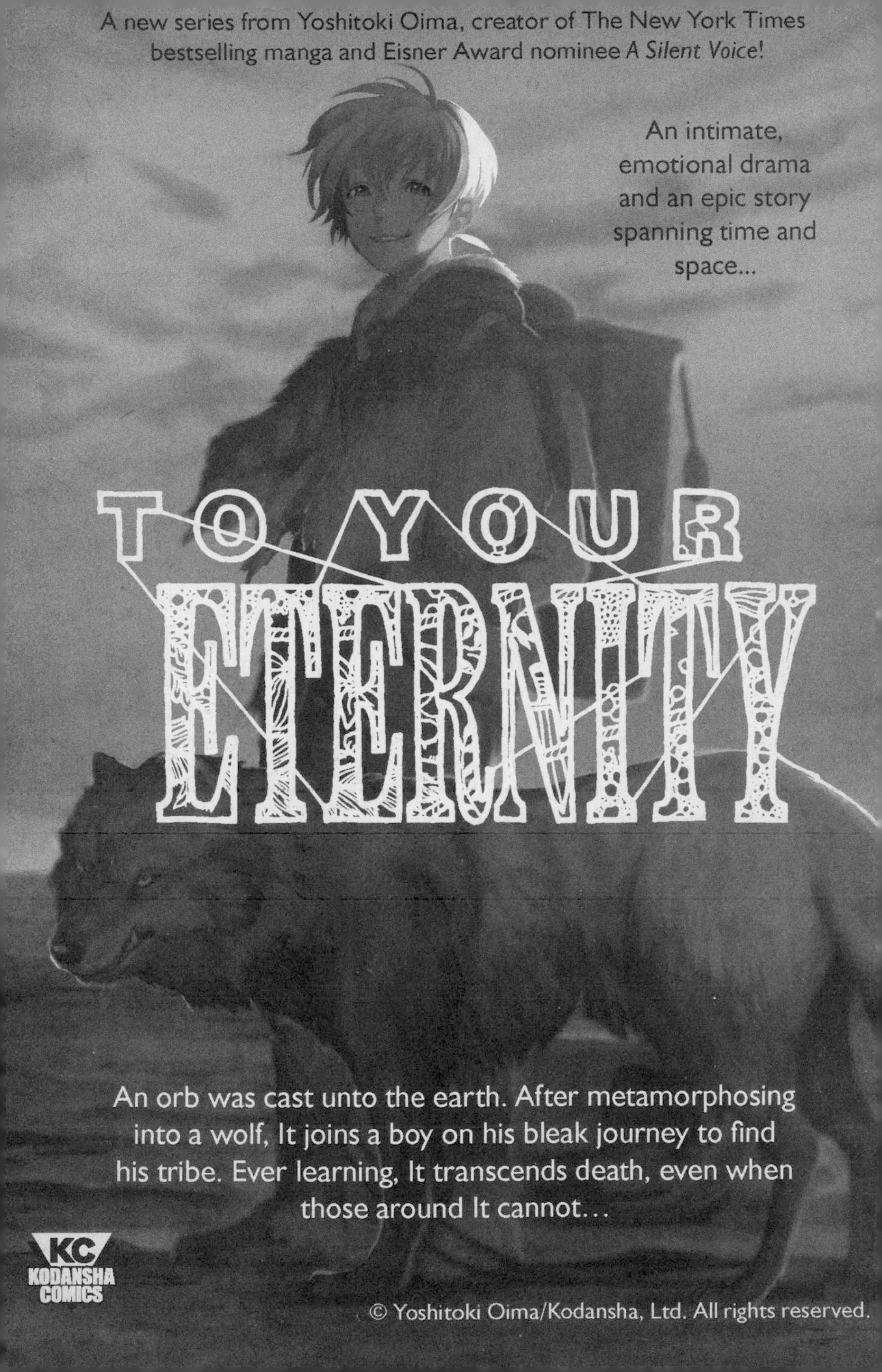
A new series from Yoshitoki Oima, creator of The New York Times bestselling manga and Eisner Award nominee *A Silent Voice*!
An intimate, emotional drama and an epic story spanning time and space...
TO YOUR ETERNITY
An orb was cast unto the earth. After metamorphosing into a wolf, It joins a boy on his bleak journey to find his tribe. Ever learning, It transcends death, even when those around It cannot...
KC KODANSHA COMICS
© Yoshitoki Oima/Kodansha, Ltd. All rights reserved.

From the creator of *The Ancient Magus' Bride*
comes a supernatural action manga in the
vein of *Fullmetal Alchemist*!

More than a century after an eccentric scholar made an infamous deal with a
devil, the story of Faust has passed into legend. However, the true Faust is not
the stuffy, professorial man known in fairy tales, but a charismatic, bespectacled
woman named Johanna Faust, who happens to still be alive. Searching for
pieces of her long-lost demon, Johanna passes through a provincial town, where
she saves a young boy named Marion from a criminal's fate. In exchange, she
asks a simple favor of Marion, but Marion soon finds himself intrigued by
the peculiar Doctor Faust and joins her on her journey. Thus begins the strange
and wonderful adventures of *Frau Faust*!